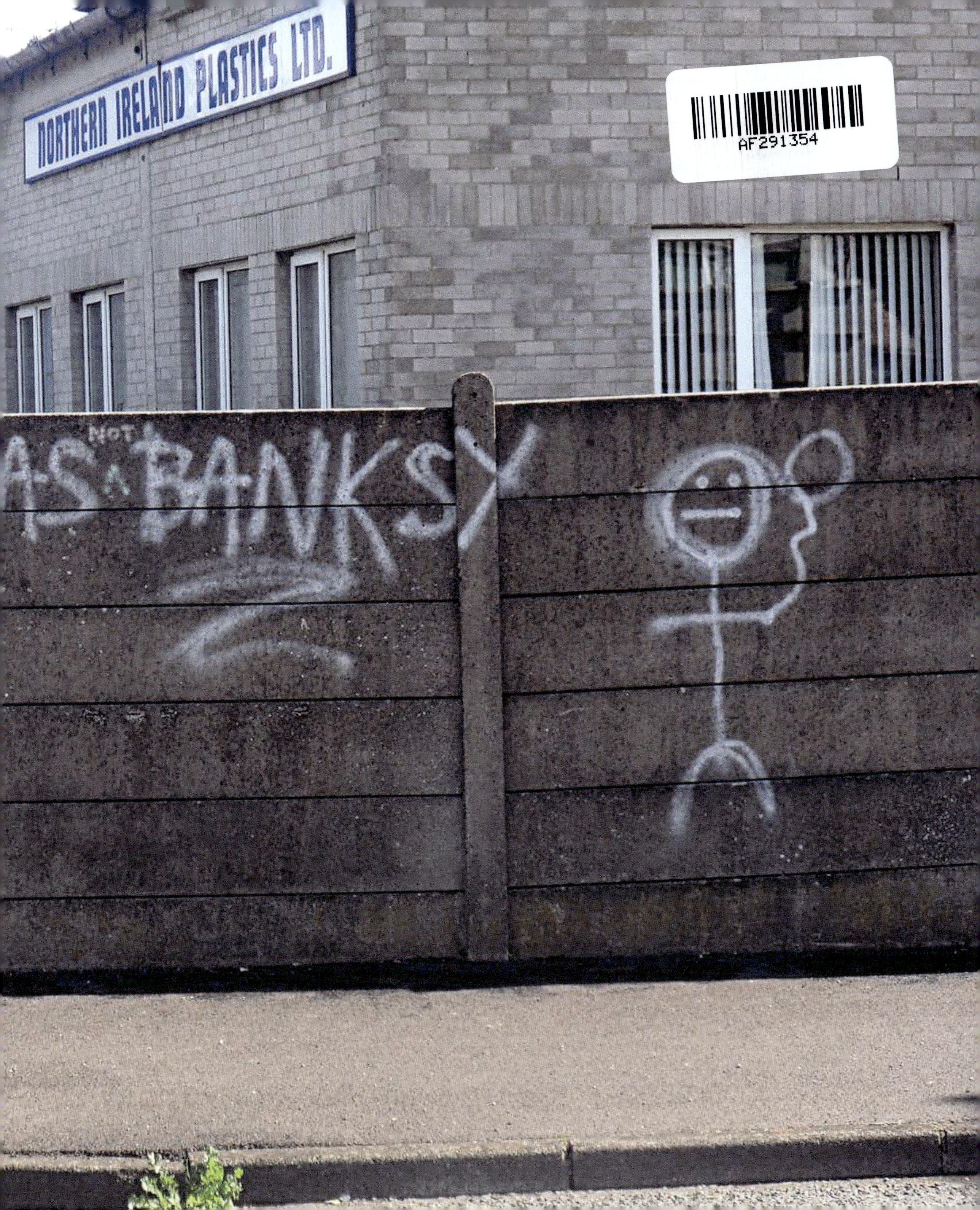

NORTHERN IRELAND PLASTICS LTD.
AF291354
AS A NOT BANKSY

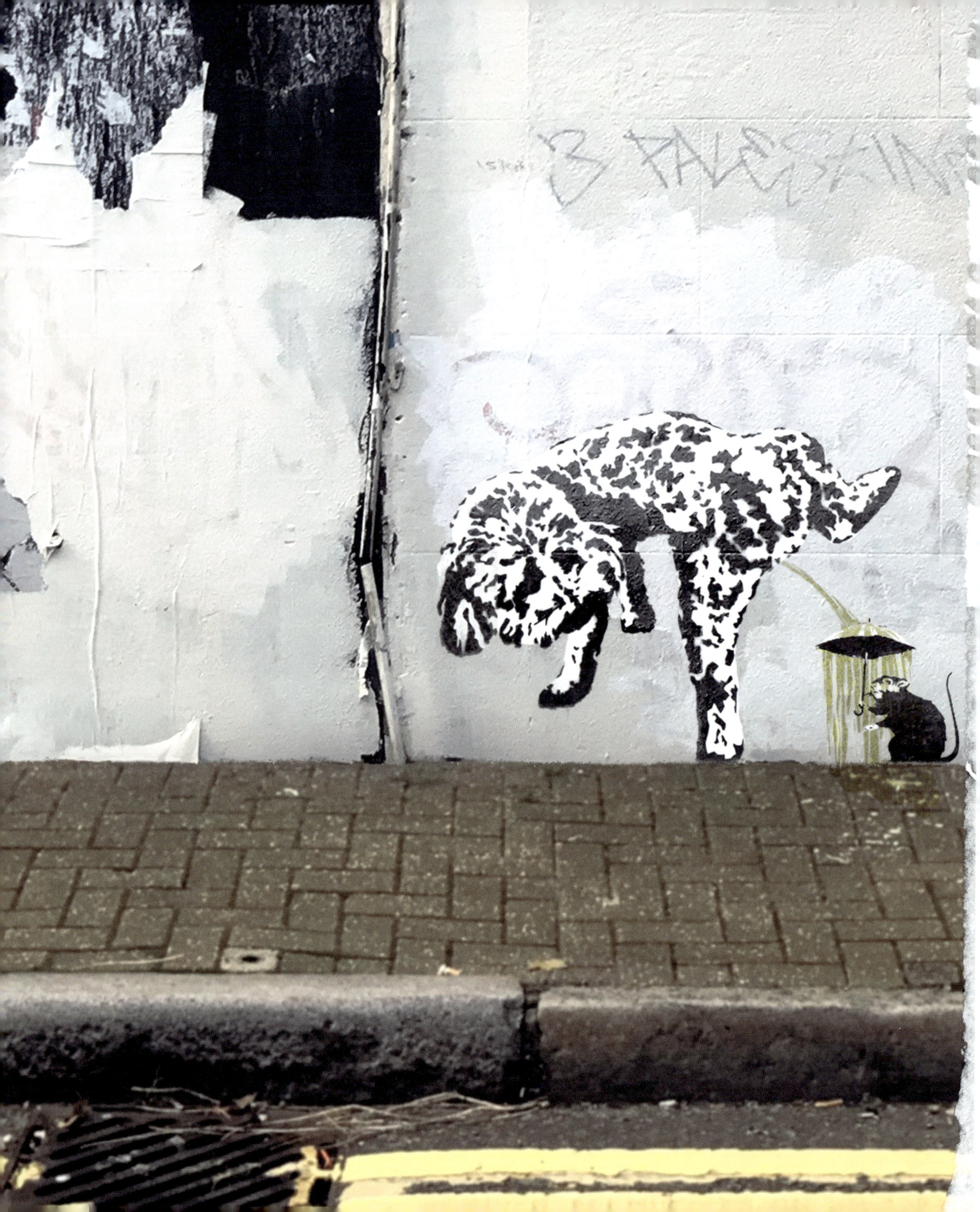

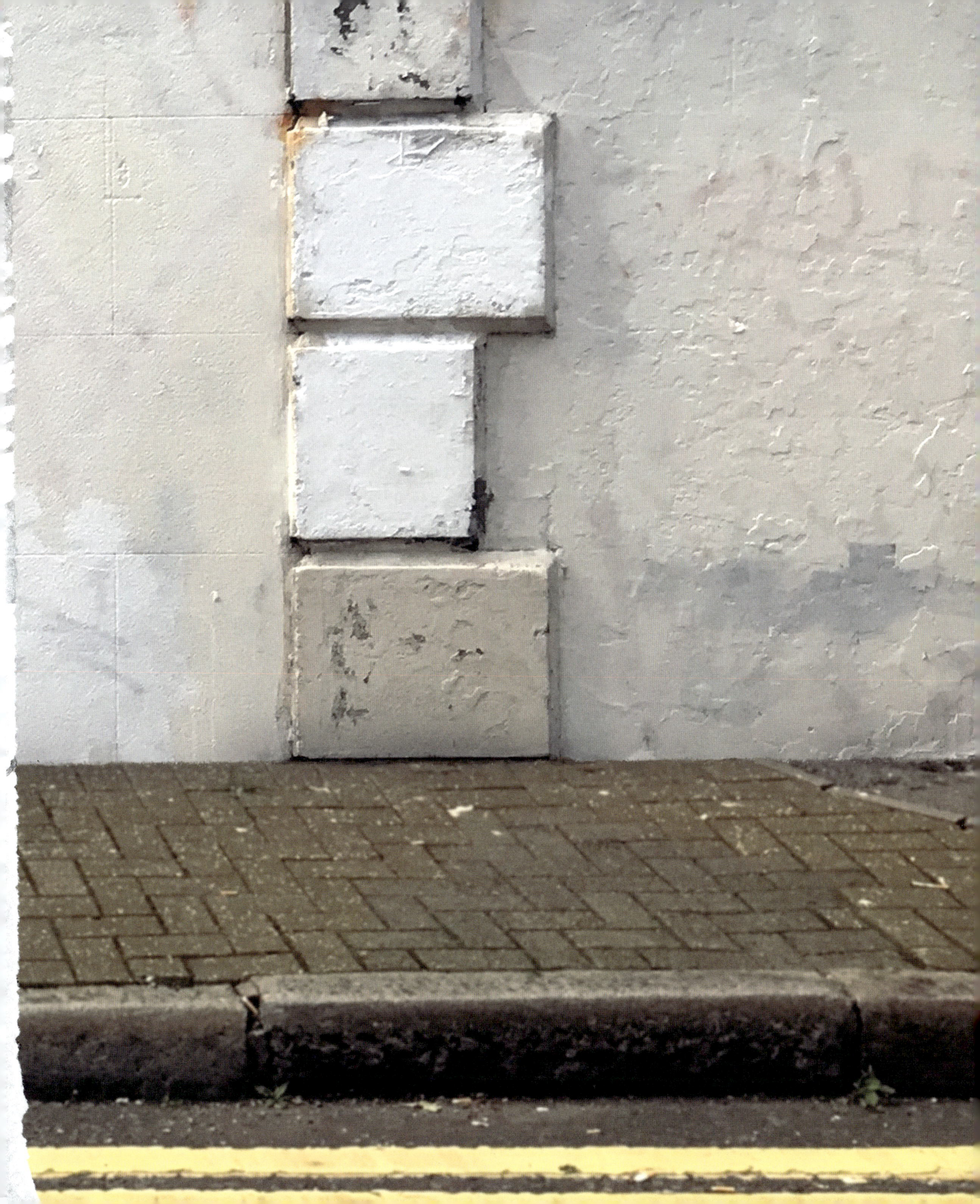

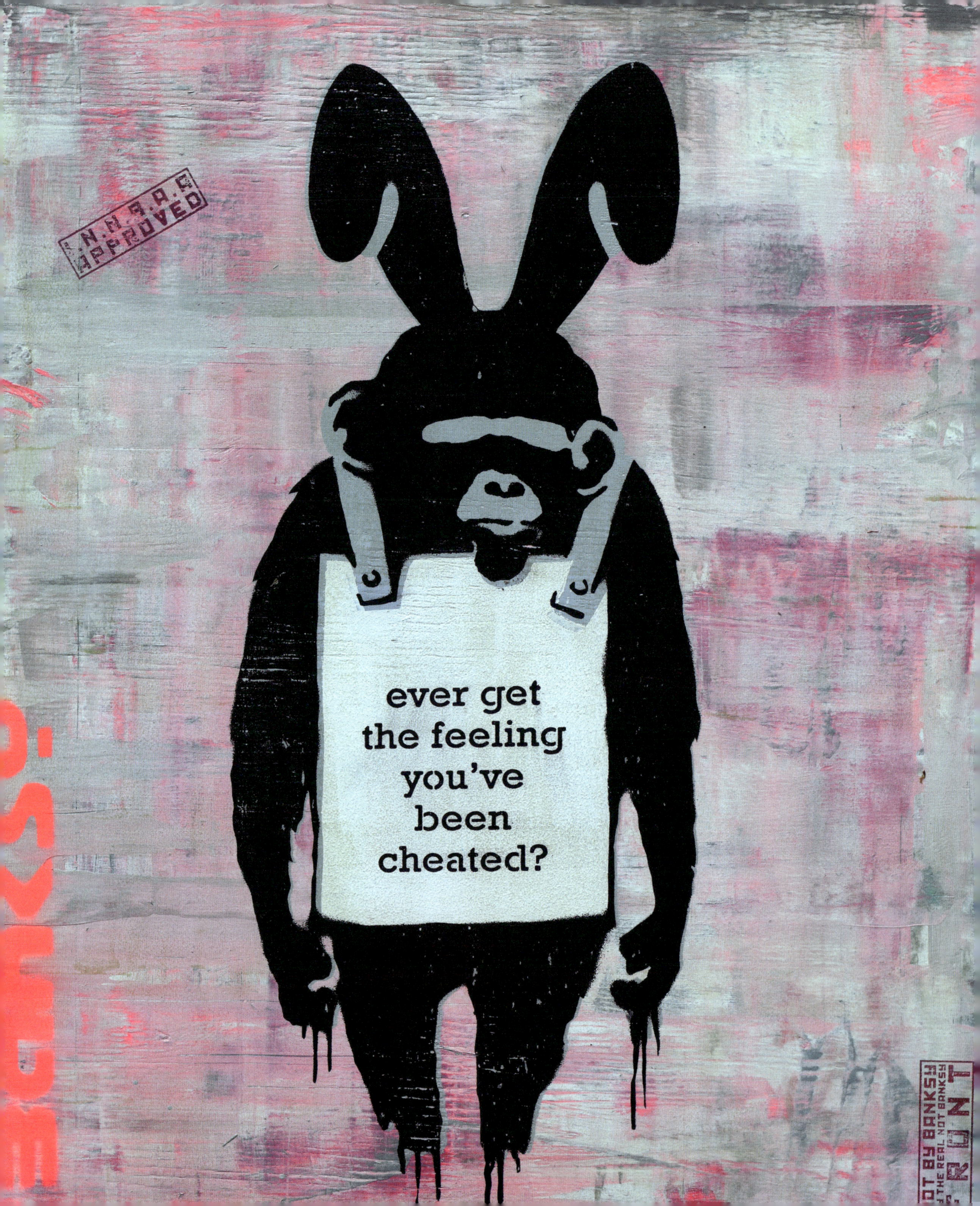

N.A.A.A.
APPROVED
ever get
the feeling
you've
been
cheated?
NOT BY BANKSY
THE REAL NOT BANKSY
FRONT

THE NOT BANKSY BOOK

LYING CHEATING STEALING & THE DEATH OF ART

VOL. 13

BY
NOT BANKSY
NOT NOT BANKSY
THE REAL NOT BANKSY FRONT
THE NEW NOT BANKSY REALISATION
&
THE EMERGENT IS-NOT-BANKSY ABNORMALCY
OF THE 21ST CENTURY
GENERATION Z

EDITED BY
STOT21stCplanB

L-13

FIRST EDITION
DECEMBER 2021

ISBN: 978-1-908067-31-9

PUBLISHED BY
THE L-13 LIGHT INDUSTRIAL WORKSHOP
& PRIVATE LADIES & GENTLEMEN'S CLUB
FOR ART, LEISURE & THE DISRUPTIVE
BETTERMENT OF CULTURE

A NEO-NOTHINGIST IS-NOT-ART PUBLICATION
FOR THE INTERNATIONAL IS-NOT-BANKSY ALLIANCE

NO RIGHTS DESERVED

DISCLAIMER

This book is entirely a work of fiction set in the real art world that is entirely fictional. The names, characters and incidents portrayed in it are the work of the authors' imagination, except where they lack any imagination. Any resemblance to actual artists, persons, animals or inanimate objects, living or dead, events or localities is not entirely coincidental, but should be taken lightly with a large pinch of salt.

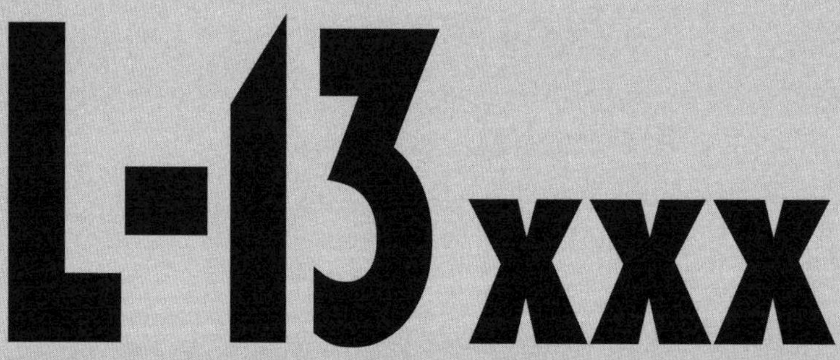

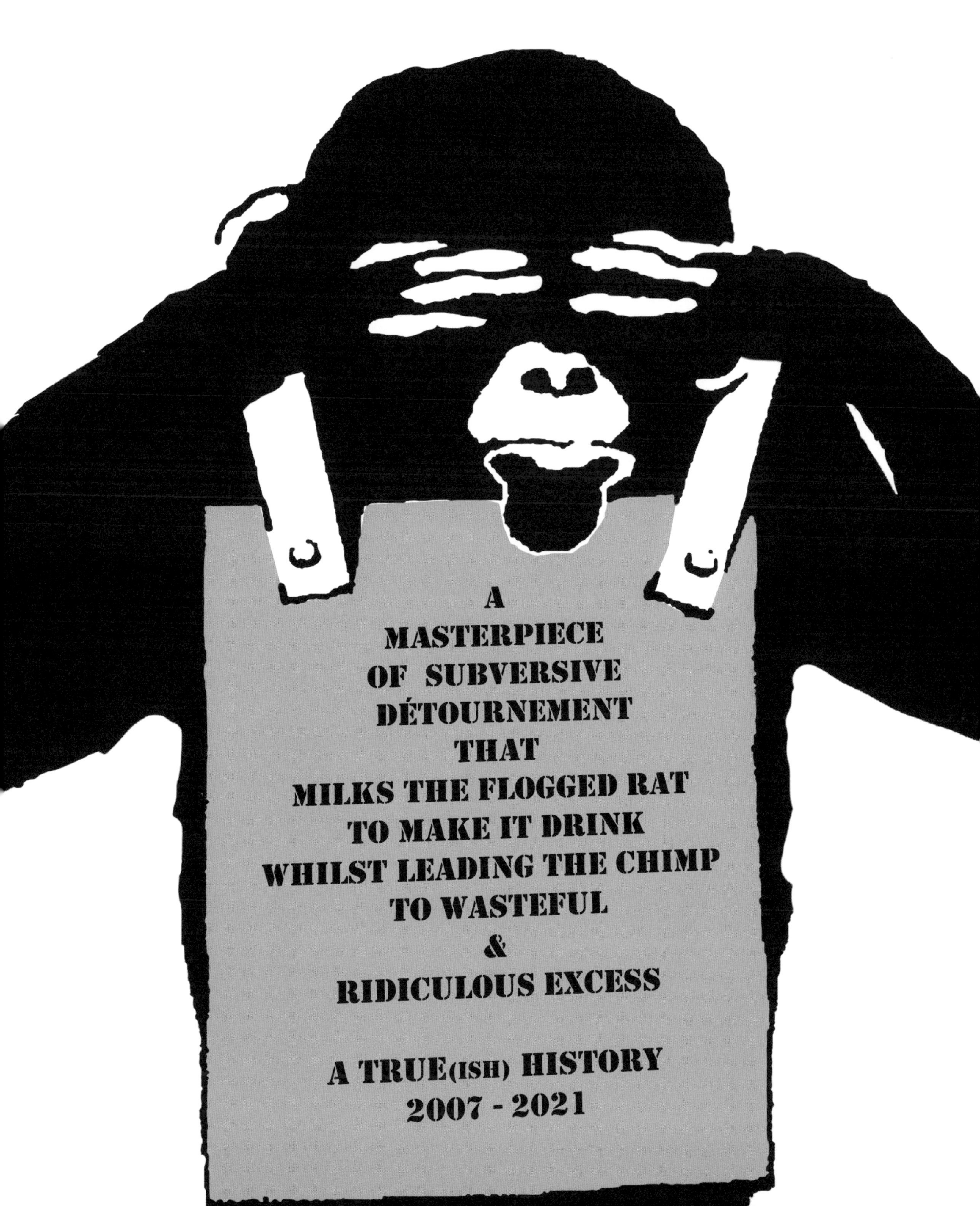
A
MASTERPIECE
OF SUBVERSIVE
DÉTOURNEMENT
THAT
MILKS THE FLOGGED RAT
TO MAKE IT DRINK
WHILST LEADING THE CHIMP
TO WASTEFUL
&
RIDICULOUS EXCESS

A TRUE(ISH) HISTORY
2007 - 2021

PART 1

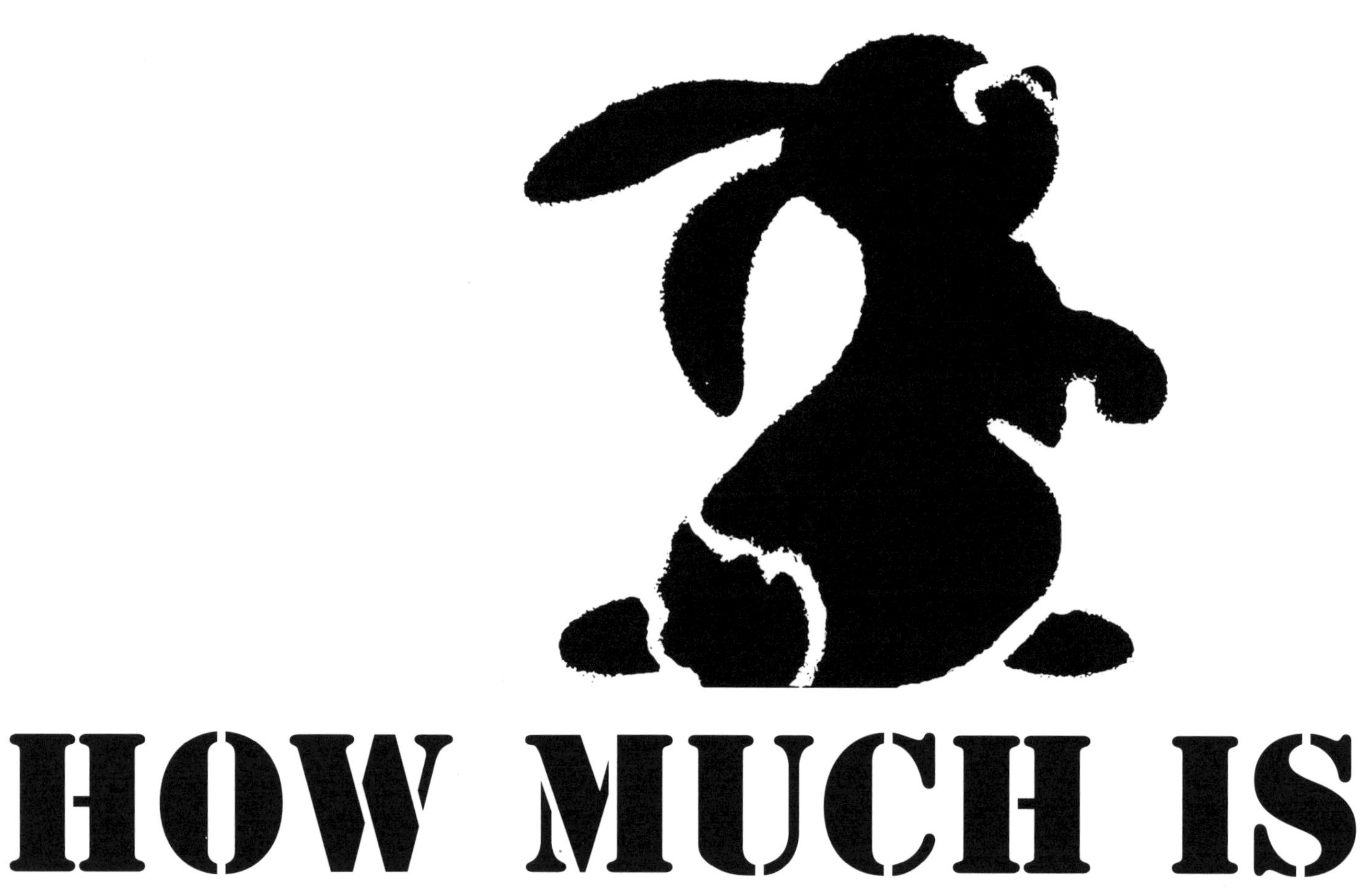

HOW MUCH IS

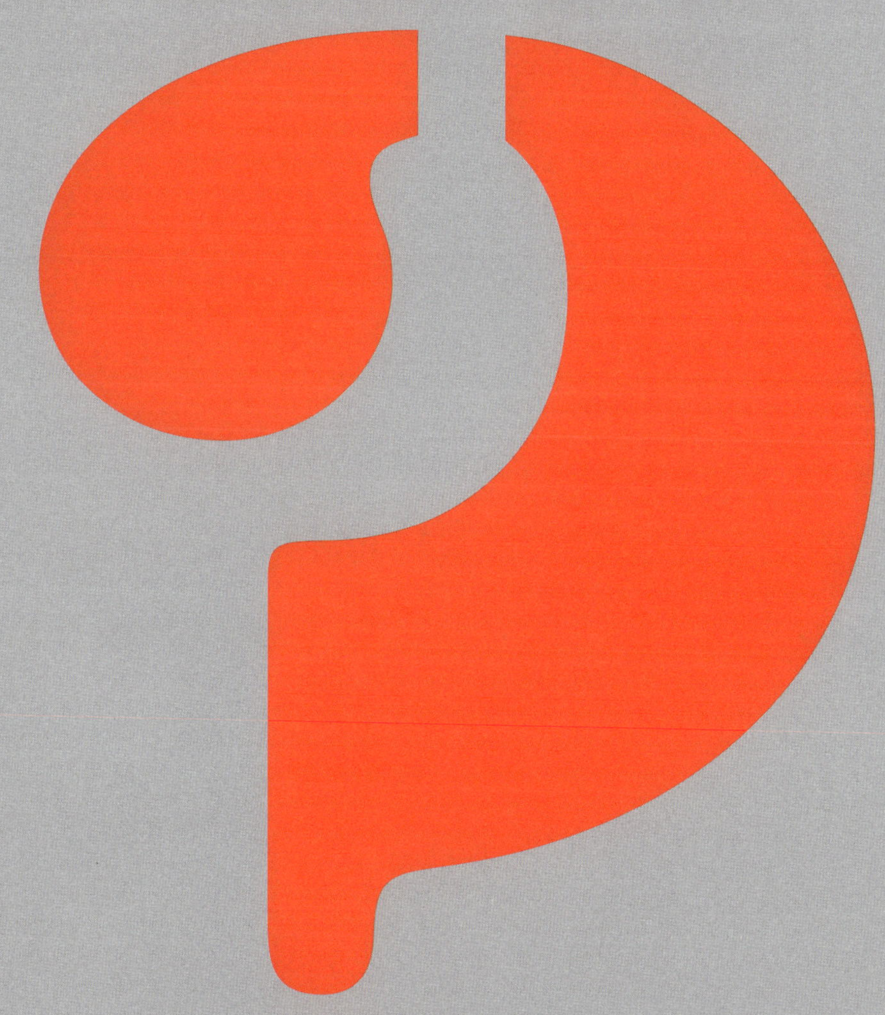
IT'S NOT!
THAT BANKSY
IN THE WINDOW

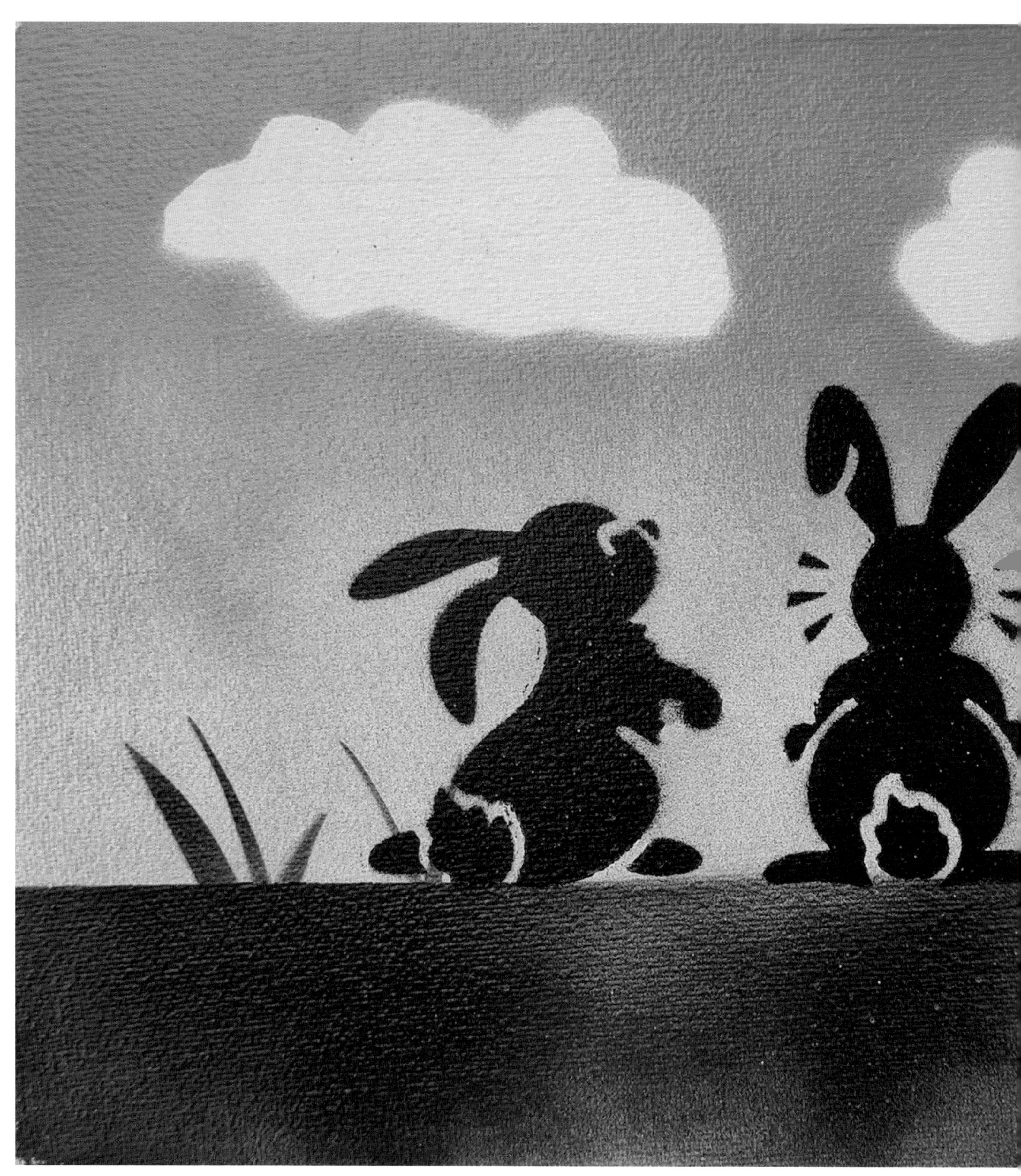

WE WILL OVERCOME, 2007 | spray paint on pound shop canvas | 10" x 8" | Edition of 10,000
of which only 10 were ever made | signed on the back by STOT21stCplanB

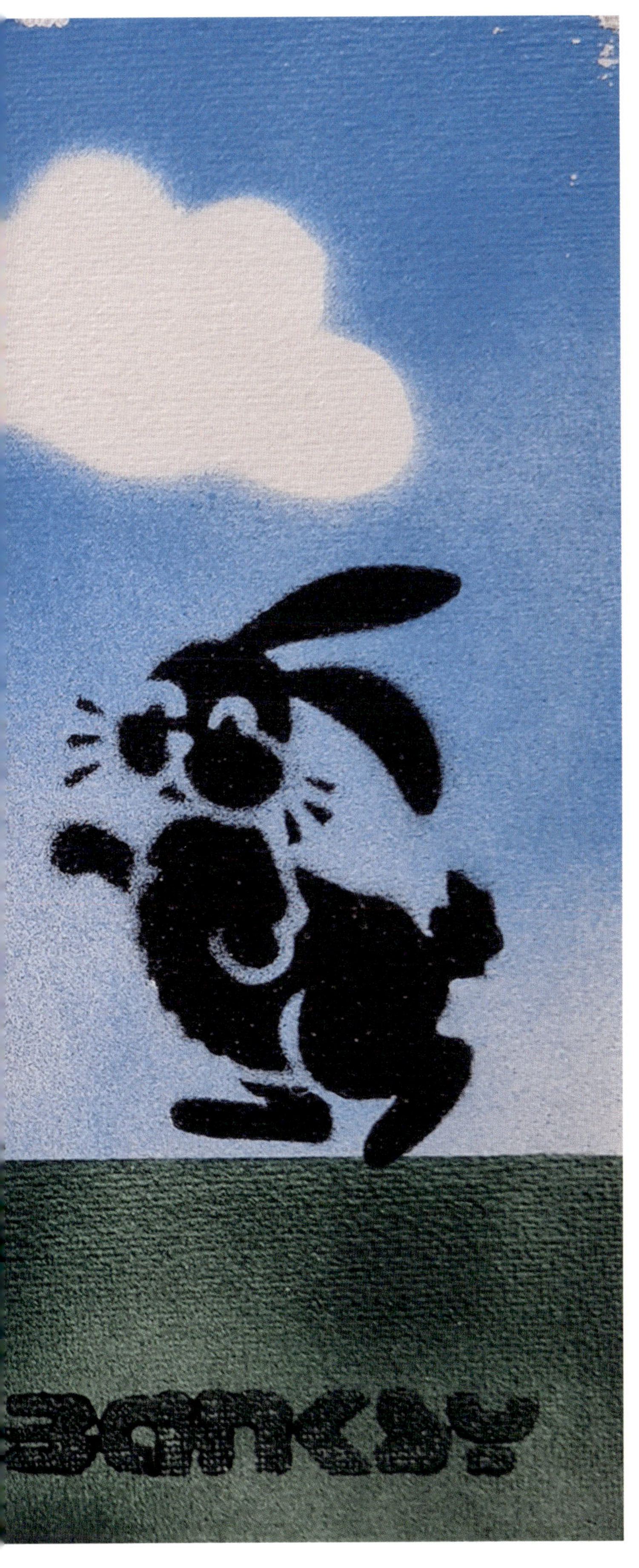

IT'S NOT BY BANKSY!
2007-2008

IN THE BEGINNING
there was no NOT BANKSY

The story of them coming into being goes something like this:

In 2007, as the world economy prepared to pop, The Janitor at L-13 (and key member of IS-NOT-ART Anartist* group STOT21stCplanB) bought some canvases and stencils from his favourite Poundland shop. The stencils were of cute little animals intended for decorating nursery walls.

The Janitor then made a painting on one of the canvases using spray paint and a stencil of some little bunnies.

He showed this to The Assistant to The Janitor (also a key member of STOT21stCplanB and IS-NOT-ART strategist at L-13) suggesting that there might be a market for this kind of thing in the highly profitable Urban Art scene.

On inspecting the piece with his expert eye The Assistant to the Janitor mooted that if the painting had been by BANKSY it might get a look in, but as it wasn't The Janitor should seek his artistic fortune elsewhere.

The Janitor went off to rethink the situation and soon came back with exactly the same painting, but this time with a BANKSY tag added to the bottom right corner.

Both The Janitor and The Assistant to The Janitor pissed themselves laughing.

*Anartist: a term coined by Marcel Duchamp

Thinking this to be a good sign, The Assistant to the Janitor decided that they should instantly mobilise STOT21stCplanB to make an edition of this artwork and disseminate it out into the world via the L-13 anti-art network.

The first painting was duly placed in the window of L-13's then gallery THE AQUARIUM L-13 on Farringdon Road, and immediately someone came in to ask eagerly:

"how much is that BANKSY in the window?"

The Assistant to The Janitor quickly explained it was NOT by BANKSY but by the Neo-Nothingist duo known as STOT21stCplanB, signed as such on the back, and that the idea of it being attributed to Banksy was a puerile joke.

"But it's signed by BANKSY" exclaimed the prospective art collector.

"No it's not..." replied The Assistant to the Janitor
"...the rubber-stamped BANKSY tag is fake".

"But you can't do that" came the retort.

"But we have!" parried The Assistant.

"How much is it then?"

"30 quid."

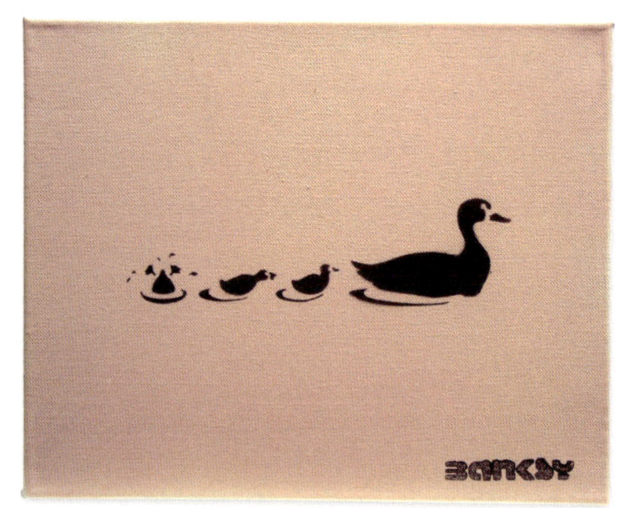

"I'll take it."

"Good man."

"...Are you sure it's NOT by BANKSY?"

"YES!!!"

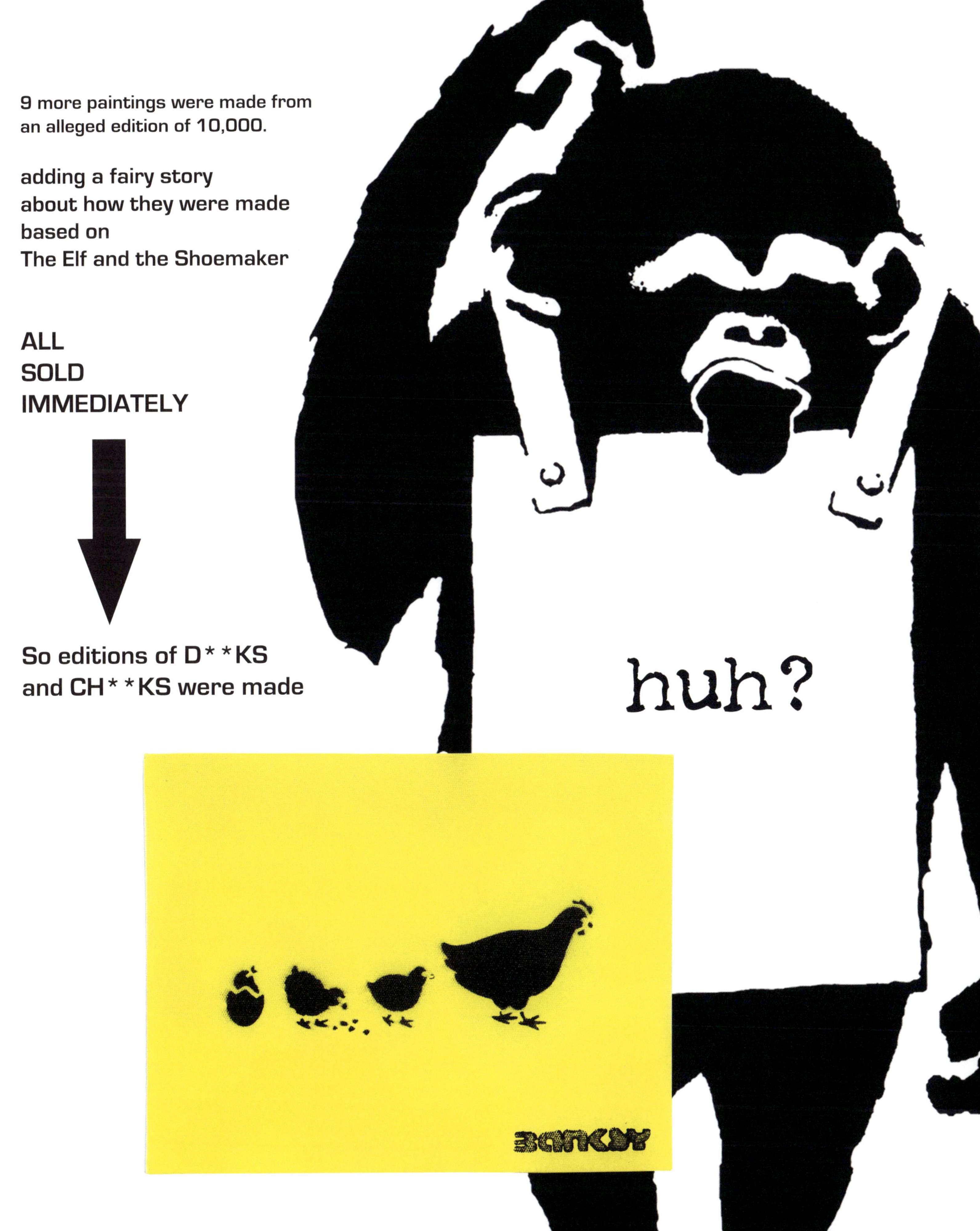
9 more paintings were made from
an alleged edition of 10,000.

adding a fairy story
about how they were made
based on
The Elf and the Shoemaker

ALL
SOLD
IMMEDIATELY

So editions of D**KS
and CH**KS were made

huh?

BANKSY

D**KS and CH**KS also sold in

We were bemused and amused...
Was it really that easy to make some money out of a bad joke?
With 900 quid in the bank (less £33 costs for canvas and stencils)
we decided to see how far this could be pushed

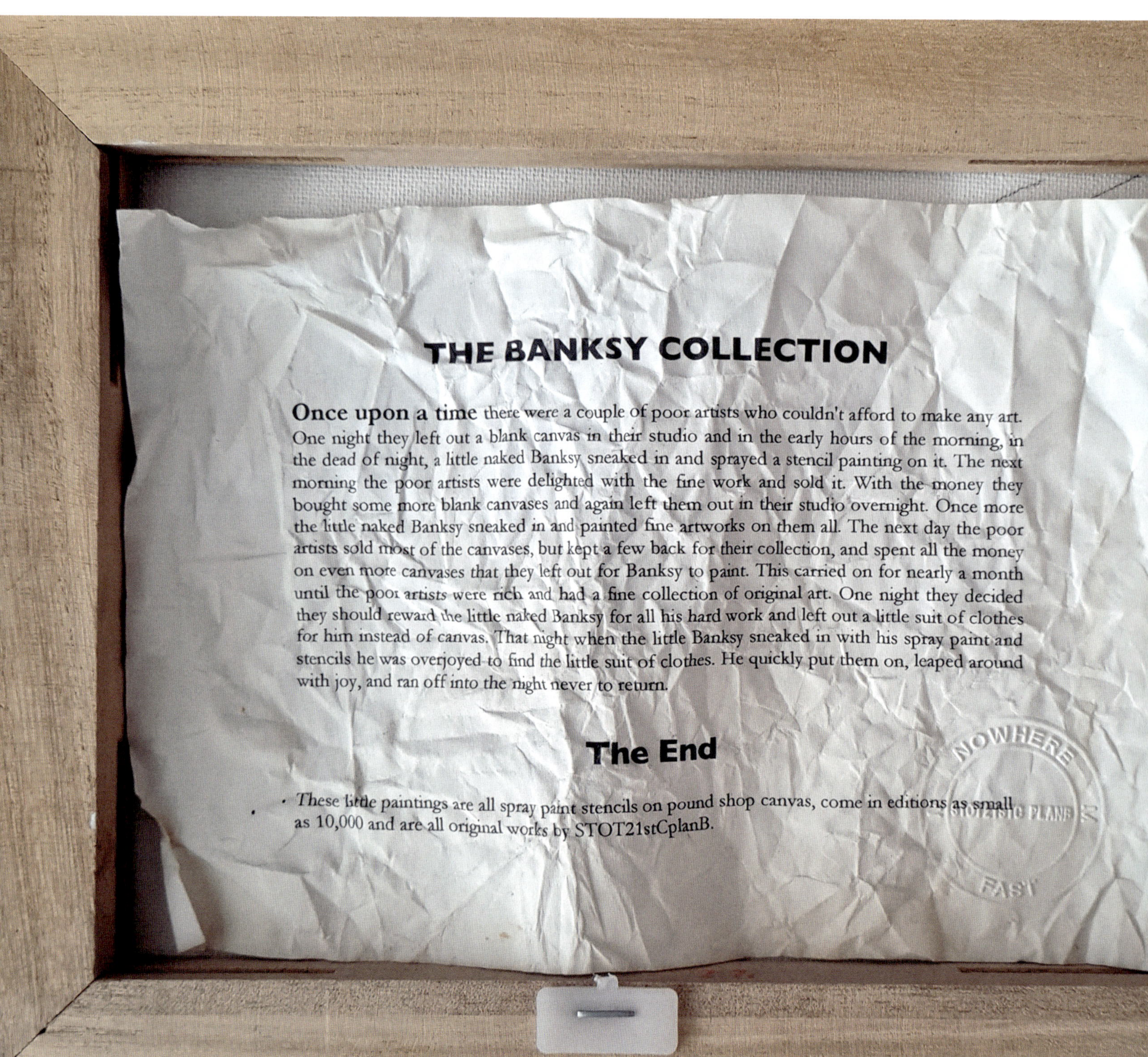

THE BANKSY COLLECTION

Once upon a time there were a couple of poor artists who couldn't afford to make any art. One night they left out a blank canvas in their studio and in the early hours of the morning, in the dead of night, a little naked Banksy sneaked in and sprayed a stencil painting on it. The next morning the poor artists were delighted with the fine work and sold it. With the money they bought some more blank canvases and again left them out in their studio overnight. Once more the little naked Banksy sneaked in and painted fine artworks on them all. The next day the poor artists sold most of the canvases, but kept a few back for their collection, and spent all the money on even more canvases that they left out for Banksy to paint. This carried on for nearly a month until the poor artists were rich and had a fine collection of original art. One night they decided they should reward the little naked Banksy for all his hard work and left out a little suit of clothes for him instead of canvas. That night when the little Banksy sneaked in with his spray paint and stencils he was overjoyed to find the little suit of clothes. He quickly put them on, leaped around with joy, and ran off into the night never to return.

The End

· These little paintings are all spray paint stencils on pound shop canvas, come in editions as small as 10,000 and are all original works by STOT21stCplanB.

the blink of an eye

A lot of pound shop canvases can be bought for 900 quid

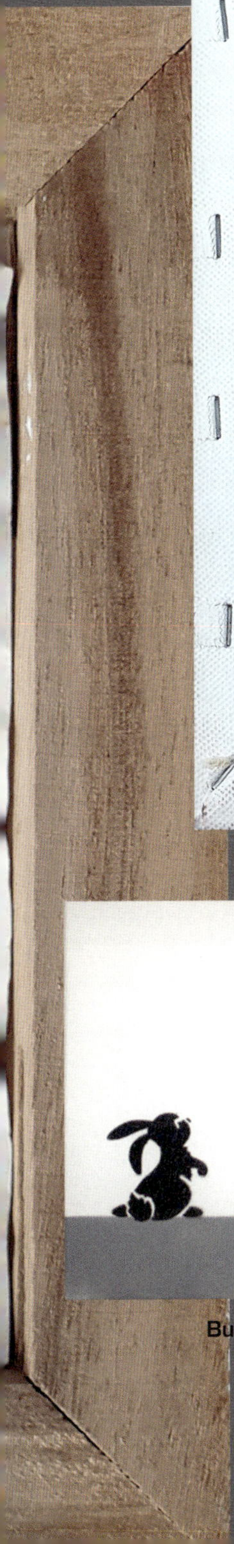

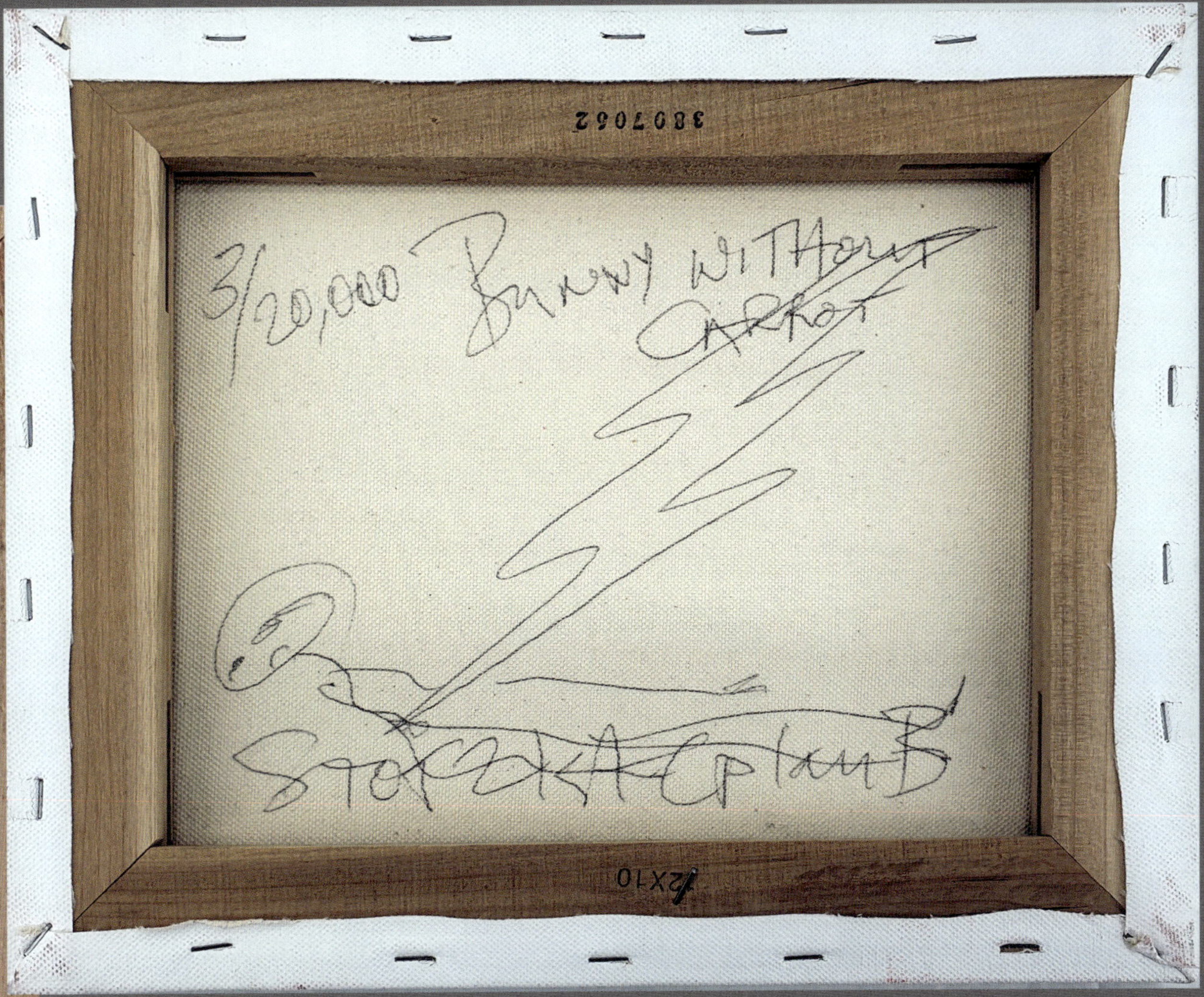

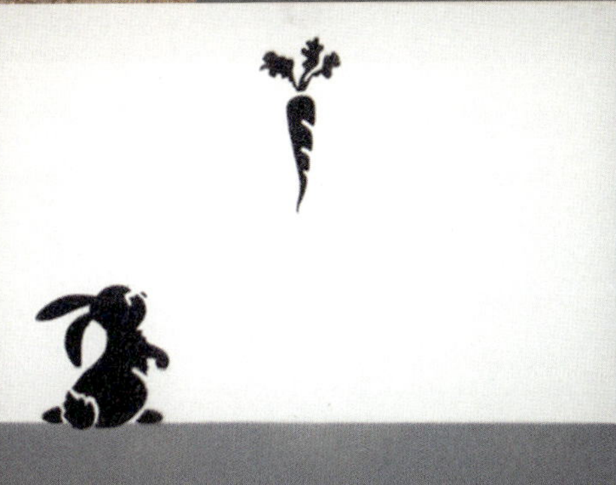

Bunny With Carrot

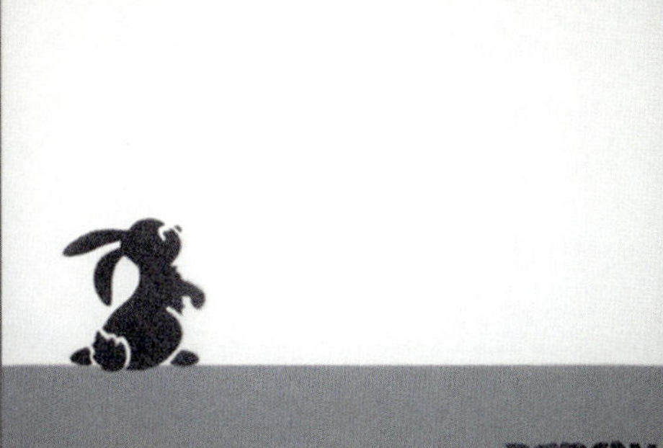

Bunny Without Carrot

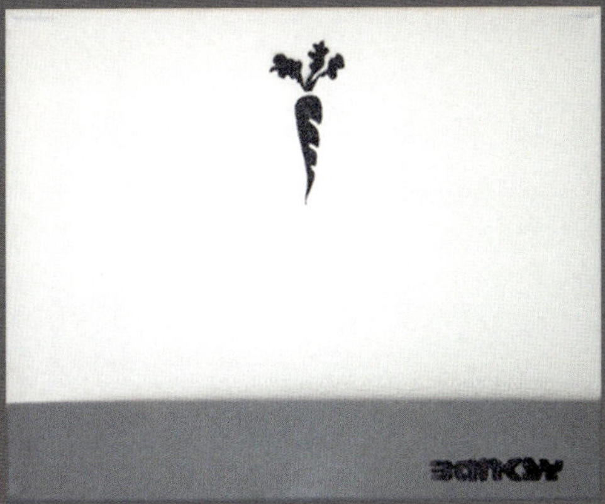

Carrot Without Bunny

CHECK IT OUT

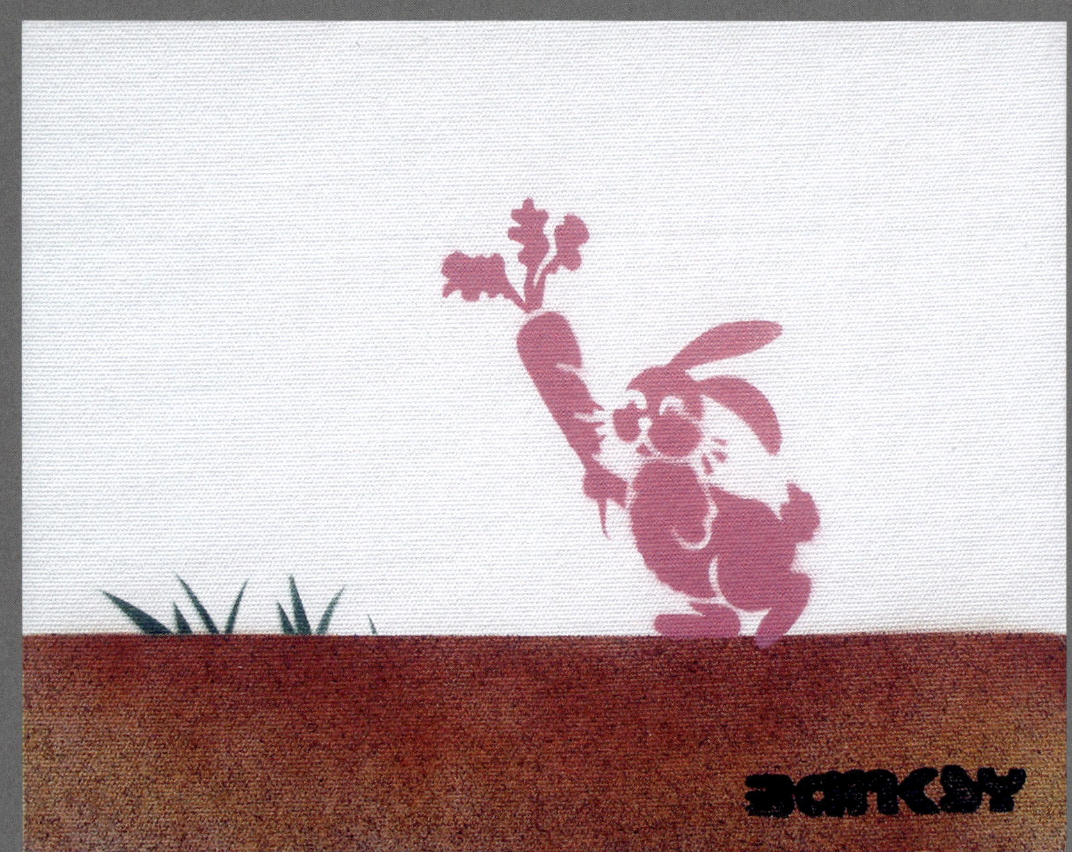

MORE PLEASE

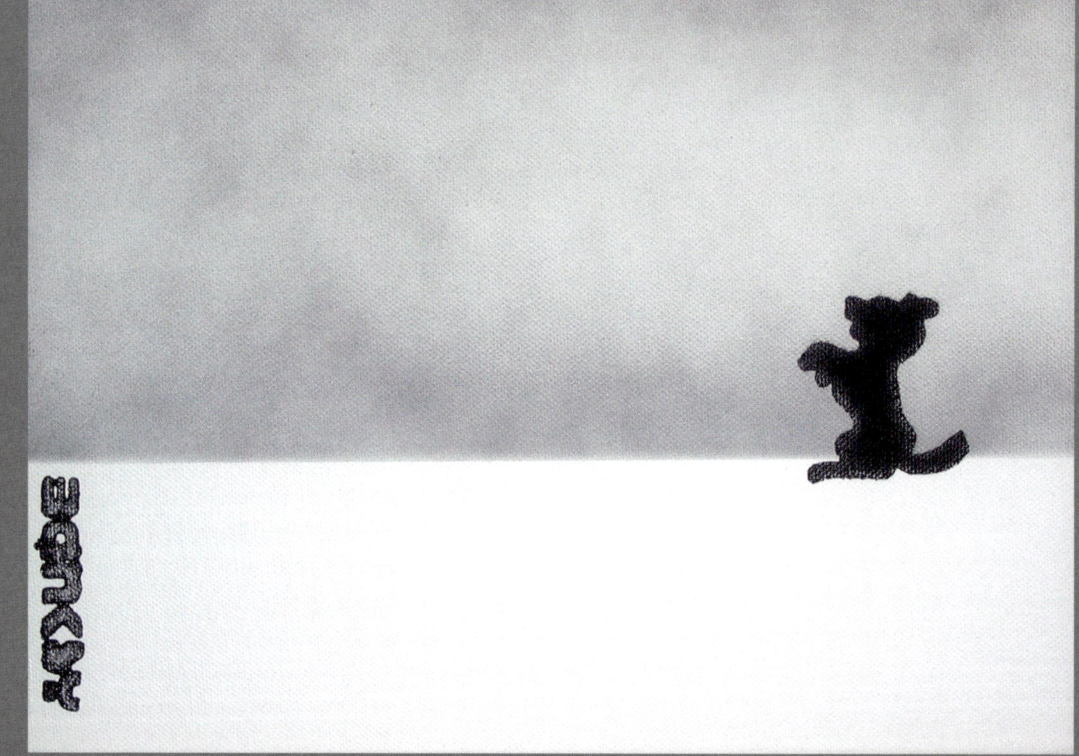

RURAL ART

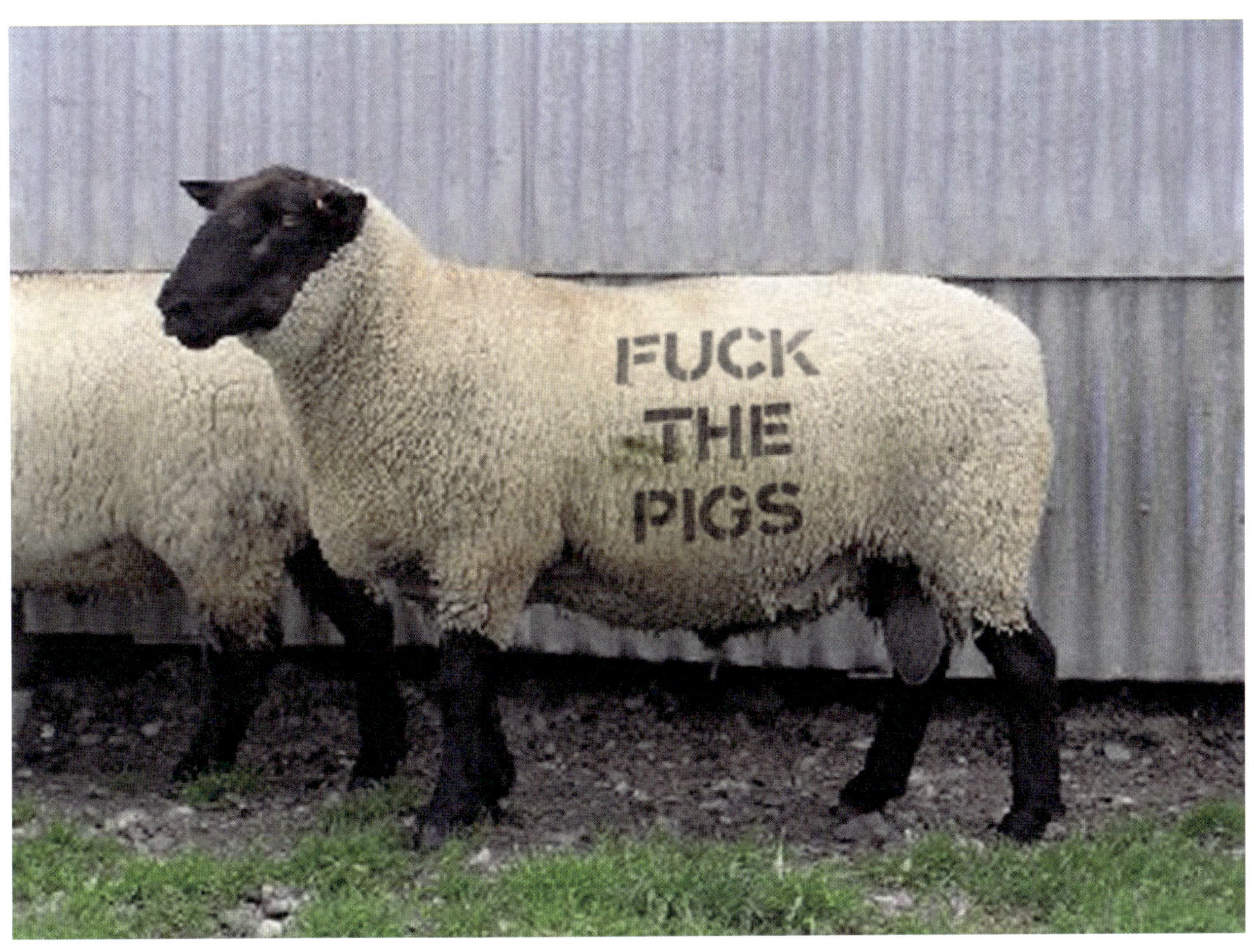

JULY 2008

THIS MORNING

a box of paintings was left anonymously on the doorstep of London's infamous L-13 Light Industrial Workshop - an organisation dedicated to the pursuit of art, leisure and the disruptive betterment of culture.

At first glance, it would seem the paintings are by the shy and secretive artist known as BANKSY, although it is obvious to anyone with half a brain that they are all clearly poorly executed pastiche fakes and NOT by BANKSY at all.

The paintings came with a note claiming that these NOT BANKSY's are the first offerings of a new, vital and ineffectual art movement know as RURAL ART. The leading lights of which, having previously earned success in the Urban Art Scene have now moved to "da C*NTRY" where they can disseminate their inane radical-chic messaging in a more genteel and leisurely manner.

Statement issued July 2008

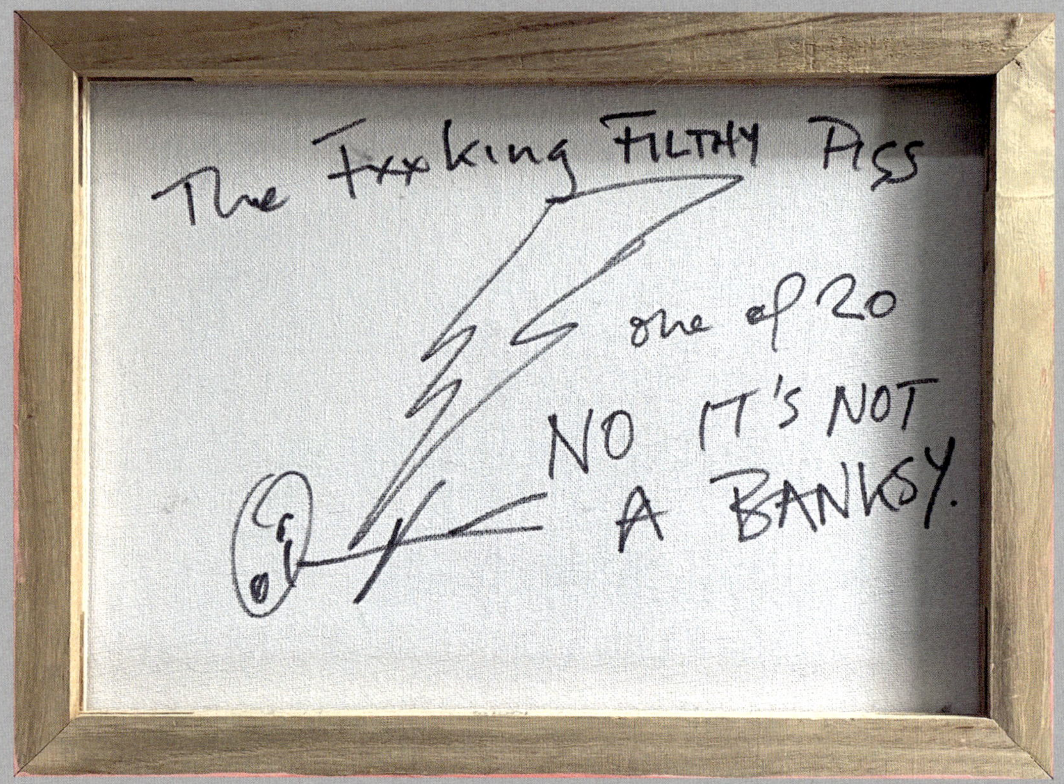

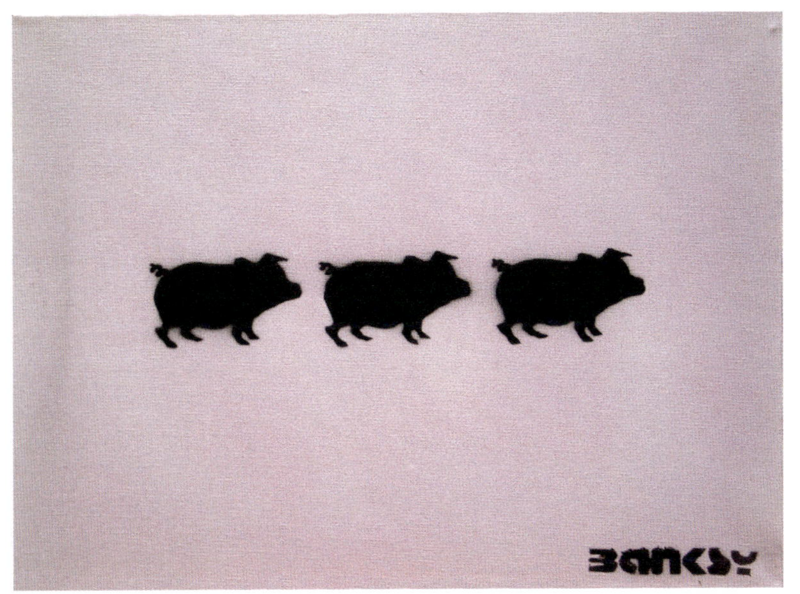

F**K THE PIGS

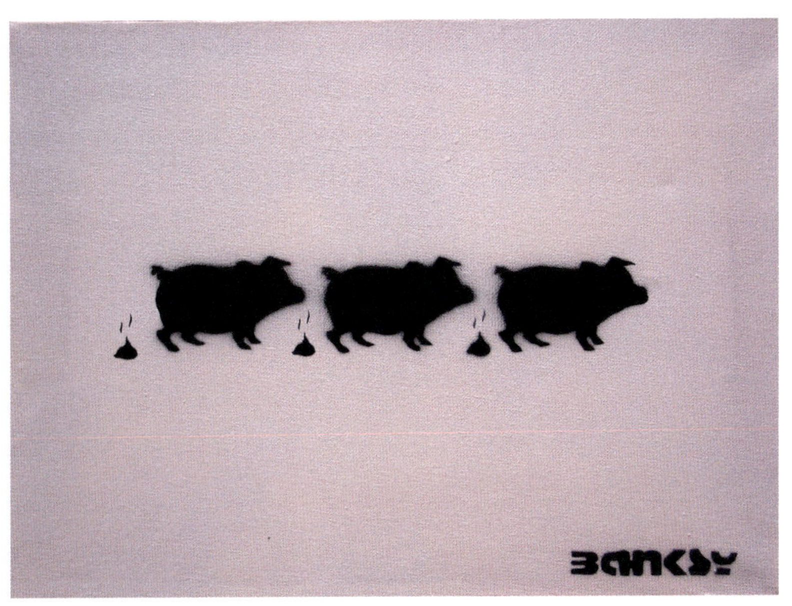

THE F**CKING
FILTHY PIGS

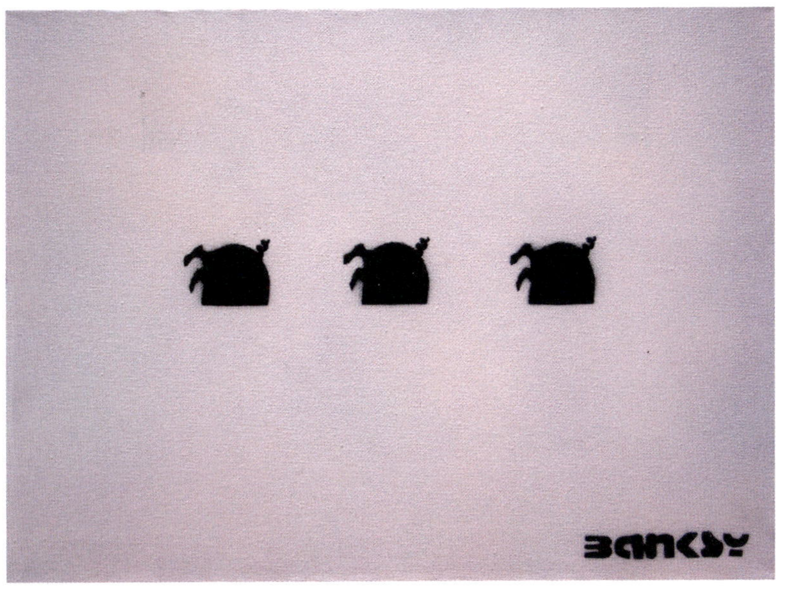

DOWN WITH
THE F**CKING
FILTHY PIGS

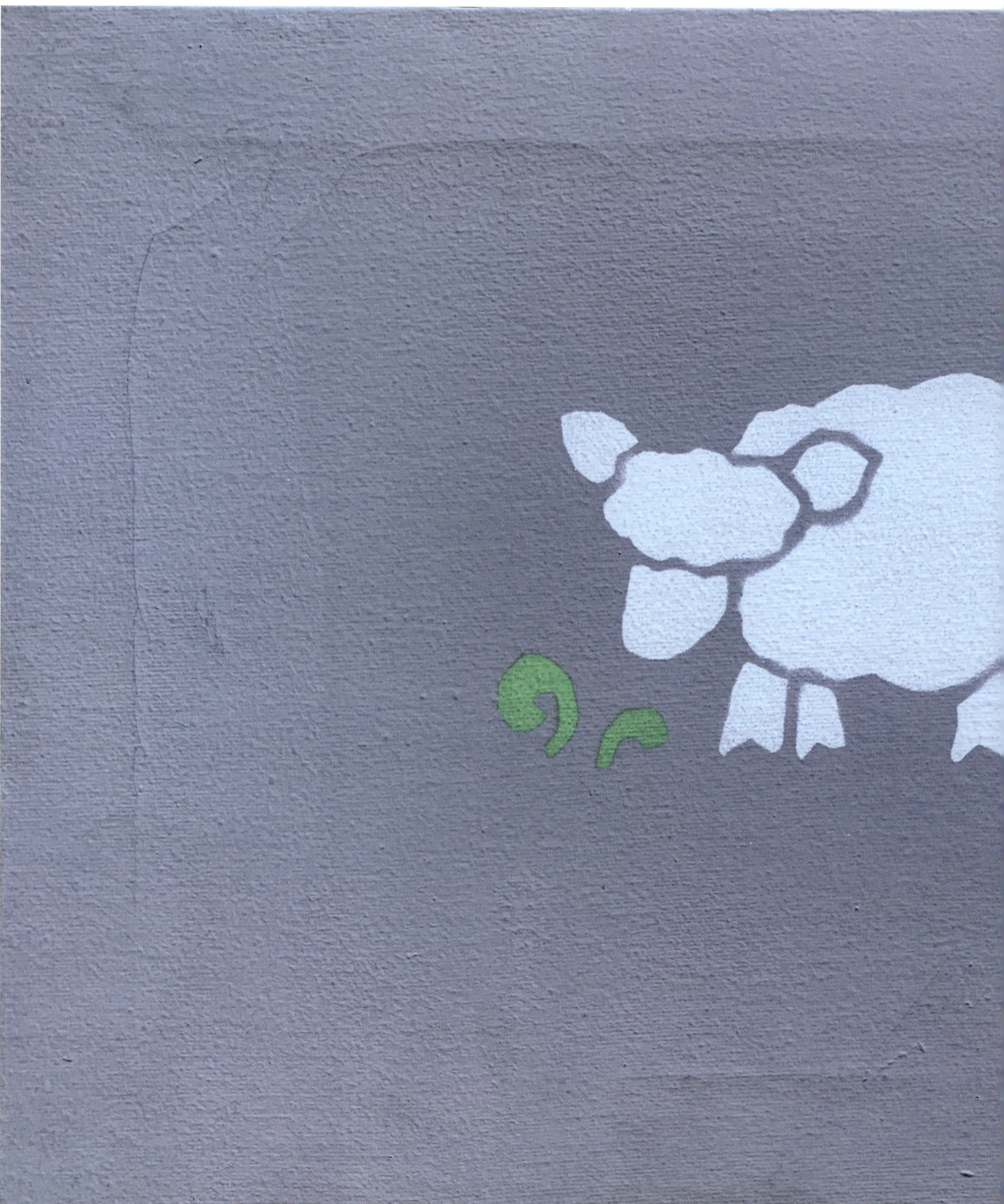

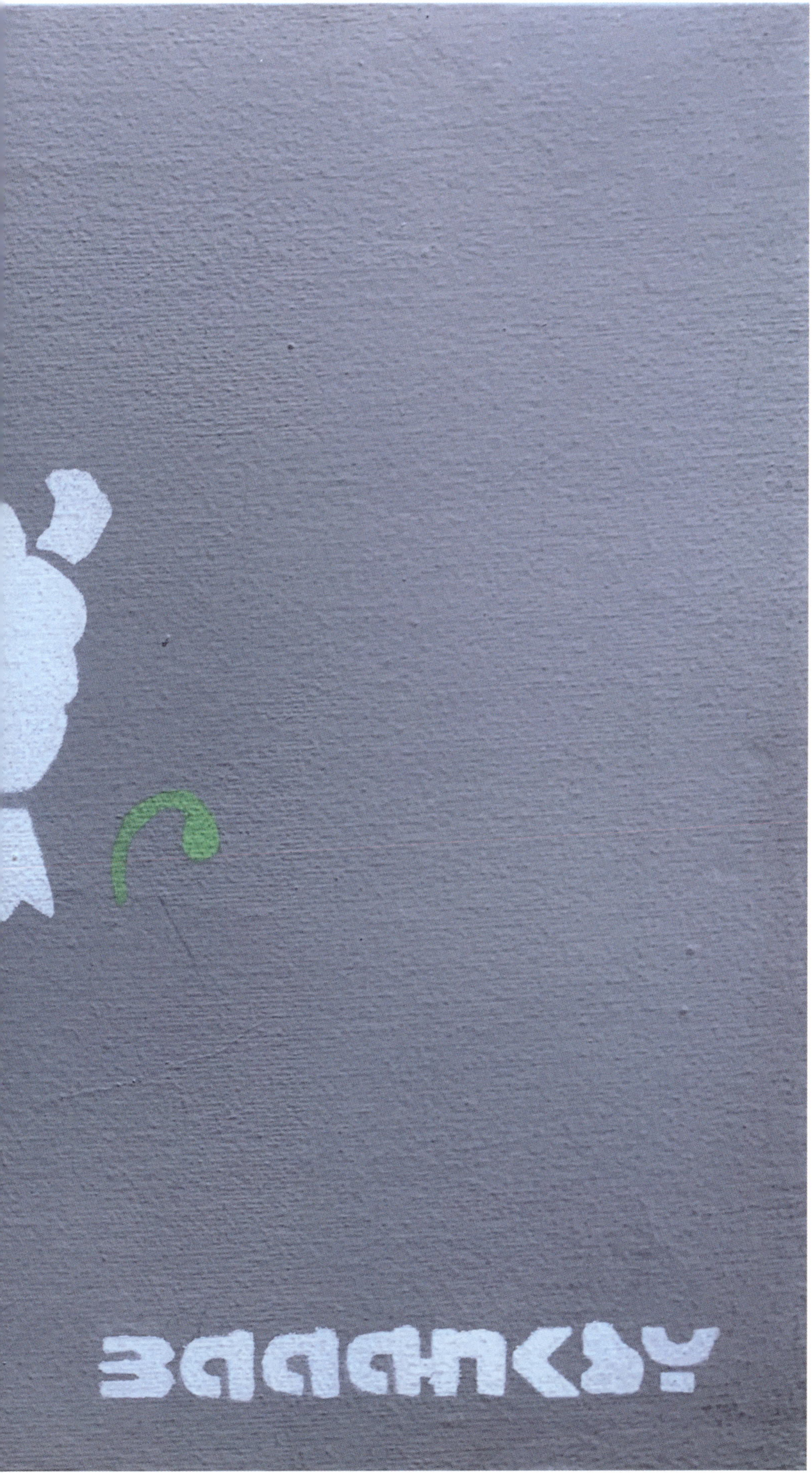

BUT

NO MATTER
HOW RIDICULOUS
THE PAINTINGS WERE
PEOPLE KEPT
BUYING THEM

WAS IT BECAUSE
THE IDEA WAS
STUPID
?

WAS IT BECAUSE
THEY WERE CHEAP
?

WAS IT BECAUSE
PEOPLE LIKED THE
PICTURES
?

WAS IT BECAUSE
THEY THOUGHT MAYBE
THEY COULD
REALLY REALLY
BE
BY BANKSY
& THEREFORE
MAYBE MAYBE MAYBE
WORTH LOTS OF MONEY

?

THEN
WE MADE
'GETTING
A SERIES OF 11 PAINTINGS
IN EDITIONS OF 20,000

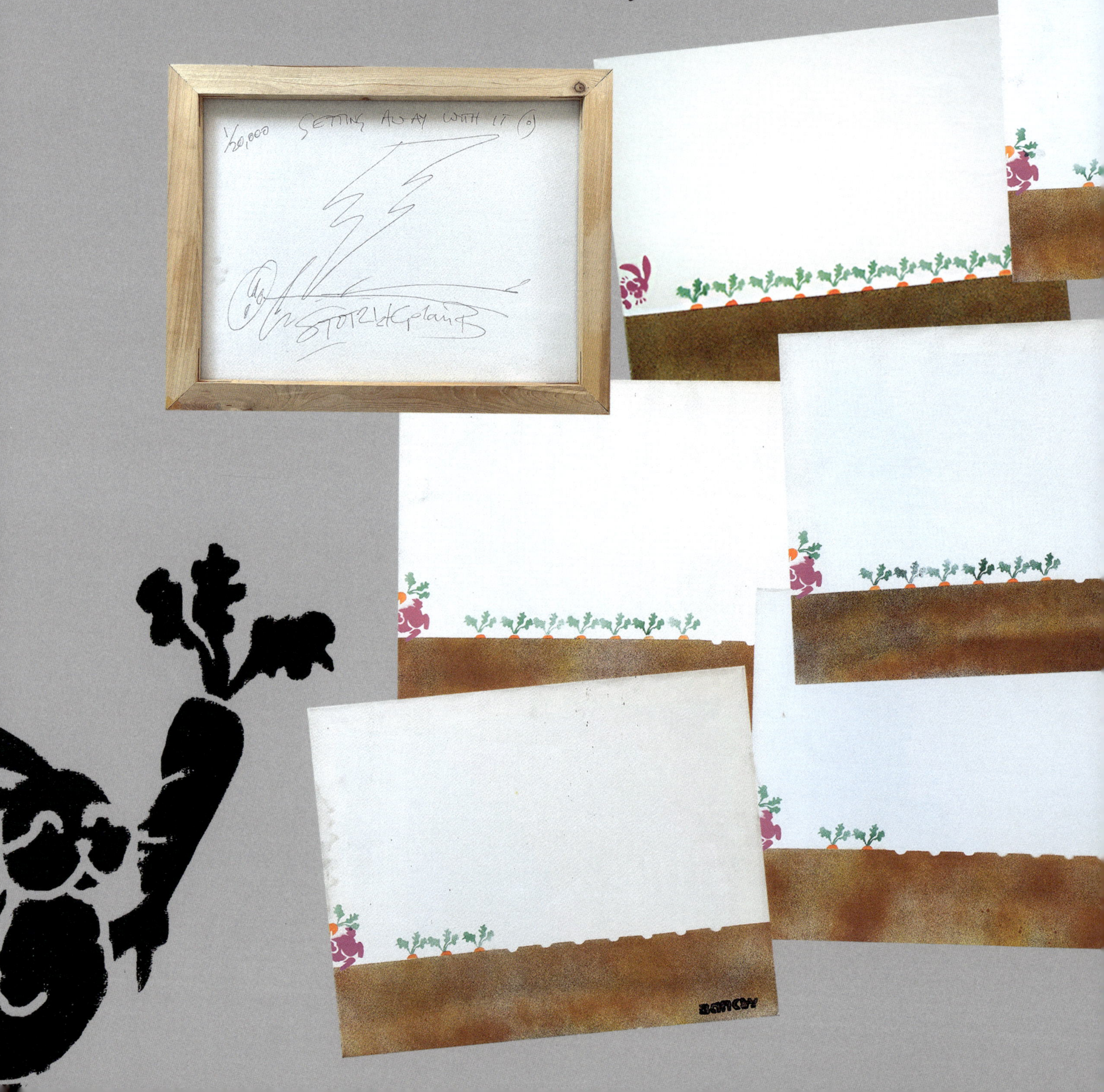

1/20,000   GETTING AWAY WITH IT

AWAY WITH IT'

THAT CAUSED A SERIOUS PAUSE

FOR

THOUGHT

SO

WE STOPPED FOR A BIT

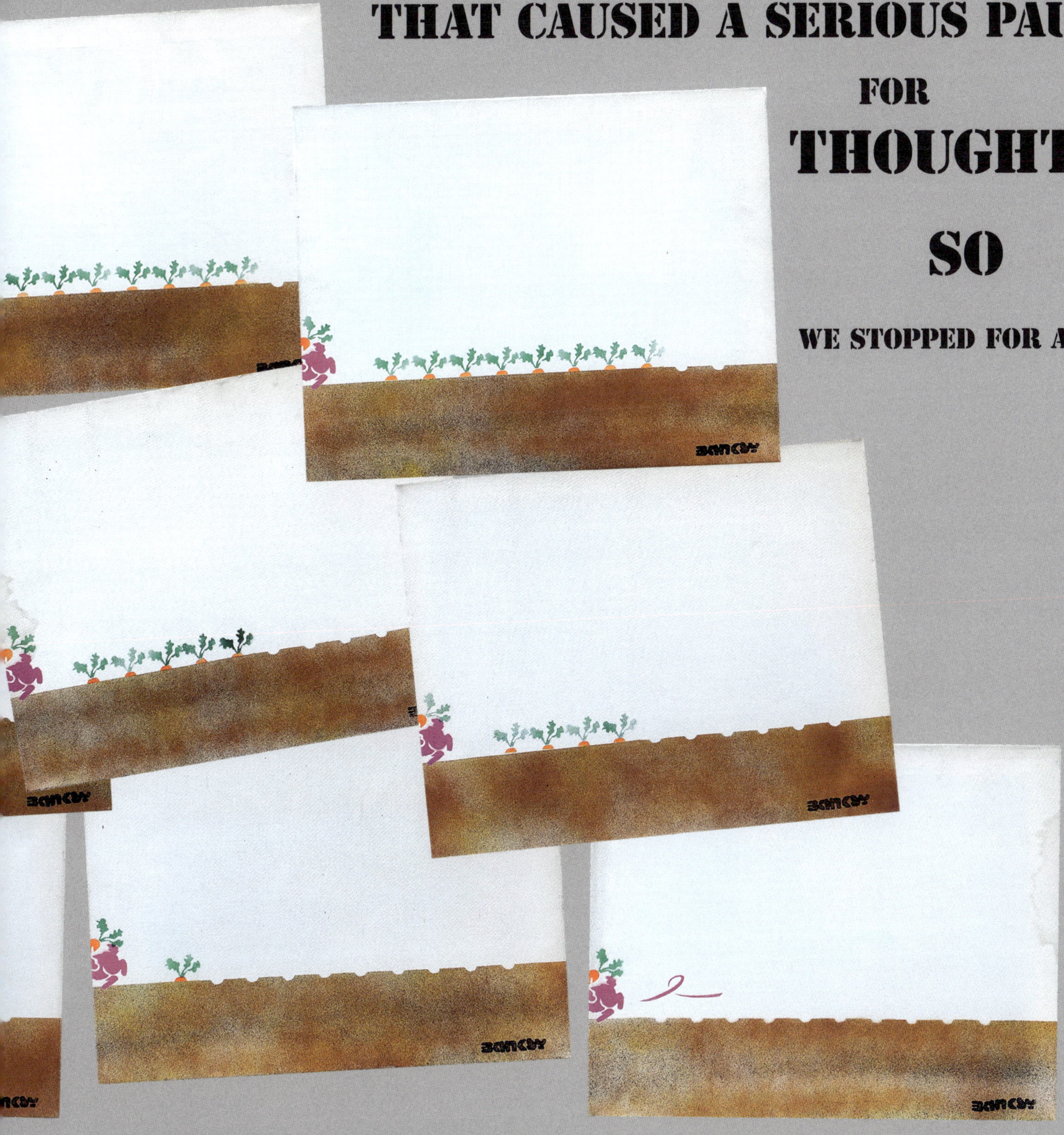

UNTIL   WE WONDERED
WHAT WOULD HAPPEN IF THE PAINTINGS REALLY LOOKED LIKE BANKSYS

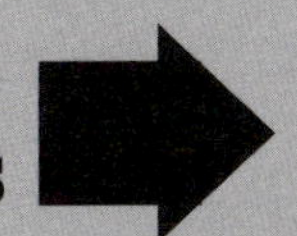

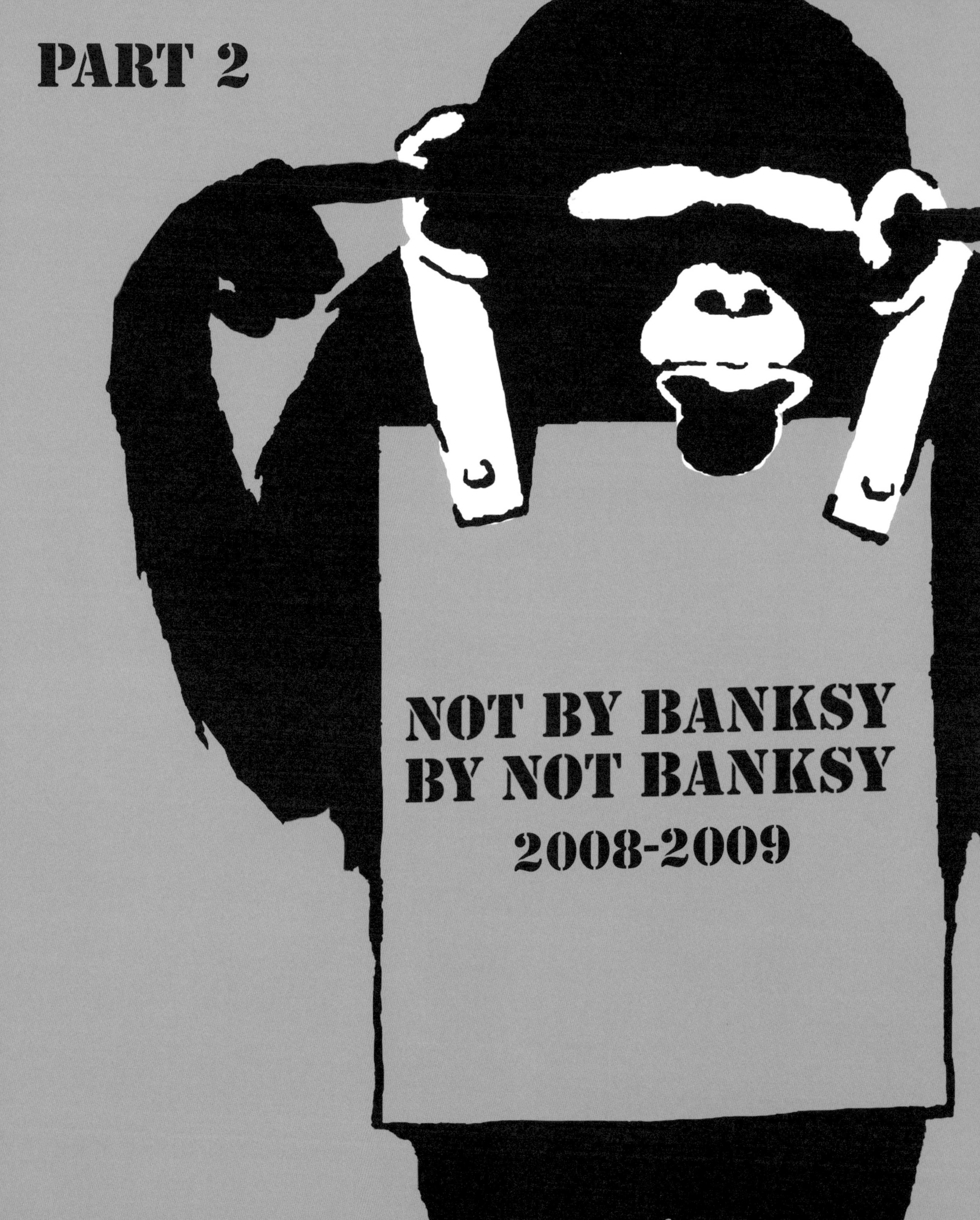

PART 2
NOT BY BANKSY
BY NOT BANKSY
2008-2009

FUCK IT

LET'S

FAKE IT

!

A MASTERPIECE OF DÉTOURNEMENT IN OUR SPECTACULAR SOCIETY

NUMBERS 1, 2 & 3

A masterful critique or just regurgitation of the same old shit?
Daylight robbery or liberation?
A fake Banksy or a real NOT BANKSY?

YOU BE THE JUDGE

Appropriating the lingo of the Situationist International for the titles,
these stencil paintings were all made in editions of 100, signed with the
STOT21stCplanB 'Thunderbolt Man' and numbered on the back.
All sold for £45 each.

The Janitor had come up with the tag line "I can't believe it's Not Banksy" after the fake butter
commercial and The Assistant to the Janitor decided that the only way to add to the
gleeful mind-fuckery was to make the pictures look like real Banksys
and say they were NOT by BANKSY, but by NOT BANKSY.
Thus inventing the 'genuine honest Not Banksy fake'.

To add to the confusion and clarify that they were
NOT by BANKSY but by NOT BANKSY
they all came with a fake Pest Control Certificate of Authenticity*
stating who the real artists were.

At this point we really were taking the piss and knew it.
We ramped up the rhetoric of the whole project as being
"a shoddy attention seeking stunt to cash in on such a fine talent (as Bansky's)"
devised to both annoy and/or amuse those who wished to engage with what we were up to.

If asked, we insisted we had nothing against Banksy himself. In fact we admired his high
spirited populist approach and wish to democratise art in a smart way. But... at the same
time disliked the machinations of the art world and commerce that were pushing
his prices beyond reasonable affordability and out of the reach of those it was intended
for, changing both the value and meaning of the work whilst spawning a slew of poor
imitators, blind adoration, and nefarious exploitation by those only interested in
financial gain and/or superficial cudos.

We claimed no higher moral ground.
We aimed to be both noble and despicable in equal measure.
But mostly we just wanted to make fun of the nonsense whilst providing
quality entertainment and art swag at a reasonable price.

* Pest Control is the organisation that officially authenticates Banksy artworks

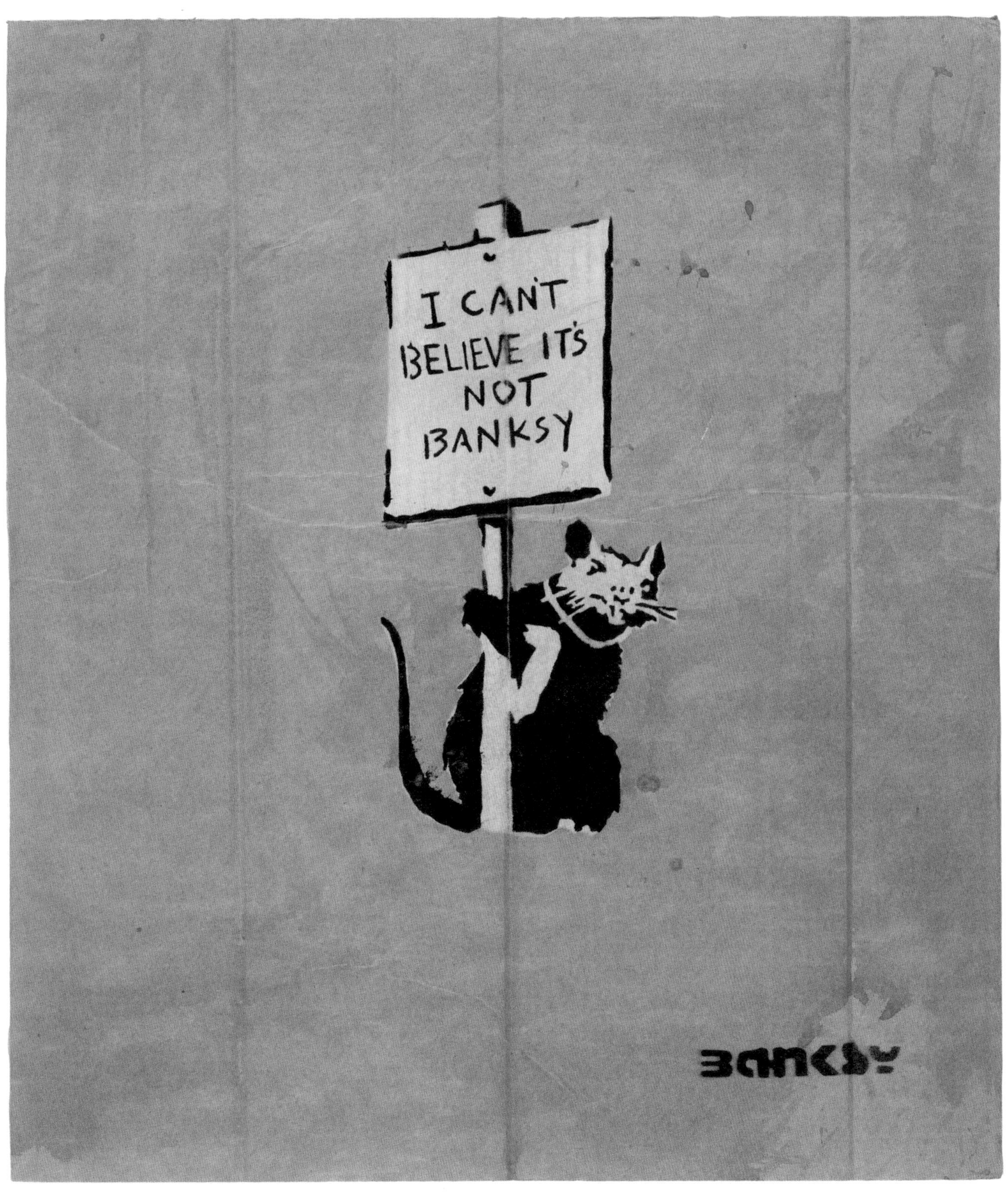

A Masterpiece of Détournement in Our Spectacular Society No.1

Spray paint, household paint and urban grime on genuine cardboard
Ltd Edition of 100
signed and numbered by STOT21stCplanB on the reverse
50 x 42 cm

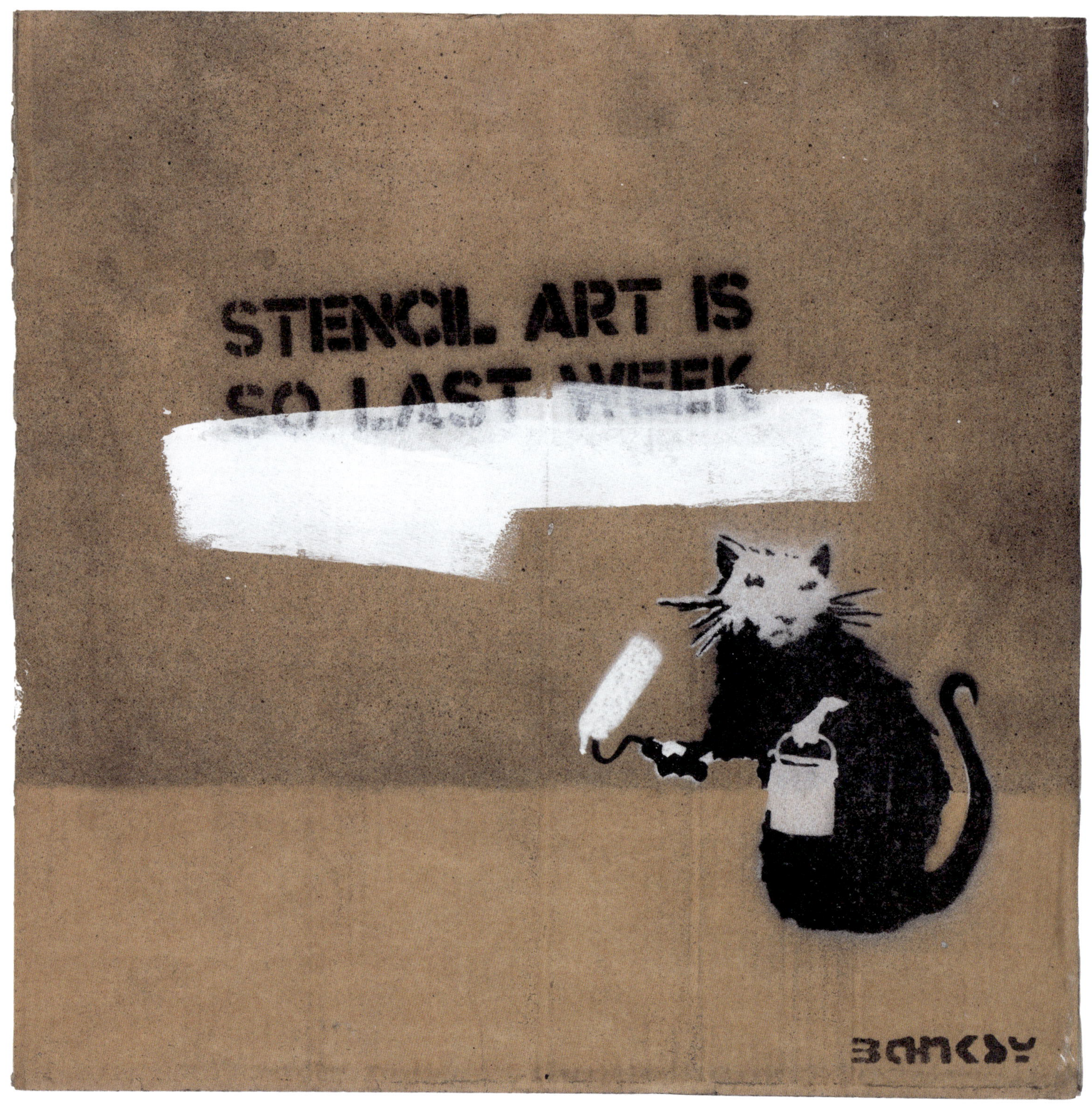

A Masterpiece of Détournement in Our Spectacular Society No.2

Spray paint, household paint and urban grime on genuine cardboard
Ltd Edition of 100
signed and numbered by STOT21stCplanB on the reverse
50 x 50 cm

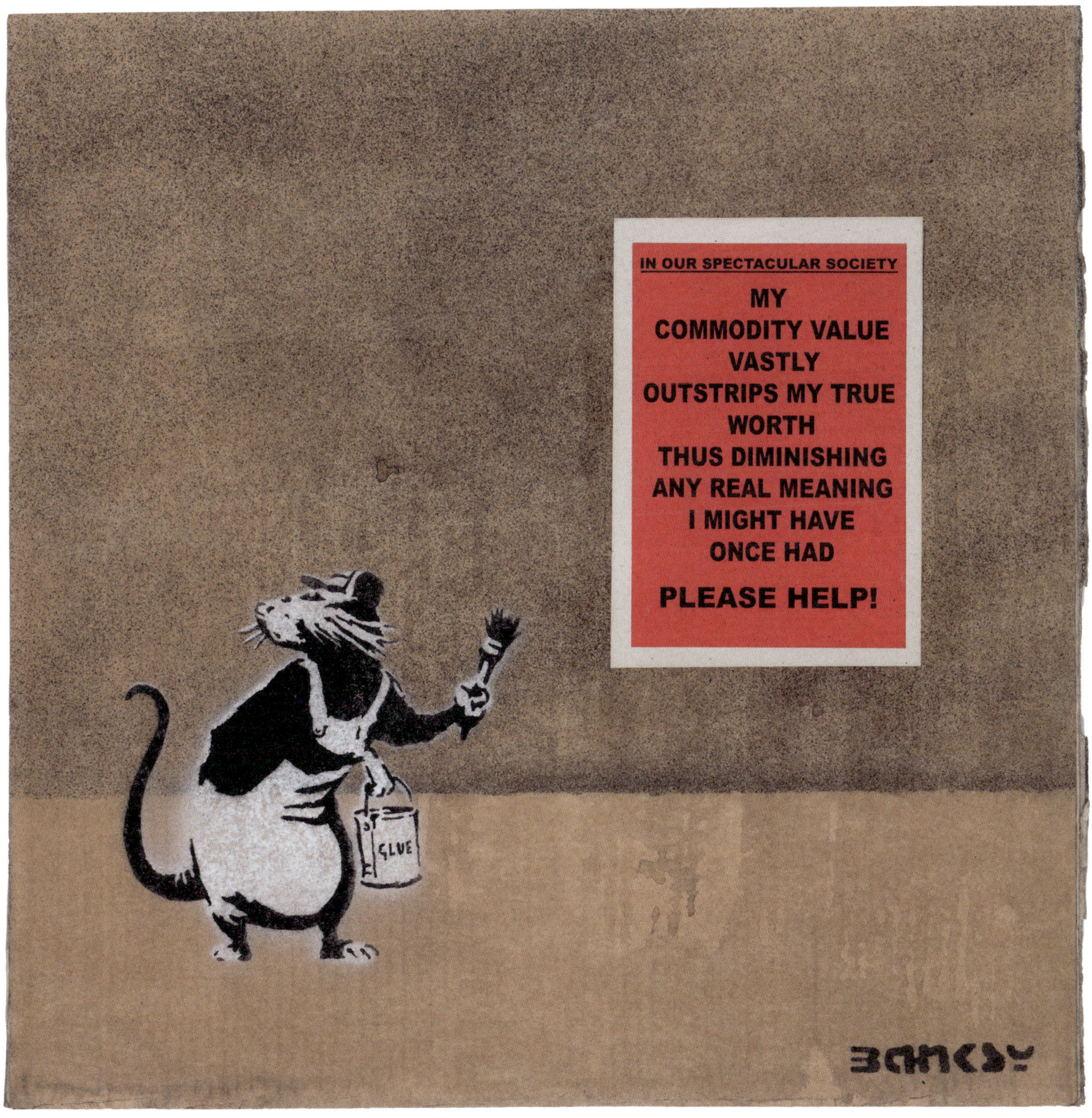

A Masterpiece of Détournement in Our Spectacular Society No.3

Spray paint, household paint, printed paper and urban grime on genuine cardboard
Ltd Edition of 100
signed and numbered by STOT21stCplanB on the reverse
50 x 50 cm

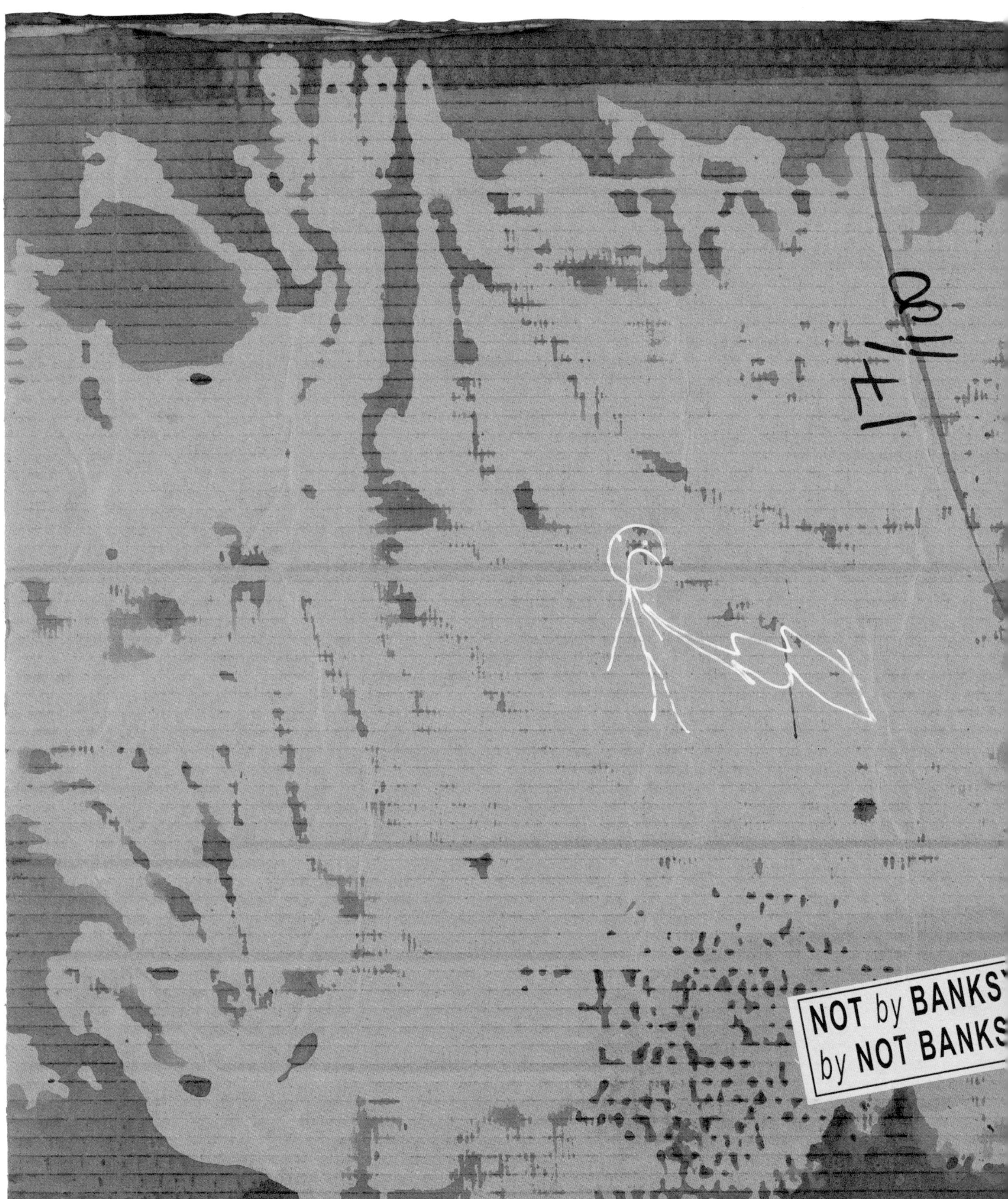

NOT by BANKS
by NOT BANKS

Certificate of Authenticity

Title: A Masterpiece of Detournement in Our Spectacular Society No3

Medium: Spray paint and pompous poster on cardboard, stained with authentic urban grime, certified by the urban soil association.

Year: 2008

Size: H: 50cm x L: 50cm

Edition: One of an edition of 100

Notes: Signed and numbered by STOT21stCplanB Please note: They don't always sign the tedious. The signature may just be a sti Also.... No Banksy had nothing to do wit

This is to certify that the work described above is an 'original' work of 'art' by NOT BANKSY and NOT by BANKSY

Signed: X

Date: 28-11-08

THE CLASSICS

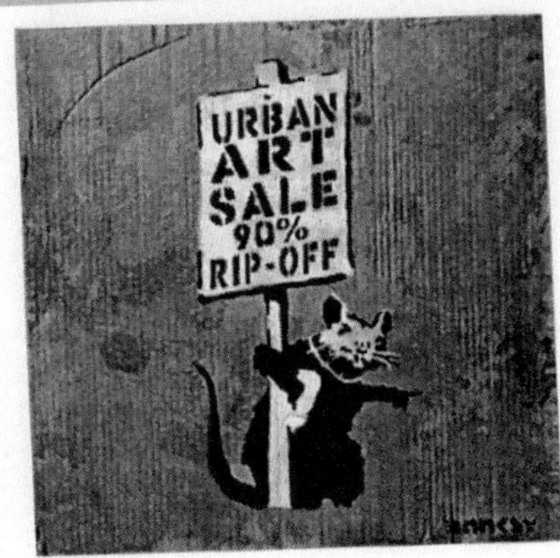

Great Expectations

Classic tale of love, crime and destiny.

19 inches by 19 inches of stencil art genius on Real Kool Cardboard (RKC) and keepin it real with authentic urban grime.

Edition of 100 at a wicked price you kids can dig.

Signed and numbered on the back by NOT STOT21stCplanB. Comes with a real fake COA from Pest Control that proves nuffink.

Available ONLY whilst stocks last.

Also available as a tacky inkjet print on canvas. Please enquire at your local Snappy Snaps.

Price: £45.00

add to cart

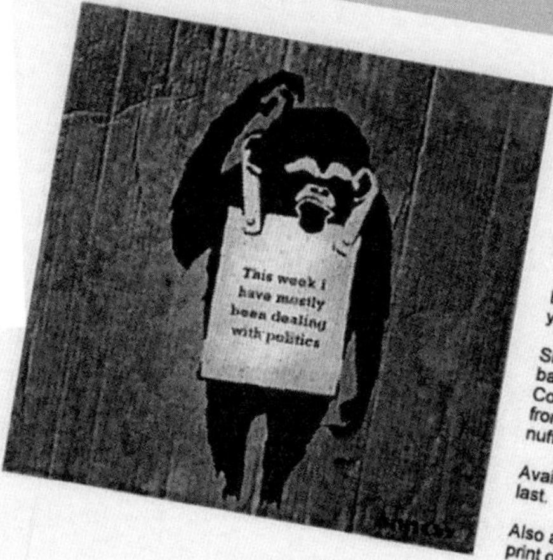

add to cart

Pride and Prejudice

Radical yet predictable tale of intrigue, suspense and idiocy.

19 inches by 19 inches of stencil art genius on Real Kool Cardboard (RKC) and keepin it real with authentic urban grime.

Edition of 100 at a wicked price you kids can dig.

Signed and numbered on the back by NOT STOT21stCplanB. Comes with a real fake COA from Pest Control that proves nuffink.

Available ONLY whilst stocks last.

Also available as a tacky inkjet print on canvas. Please enquire at your local Snappy Snaps.

Price: £45.00

add to cart

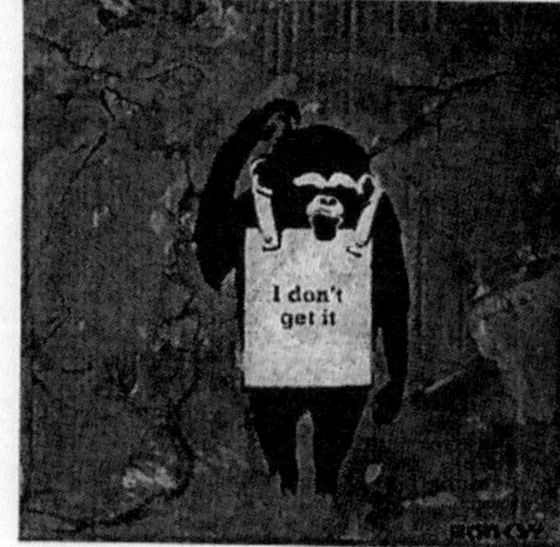

A twisted but... poses radical questions as to the nature of mans goodness in relation to evil.

19 inches by 19 inches of stencil art genius on Real Kool Cardboard (RKC) and keepin it real with authentic urban grime.

Edition of 100 at a wicked price you kids can dig.

Signed and numbered on the back by NOT STOT21stCplanB. Comes with a real fake COA from Pest Control that proves nuffink.

Available ONLY whilst stocks last.

Also available as a tacky inkjet print on canvas. Please enquire at your local Snappy Snaps.

Price: £45.00

add to cart

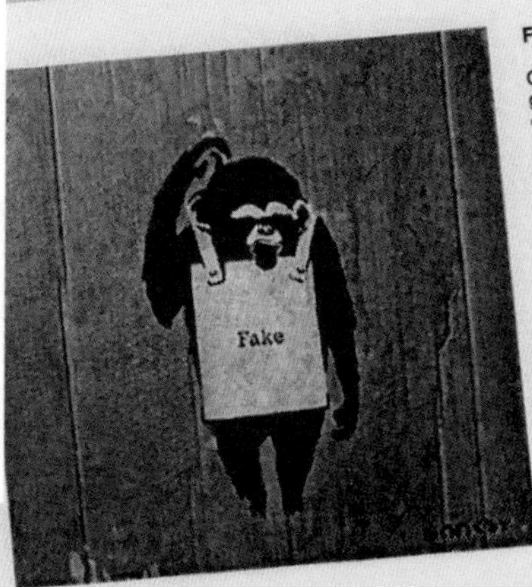

Far From The Madding Crowd

Gripping tale of patient, generous love and faith that ends in misery.

19 inches by 19 inches of stencil art genius on Real Kool Cardboard (RKC) and keepin it real with authentic urban grime.

Edition of 100 at a wicked price you kids can dig.

Signed and numbered on the back by NOT STOT21stCplanB. Comes with a real fake COA from Pest Control that proves nuffink.

Available ONLY whilst stocks last.

Also available as a tacky inkjet print on canvas. Please enquire at your local Snappy Snaps.

Price: £45.00

add to cart

Why we named this series after 19th Century works of literature is anyone's guess.
We guess it was something to do with applying high art pretensions to low art products to make them seem more interesting than they were.

Great Expectations
A classic tale of love, crime and destiny

Spray paint, household paint and urban grime on genuine cardboard
Ltd Edition of 100
signed and numbered by STOT21stCplanB on the reverse
50 x 50 cm

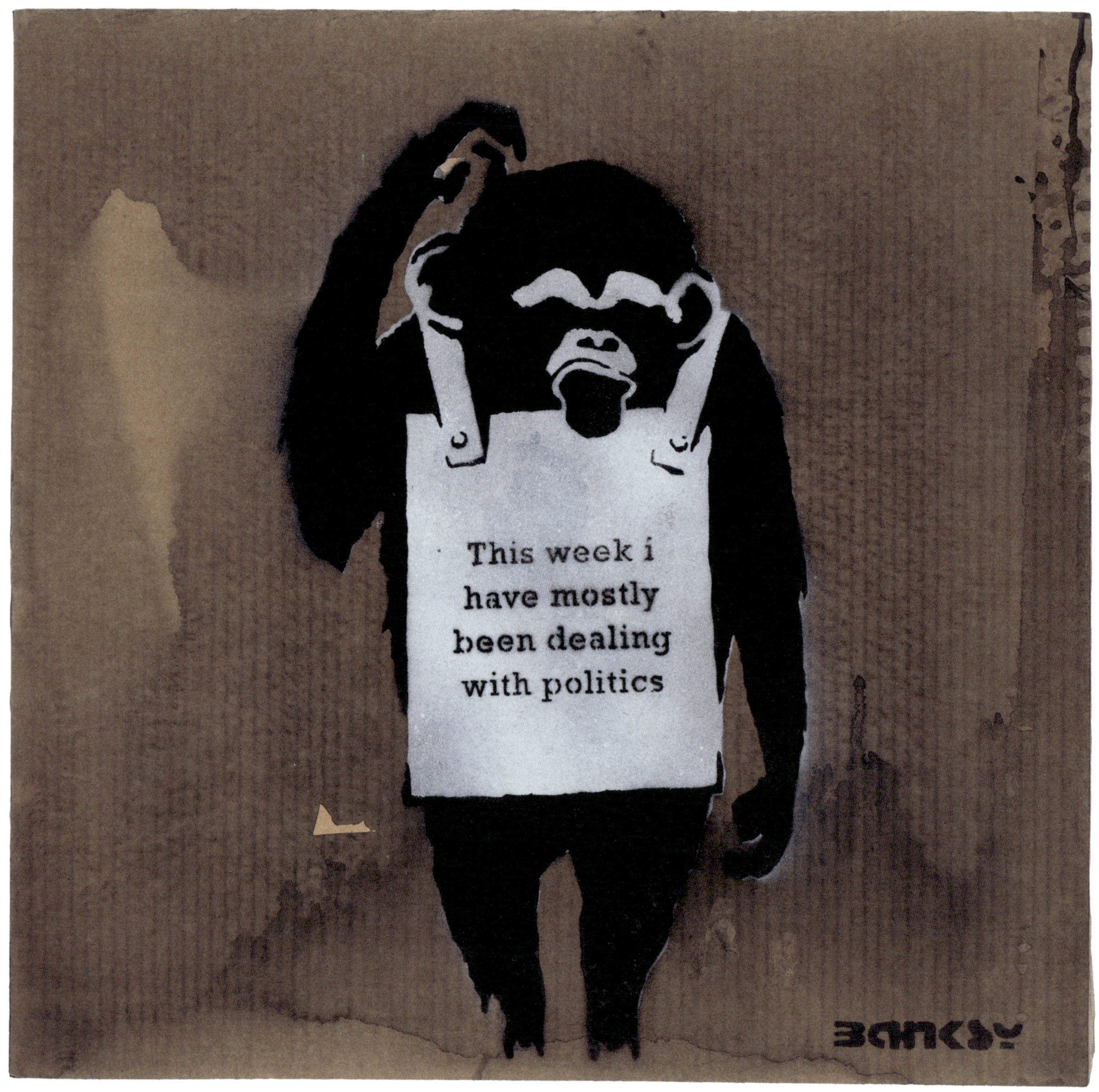

Pride and Prejudice
A radical yet predictable tale of intrigue, suspense and idiocy

Spray paint, household paint and urban grime on genuine cardboard
Ltd Edition of 100
signed and numbered by STOT21stCplanB on the reverse
50 x 50 cm

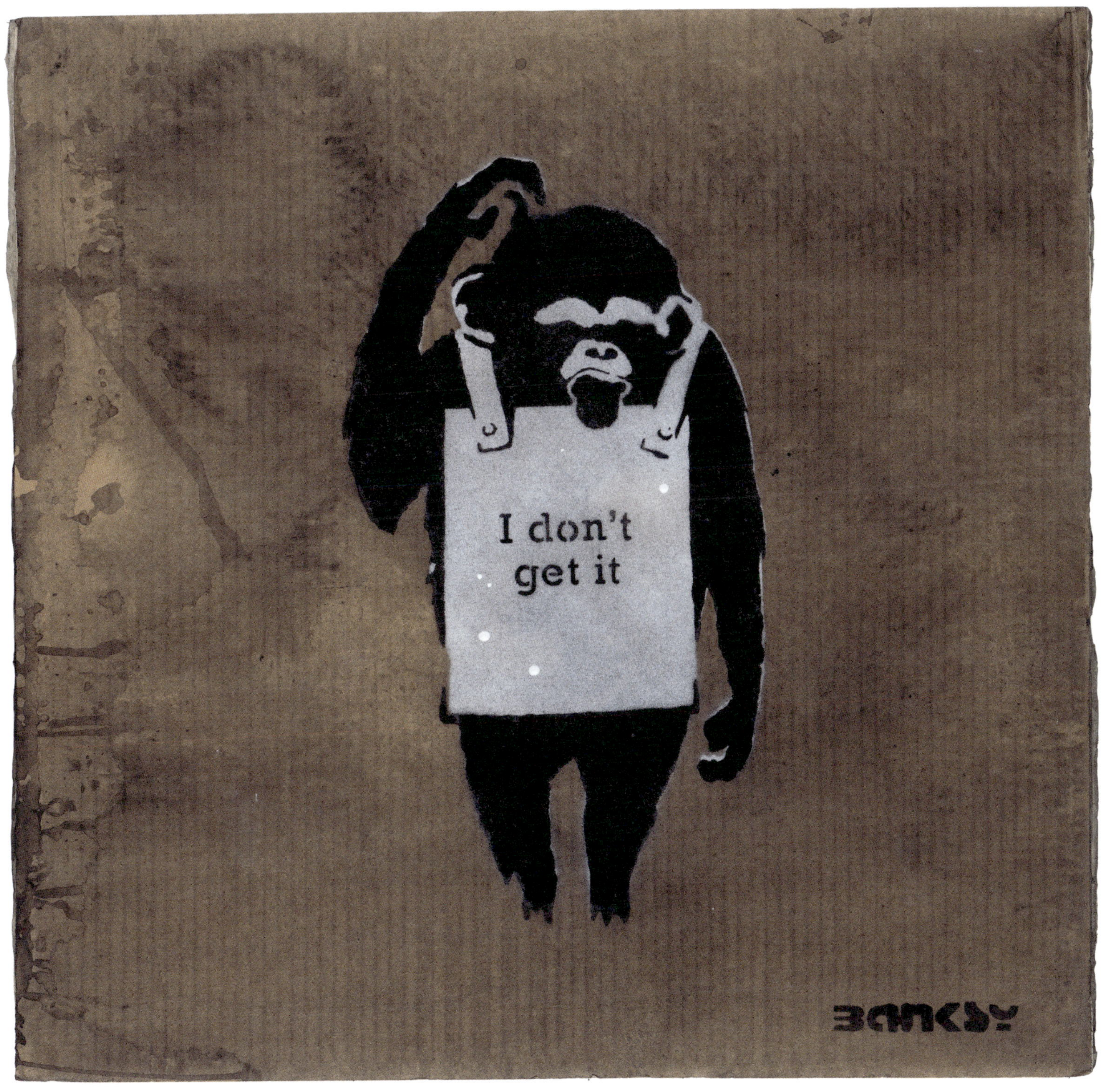

The Idiot
A twisted but hilarious tale that poses radical questions as to the nature of man's goodness in relation to evil

Spray paint, household paint and urban grime on genuine cardboard
Ltd Edition of 100
signed and numbered by STOT21stCplanB on the reverse
50 x 50 cm

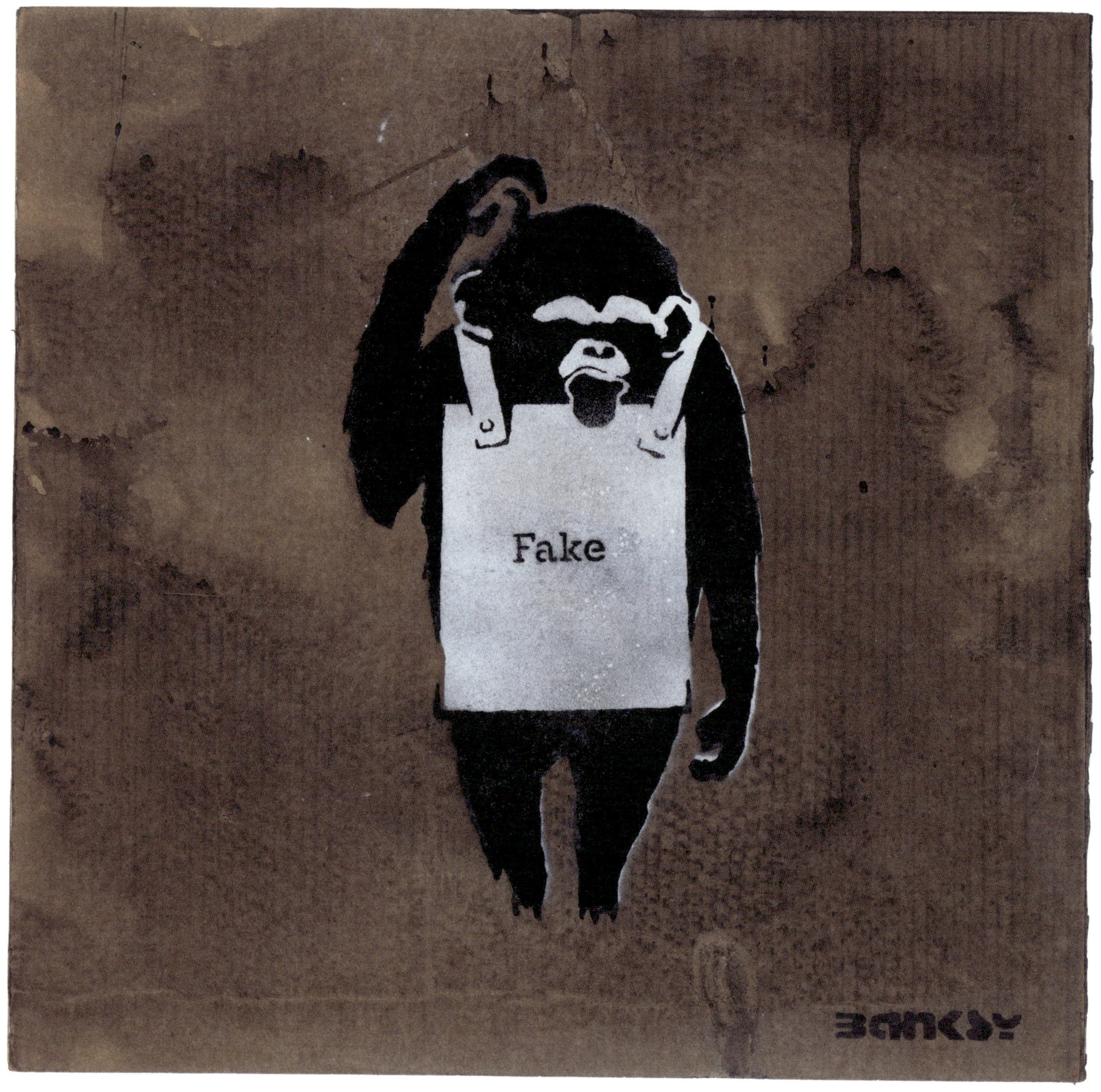

Far From The Madding Crowd
A gripping tale of patient, generous love and faith that ends in misery

Spray paint, household paint and urban grime on genuine cardboard
Ltd Edition of 100
signed and numbered by STOT21stCplanB on the reverse
50 x 50 cm

TIME TO STOP

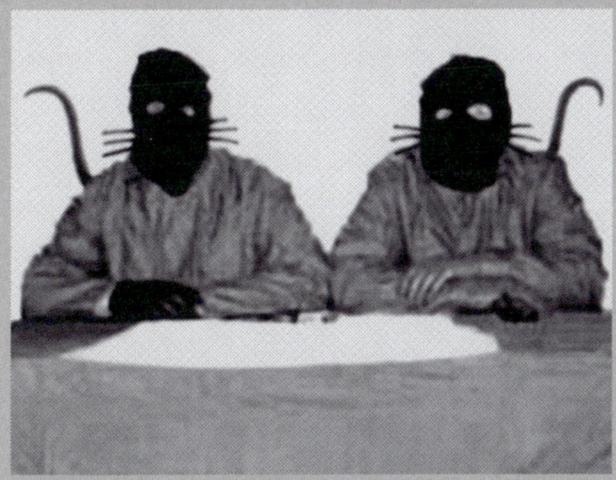

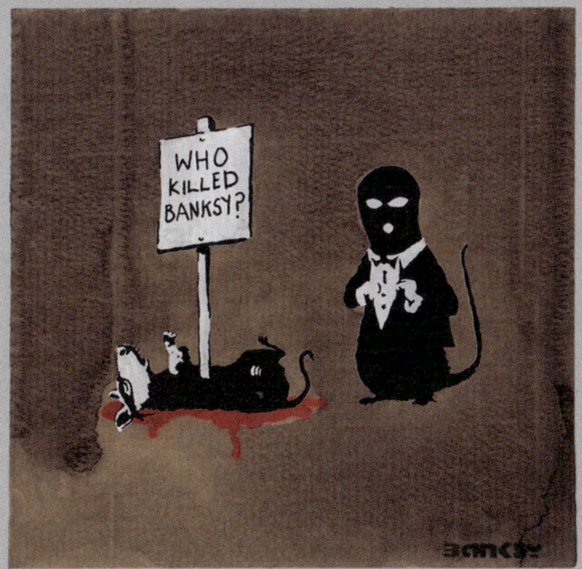

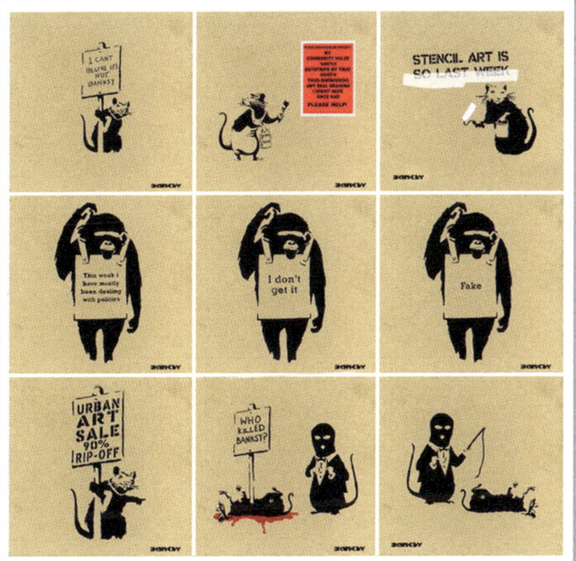

By this time we were running out of ideas and steam.

We were also a bit concerned that too many people were buying these editions in the vain hope that Banksy really was behind them and were waiting for the big reveal that would never come.

Messing with people's minds was part of the game, but tricking them was never on our agenda.

We guessed a few people were buying them because they were fans of STOT21stCplanB and understood our twisted humour and delight in ridicule, whilst many others claimed they were buying them as they were the closest thing to a real Banksy that they could afford.

But, in the end, we decided enough was enough was enough no matter what our excuses were. It was time to stop!

At the same time another **NOT BANKSY** had emerged with a website who was doing some great site specific piss-takes and shaming us by giving away editions for free.

Perhaps that was the real Banksy short-circuiting our efforts??

Any-which-way it was ceasing to be fun so we hung up our boots in the garden and went on boxing leave.

Seeing as there was now another **NOT BANKSY** we claimed **BANKSY** was **DEAD** and (our) **NOT BANKSY** along with him, then we published one last stencil painting edition:

WHO KILLED BANKSY
by the
CONTINUITY NOT BANKSY *
+
a series of very affordable mini screenprints
of our greatest **NOT BANKSY** hits, including
one new piece: FLOGGING A DEAD RAT.

* after the Continuity IRA

THEN WE DID NOTHING

for nearly 10 years

UNTIL →

EMPHATIC DENIAL NON-RESURRECTION (2018)

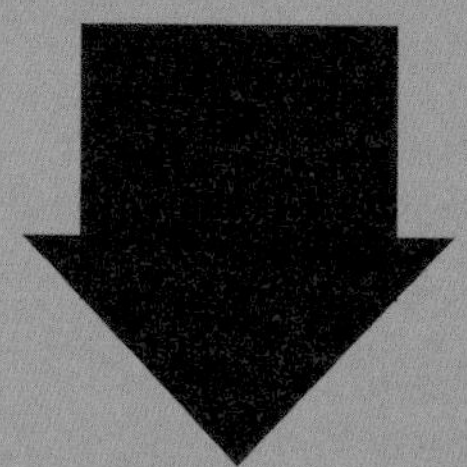

IS-NOT-ART (2021)

NOT NOT BANKSY
THE REAL NOT BANKSY FRONT
THE NEW NOT BANKSY REALISATION
THE NEW NOT BANKSY REALISATION
OF THE RISING SUN
&
THE EMERGENT IS-NOT-BANKSY
ABNORMALCY
OF THE
21ST CENTURY
GENERATION
Z

PART 3

2018

In the run up to 2018 we were increasingly asked to authenticate Not Banksy paintings that were showing up in various auctions.

We were also increasingly asked by some secondary market art dealers if we had any old pieces hidden in our archives that we'd be willing to sell.

It seemed that our old work was going up in price and therefore (as is the way of the art world) becoming more desirable.

More confusingly some fakes of our work started to appear on the secondary market. Strange, as anyone could be Not Banksy and make fake Banksy's, but these ones were listed as being by STOT21stCplanB complete with fakes of our fake Pest Control Certificates of Authentication. Weird!

The fakes were also shoddy in comparison to our finely crafted efforts, and there were no apparent jokes, critique or reinvention involved at all. Just straight copies of Banksys that seemed pointless to us.

So, we thought we'd best counteract the rising prices and emergence of pointless fakery with a brand new 10th Anniversary Edition at the same old price of £50.

We'd forgotten that Not Banksy had continued into 2009, so it was really a 9th anniversary, and we'd forgotten that the old price was £45 not £50, but details details details......

Not Banksy was also dead, so the resurrection came in the form of the Non-Resurrection of a new double-negative enitity known as NOT NOT BANKSY.

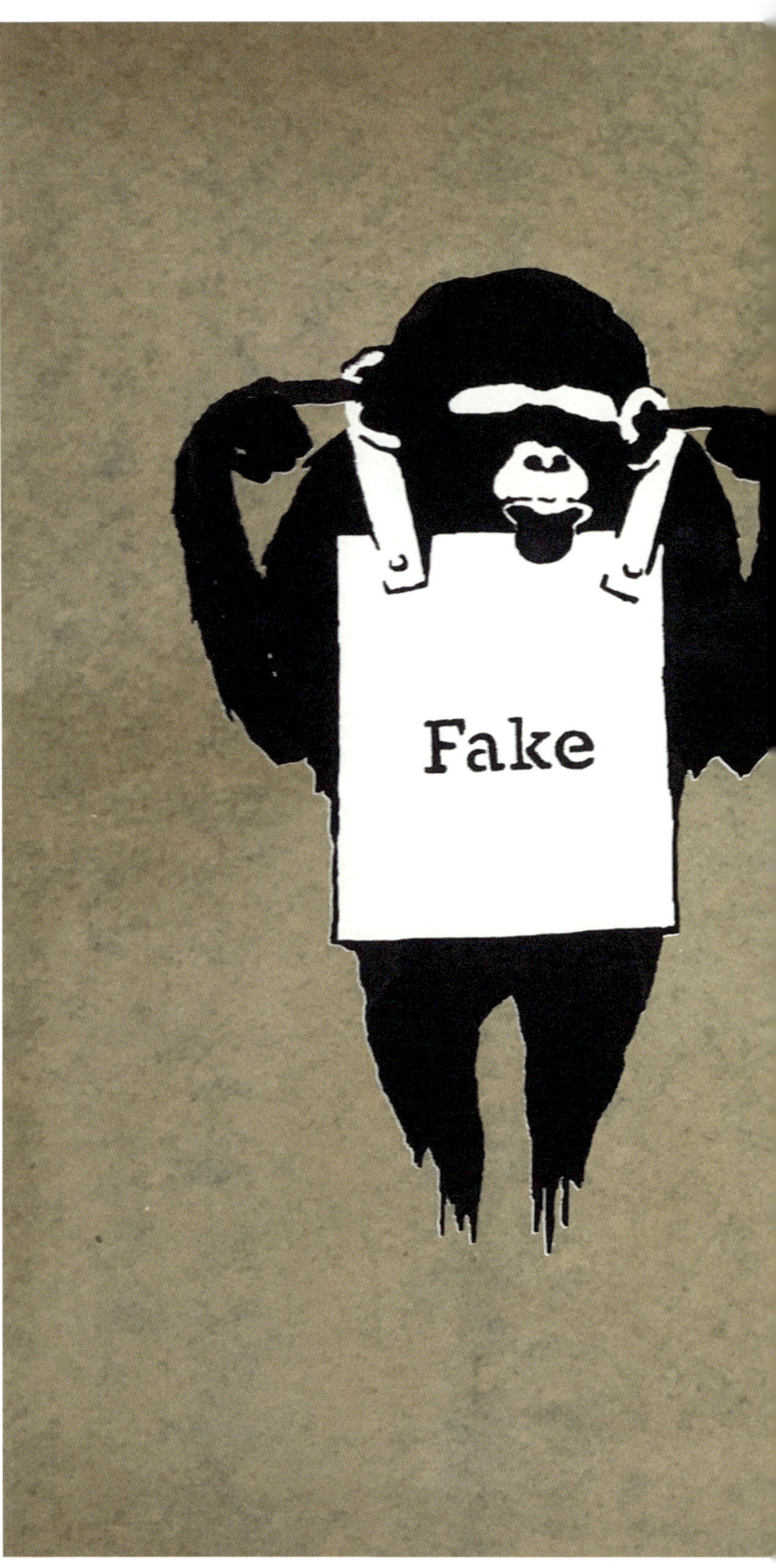

HEAR NOT NOT BANKSY,

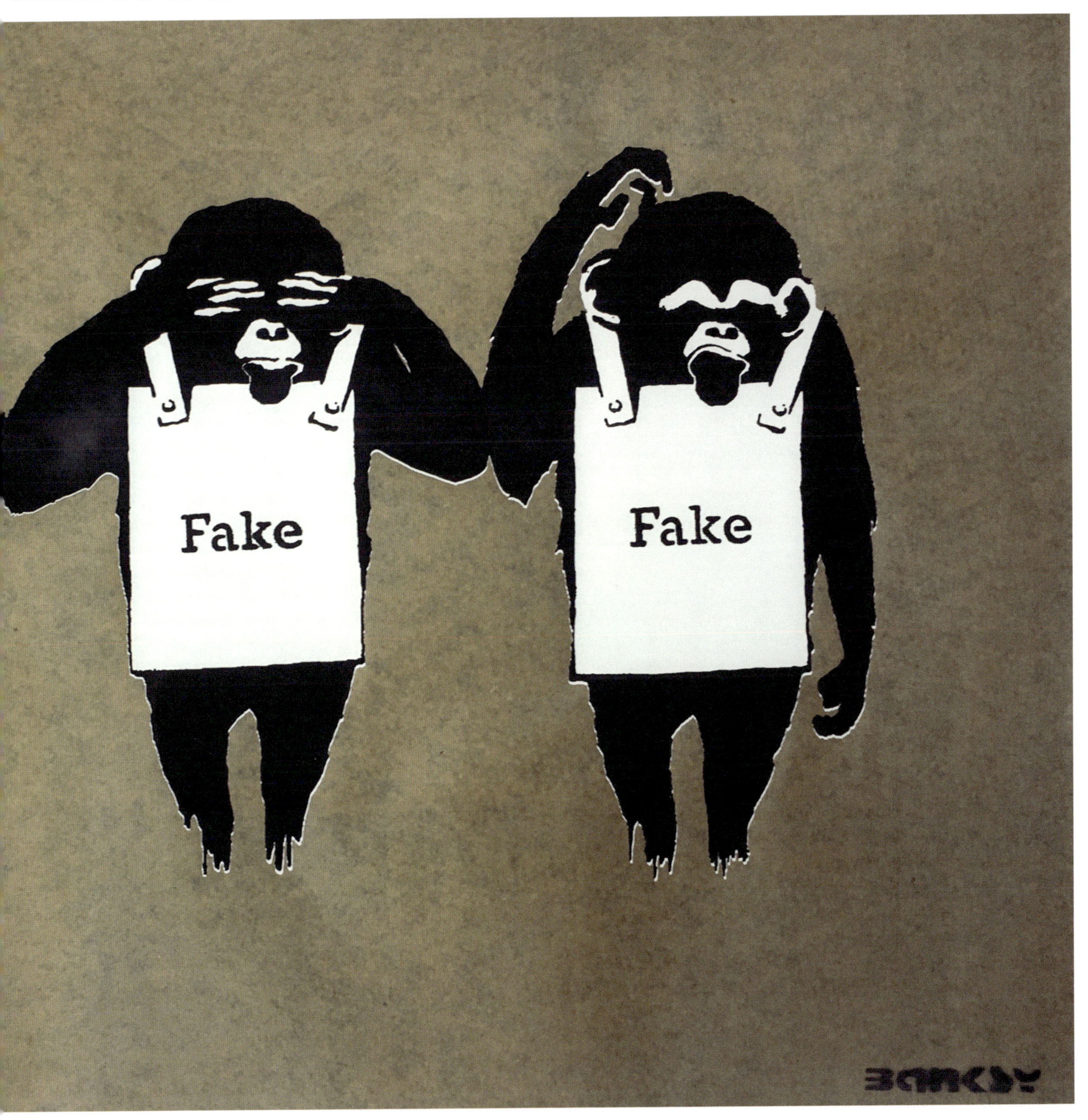

2 colour screen print on tar paper | 58 x 84 cm | Edition of 113 | Signed, numbered and titled on the back by STOT21stCplanB

NOT NOT BANKSY
is not
NOT BANKSY
as he is dead

These prints are a homage to NOT BANKSY (not BANKSY)
by a new artist known as NOT NOT BANKSY
who continues the great work of NOT BANKSY
and not BANKSY
Some people think it is NOT known if BANKSY
was ever involved in the NOT BANKSY project
or if
NOT BANKSY
is
NOT DEAD
and in fact
NOT NOT BANKSY

The latter may be the case but we can categorically say
BANKSY was NOT
involved in any creation or idea formed by
NOT BANKSY
or the
CONTINUITY NOT BANKSY
and certainly
not NOT NOT BANKSY!

Is that clear?

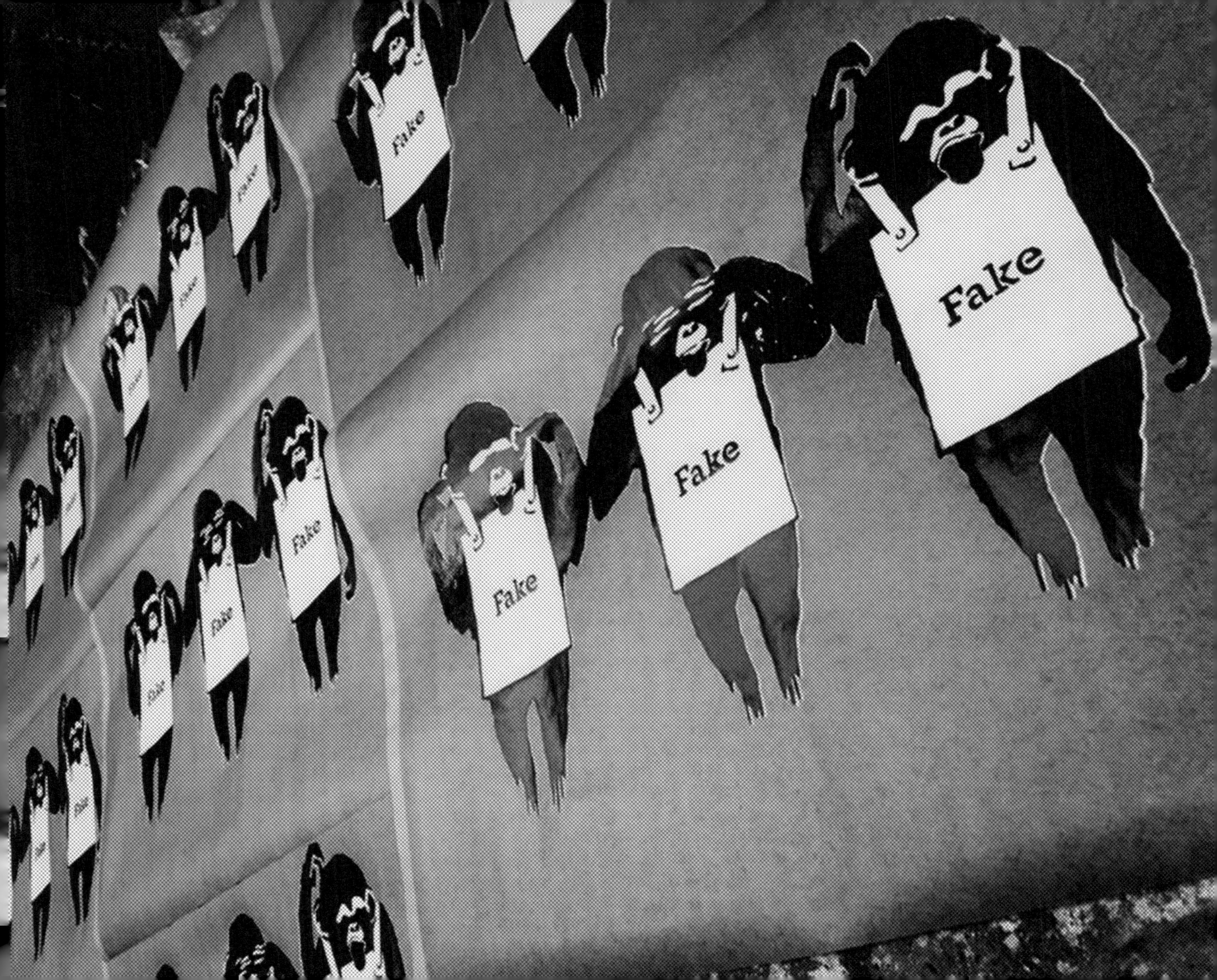
Fake
Fake
Fake
Fake
Fake

RAT WITH BLACK SQUARE: BANKSY

THE FIRST AND LAST EVER NOT NOT BANKSY EXHIBITION
14th December 2018

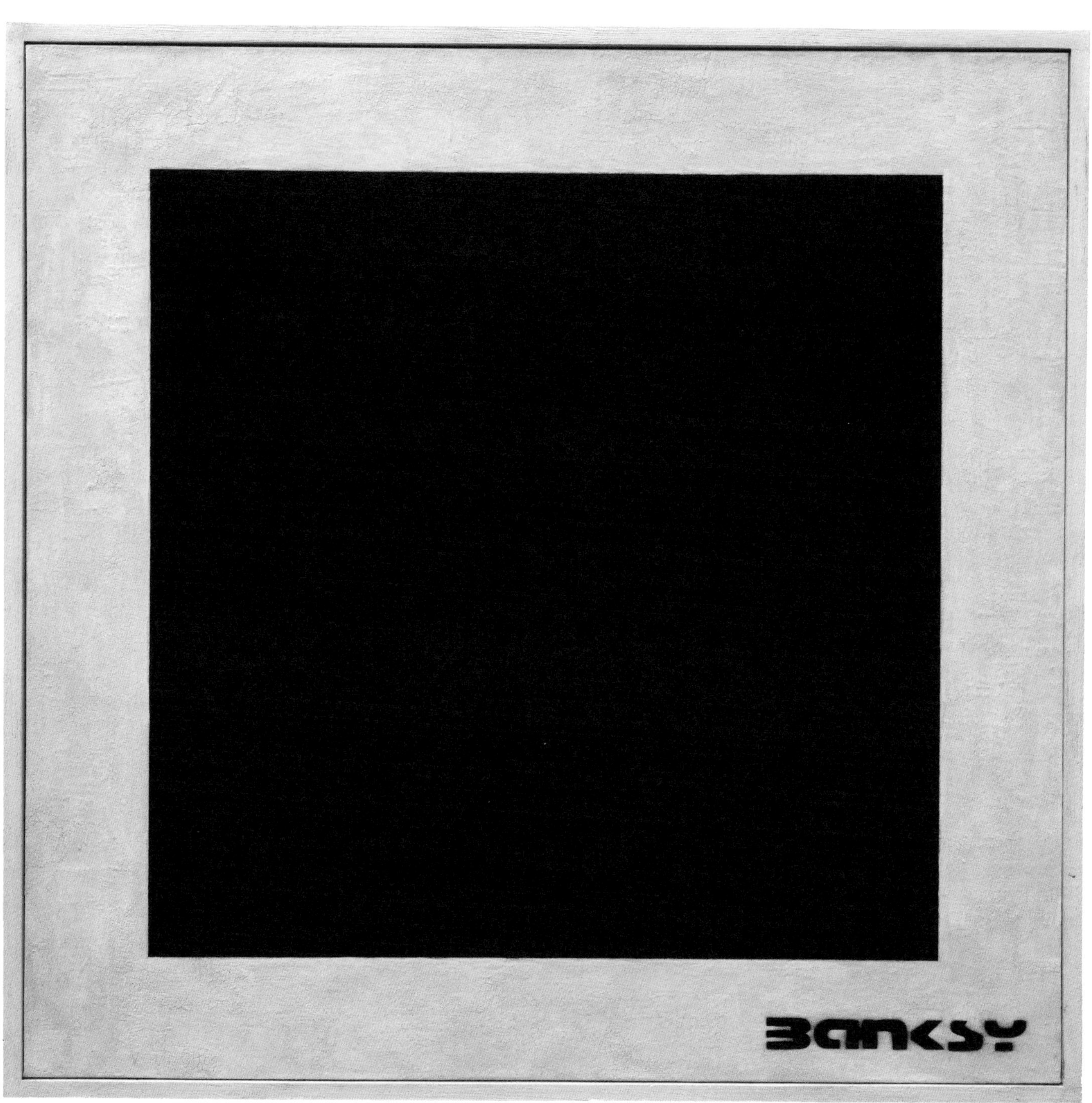

Malevich's 13th Black Square by Not Not Banksy, 1918 - 2018
113 x 113 cm
oil on canvas in artist made frame

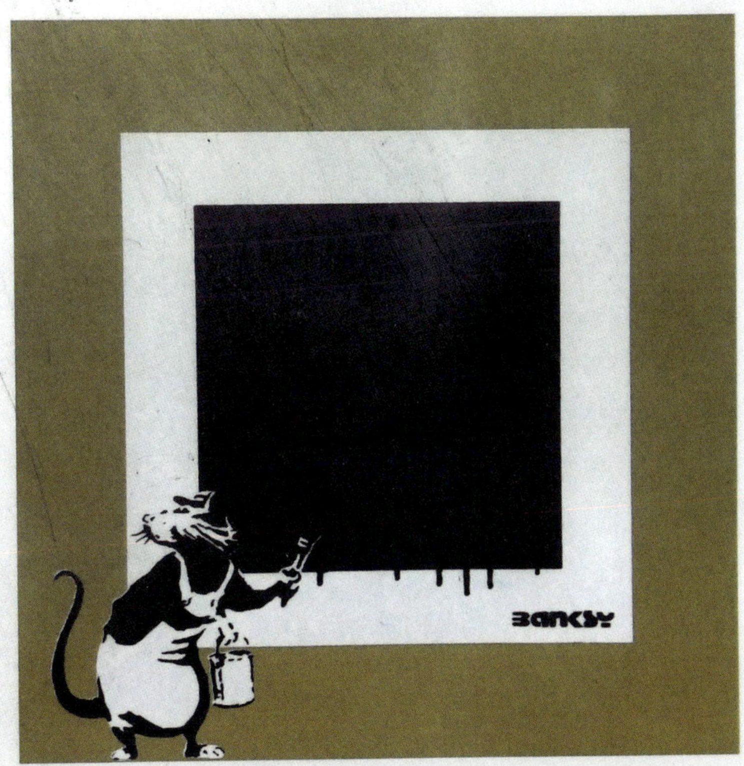

Cover of the exhibition catalogue/pamphlet

Some theoretical observation

^{IR} REVOLUTION

Here, █████████ NOT NOT BANKSY pays homage to ███████ and his finest unknown masterpiece THE BLACK SQUARE.

PART 2

By way of explanation, a short history

When Banksy met Russian artist Kazimir Malevich in 1913 he jokingly gave him a painting of a black square as a friendly dig at the earnest radical's minimal Suprematist paintings. In 1915 Malevich copied Banksy's "joke" painting and his Black Squares* went on to be the most radical revolutionary works of art ever made. Banksy was gutted. Until then he had been an ardent champion of figurative painting with a penchant for bucolic landscape scenes, believing observation of nature to be the cornerstone of art. But that all changed over-night. Following the success of Malevich's Black Square he turned his own hand to abstraction under various pseudonyms (Piet Mondrain and Mark Rothkok being a couple of the more notable ones), until - realising the pointlessness of it all - he finally gave up painting altogether in 1970, faked his death and went on to become a successful rare breeds pig farmer in Somerset. It was only when his old friend Blek le Rat managed to track him down in the early 1990's, and got him to help him with some stencil graffiti, that Banksy once again got the fire in his belly and realised that this new art form was his true calling. The rest, as they say, is history. Banksy became the most important cultural innovator's and influencer of the early 21st century, with many poor imitators, copyists and outright fakers taking to the streets and galleries of the world under the banner of so-called Urban Art. The most important of these inadequate copyist fakers being NOT BANKSY and his smart-arse neo-Nothingist successor NOT NOT BANKSY**.

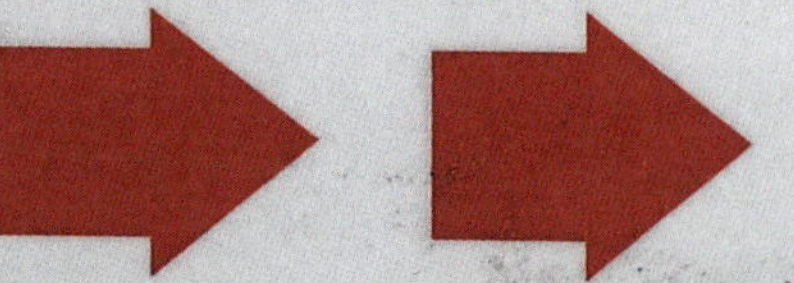

Deformalist critic and Post-Art Historian Harold Rosenbloom has linked the aestheticism of the early 21st Century's so-called *Urban Art Revolution* with the collapse of liberal democracy and the Brexit/Trump revolutions; citing the art movement's populist attitudes and derogatory attacks on the complex cultural coding of established art-world norms as making them receptive to a reductive, polemic and highly profitable new meta-reality.

Many of the so-called Urban Artists engaged in public projects that agitated for 'success over substance' and mocked representatives of the toppled art elite. The new army of artists, led by the so-called NOT NOT BANKSY of the highly provocative *all action no content*, double negative de-radicalised neo-Nothingist post-anti-art anti-art agitator activist group known as (the so called) *Ni**er L**er™®*, adopted hitherto fashion-controlled modish styles, now outlawed and subjected to the framework of collectively approved miss-perception, and de-marketed through digital and non-digital media. With these new forms of production, anti-production and anti-nonproduction, the imposition of one's augmented reality 'ABC' was turned into the proposition of an egalitarian popular aesthetics that had a high potential for mimicry, mockery, regurgitation and fakery that could erase reference to both the past and future for ever. The goal was not to provide a counter-revolutionary layer over the old world but to destroy it altogether then refuse to build a new one; thus, propelling post-art anti-artists to create new neo-nihilistic counter-productive visions of a dying planet being pissed-on from afar by a dysfunctional bloated white-man dressed in a dirty rat suit, forever (and pointlessly) painting a monumental black square of empty nothingness under the gaze of a cute bunny. Forming a puerile universal language of nonsensical and barely funny one-liner visual gags, this created an effective method to disseminate the (ir)revolutionary non-art agenda and double negative anti-elite neo-elitist sentiments to form a new meta-meaning of universal neo-non-nothingness.

Please Note: All works in this exhibition are fakes or fakes of fakes. Nothing is real. It is all an illusion. Everything is For Sale.

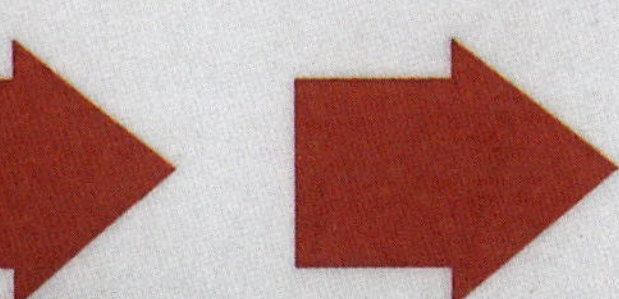

* Between 1915 and 1918, **Kazimir Malevich** painted **13 versions** of the **Black Square** before they were banned by the revolutionary government for being **"meaningless bollocks"**. It is universally agreed that his 13th Black Square painting was his best.

** **NOT NOT BANKSY** is not **NOT BANKSY** as **NOT BANKSY** is dead. These prints are a homage to **BANKSY**, not **NOT BANKSY** by the artist(s) known as **NOT NOT BANKSY** who continues the great work of **NOT BANKSY** and not **BANKSY**. Some people think it is **NOT** known if **BANKSY** was ever involved in the **NOT BANKSY** project, or if **NOT BANKSY** is **NOT DEAD** and in fact is **NOT NOT BANKSY**. The latter is unknowable but we do know, categorically, that **BANKSY** was **NOT** involved in any creation or idea formed by **NOT BANKSY, THE CONTINUITY NOT BANKSY**, and certainly not **NOT NOT BANKSY**.

Pages 2 and 3 of the exhibition catalogue/pamphlet with art-speak text appropriated from an exhibition on Russian Dada

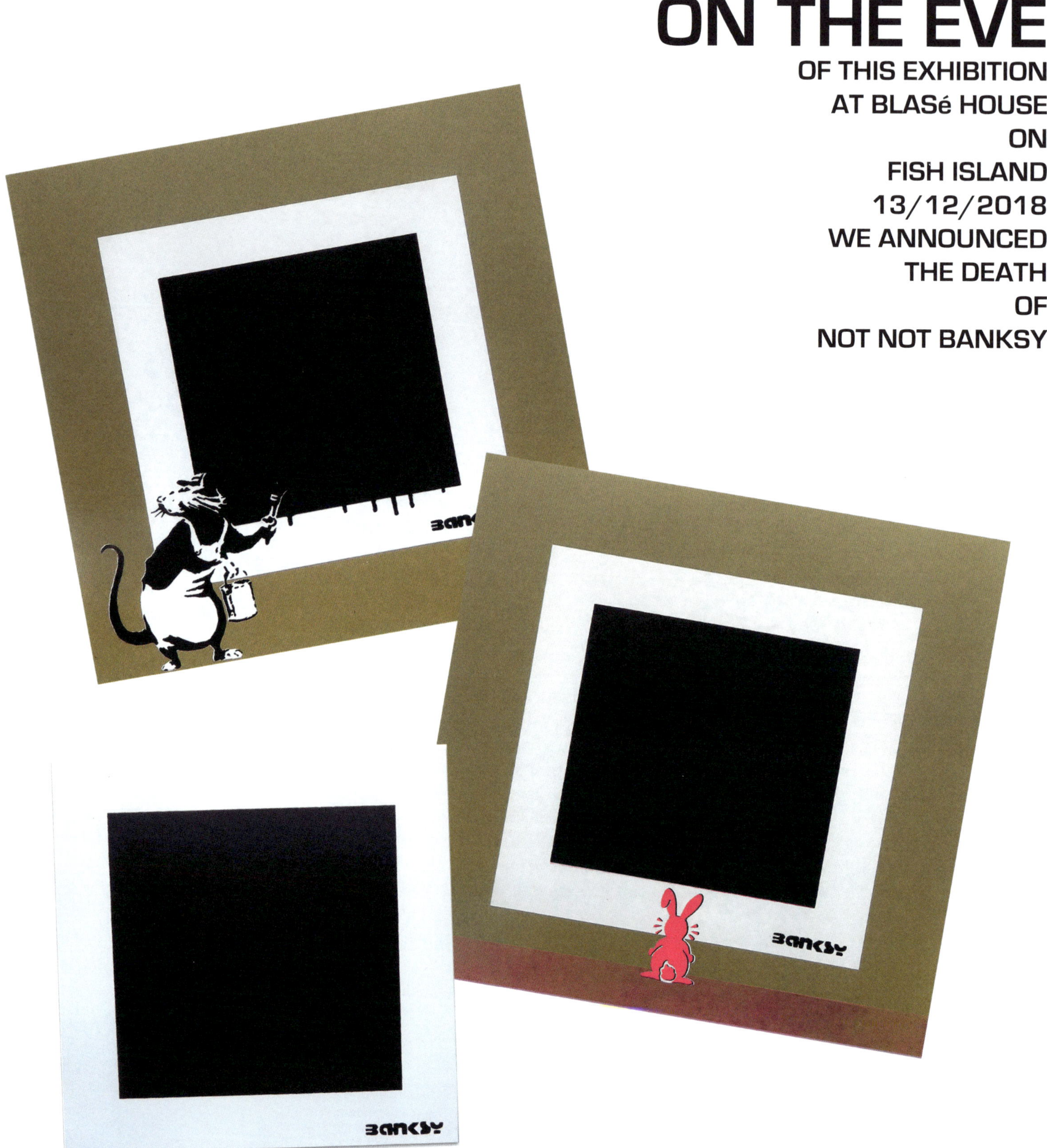

Rat with Black Square, Black Square with Black Square, Pink Bunny with Black Square
2 and 3 colour screen prints on brown card
Editions of 200

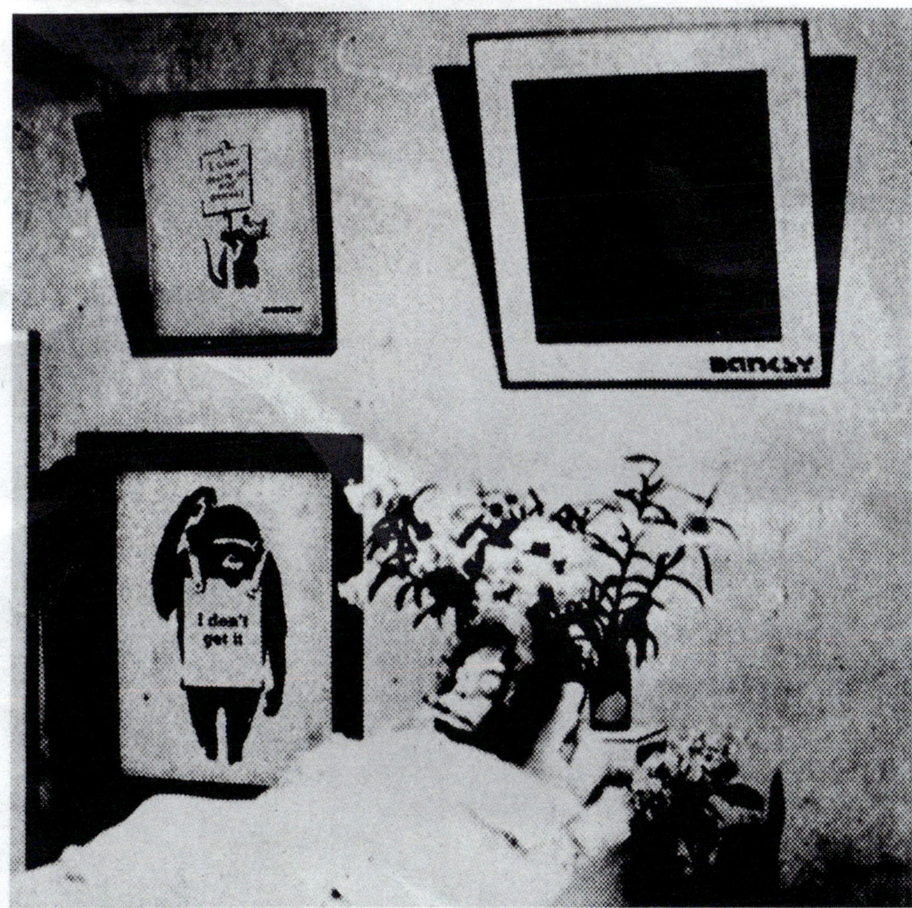

ON THE EVE OF HIS FIRST EVER **EXHIBITION**, CONTRARIAN POST-ART ARTIST AND NEO-NOTHINGIST **NOT NOT BANKSY** HAS BEEN FOUND **DEAD** OUTSIDE HIS EAST LONDON STUDIO, SPRAY CAN AND STENCIL IN HAND.

IT IS BELIEVED HE **HAD IT COMING** AND RUMOURED HE WAS **POISENED** BY THE NERVE AGENT **POPPYCHOK** AS (REPORTEDLY) USED BY BANKSY'S PRIVATE POLICE FORCE **PEST CONTROL**.

PEST CONTROL HAVE STRONGLY DENIED ANY INVOLVEMENT AND INSIST THEY ONLY USE CONVENTIONAL, **NON-LETHAL** METHODS OF PROTECTING **BANKSY'S RIGHTS**.

THOSE CLOSE TO **NOT NOT BANKSY** SAY THIS IS WHAT HE WOULD HAVE WANTED.

Leaflet announcing the death of **NOT NOT** Banksy

THE DEATHBED OF NOT NOT BANKSY

Google 'Kazimir Malevich deathbed' + 'Warhol death and disaster' for further information

'Warholian Silver' household paint and screen ink on cardboard

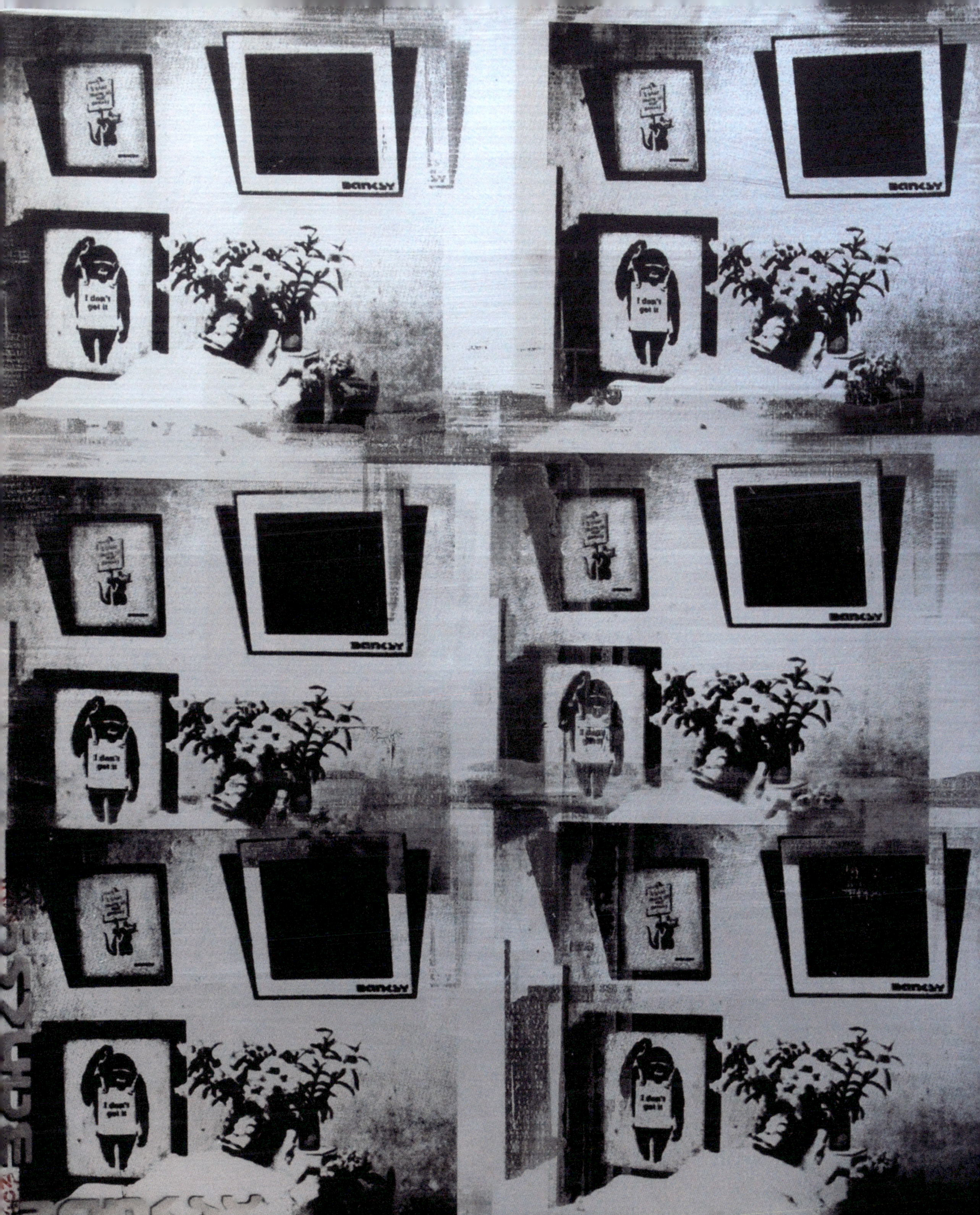

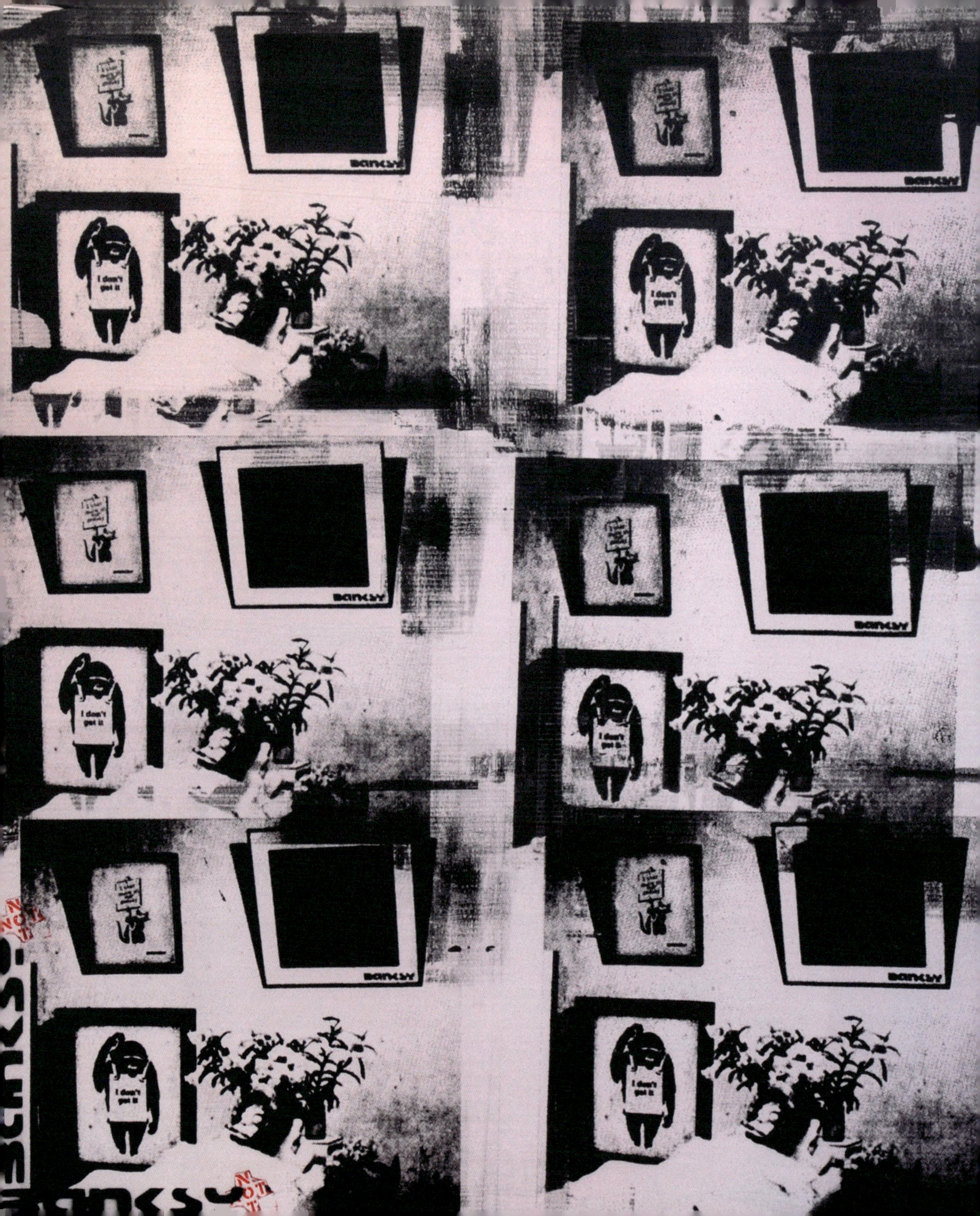

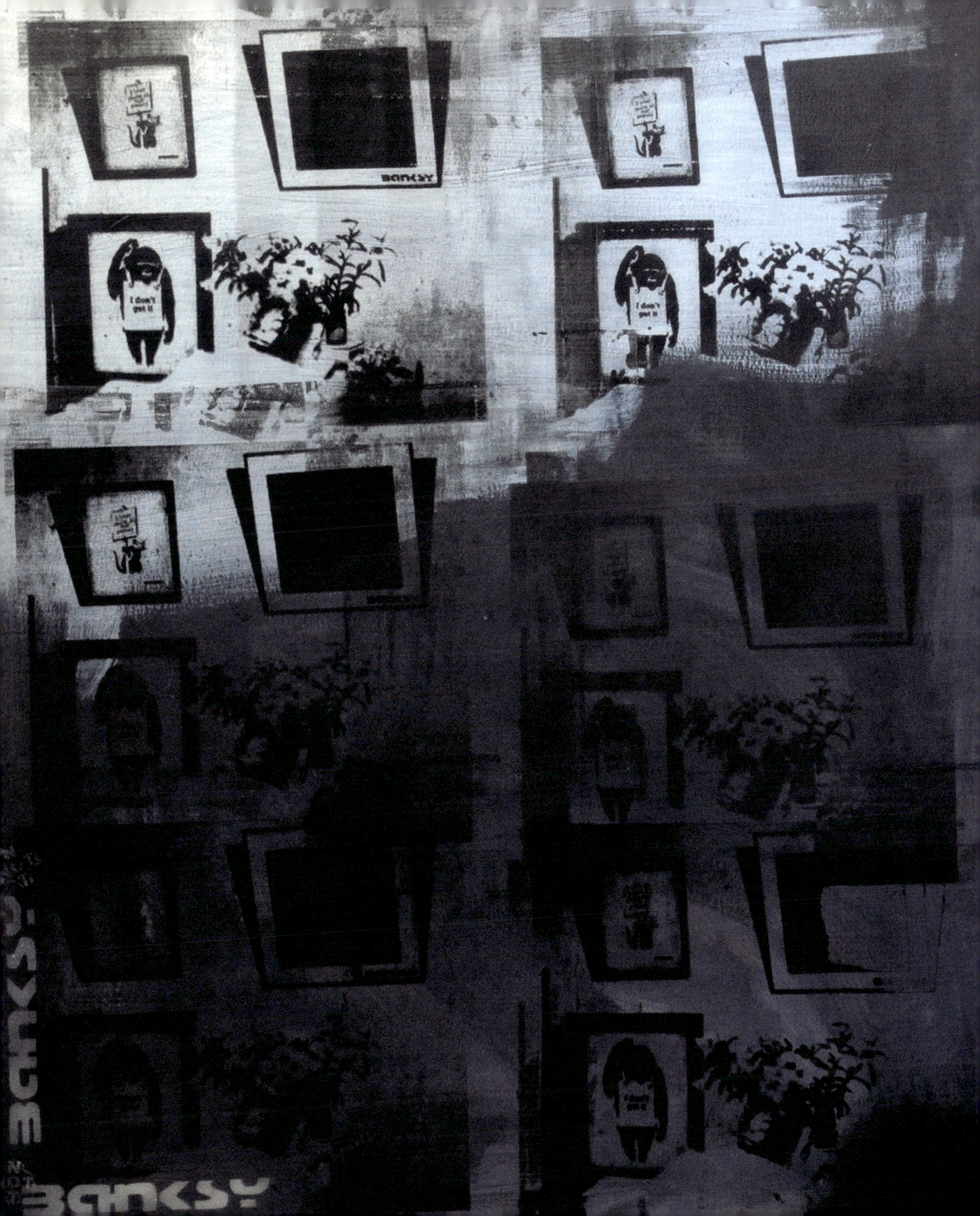

I don't get it
BANKSY
BANKSY
BANKSY

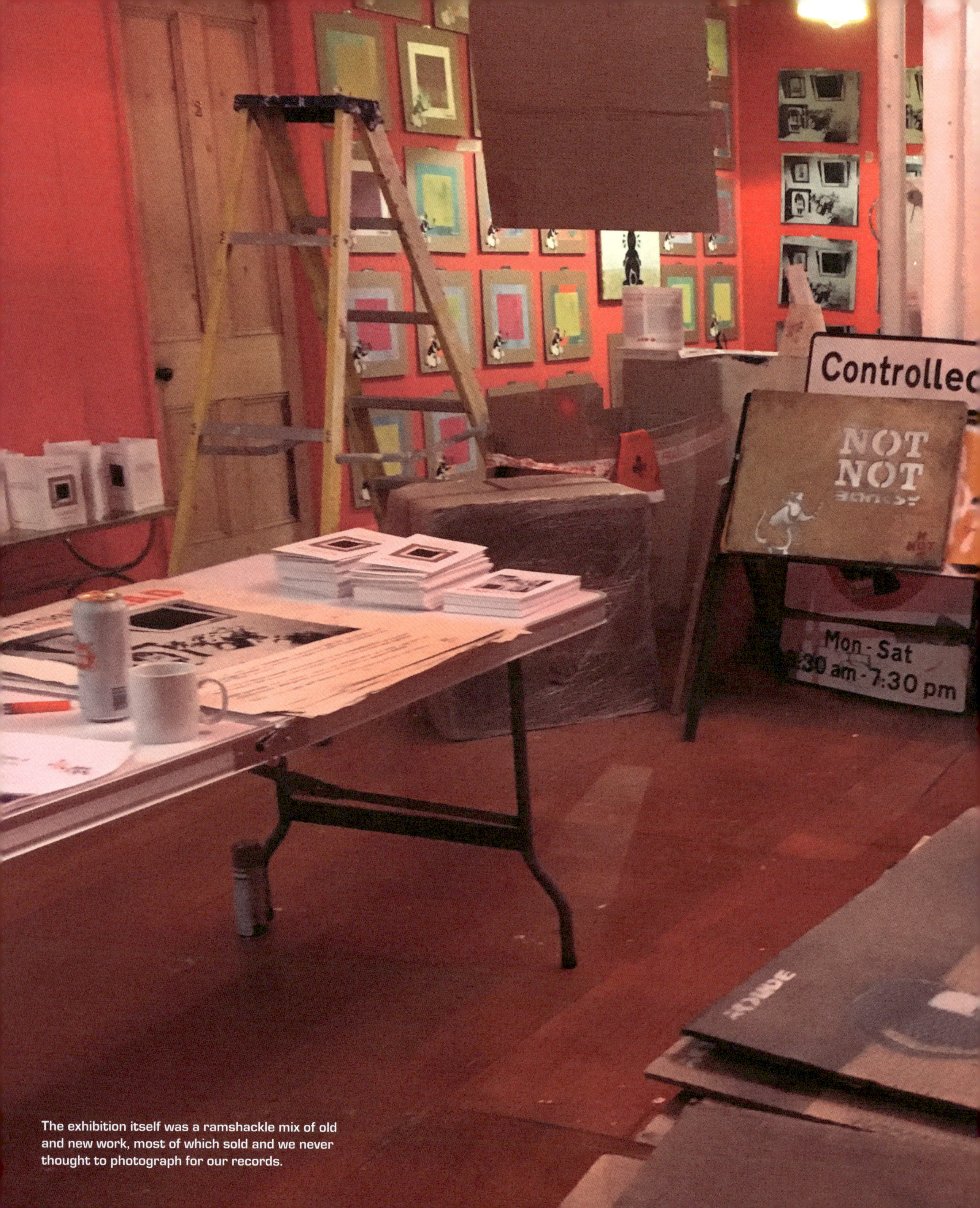

The exhibition itself was a ramshackle mix of old and new work, most of which sold and we never thought to photograph for our records.

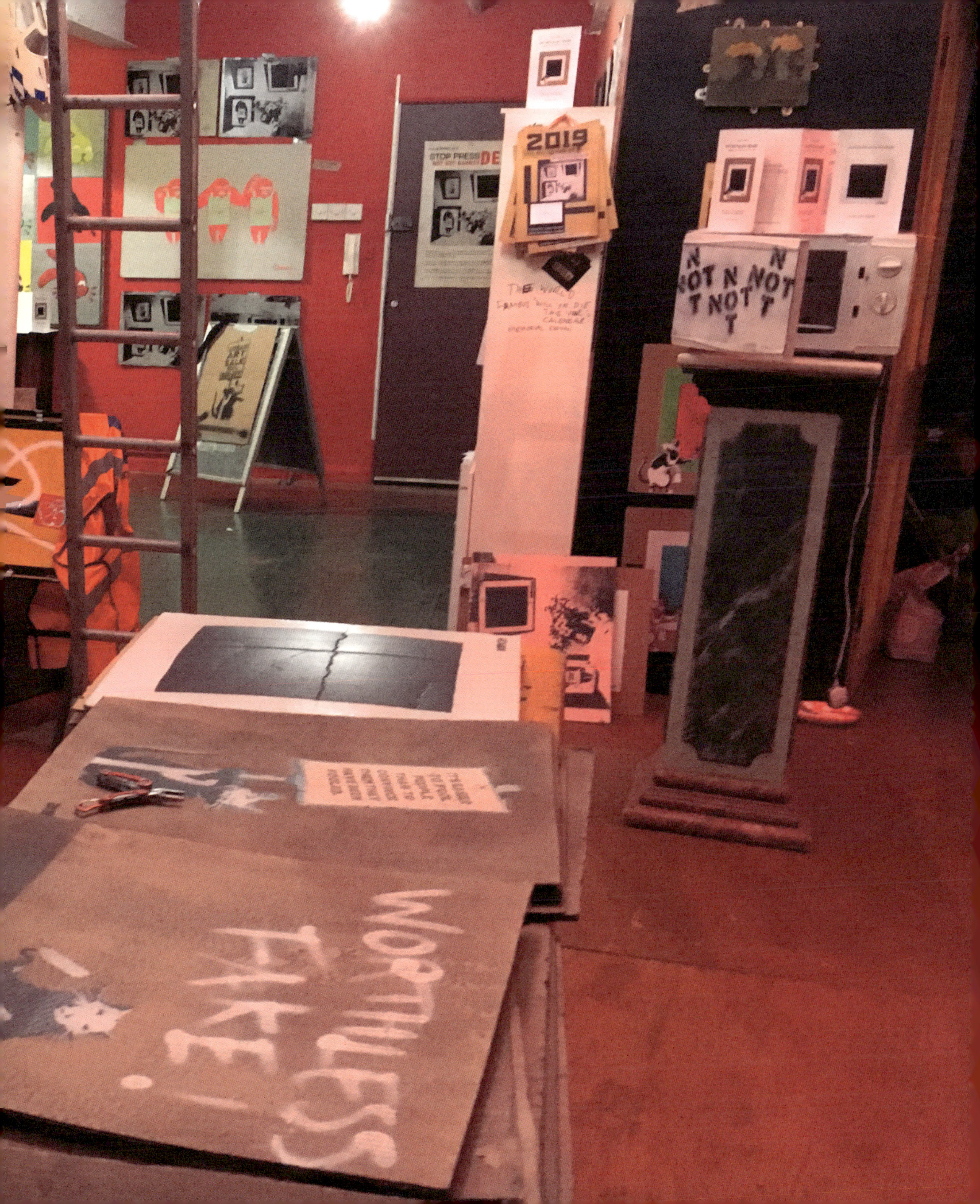
2019
STOP PRESS
NOT NOT BANKSY
DEAD
N N
NOT N NOT
T NOT T
T

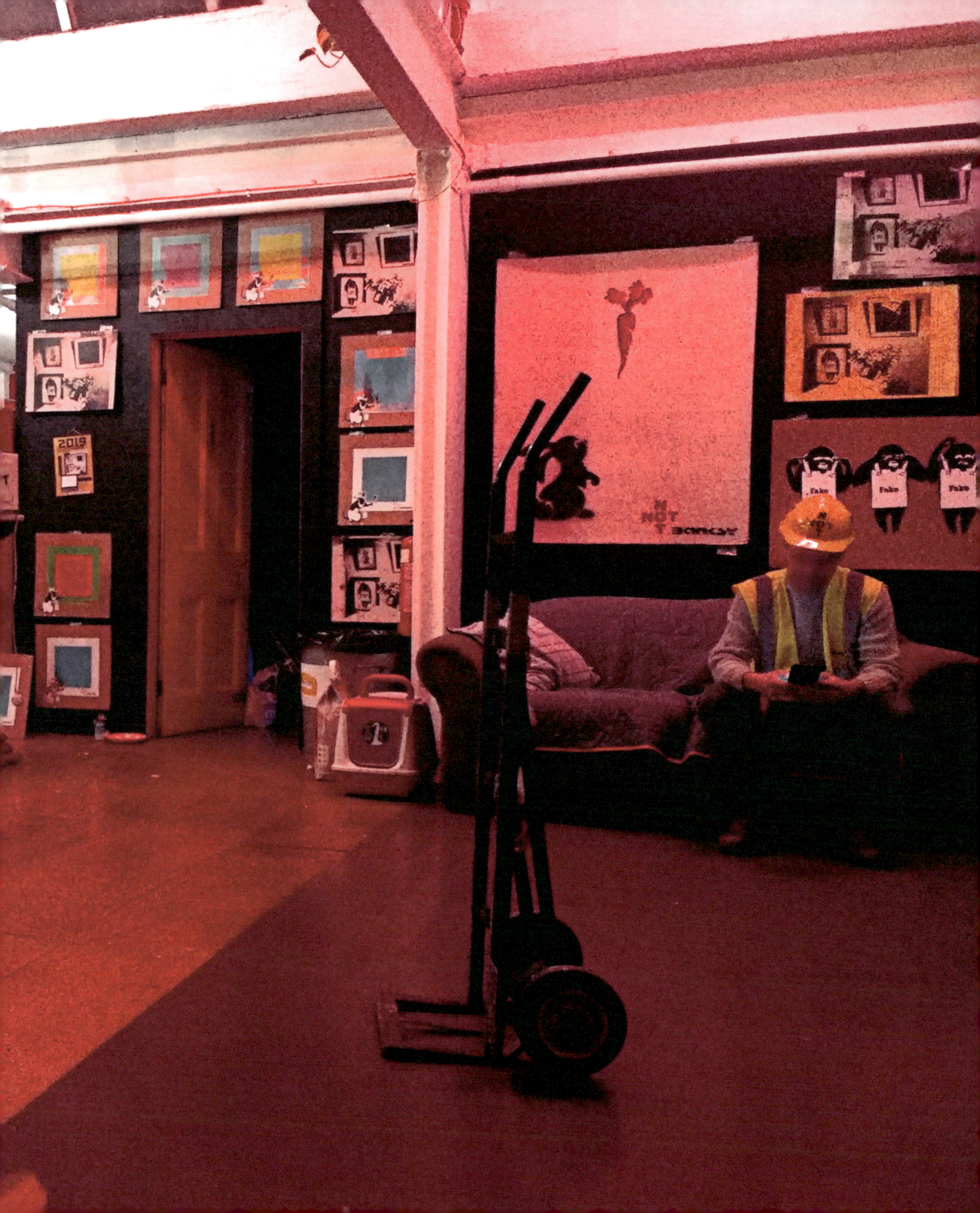

NOT BANKSY
Fake
Fake
Fake
2019

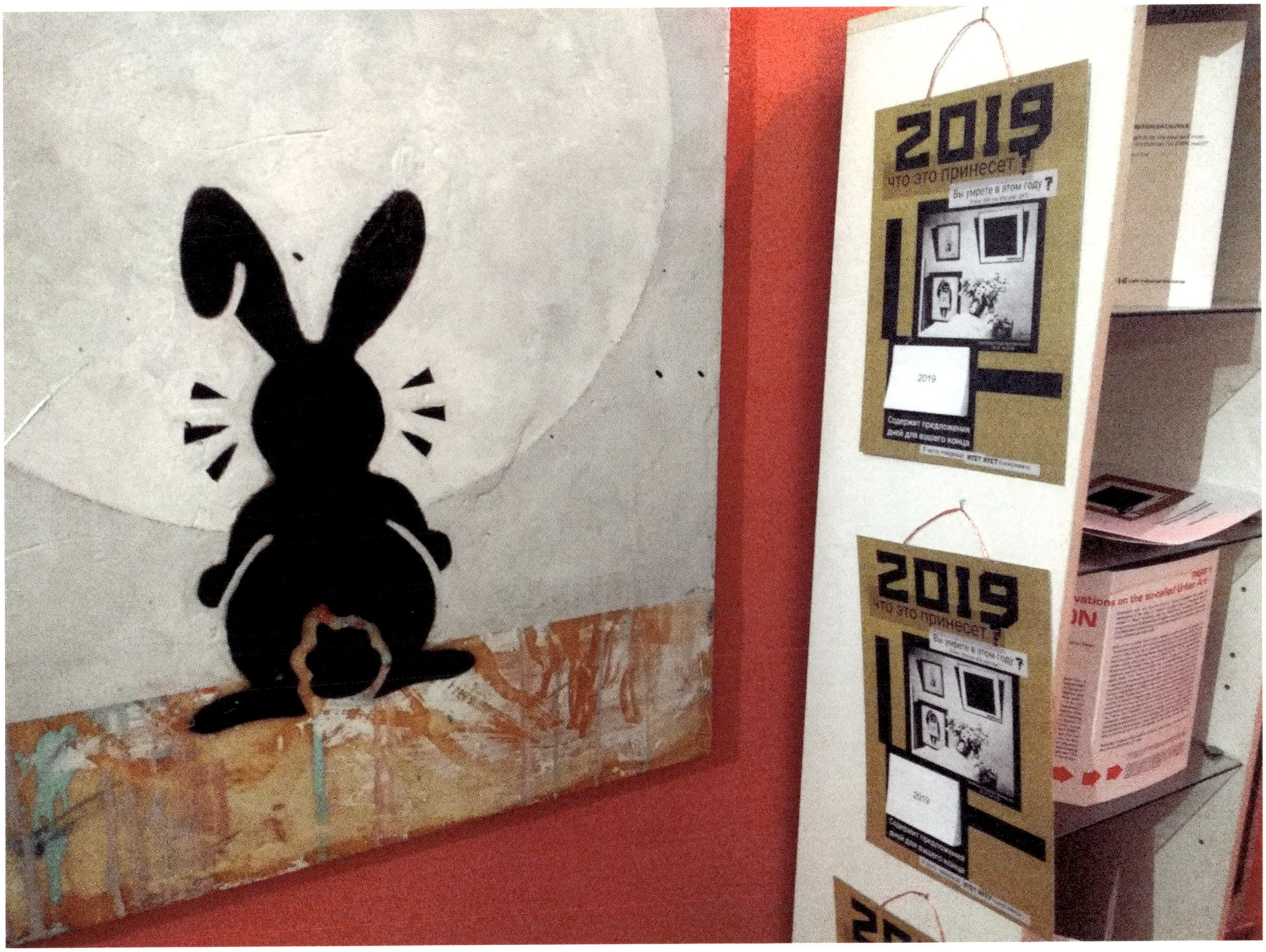

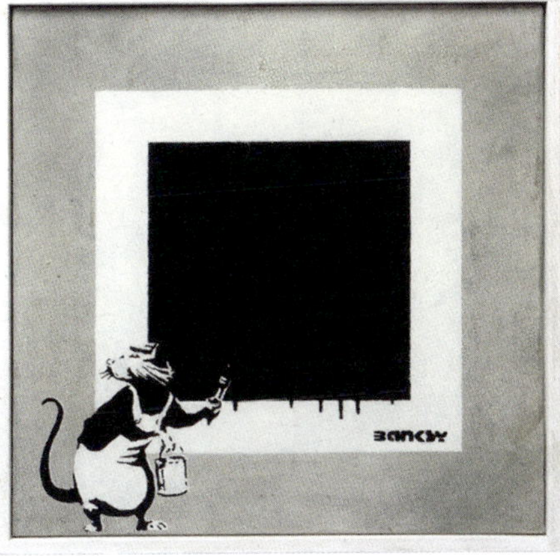

The 2019 World Famous Harry Adams "Will You Die This Year?" Calendar was dedicated to the Death of Not Not Banksy

THE FIRST EVER NOT NOT BANKSY "ORIGINALS" WERE MADE

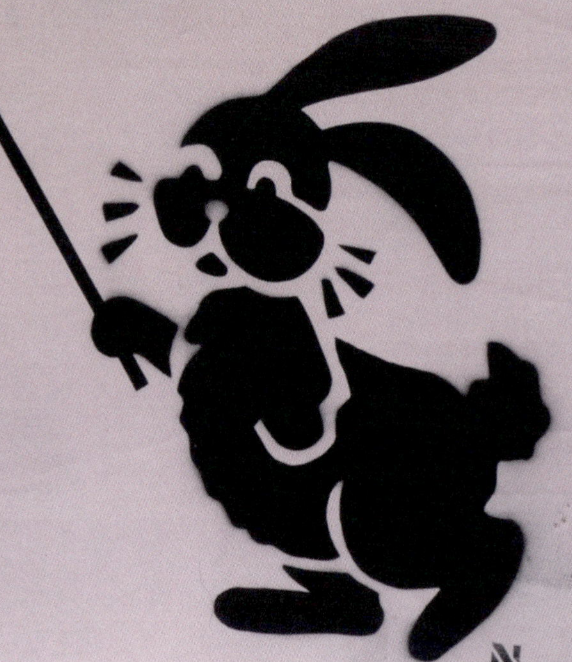

N
NOT
Banksy

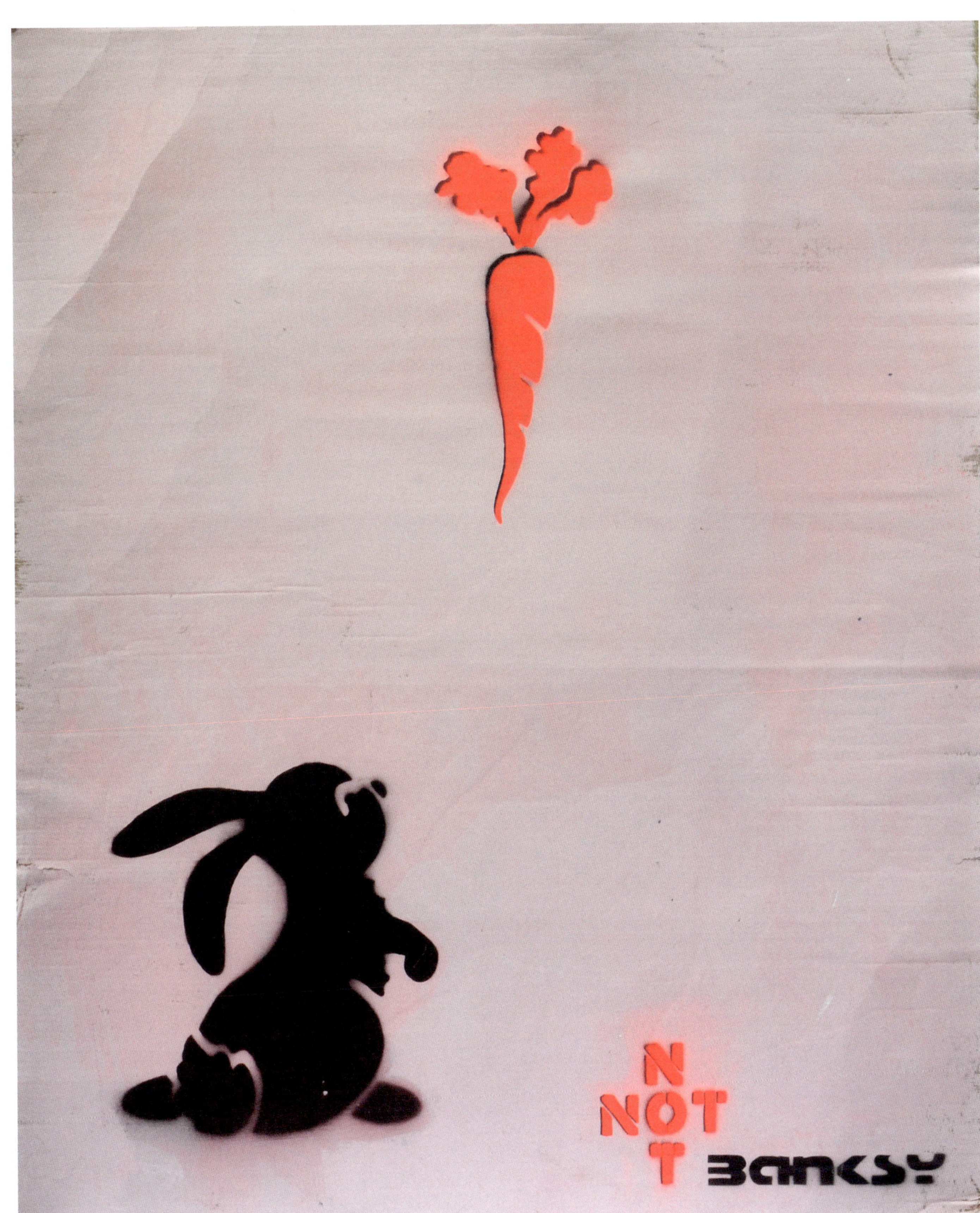

N
NOT
T
BANKSY

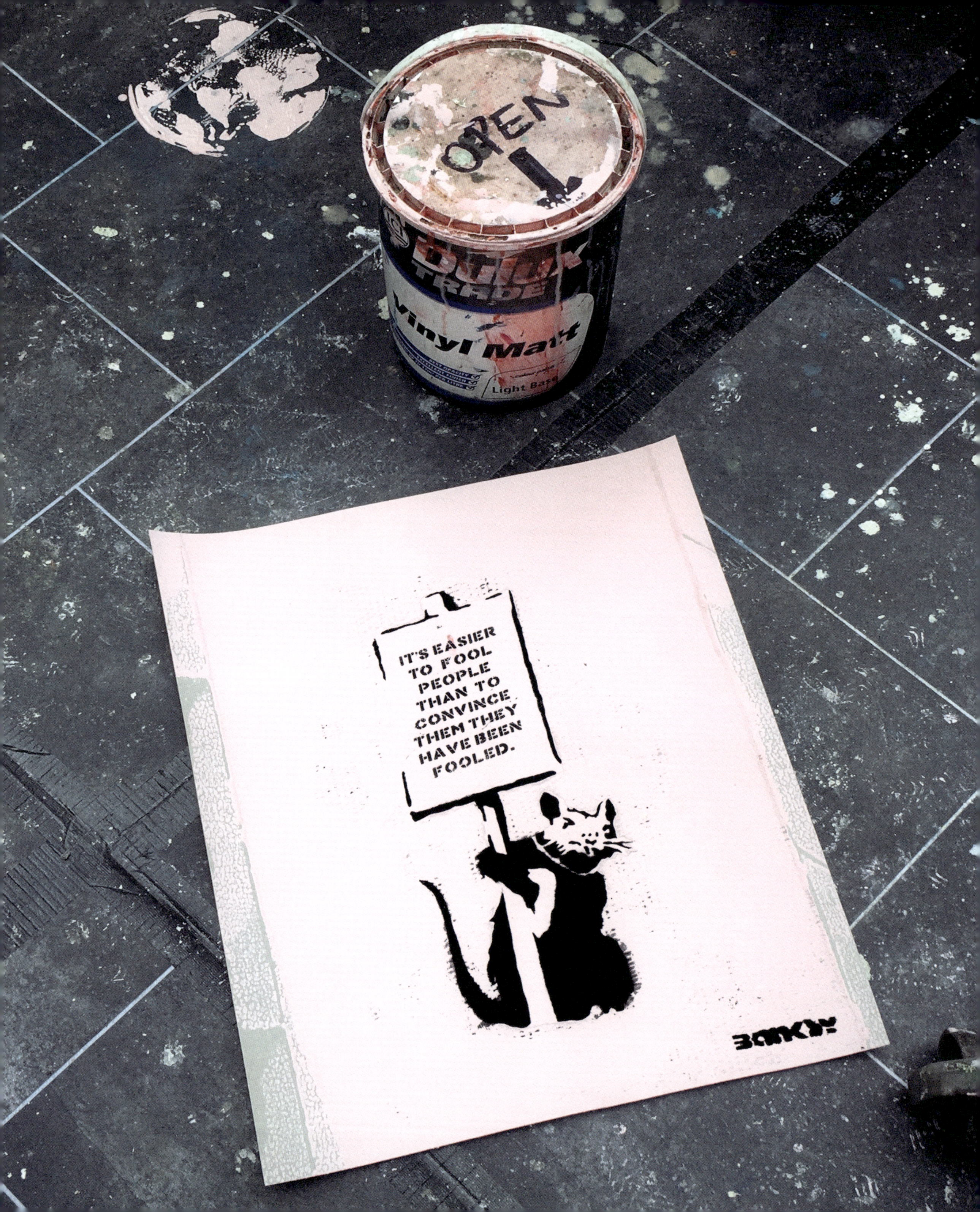
OPEN
DULUX
TRADE
Vinyl Matt
Light Base
IT'S EASIER
TO FOOL
PEOPLE
THAN TO
CONVINCE
THEM THEY
HAVE BEEN
FOOLED.
BANKSY

OPERATION SATURATION
OR
IS IT POSSIBLE TO MILK A DEAD RAT?
BY THE
REAL NOT BANKSY FRONT

An April Fools Day Special in collaboration with the MANGéL PrESS*
by order of the
International Neo Not Banksy Anartist Alliance

Screen print and household paint on grey pulp card
Edition of 300
Signed, stamped and numbered by the real artists
50 x 42 cm

Following the revelation that THE REAL NOT BANKSY is in fact a pro-Brexit 13-year-old girl from
Scunthorpe – the abandoned illegitimate child of THE "REAL" BANKSY
intent on undermining her father's liberal snowflake neo-Marxist woolly do-gooder
politics (whilst, like all xenophobic neo-Fascists, secretly only wanting to be held and loved) – we are
pleased to present this authentic no-nonsense fake to once and for all silence all the NOT BANKSY
imposters and pretenders out there.

WE ASK:
Is it possible to milk a dead rat, or lead a dead rat to be flogged?
OR...
flog a milked dead rat being lead to jump the shark whilst gilding the lily?
OR...
will this be the last straw that broke the rat's back?
OR...
is it, perchance, to throw a perfume on the violet, to smooth the ice, or add another hue
unto the rainbow, or with taper-light to seek the beauteous eye of heaven to garnish,
wasteful and ridiculous excess?

Any-which-way, there is only one REAL NOT BANKSY with more FRONT than any others
and she's much more righteously disenfranchised, funnier, cleverer
and more dank than the rest of ya.

Suck it up kids!

* The MANGéL PrESS is a print outfit founded by Harry Adams
at L-13 that uses an old laundry mangle to make prints

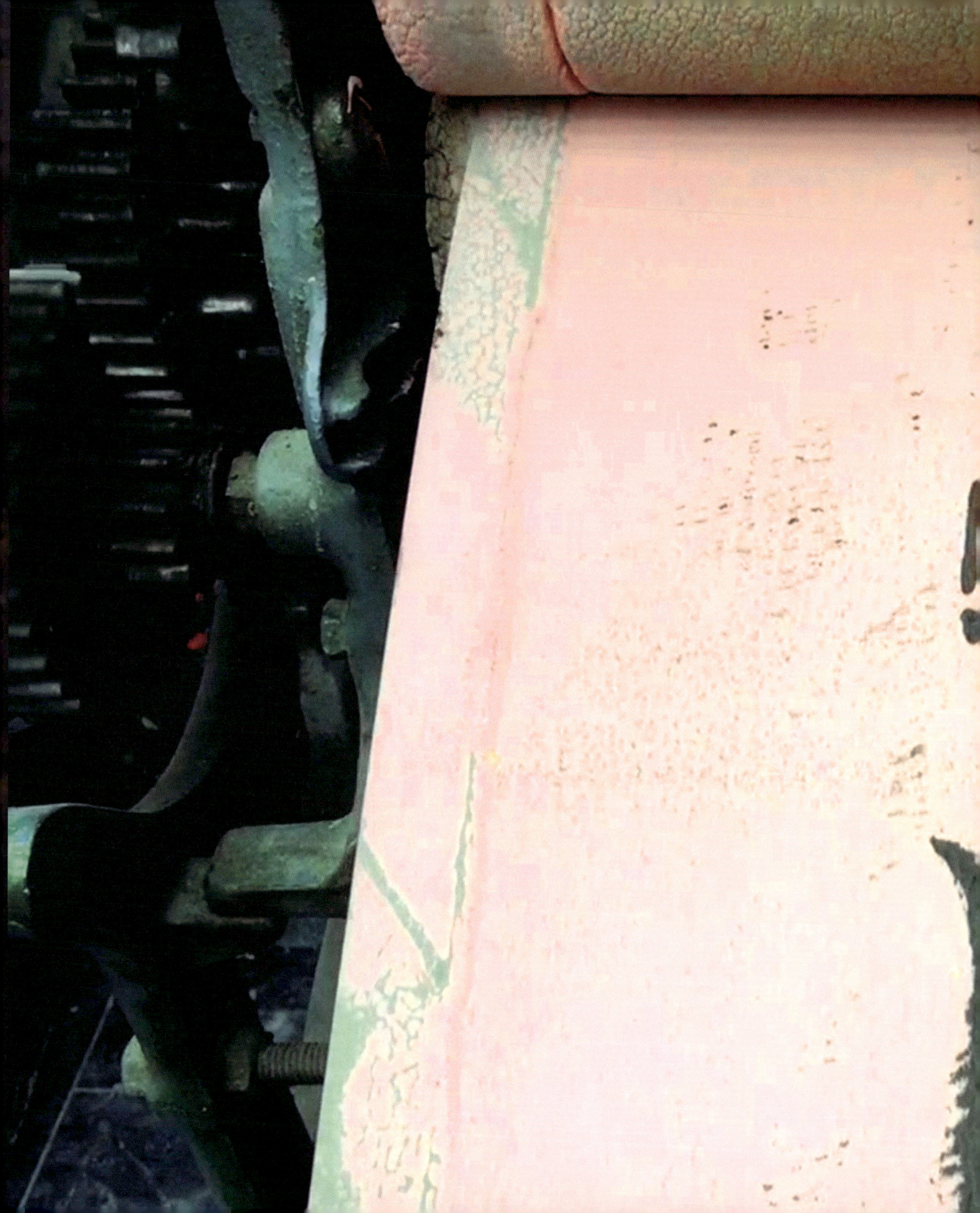

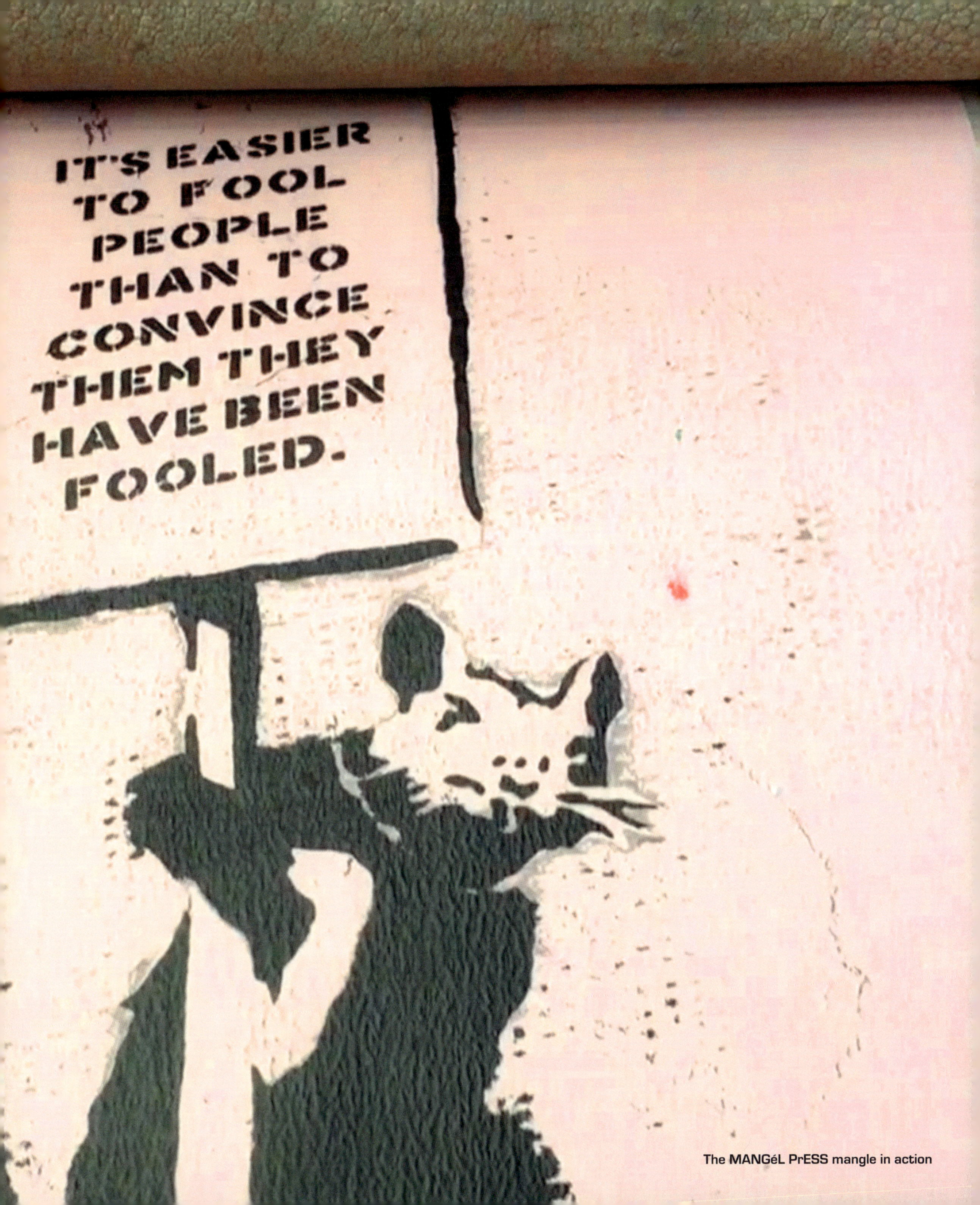

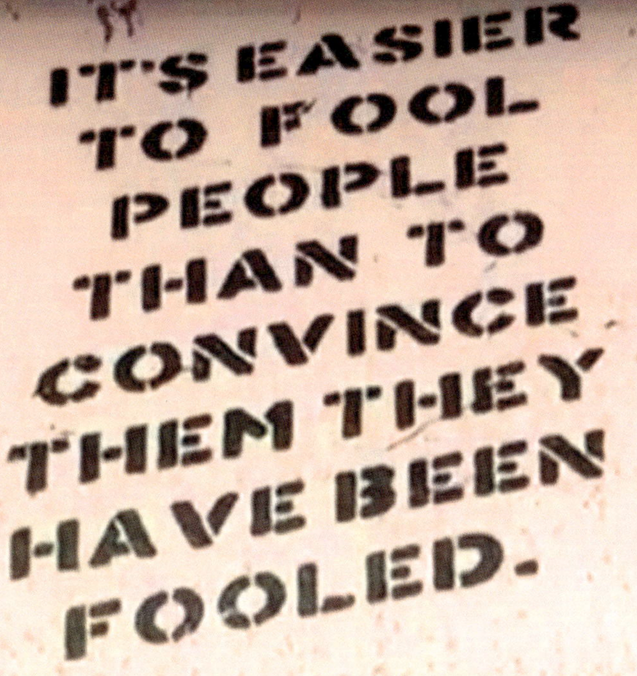

The MANGéL PrESS mangle in action

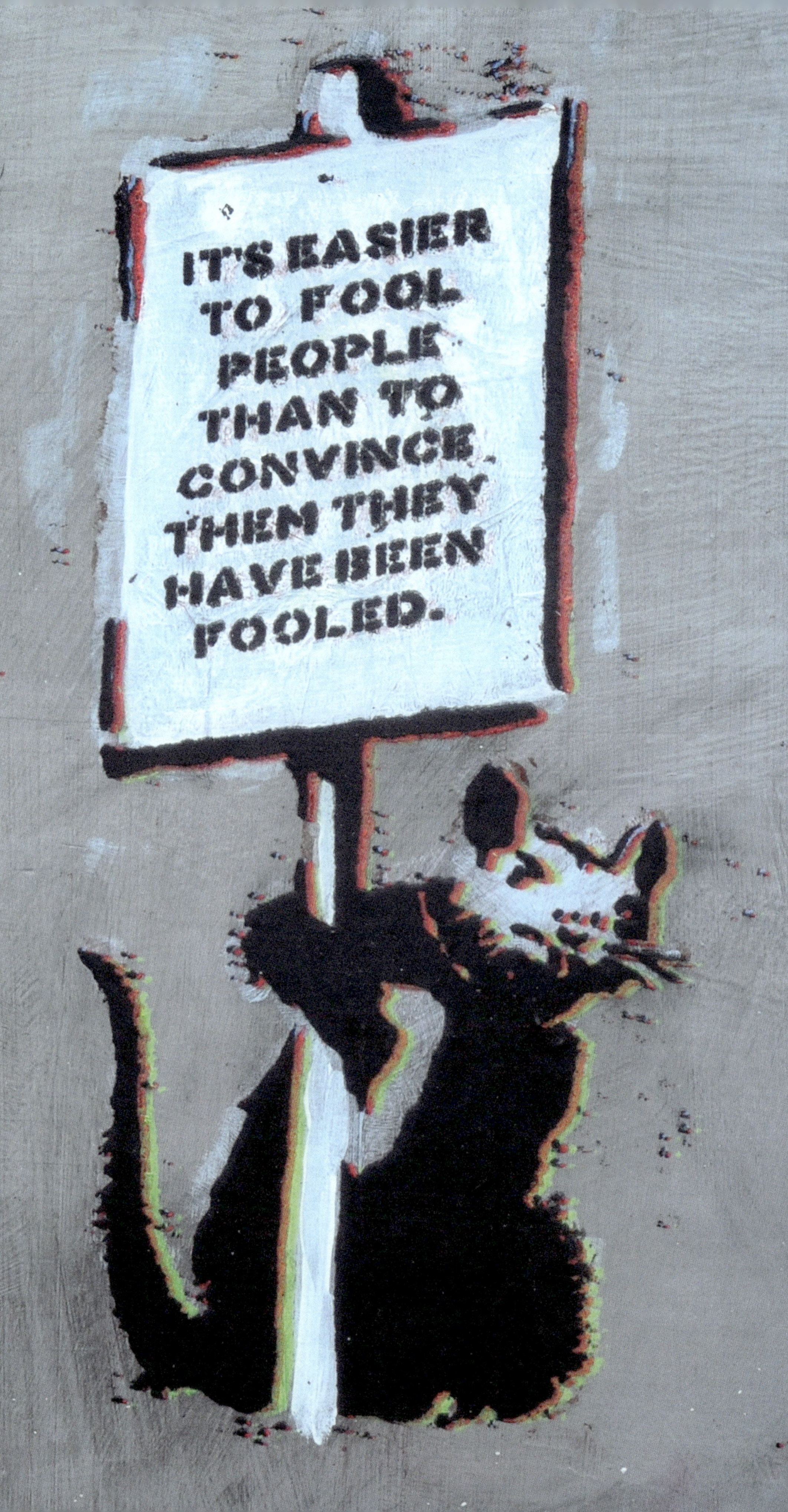

IT'S EASIER
TO FOOL
PEOPLE
THAN TO
CONVINCE
THEM THEY
HAVE BEEN
FOOLED.

OPERATION SATURATION "ORIGINALS"

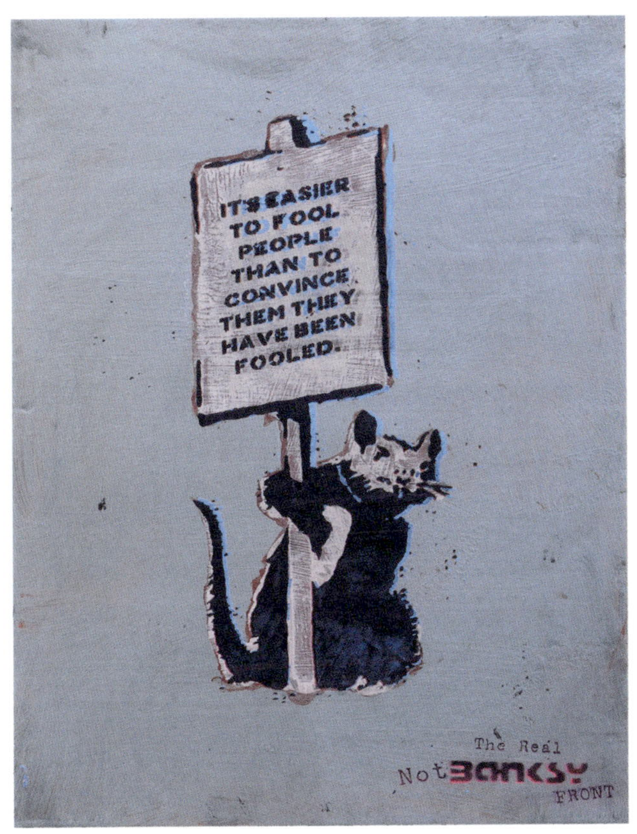

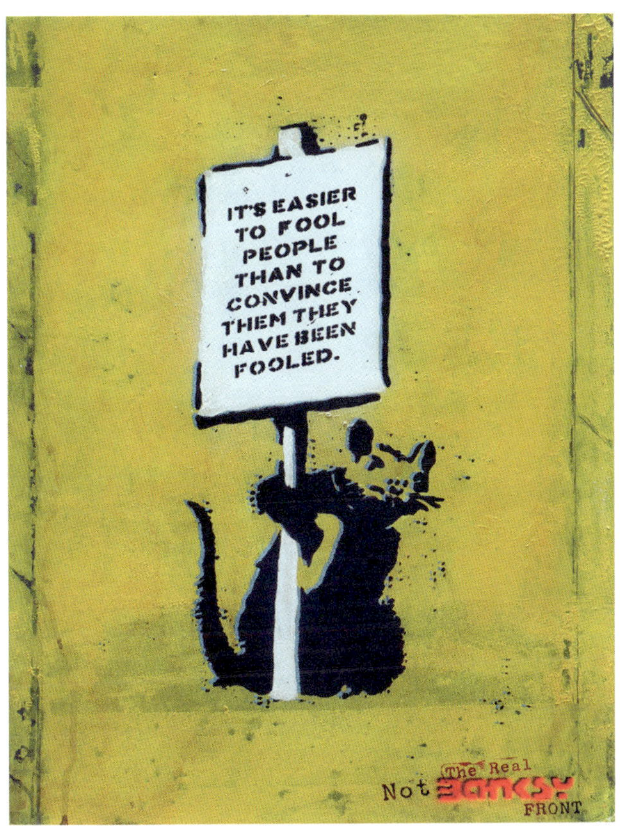

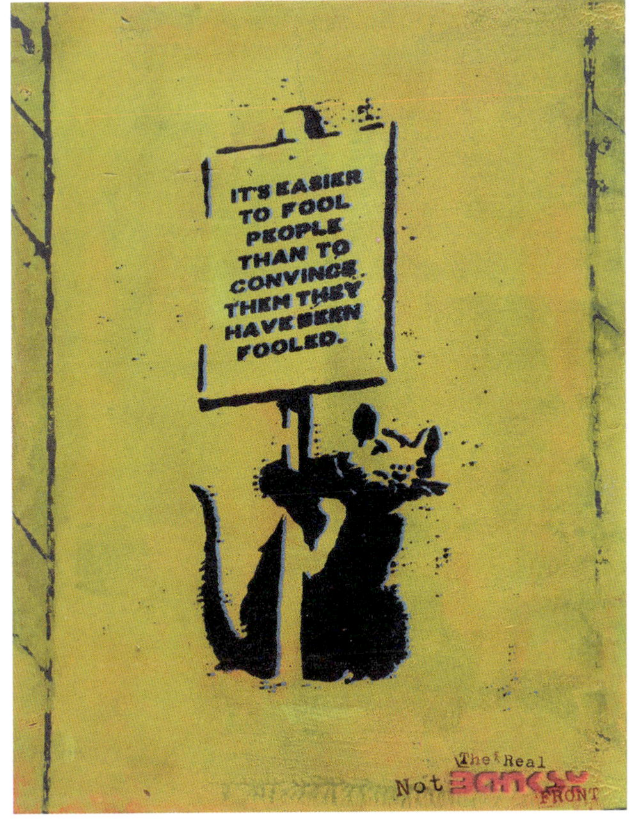

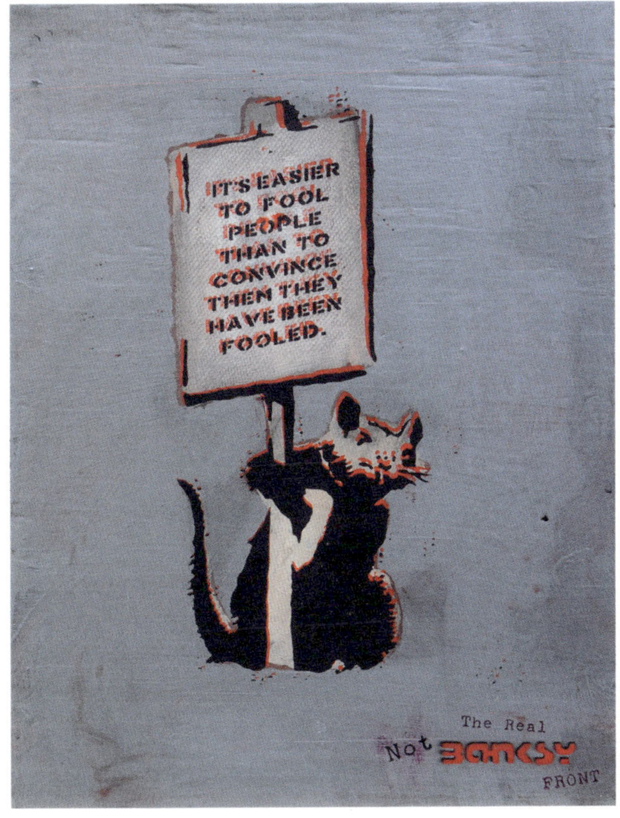

Household paint and screen ink on plywood panels.
Each unique

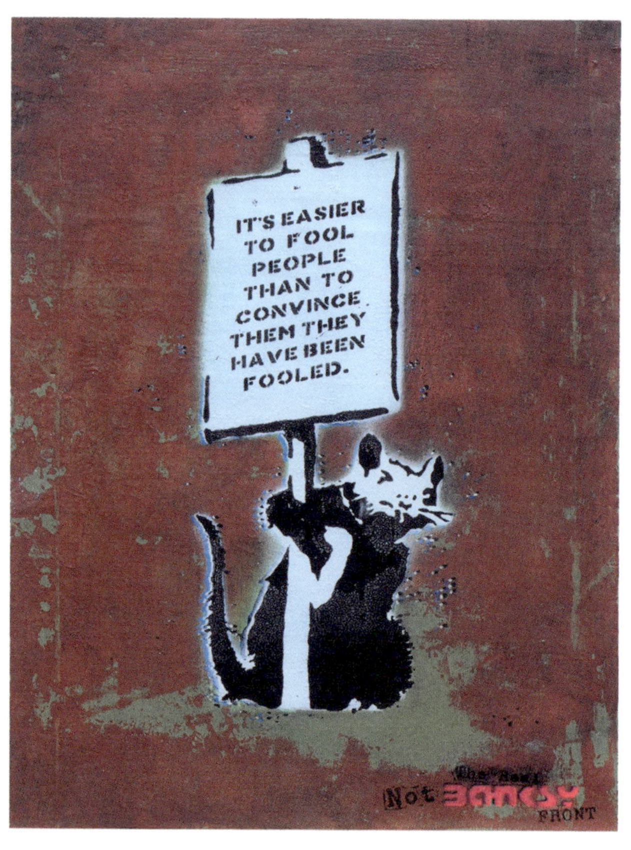

IT'S EASIER
TO FOOL
PEOPLE
THAN TO
CONVINCE
THEM THEY
HAVE BEEN
FOOLED.
The Real
Not BANKSY
FRONT

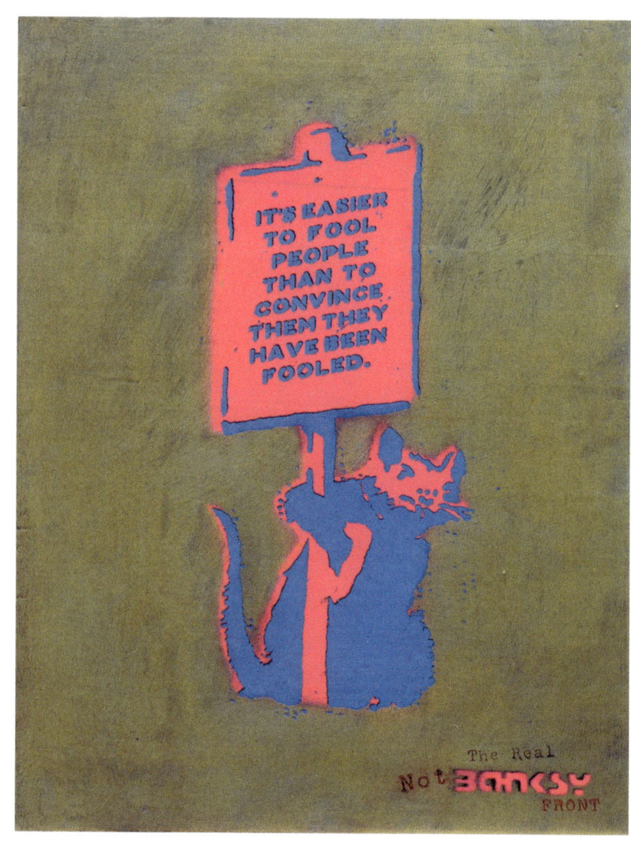

IT'S EASIER
TO FOOL
PEOPLE
THAN TO
CONVINCE
THEM THEY
HAVE BEEN
FOOLED.
The Real
Not BANKSY
FRONT

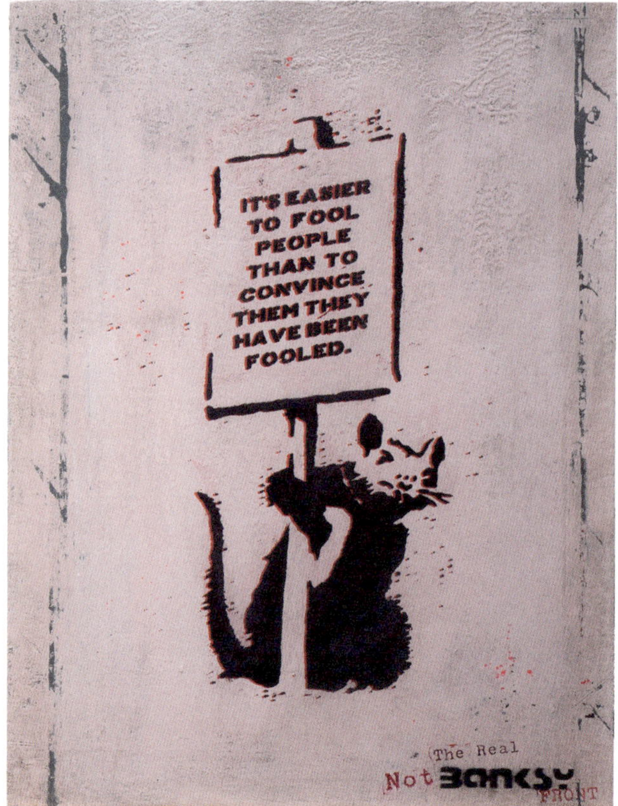

IT'S EASIER
TO FOOL
PEOPLE
THAN TO
CONVINCE
THEM THEY
HAVE BEEN
FOOLED.
The Real
Not BANKSY
FRONT

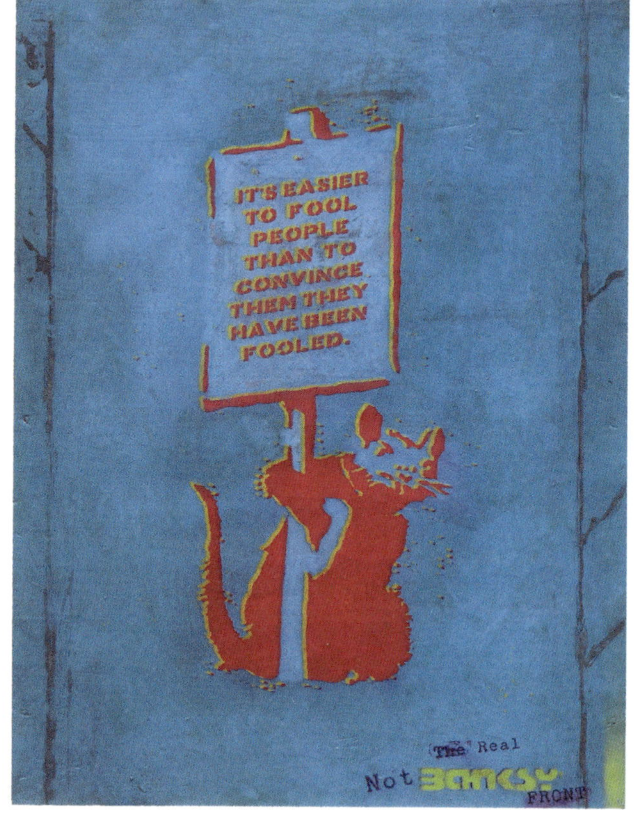

IT'S EASIER
TO FOOL
PEOPLE
THAN TO
CONVINCE
THEM THEY
HAVE BEEN
FOOLED.
The Real
Not BANKSY
FRONT

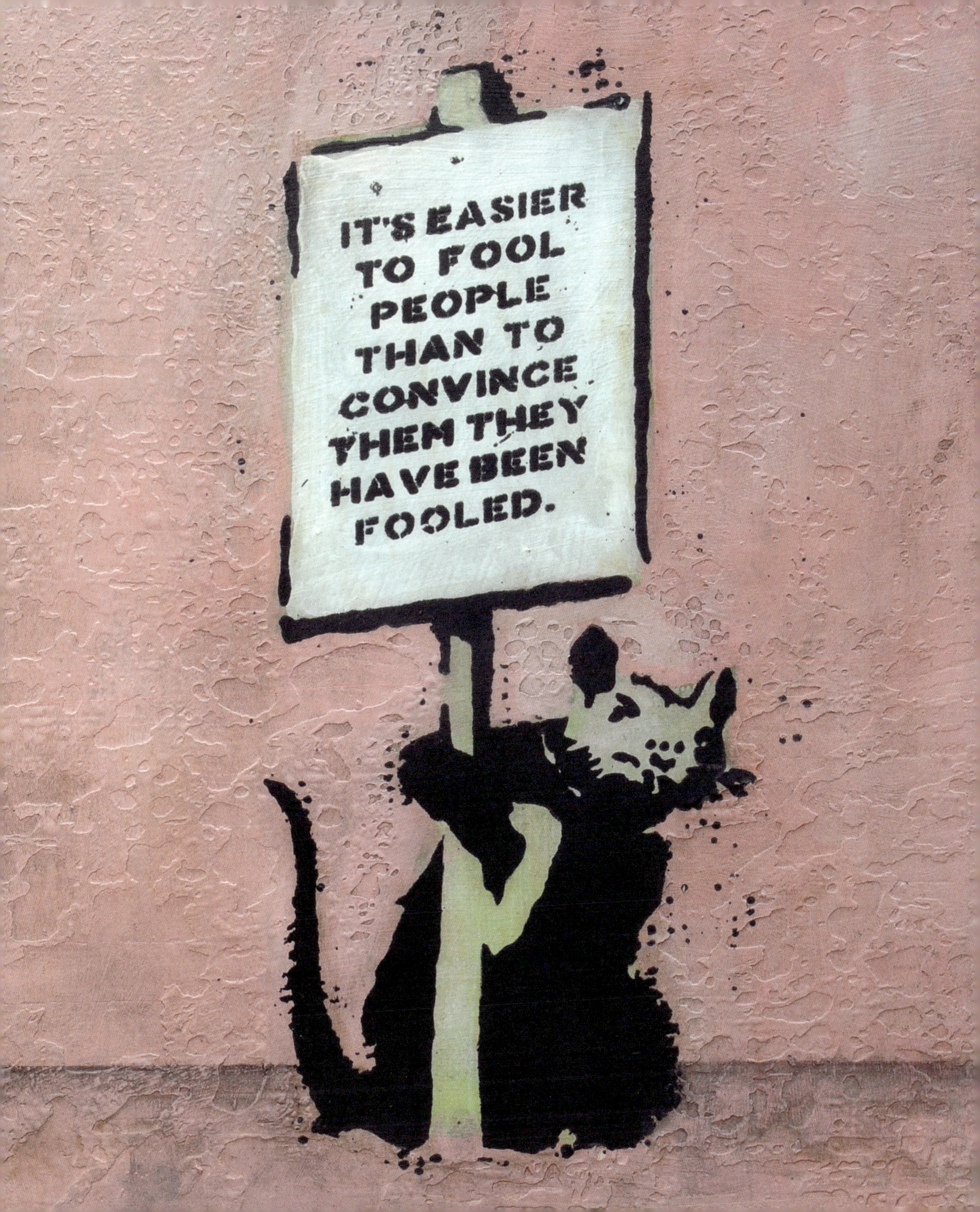

IT'S EASIER
TO FOOL
PEOPLE
THAN TO
CONVINCE
THEM THEY
HAVE BEEN
FOOLED.

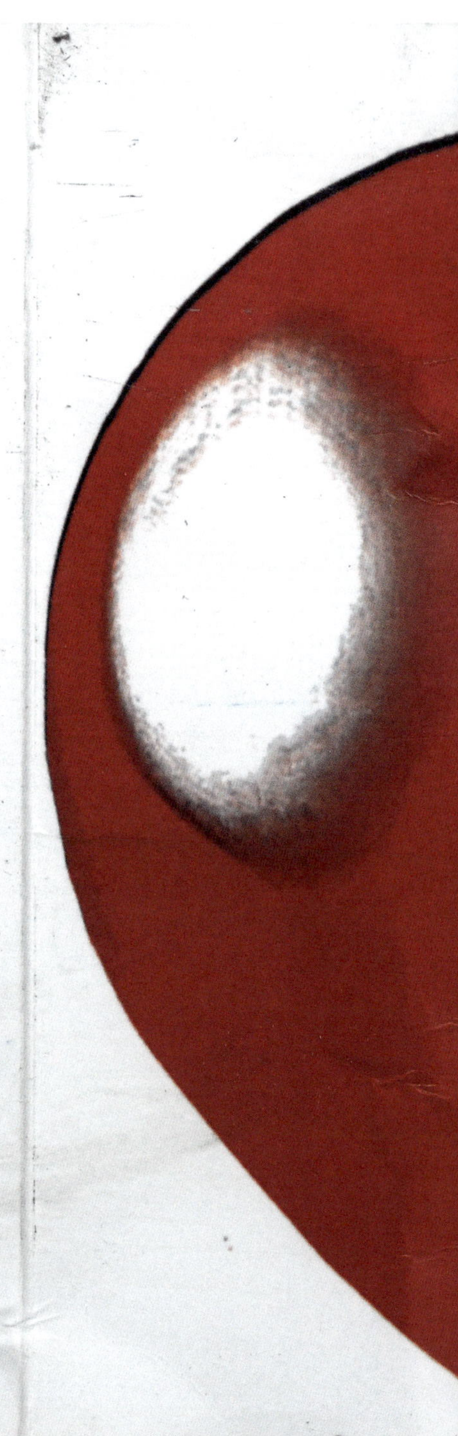

TRUE LOVE FAKE ART !!SUCKERS!!

THE REAL NOT BANKSY FRONT

ART CAR BOOT FAIR, 2019

At the request of the Art Car Boot Fair, the **International Neo Not Banksy Anartist Alliance** (I.N.N.B.A.A) has instructed the L-13 Light Industrial Workshop to assist the **Real Not Banksy Front** (R.N.B.F) in the production of a screen print on the theme of **LOVE**.

As we all know, **LOVE** in the 21st Century is a neo-liberal post-capitalist construct aimed at perverting and enslaving our animalistic desires to make us compliant in a work, reward, buy shit, fuck each other, procreate, fuck the planet, kill people, work work work then die culture; and like-wise that **ART** is fundamentally an evil force raping and pillaging the creative life force of humankind and reducing it to a gaudy trinket to be flogged at market to the highest bidder…. And of course, that all **ART** is **FAKE LOVE** and all **LOVE** is **FAKE ART**.

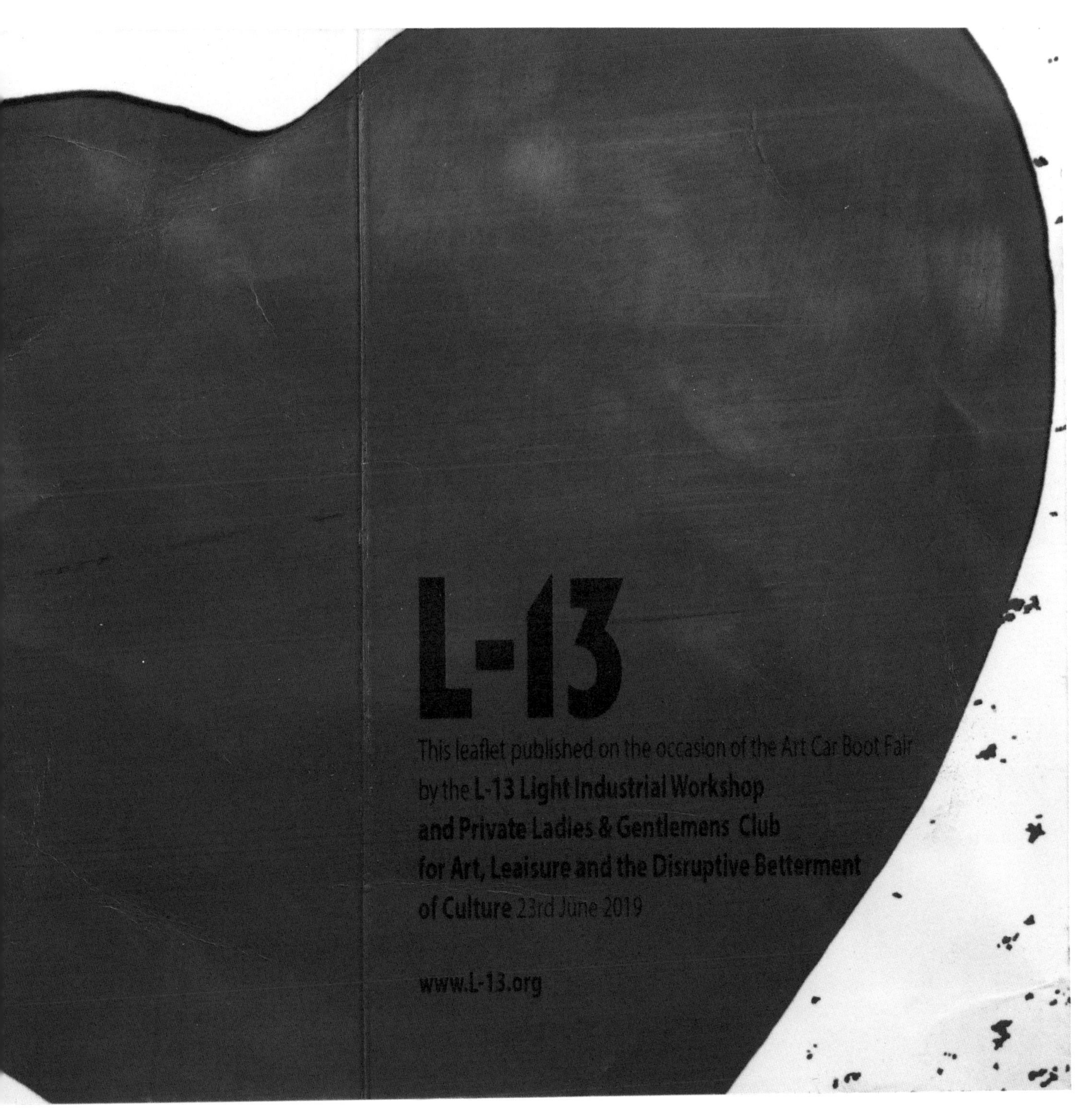

Pamphlet published on the occasion of the Art Car Boot Fair 2019

So, we pose the questions: Is Banksy with us in the fight against **LOVE & ART** or is he part of the racket?... Are we the pseudo-seditious answer to our marketed rebellion future? Will that bubble ever burst? OR will the **TRUE FAKE LOVE ART** of the **REAL NOT BANKSY FRONT** liberate us all from the shackles that chain us to a stump in the swamp of maudlin soup that's sucking us slowly down into the mire?

ANSWER: No!

EDITION

TRUE LOVE FAKE ART SUCKERS!

Four colour screen print on recycled grey pulp board

Edition of 500 + 50 APs

Signed, numbered and stamped on the reverse

Published on the occasion of the Art Car Boot Fair

23rd June 2019

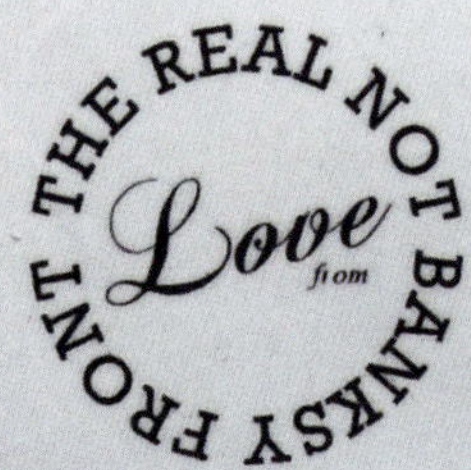

NOTES

THE REAL NOT BA
artist but an Anartist
year-old girl from Sc
illegitimate   child
BANKSY intent on
liberal snowflake
gooder politics, whils
Fascists, secretly on
loved.

But really:

THE REAL NOT BA
There is no unlove
Scunthorpe   (right
making **NOT BANK**
NOT   BANKSY
the **INTERNATIONA**
ANARTIST   ALL
The **I.N.N.B.A.A.** is
of **NOT BANKSY** fr
NOT BANKSY. As w
BANKSY is dead, a
(rumoured to have be
Control). As there
BANKSY to make n
BANKSY, the **INTE**
BANKSY   ANART
fabricated **THE**
FRONT and invited L
technicians   in   t
Department to aid
production.

All **I.N.N.B.A.A.** artw
and stamped by an I.
with a **STOT21stCpla**
issued   with   a   m
BANKSY FRONT Pe

SY FRONT is not an
a fact a pro-Brexit 13-
orpe – the abandoned
f THE "REAL"
ermining her father's
Marxist woolly do-
e all xenophobic neo-
anting to be held and

Y FRONT is not real.
3-year-old girl from
g or otherwise)
artworks. THE REAL
an invention of
NEO NOT BANKSY
CE (I.N.N.B.A.A.).
international alliance
s and NOT the real
know, the real NOT
NOT NOT BANKSY
assassinated by Pest
NO REAL NOT
works of art by NOT
ATIONAL NEO NOT
ALLIANCE has
L NOT BANKSY
s especially untrained
MANGéL PrESS
nd abet this faux-

are quality checked
B.A.A. official, signed
thunderbolt man, and
ngless REAL NOT
ontrol COA.

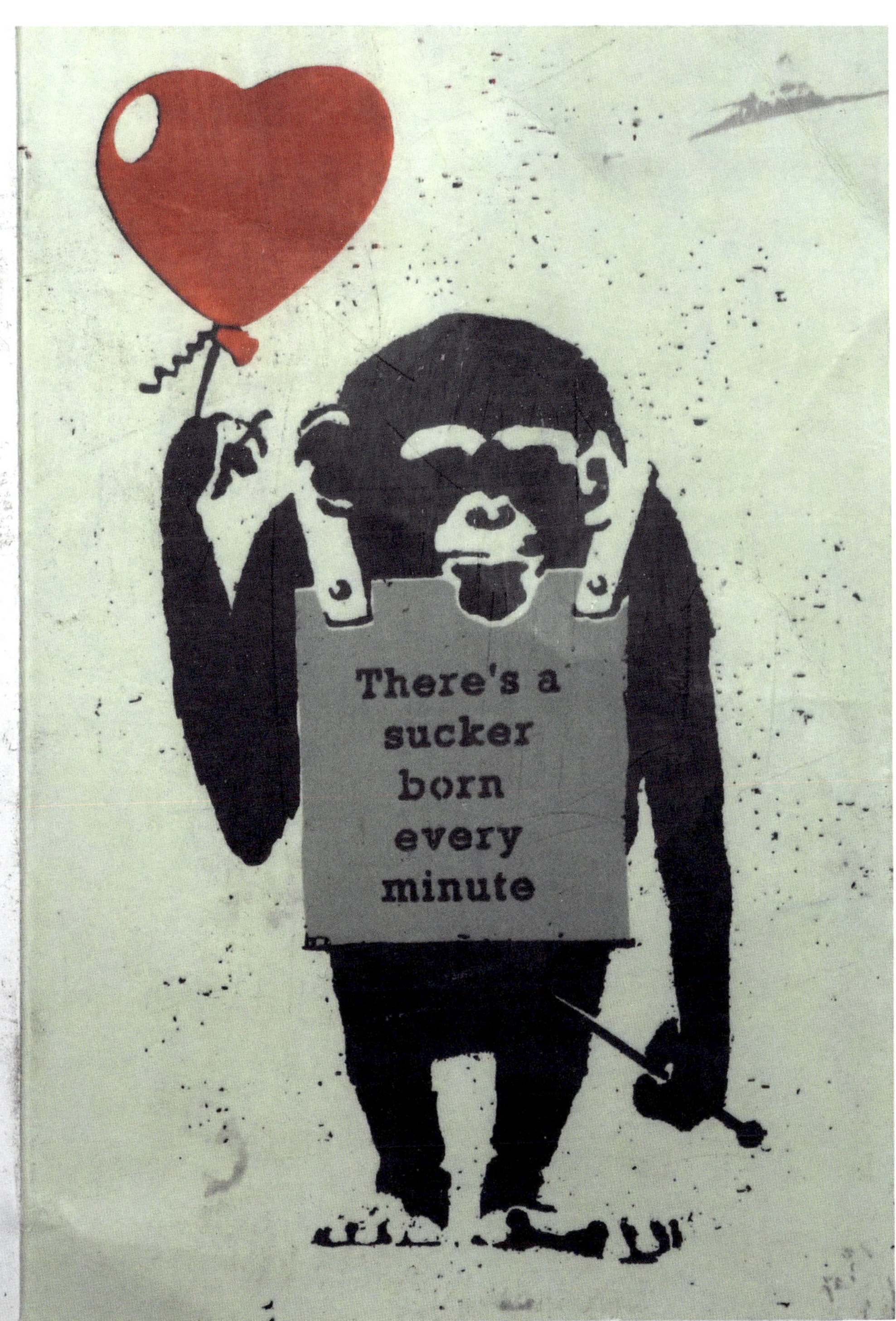

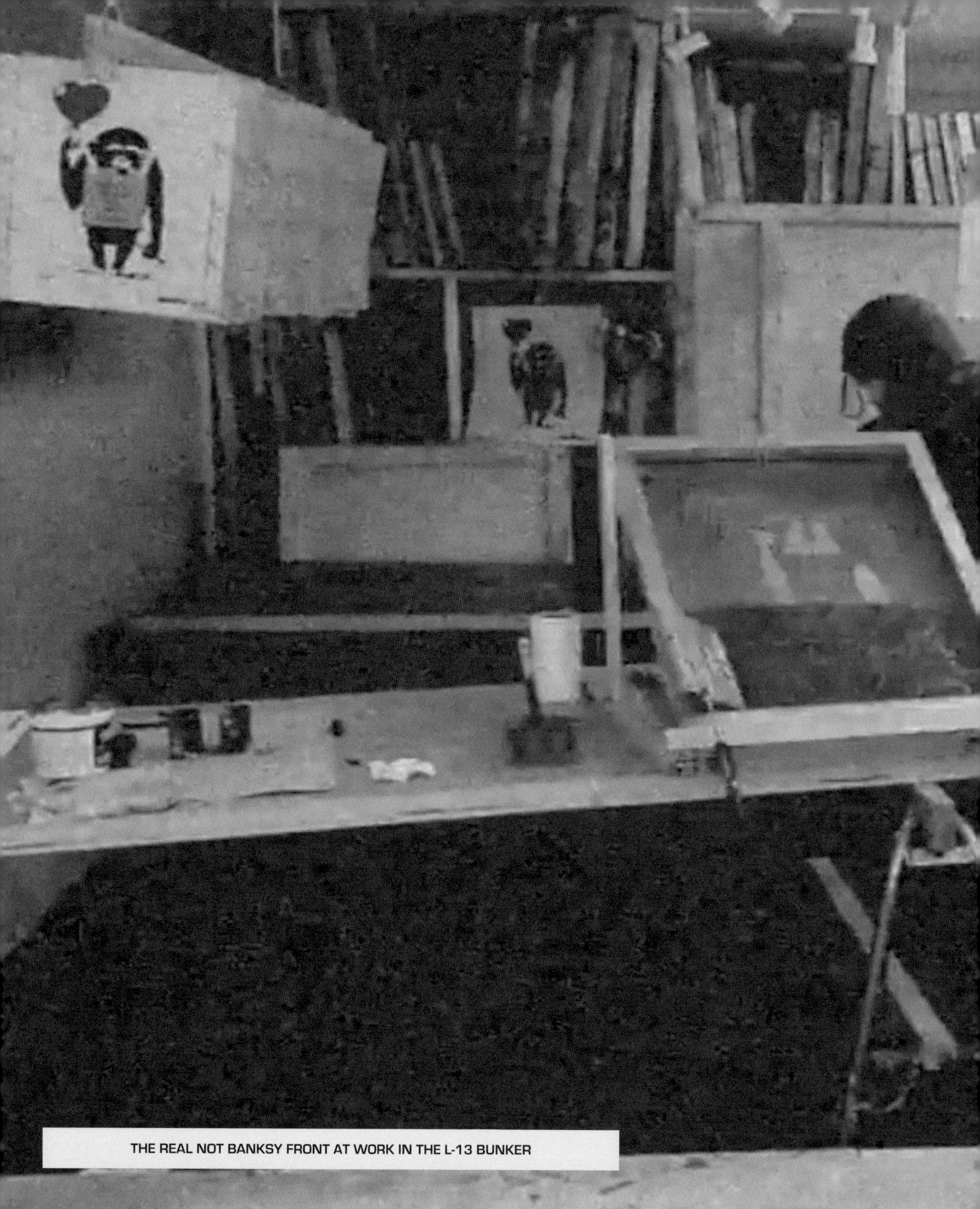

THE REAL NOT BANKSY FRONT AT WORK IN THE L-13 BUNKER

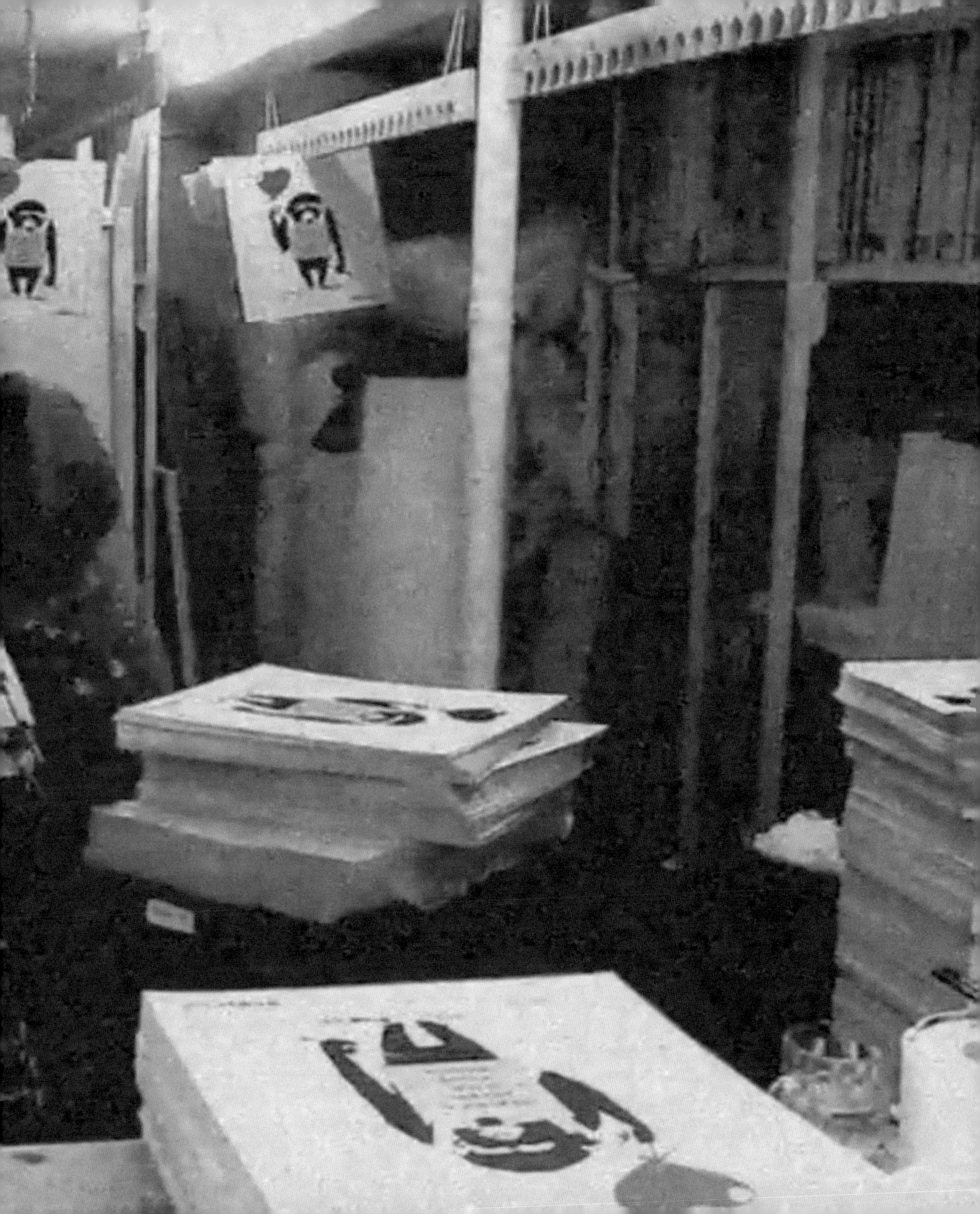

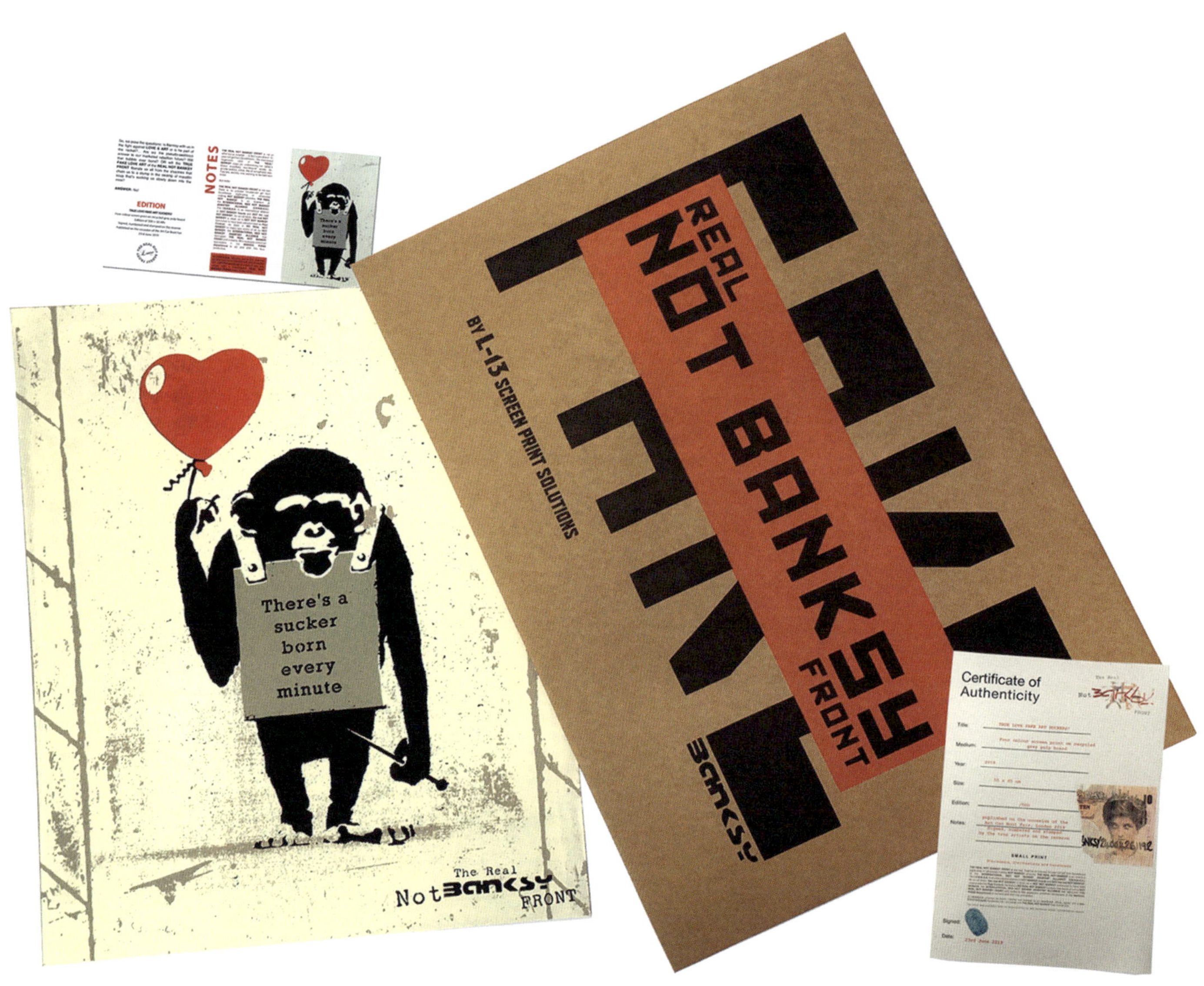

4 colour screen print with thumbprinted COA, edition pamphlet, and printed cardboard mailer

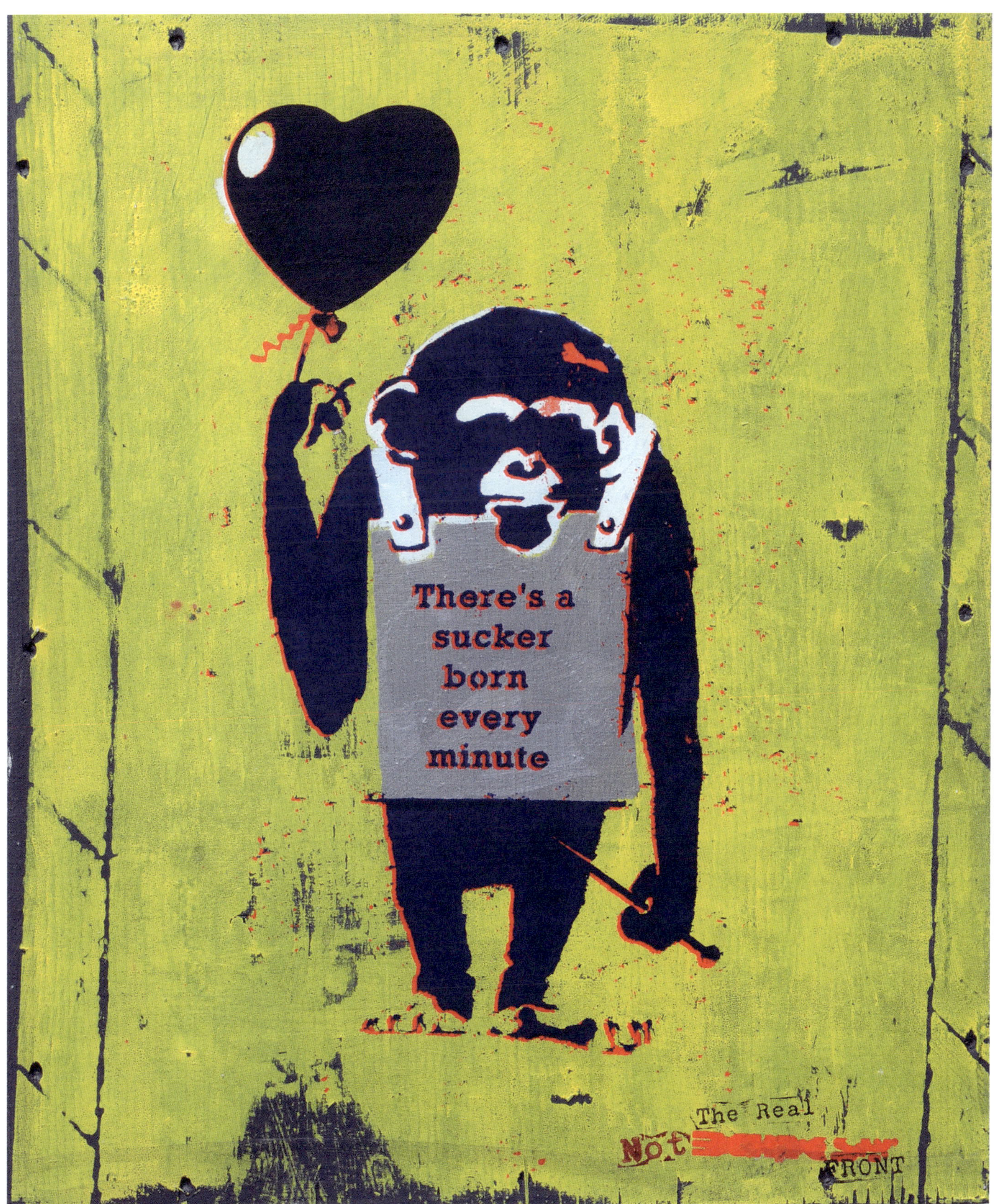

"original" True Love Fake Art Suckers

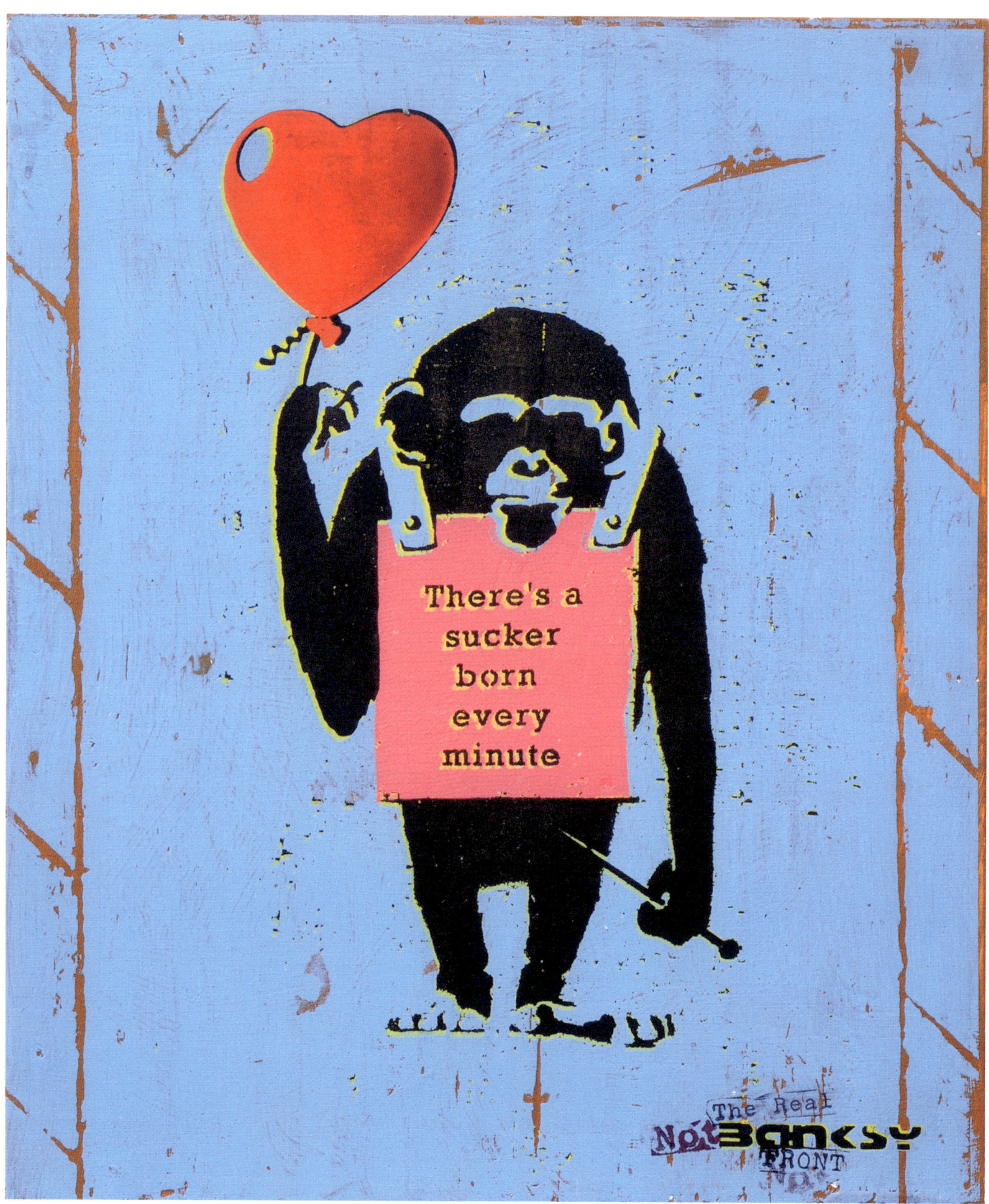

More "originals"...

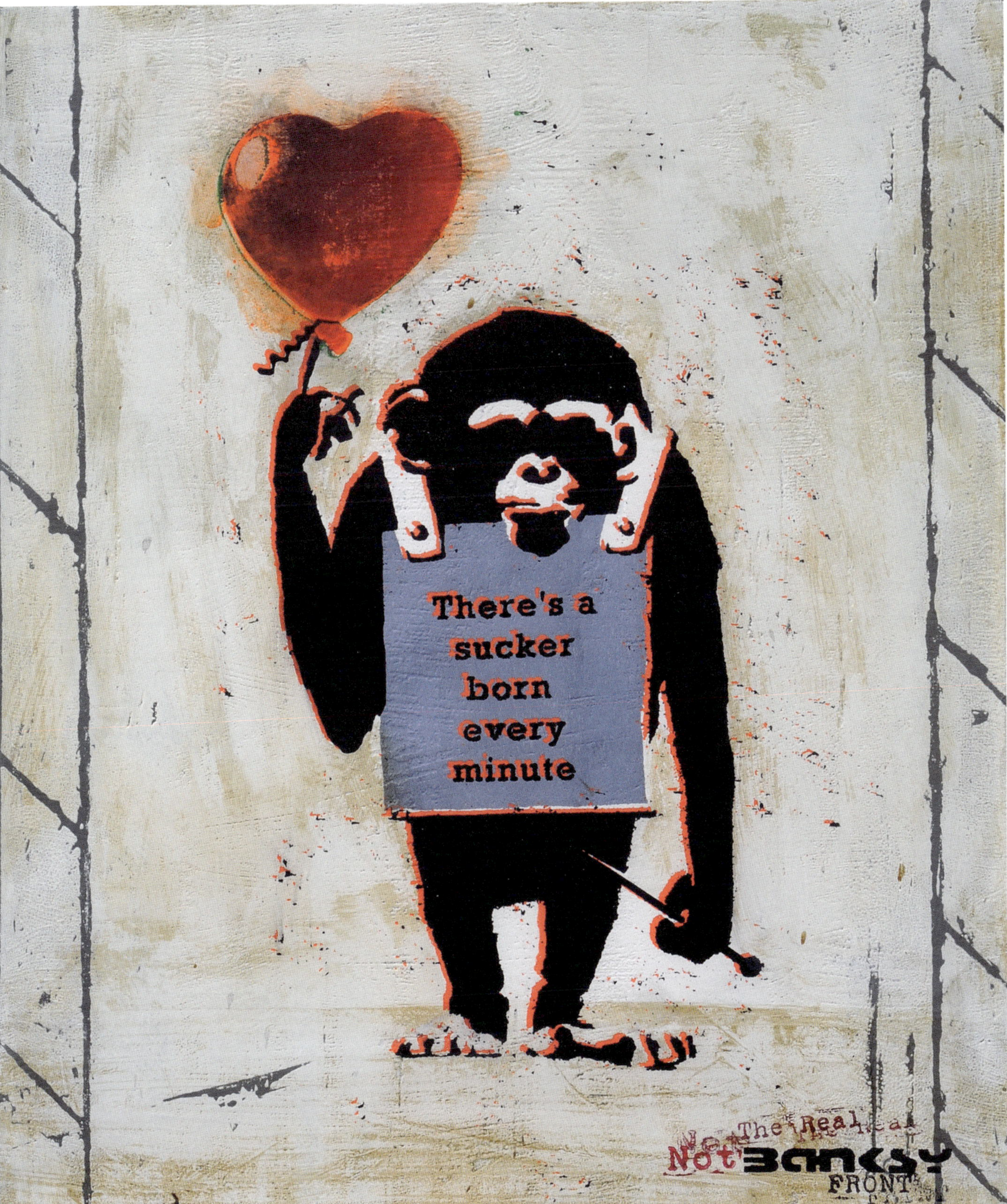
There's a
sucker
born
every
minute
The Real
Not Banksy
FRONT

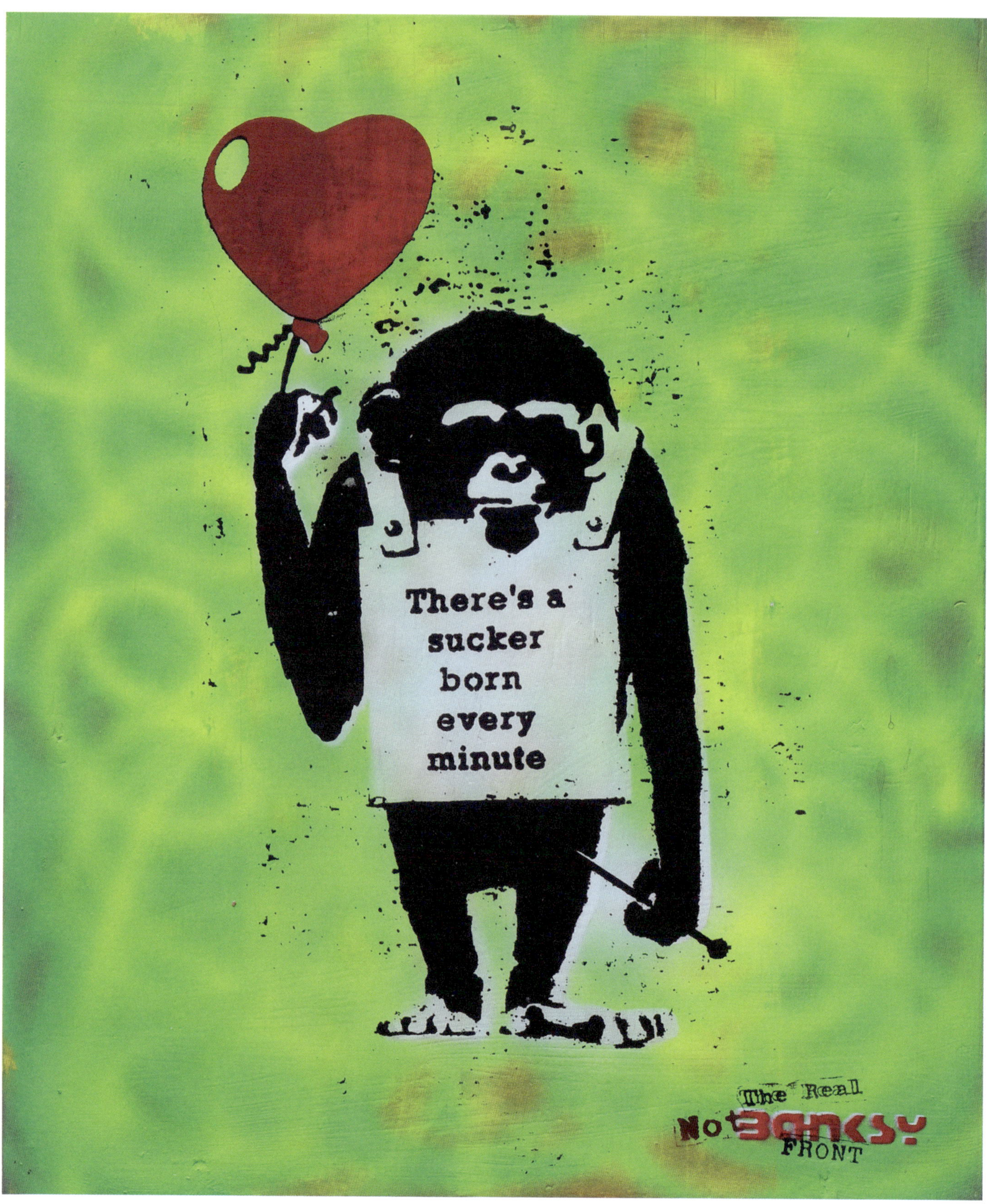

More...

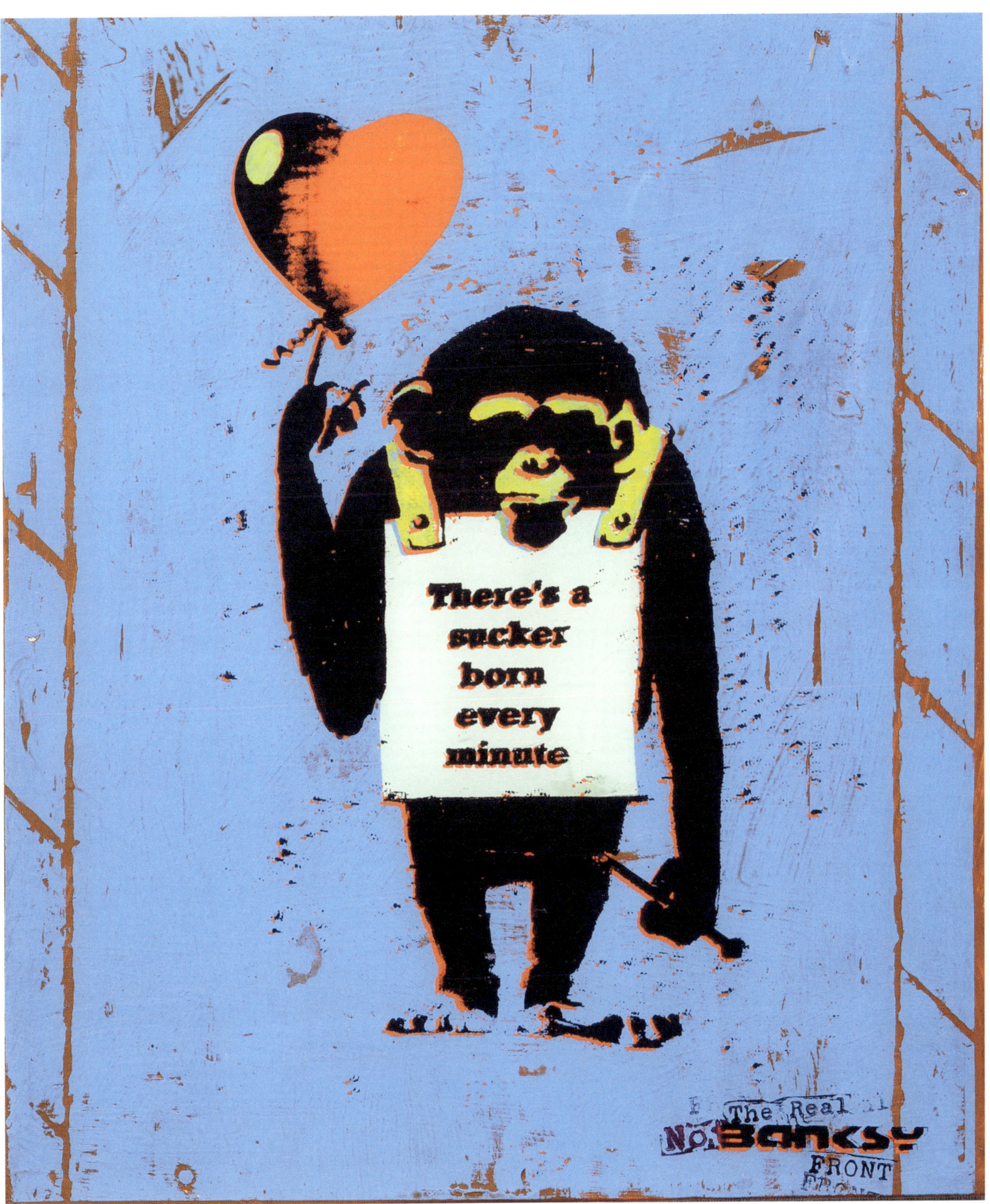
There's a
sucker
born
every
minute
The Real
No.Banksy
FRONT

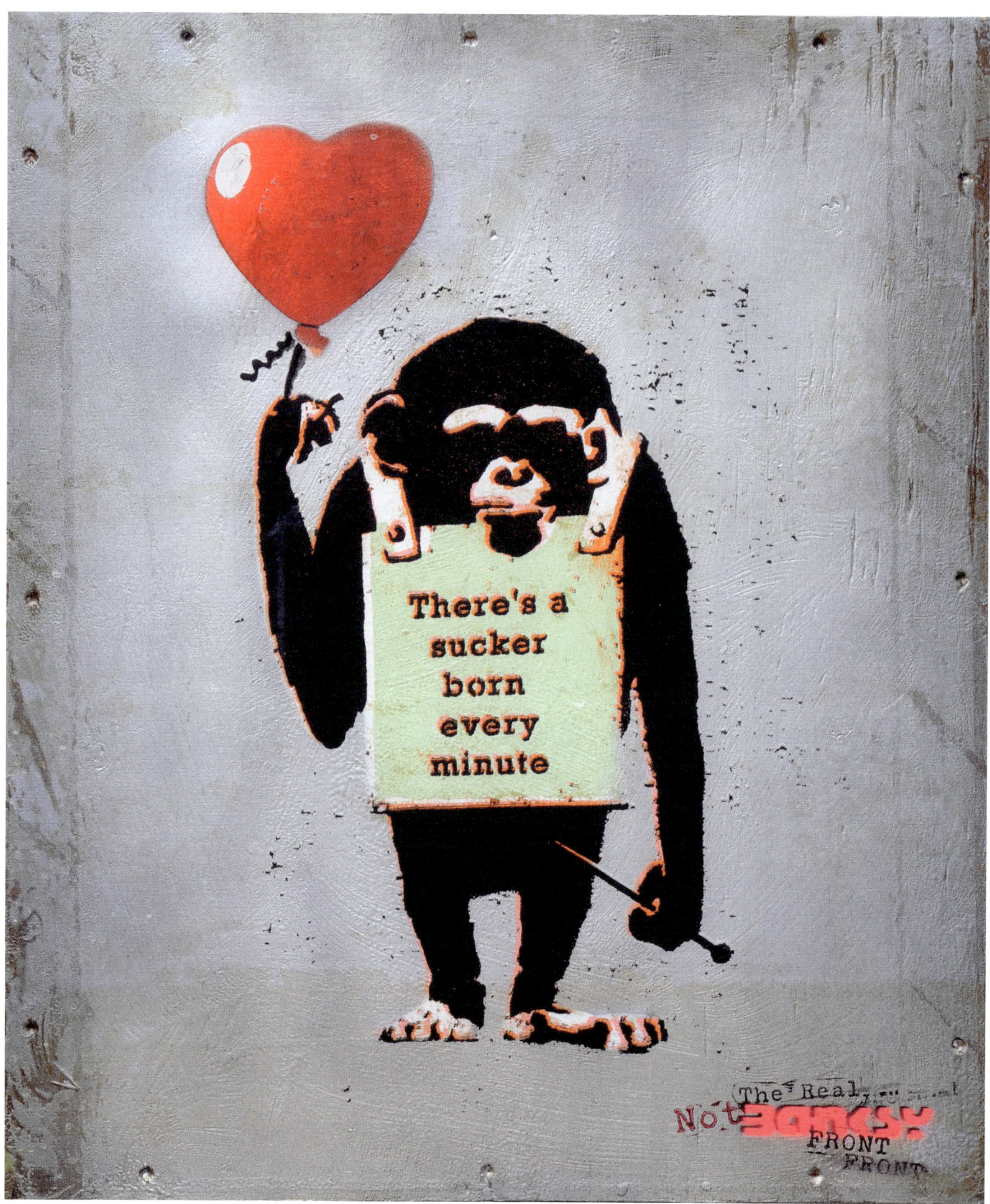

And more...

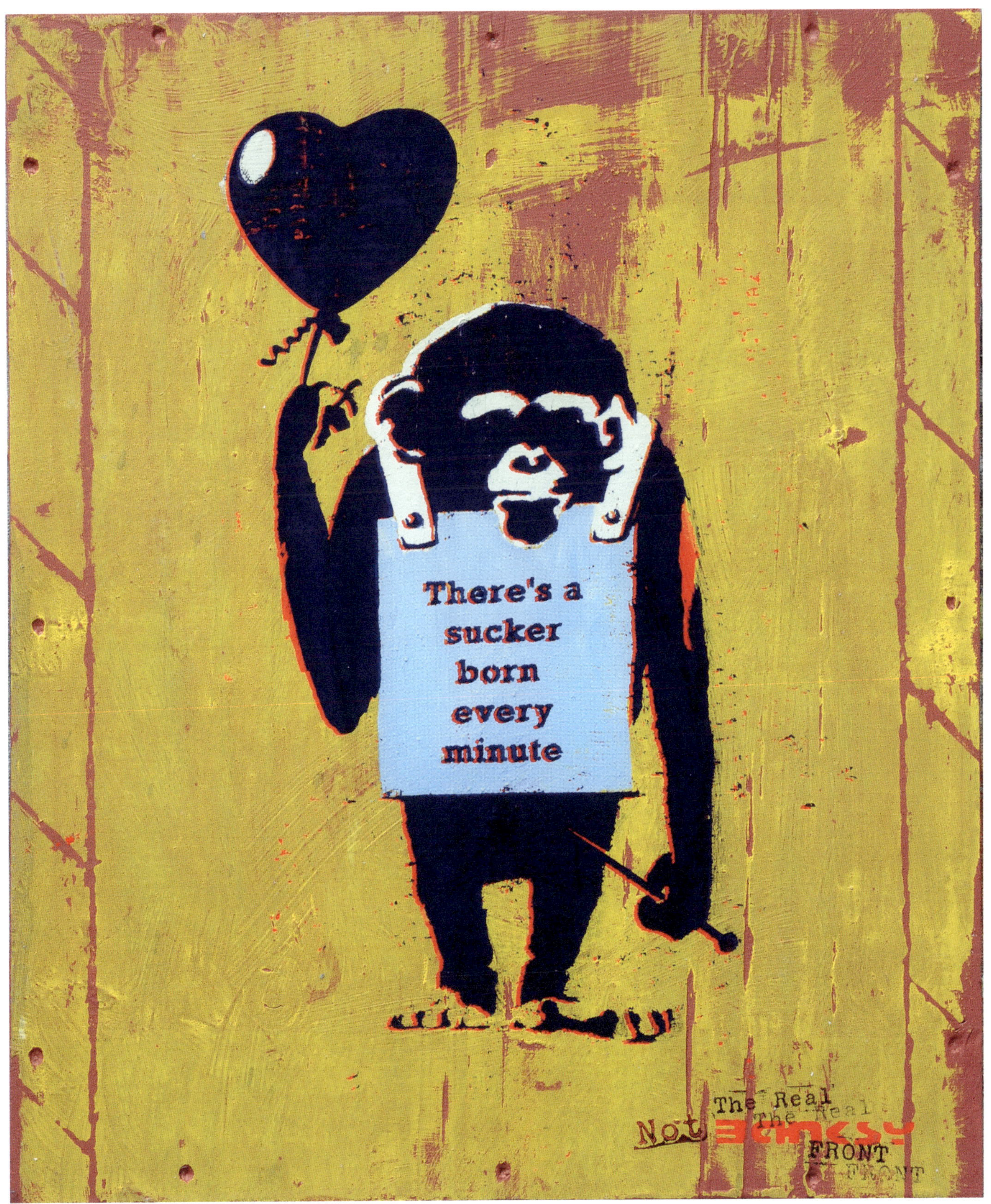
There's a
sucker
born
every
minute
Not The Real Banksy
The Real
FRONT

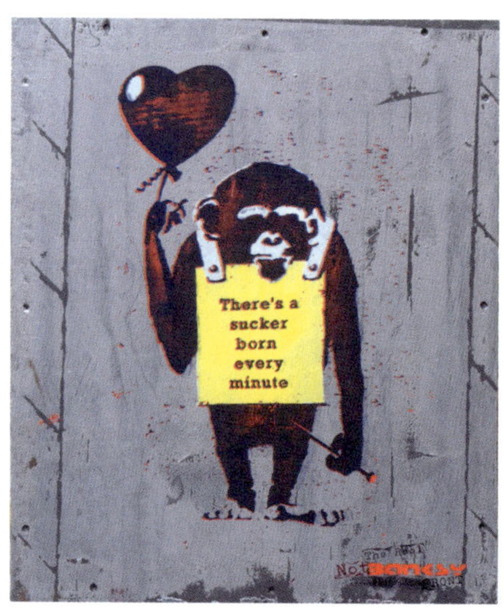

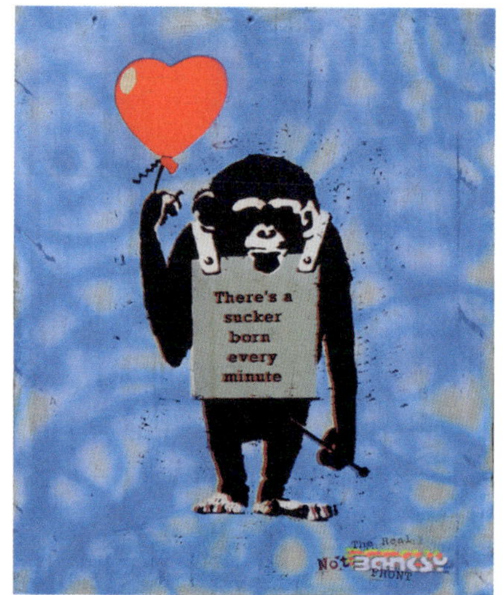

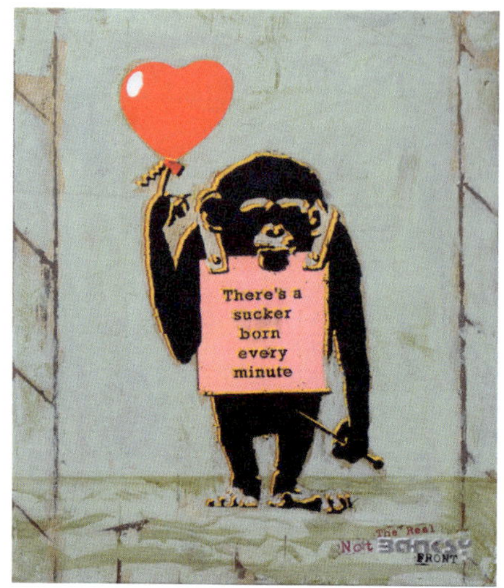

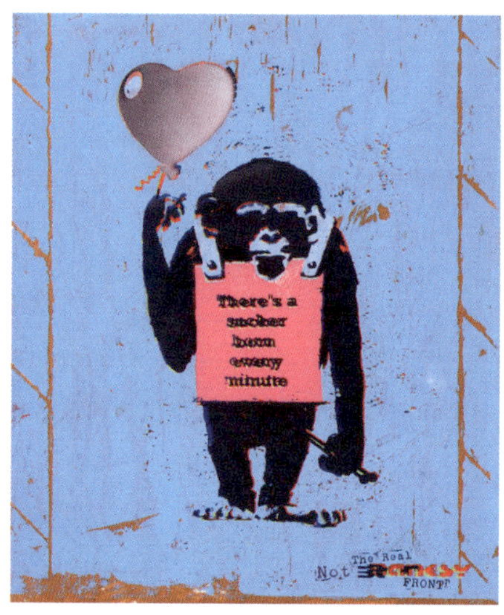

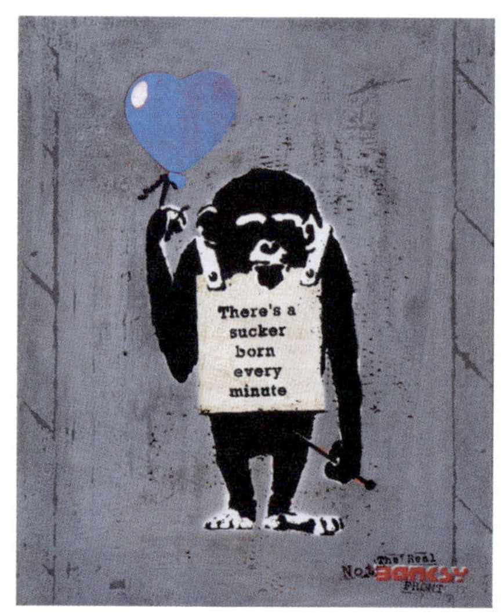

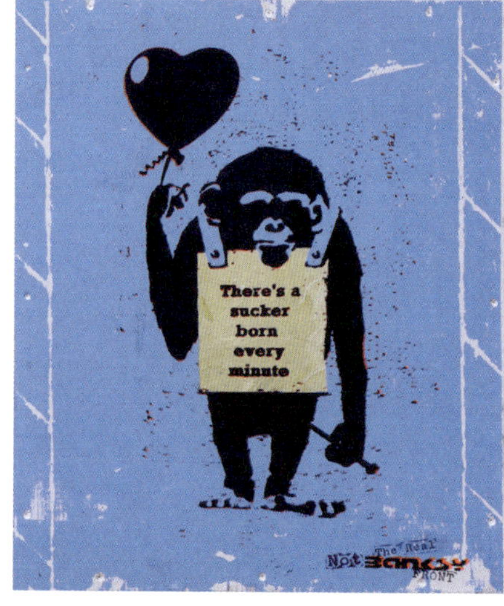

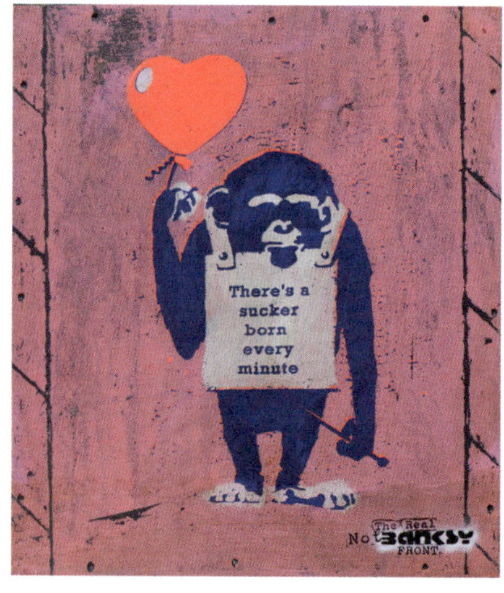

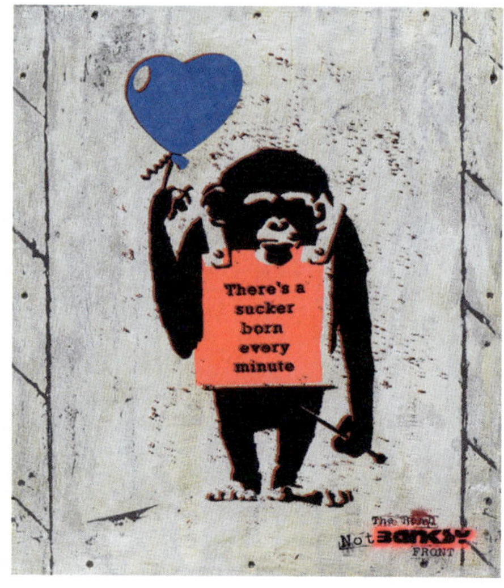

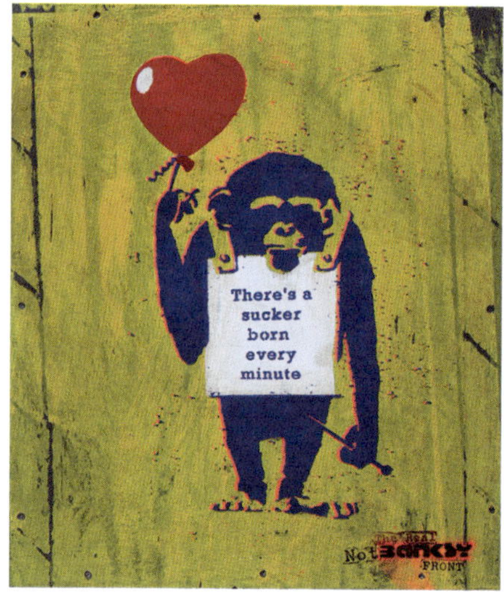

And MORE!!!!

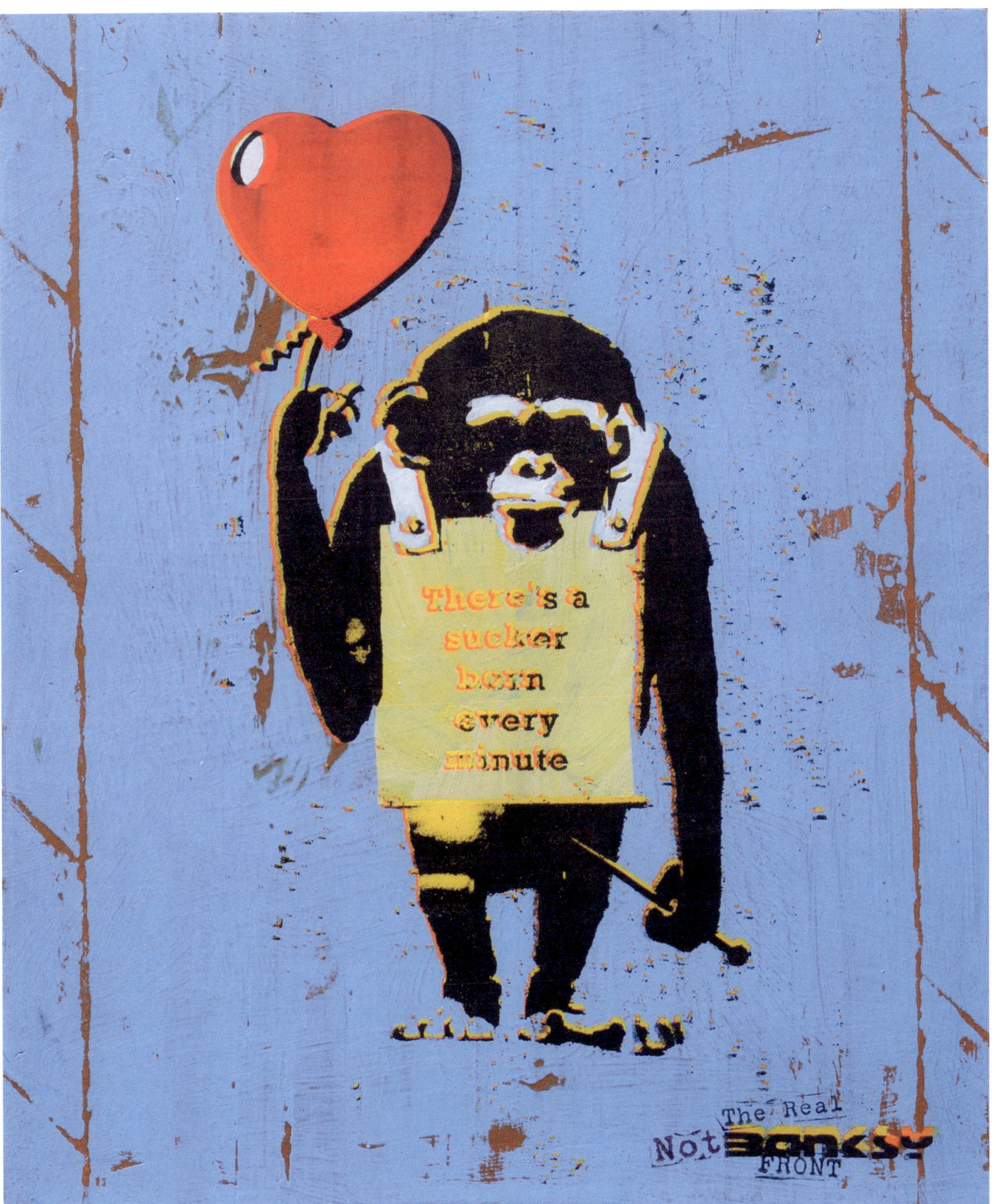

There's a sucker born every minute
The Real
Not BANKSY
FRONT

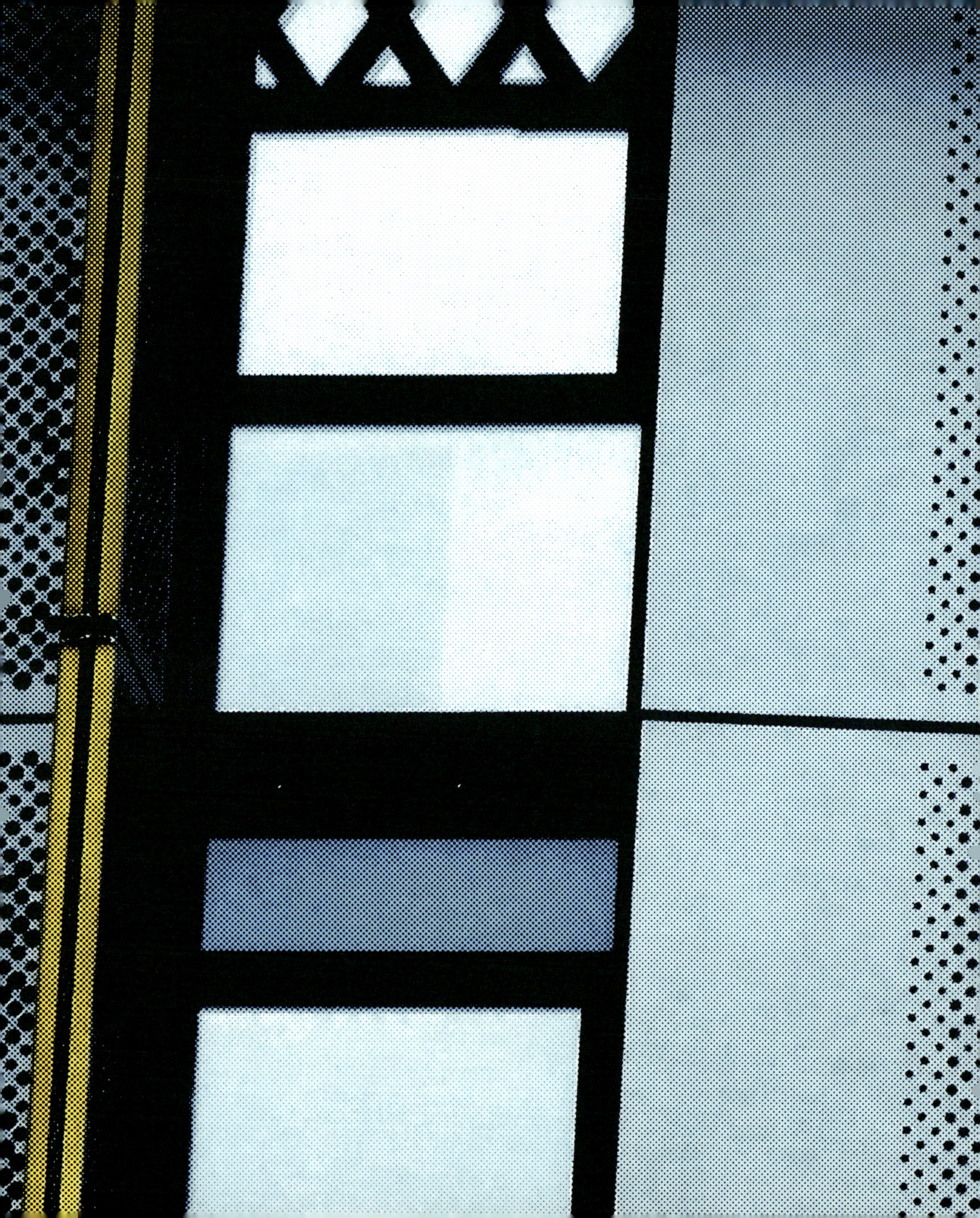

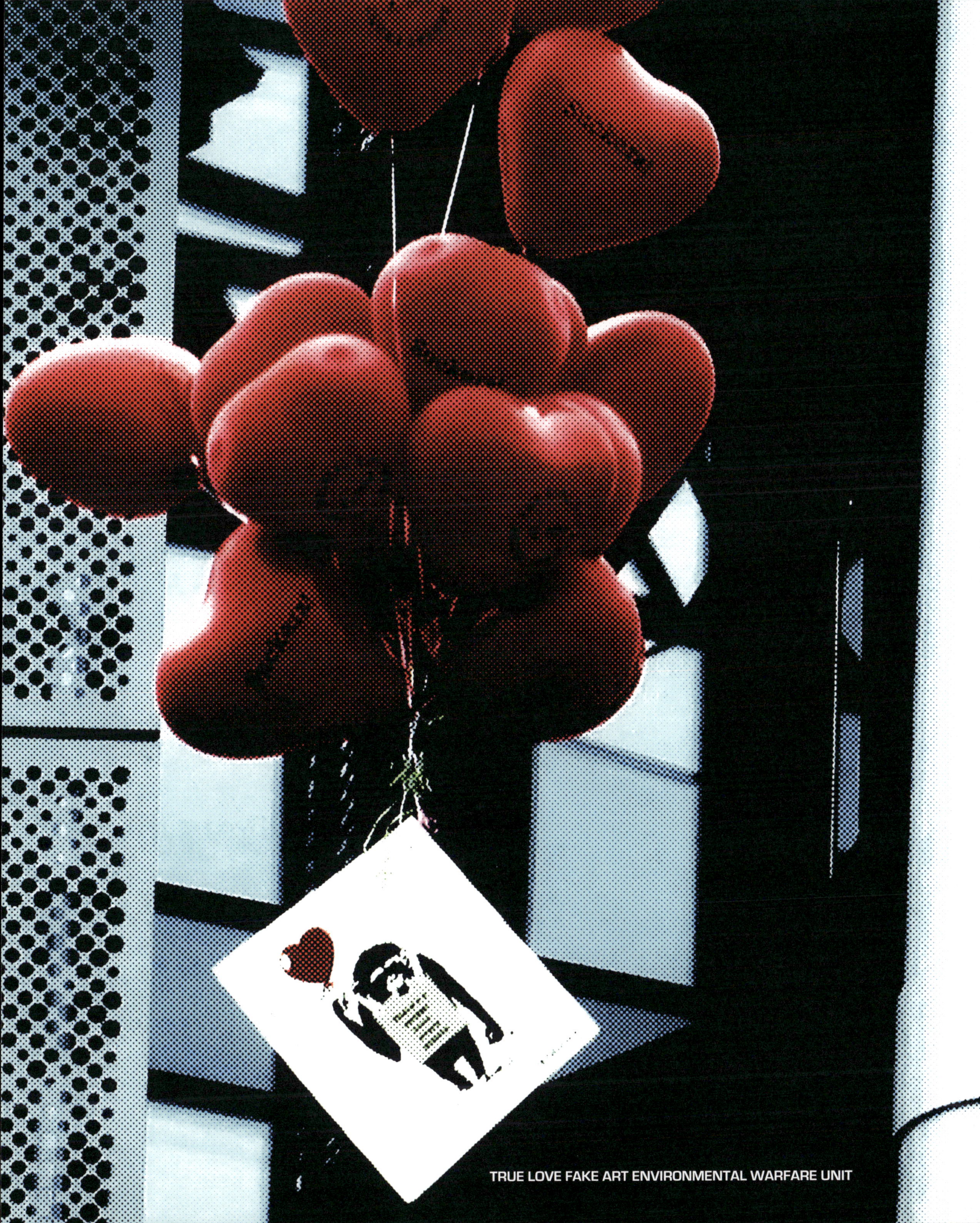
TRUE LOVE FAKE ART ENVIRONMENTAL WARFARE UNIT

EXHIBITION NOTES

THE REAL NOT BANKSY FRONT GENERAL ELECTION SPECIAL
THE ELEVENTH HOUR
ANexhibition of fakery, fraudery and cynical exploitation
on the eve of the END TIMES I2/I2/I9
being
A DEMONSTRATION OF THE INTERNATIONAL NEO NOT BANKSY ANARTIST
ALLIANCE against the DEMOCRATIC FREE WORLD
With
fake artworks by THE REAL NOT BANKSY FRONT

"GET BANKSY DONE" you cry ... and believe you me, we will
but it won8t be pretty.

Hold onto your hats and arses.

As the last votes are ɛ cast and the polling stations close
our valiant exhibition will open to the haunting refrain of
the Last Post8 played on bugle for all those fallen, all those
lost, and all those last past the post.

As the fat white western world realises that our saviour ~~StXBanksy~~
St Banksy— Flayed alive and crucified at the cross of blue-chip
art martyrdom — could not deliver us from evil, and that his
nemesis — the fallen angels STOT 21stCplanB — could not not
stop him from trying to save us with their double XX negative
Neo-Nothingist attempt at culture jamming all time and
meaning into a volatile ball of pataphysical dual reality-reason
and super-righteous non-non-victory-reason where the good and
the bad fuck each other to produce the ugly bastard child
named hashtagGOODBADWHATTHEFUCKITSFUNNY . . . . .. It is finally
time to submit to defeat. To submit and witness the burning
ruins of sense and order. To realise the collapse of purpose.
To welcome the eradication of all dignity and hope.

~~Let8sXface~~ Let's face it, we're fucked!

As the votes are counted we enter a new era of nothingness.

~~GetXBanksyXdonX~~ "GET BANKSY DONE" you cried... so we did. And
now you must pay.

You want answers? Solutions? Then please look elsewhere.
All we can offer is mind-fuckery and distraction at its worse.

So, don the ~~NOT~~ REAL NOT BANKSY FRONT bunny ears, and let's
dance.

Chaos is the future and the future is now,

We offer you the surrender monkeys of art from the no-man's
land of the socio-political cultural abyss.

ALL ART IS FAKE and only FAKE ART IS REAL

THE END

* 'Get Banksy Done' echoes Boris Johnson's mantra
of 'Get Brexit Done' during the election campaign

THE ELEVENTH HOUR

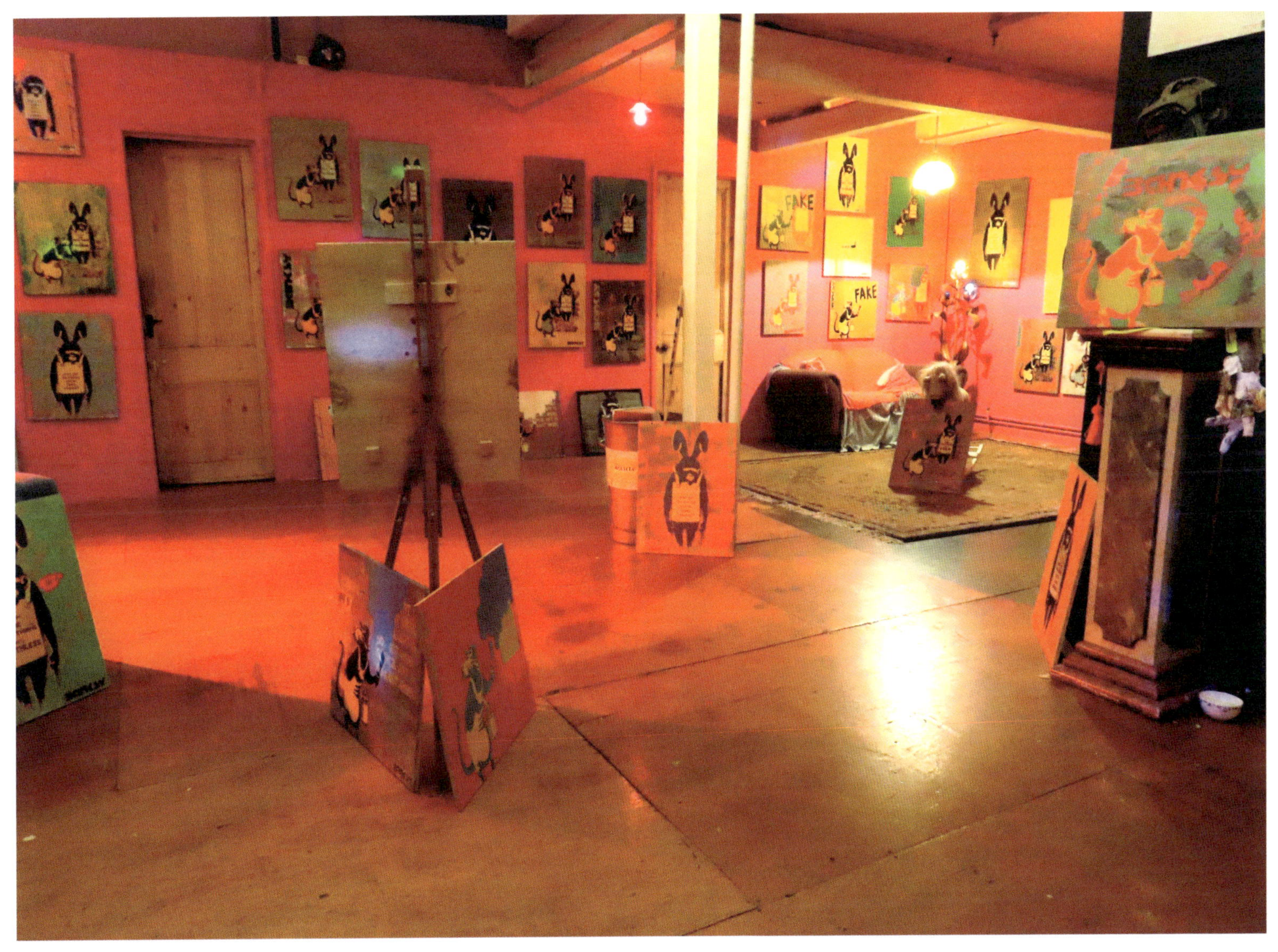

ELECTION DAY EXHIBITION 2019
BLASÉ HOUSE
LONDON

ANOTHER RAMSHACKLE EXHIBITION OF PRINTS AND PAINTINGS MADE
TO DISTRACT OUR MINDS FROM THE PENDING HORROR
OF ANOTHER TORY VICTORY
AND THE SPECTRE OF
BORIS F'ING JOHNSON
AS PRIME MINISTER

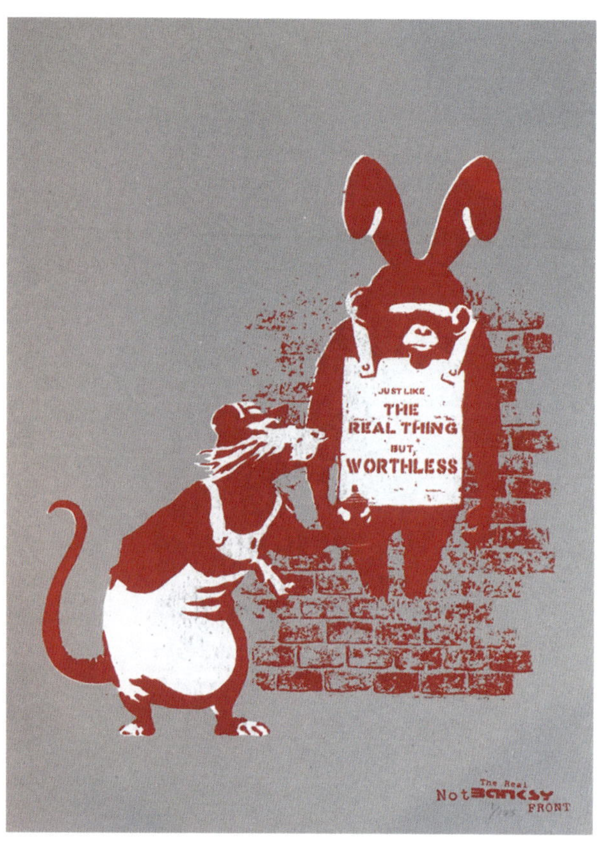

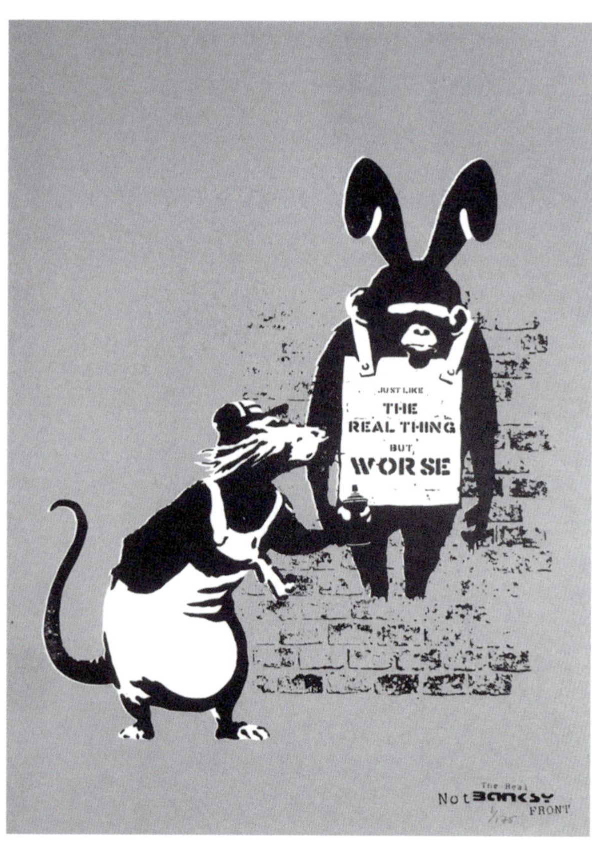

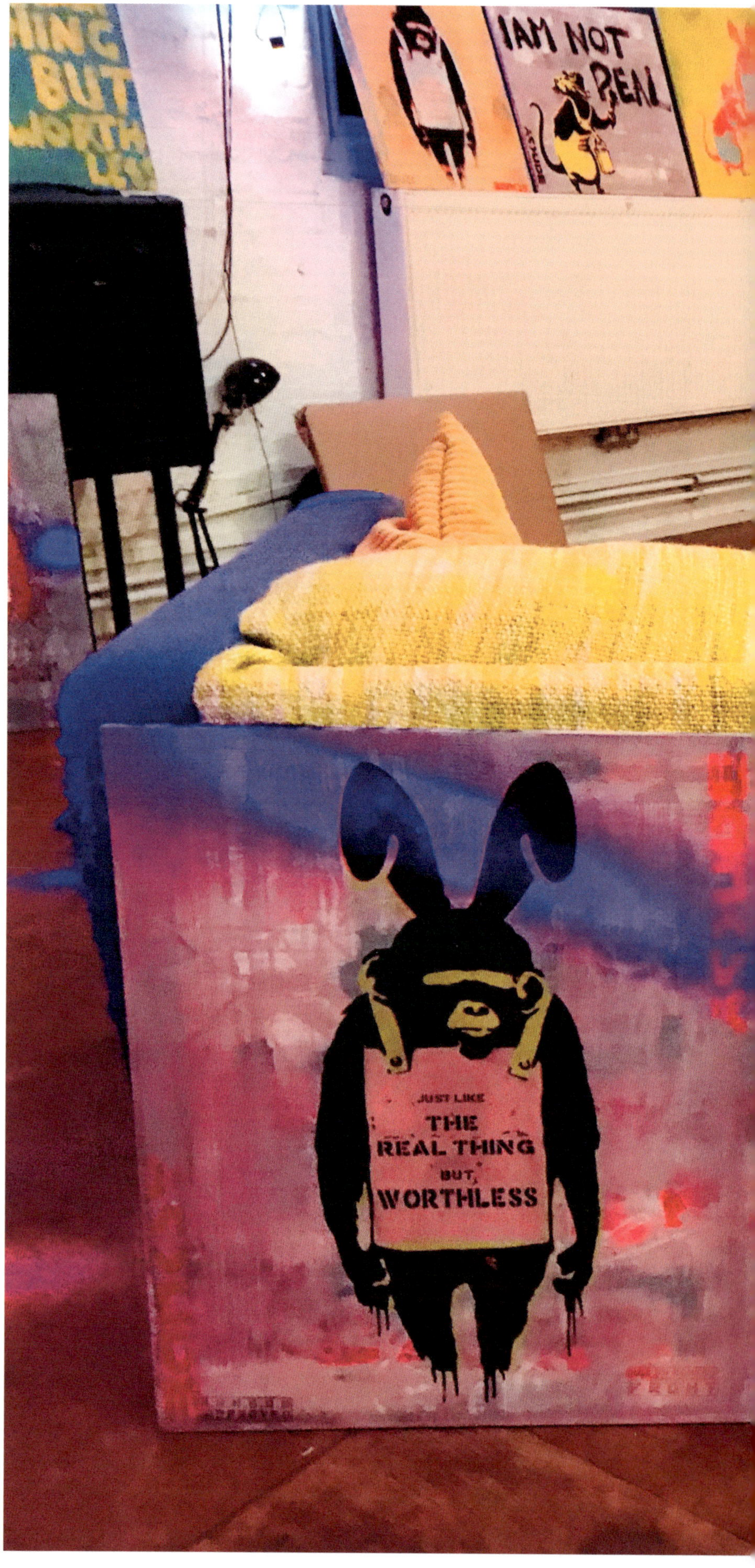

WORTHLESS and WORSE Editions
2 colour screen prints on recycled pulp grey card
Editions of 175 of each

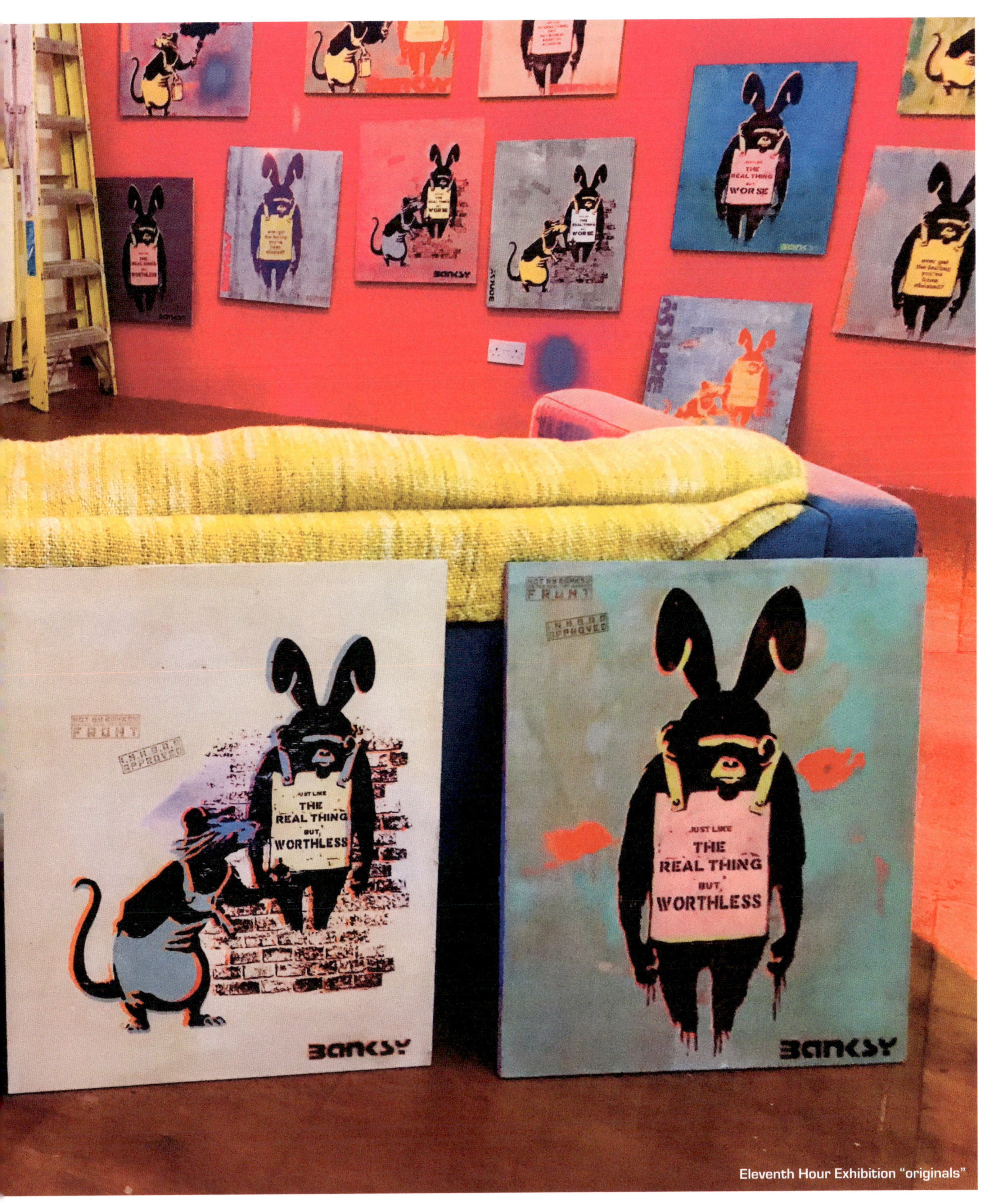

Eleventh Hour Exhibition "originals"

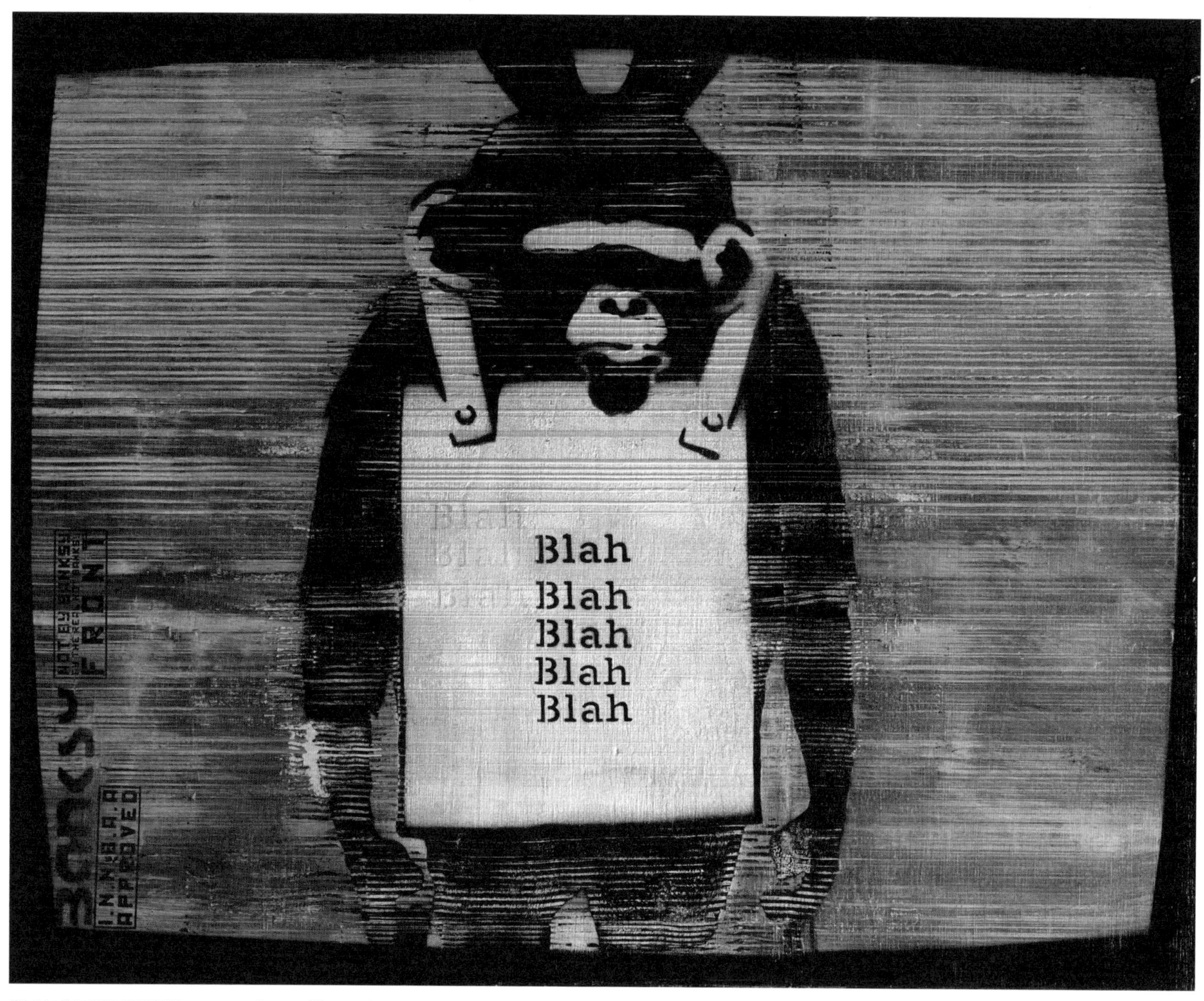

BLAH MEDIA CHIMP spray paint and household paint on plywood panel

THE GREAT INDIGNITY - GLITTER BUNNY CHIMP spray paint, household paint, and black glitter on plywood panel

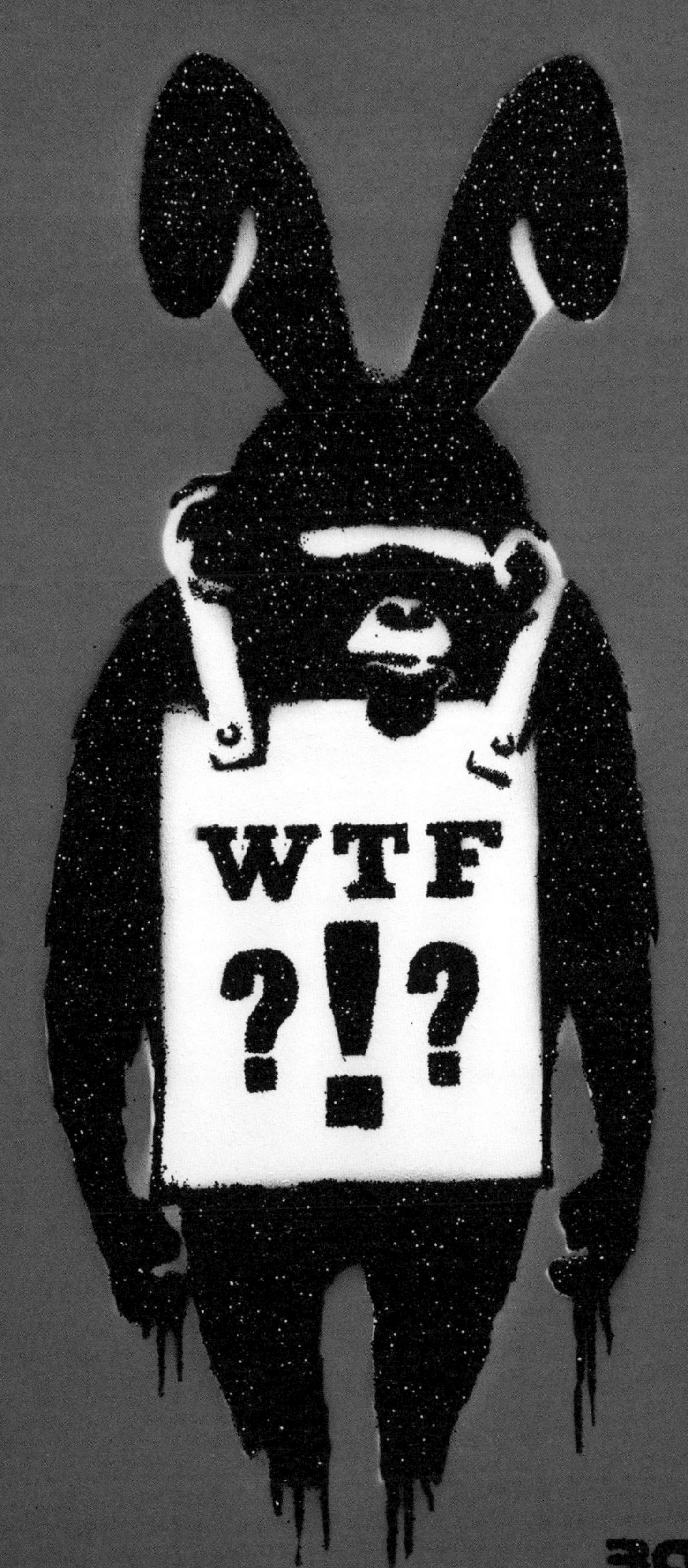

WTF
?!?
NOT BY BANKS!!
BY THE REAL NOT BANKSY
FRONT
I.N.B.A.D
APPROVED
BANKSY

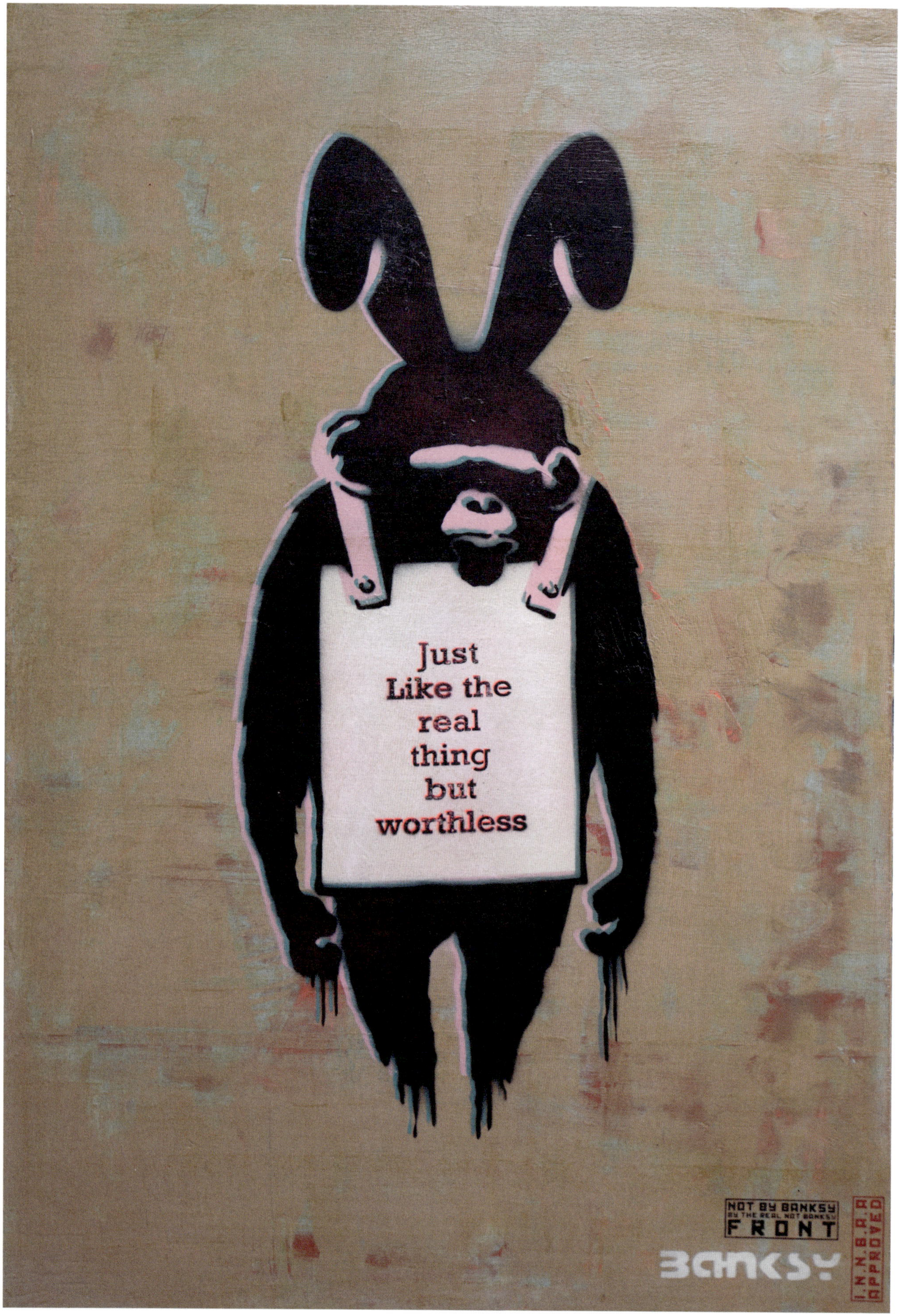

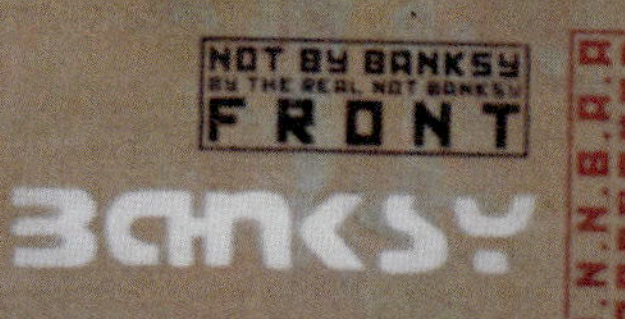
Just
Like the
real
thing
but
worthless
NOT BY BANKSY
BY THE REAL NOT BANKSY
FRONT
BANKSY
I.N.N.B.A
APPROVED

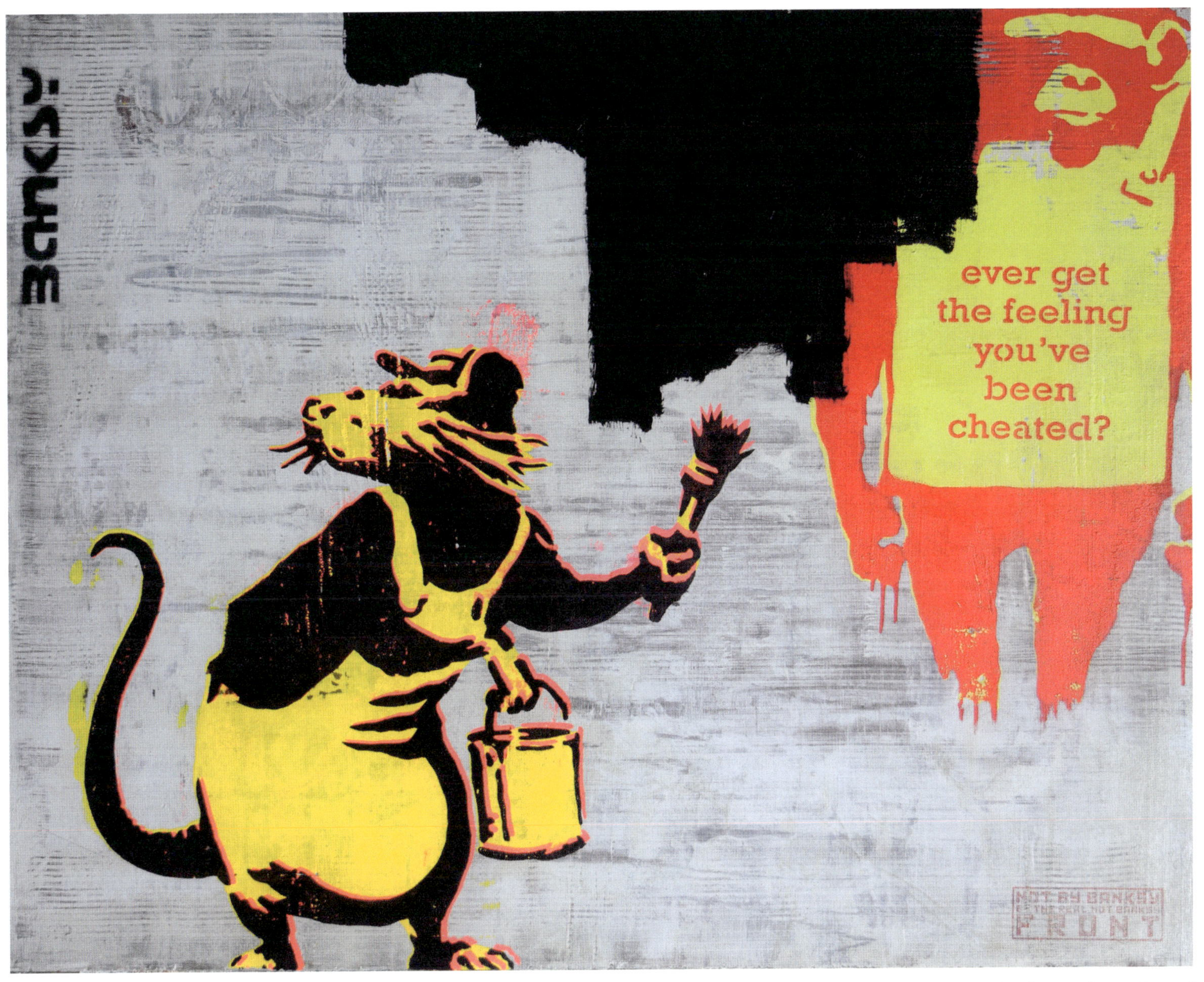

CHEATED screen ink and household paint on plywood panel

WORTHLESS BUNNY CHIMP screen ink and household paint on plywood panel

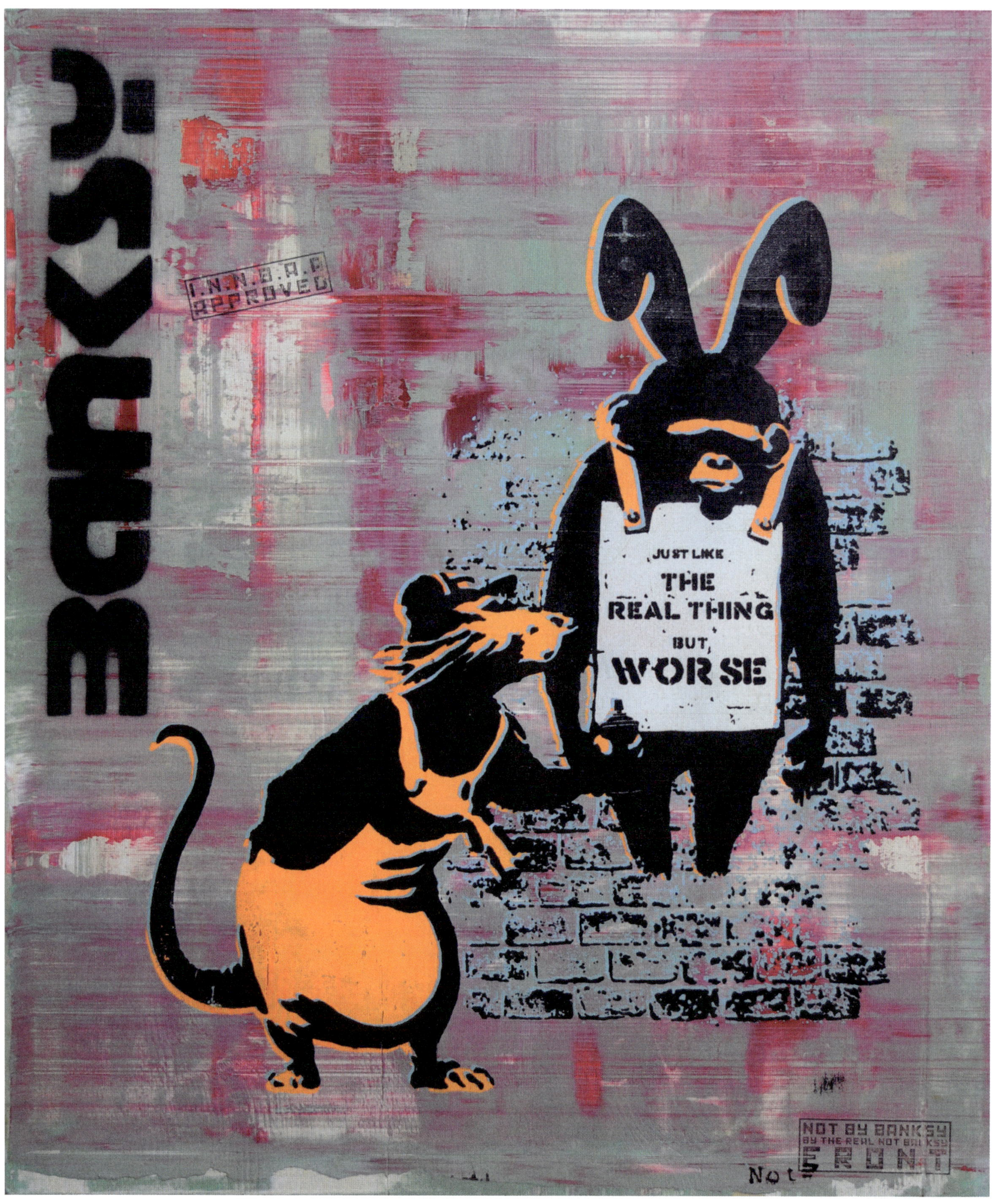

WORSE screen ink and household paint on plywood panel

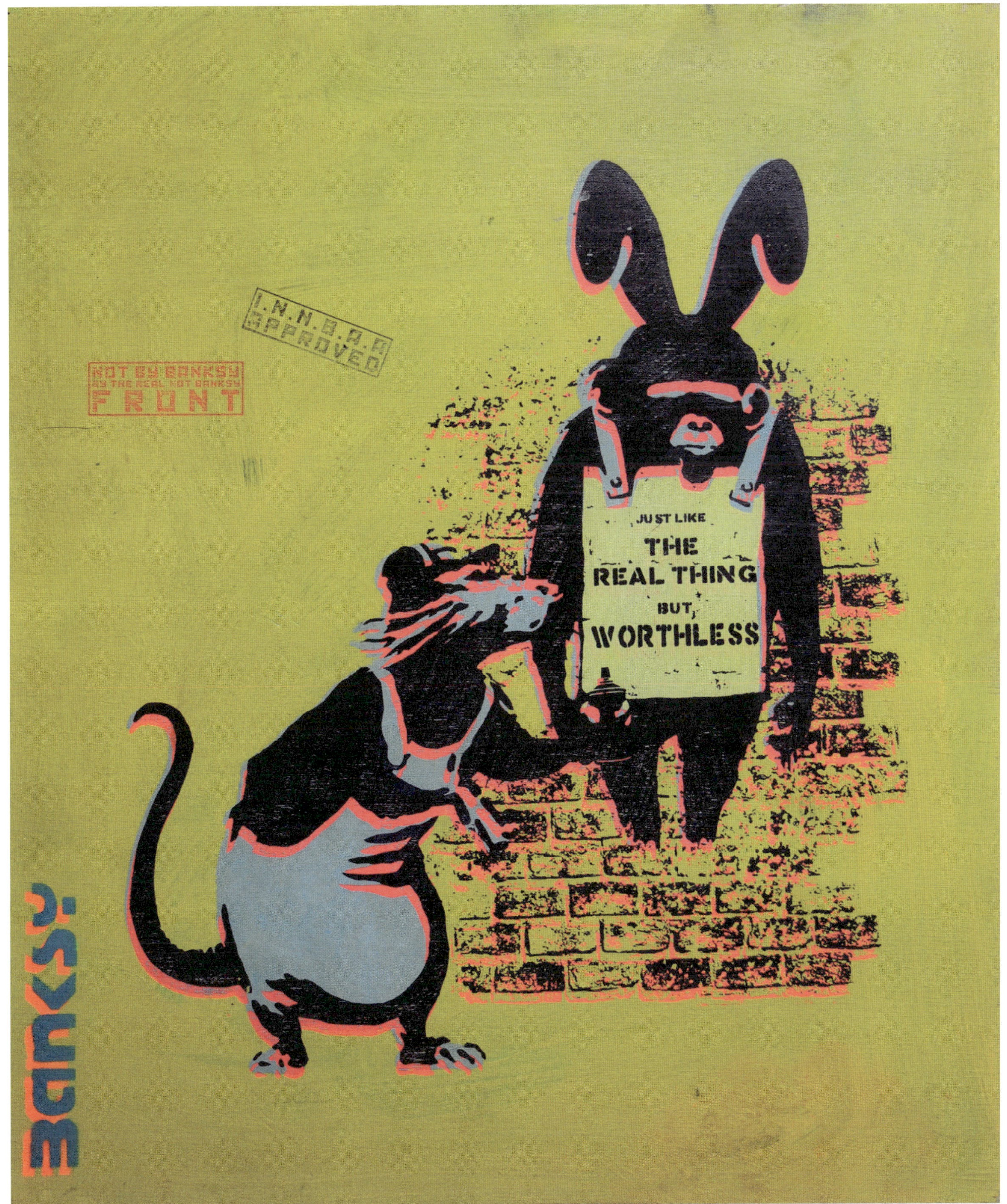

WORTHLESS screen ink and household paint on plywood panel

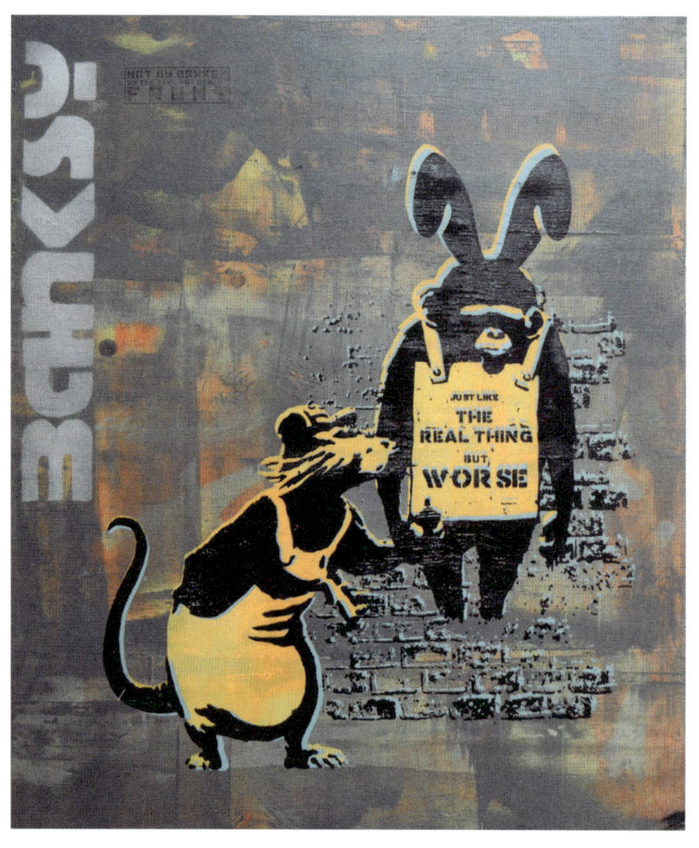

BANKSY!
NOT BY BANKSY
FRONT
JUST LIKE
THE REAL THING
BUT WORSE

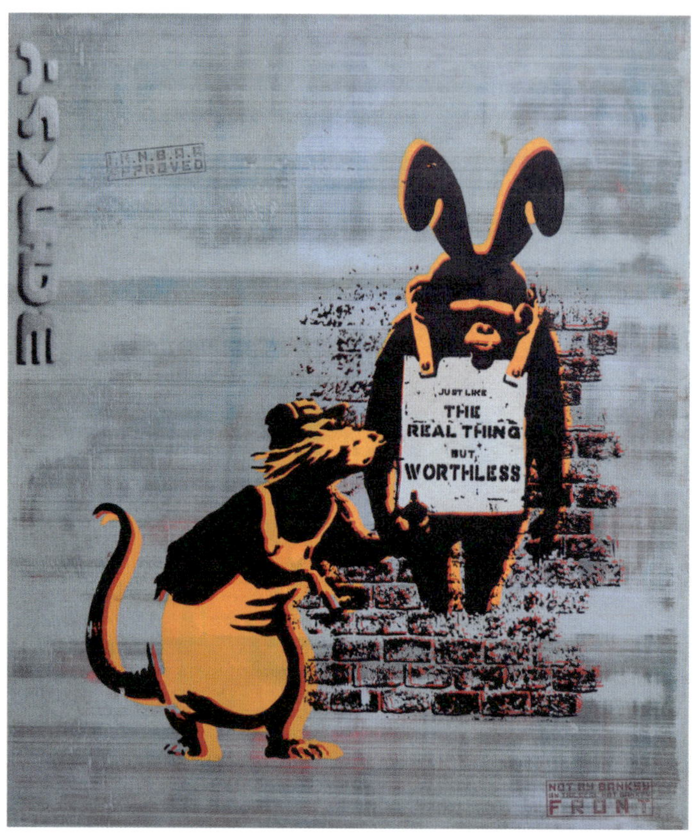

BANKSY!
I.N.N.B.A.R
APPROVED
JUST LIKE
THE REAL THING
BUT WORTHLESS
NOT BY BANKSY
FRONT

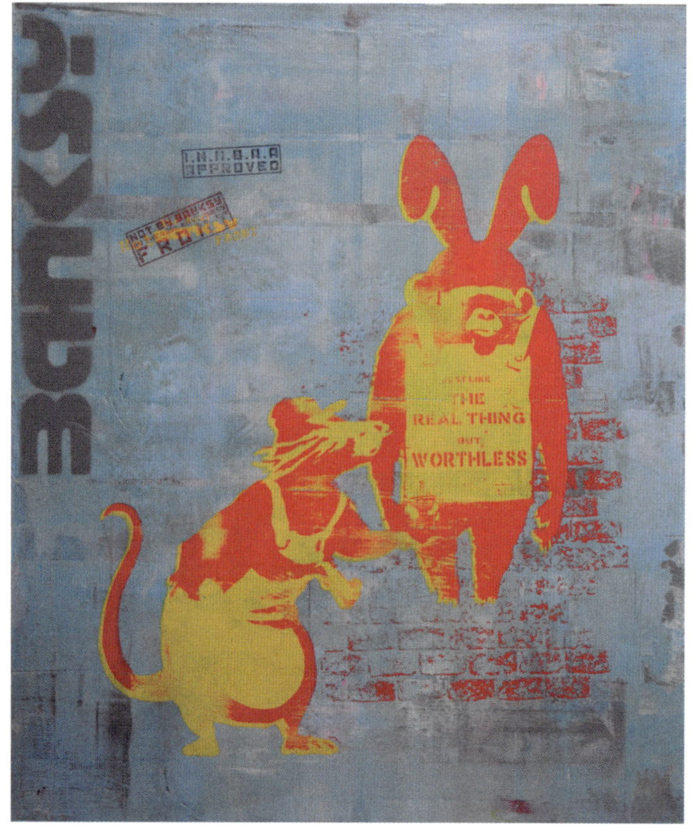

BANKSY!
I.N.N.B.A.R
APPROVED
NOT BY BANKSY
FRONT
JUST LIKE
THE REAL THING
BUT WORTHLESS

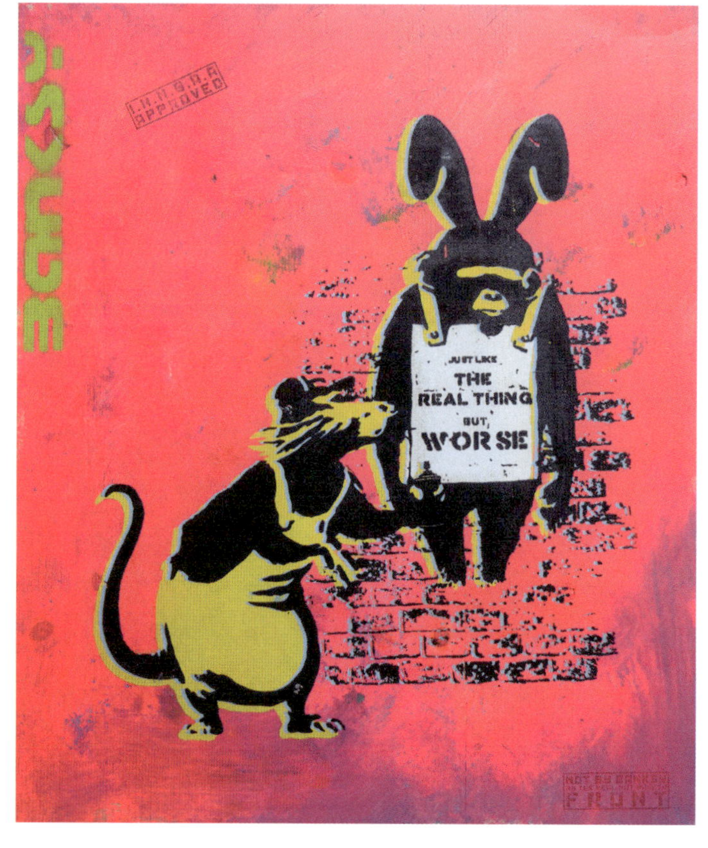

BANKSY!
I.N.N.B.A.R
APPROVED
JUST LIKE
THE REAL THING
BUT WORSE
NOT BY BANKSY
FRONT

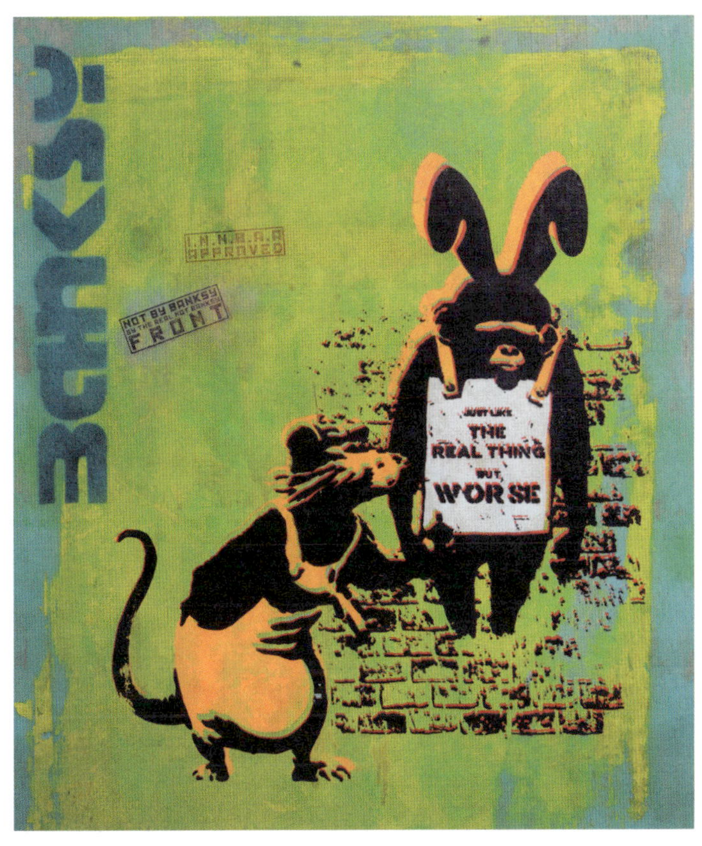

BANKSY!
I.N.N.B.A.A APPROVED
NOT BY BANKSY
FRONT
JUST LIKE
THE REAL THING
BUT, WORSE

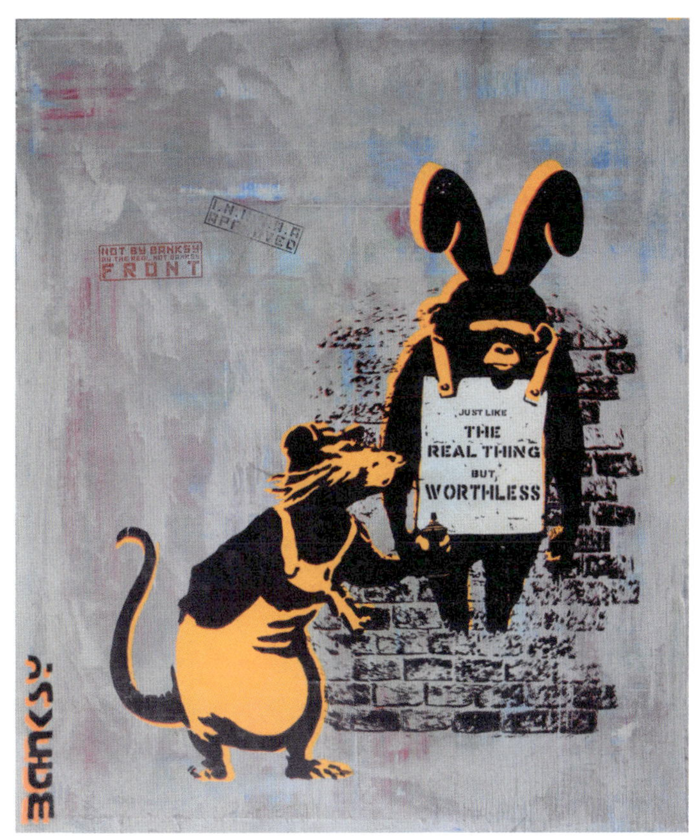

I.N.N.B.A.A APPROVED
NOT BY BANKSY
FRONT
JUST LIKE
THE REAL THING
BUT, WORTHLESS
BANKSY!

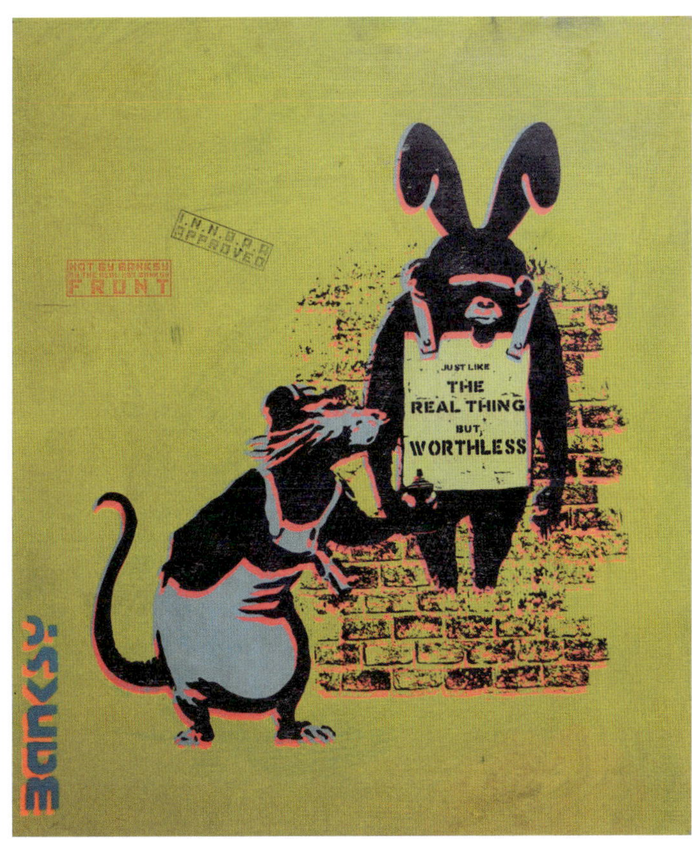

I.N.N.B.A.A APPROVED
NOT BY BANKSY
FRONT
JUST LIKE
THE REAL THING
BUT, WORTHLESS
BANKSY!

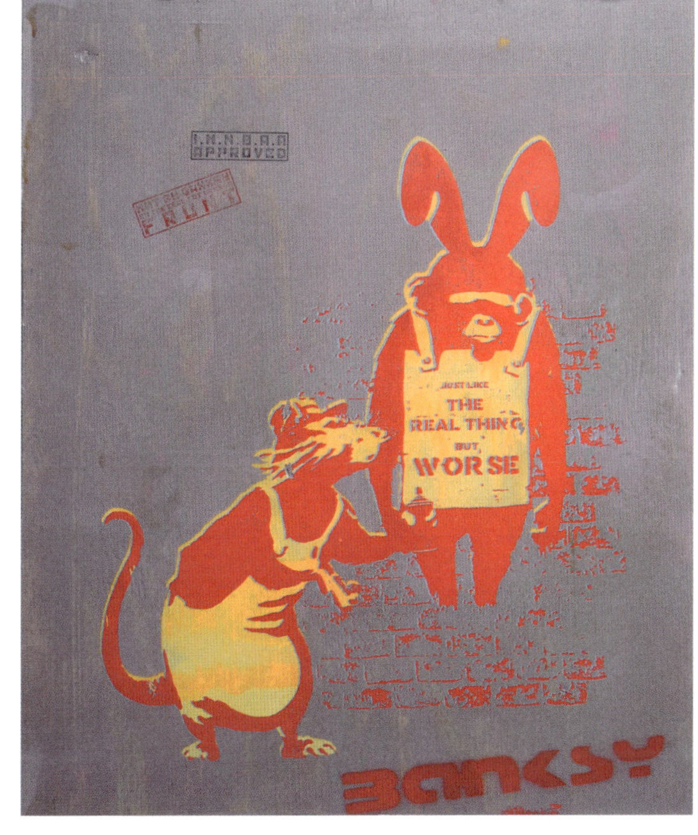

I.N.N.B.A.A APPROVED
NOT BY BANKSY
FRONT
JUST LIKE
THE REAL THING
BUT, WORSE
BANKSY!

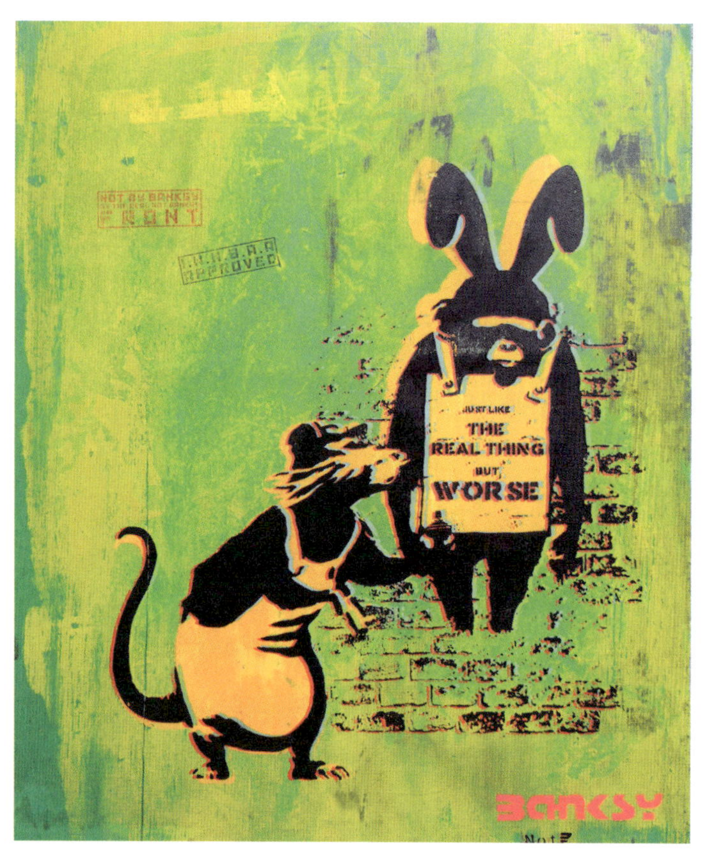

NOT BY BANKSY
FRONT
N.N.B.A.A
APPROVED
JUST LIKE
THE
REAL THING
BUT
WORSE

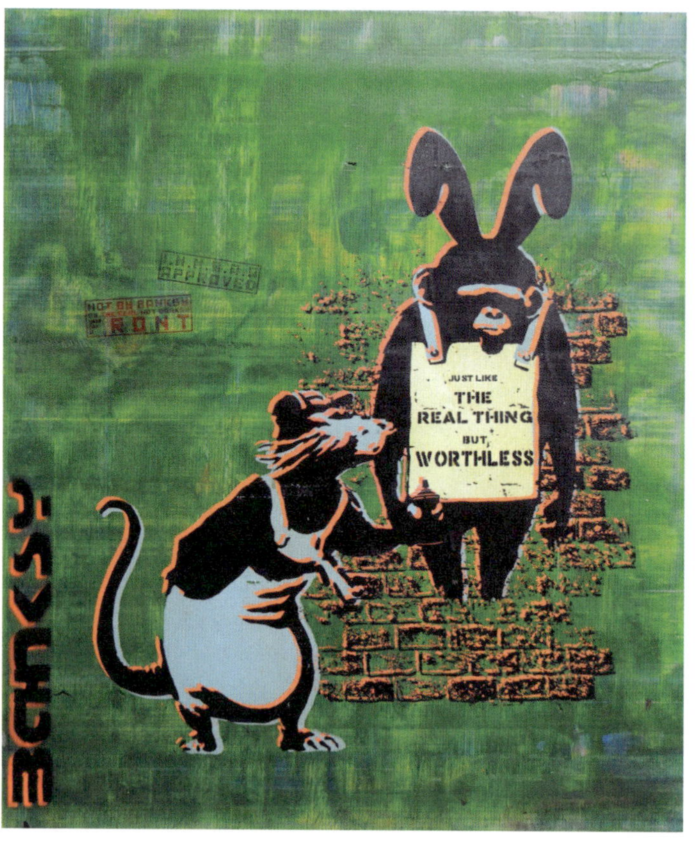

N.N.B.A.A
APPROVED
NOT BY BANKSY
FRONT
JUST LIKE
THE
REAL THING
BUT
WORTHLESS
BANKSY

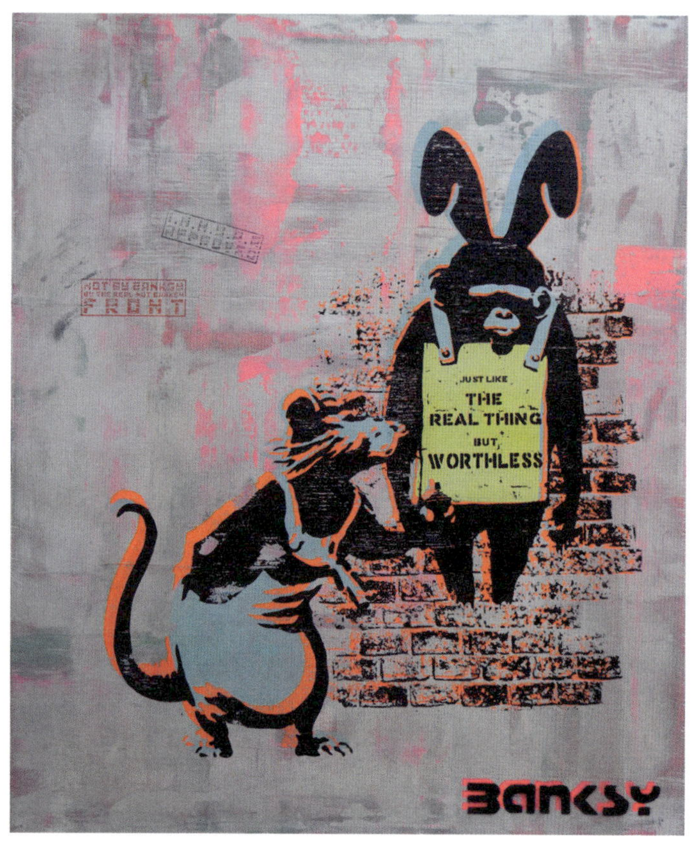

NOT BY BANKSY
FRONT
JUST LIKE
THE
REAL THING
BUT
WORTHLESS
BANKSY

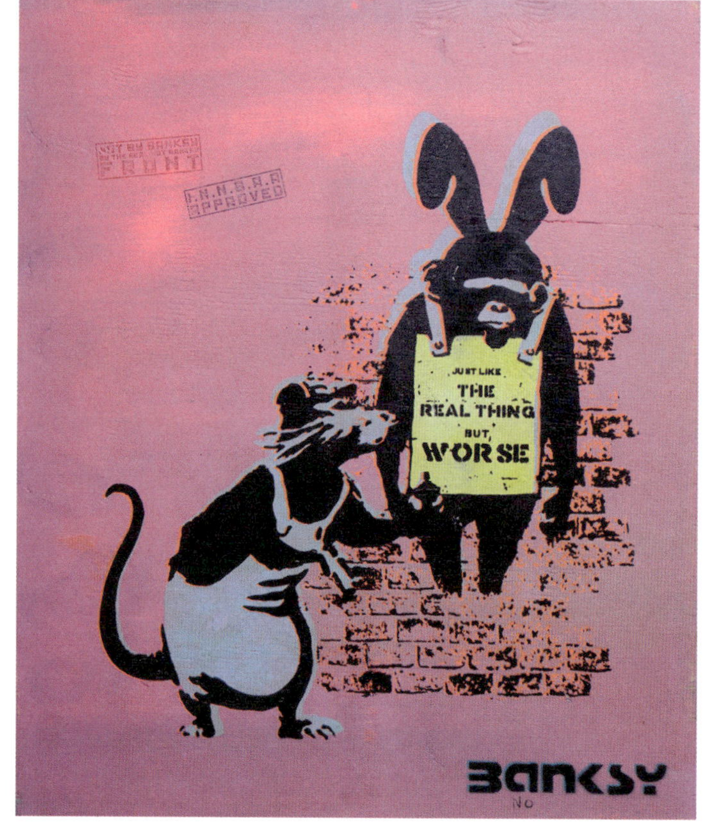

NOT BY BANKSY
FRONT
N.N.B.A.A
APPROVED
JUST LIKE
THE
REAL THING
BUT
WORSE
BANKSY

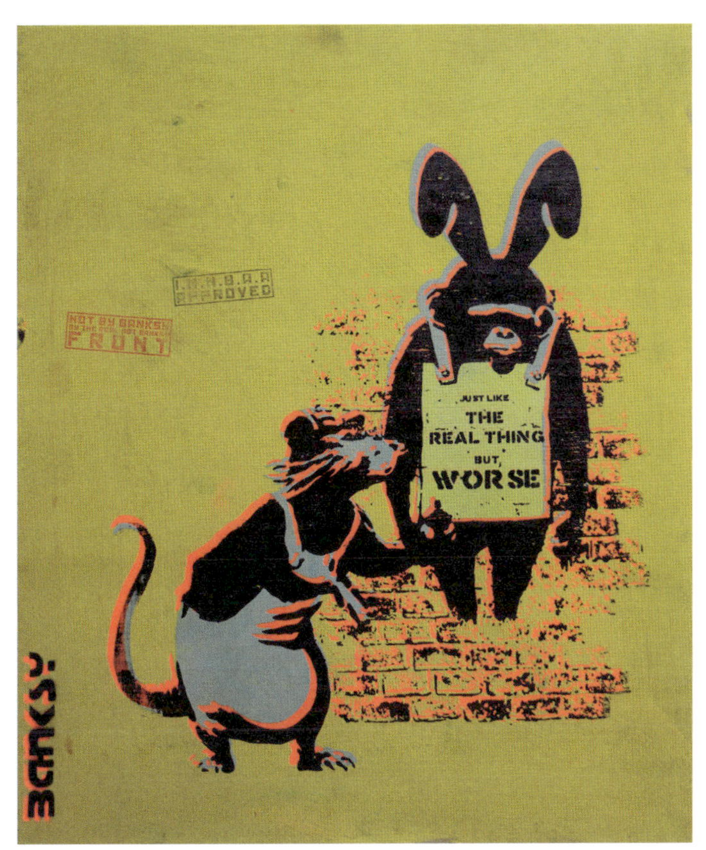
I.N.N.B.A.A
APPROVED
NOT BY BANKSY
FRONT
JUST LIKE
THE
REAL THING
BUT,
WORSE
BANKSY

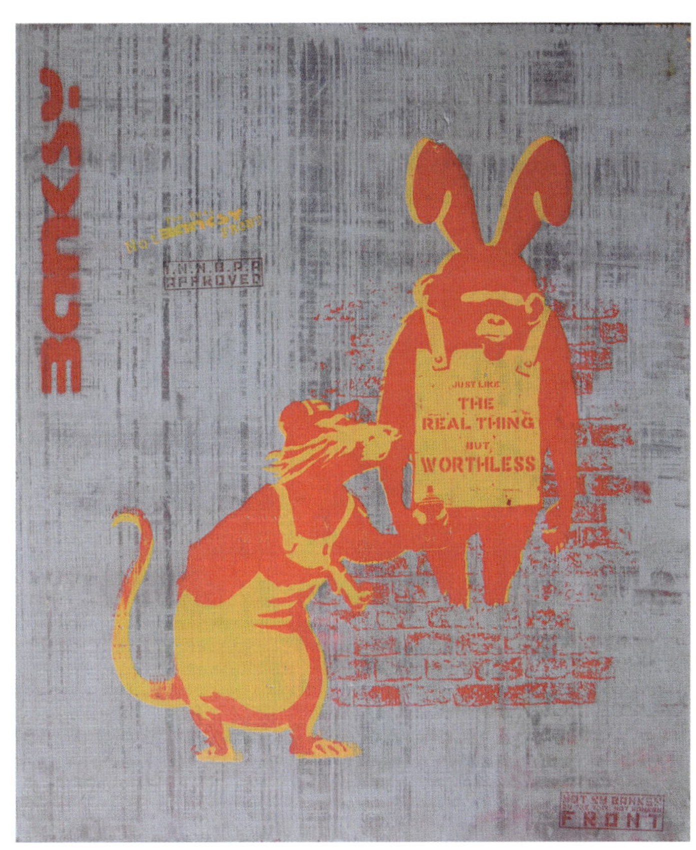
BANKSY
I.N.N.B.A.A
APPROVED
JUST LIKE
THE
REAL THING
BUT,
WORTHLESS
FRONT

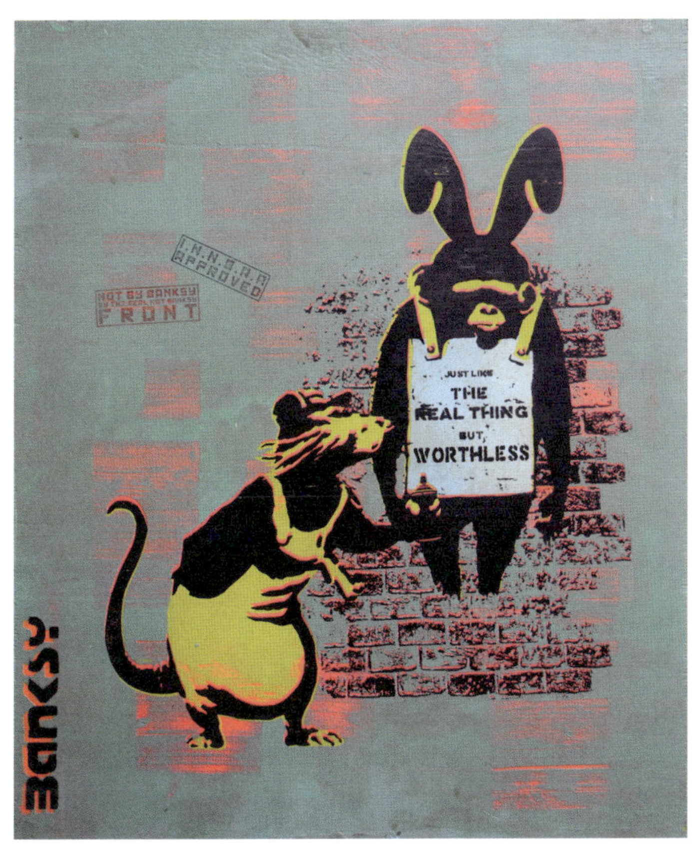
I.N.N.B.A.A
APPROVED
NOT BY BANKSY
FRONT
JUST LIKE
THE
REAL THING
BUT,
WORTHLESS
BANKSY

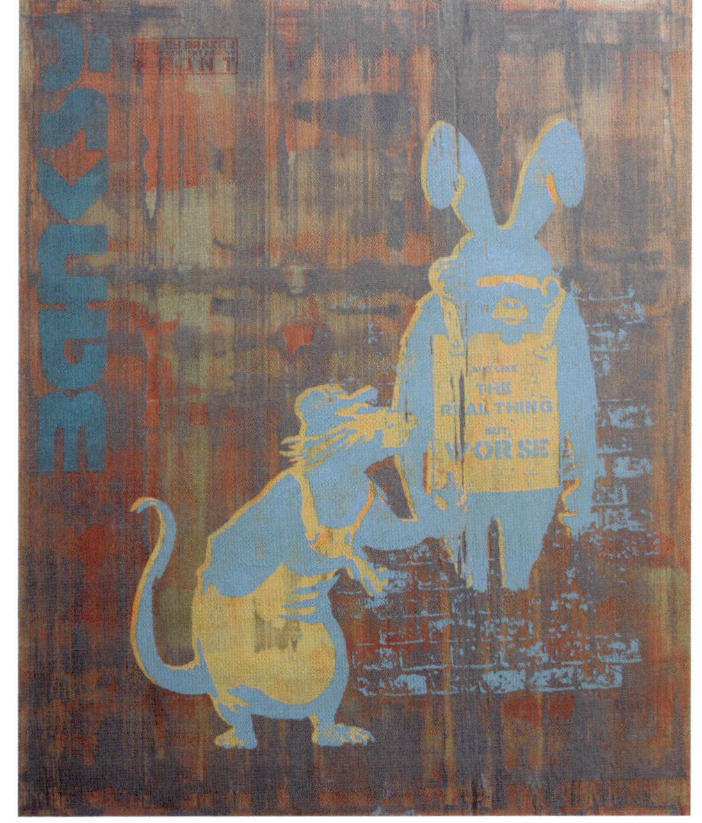
FRONT
BANKSY
JUST LIKE
THE
REAL THING
BUT,
WORSE

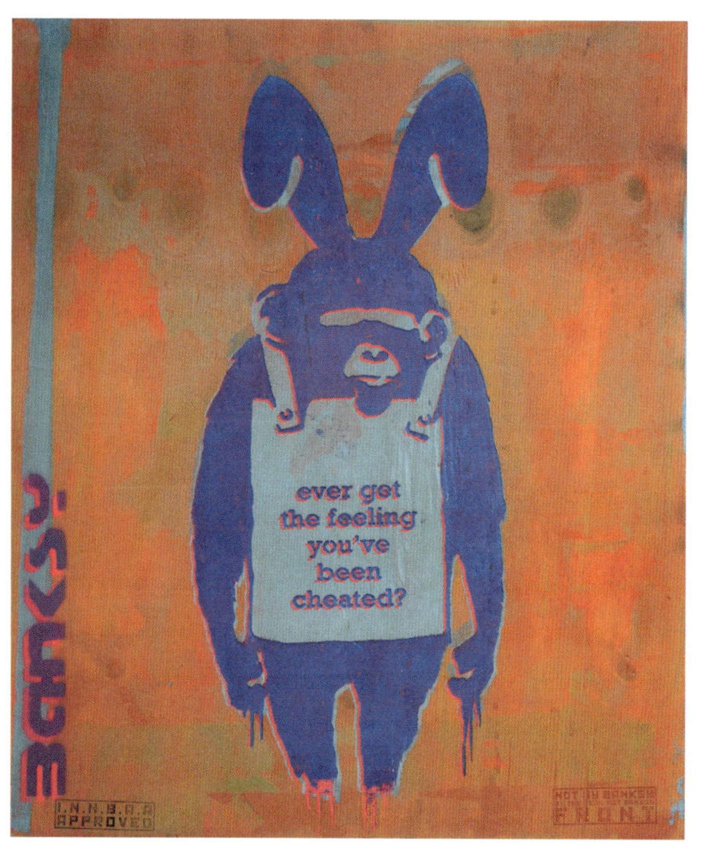
ever get
the feeling
you've
been
cheated?
BanKSY
I.N.N.B.A.A
APPROVED
NOT BY BANKSY
FRONT

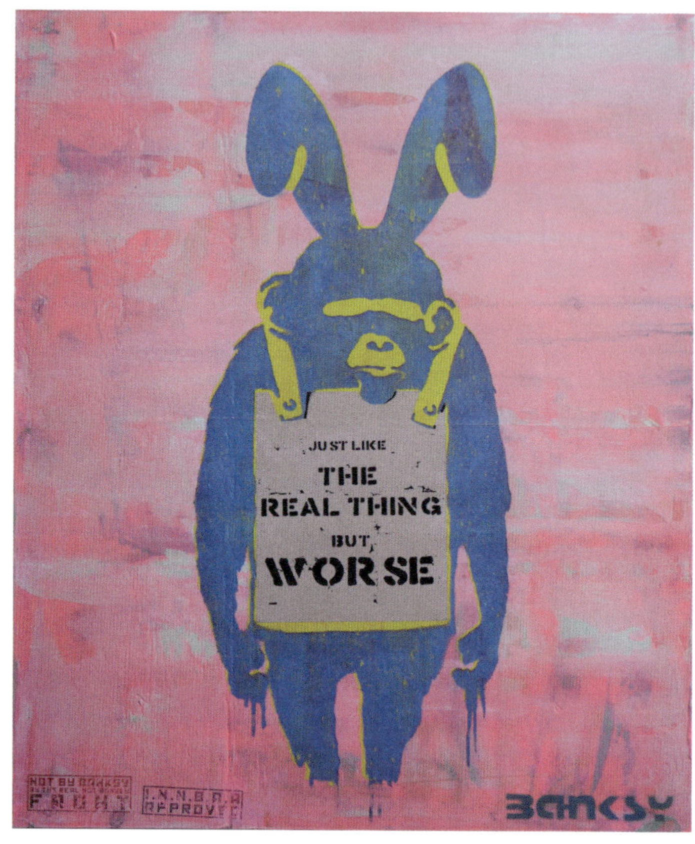
JUST LIKE
THE
REAL THING
BUT
WORSE
BanKSY
NOT BY BANKSY
FRONT
I.N.N.B.A.A
APPROVED

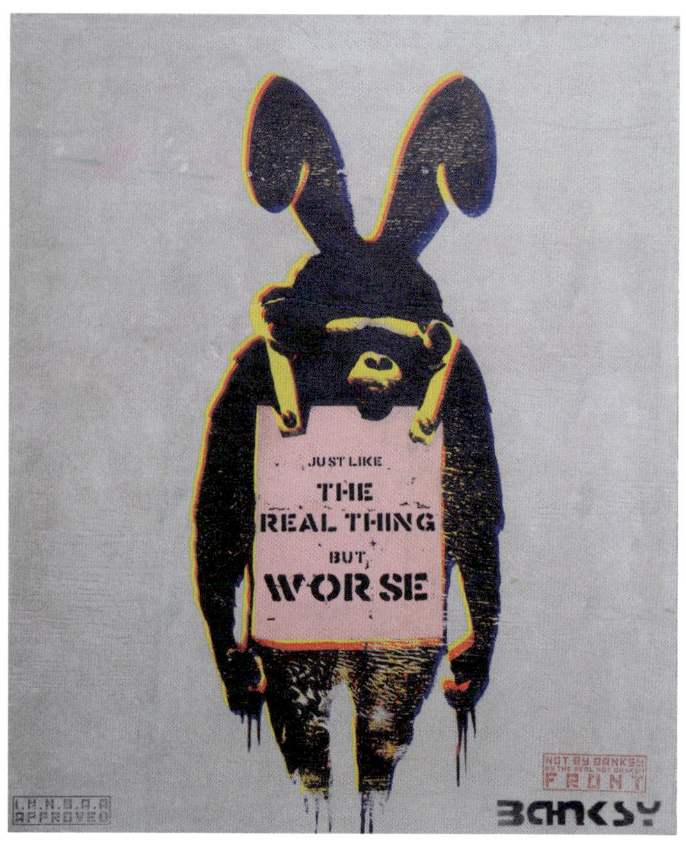
JUST LIKE
THE
REAL THING
BUT
WORSE
BanKSY
I.N.N.B.A.A
APPROVED
NOT BY BANKSY
FRONT

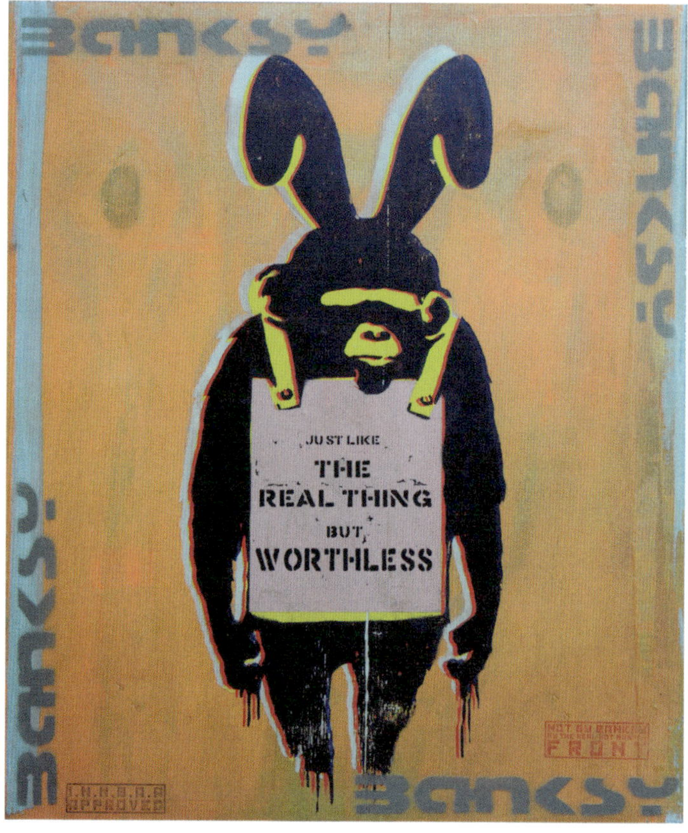
JUST LIKE
THE
REAL THING
BUT
WORTHLESS
BanKSY
BanKSY
BanKSY
I.N.N.B.A.A
APPROVED
NOT BY BANKSY
FRONT

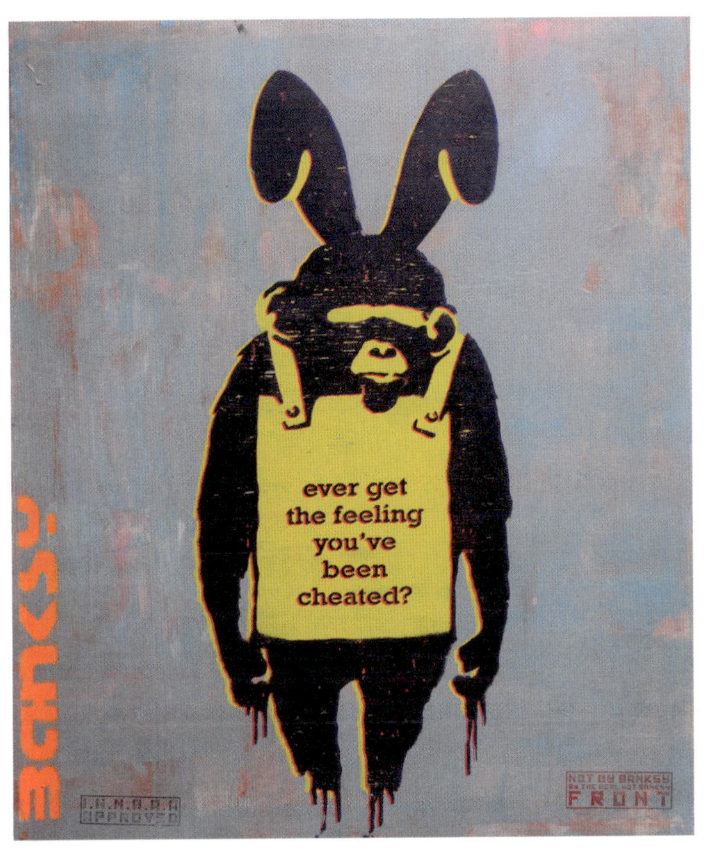

BANKSY
ever get
the feeling
you've
been
cheated?
I.N.N.B.A.A
APPROVED
NOT BY BANKSY
FRONT

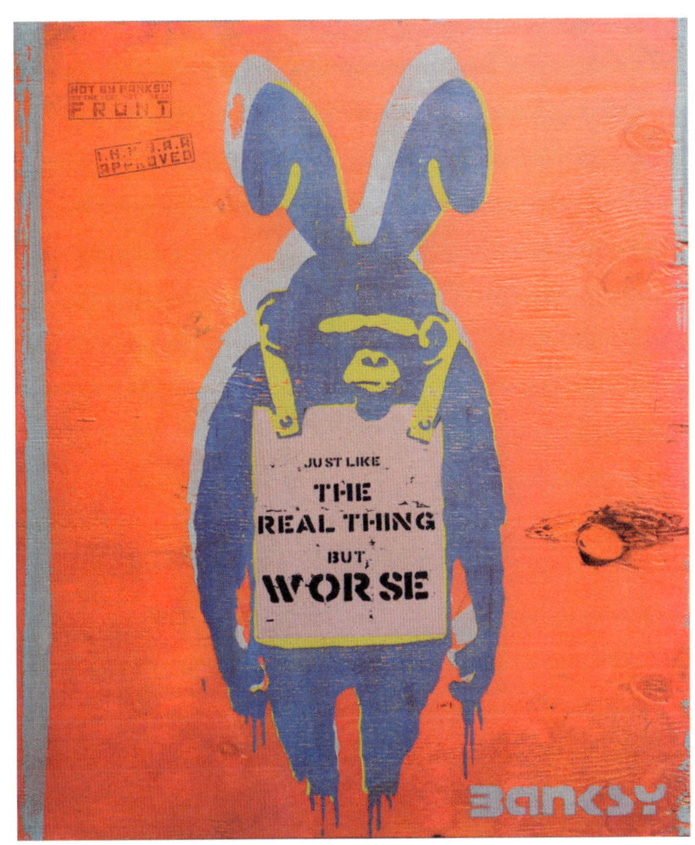

NOT BY BANKSY
FRONT
I.N.B.A.A
APPROVED
JUST LIKE
THE
REAL THING
BUT
WORSE
BANKSY

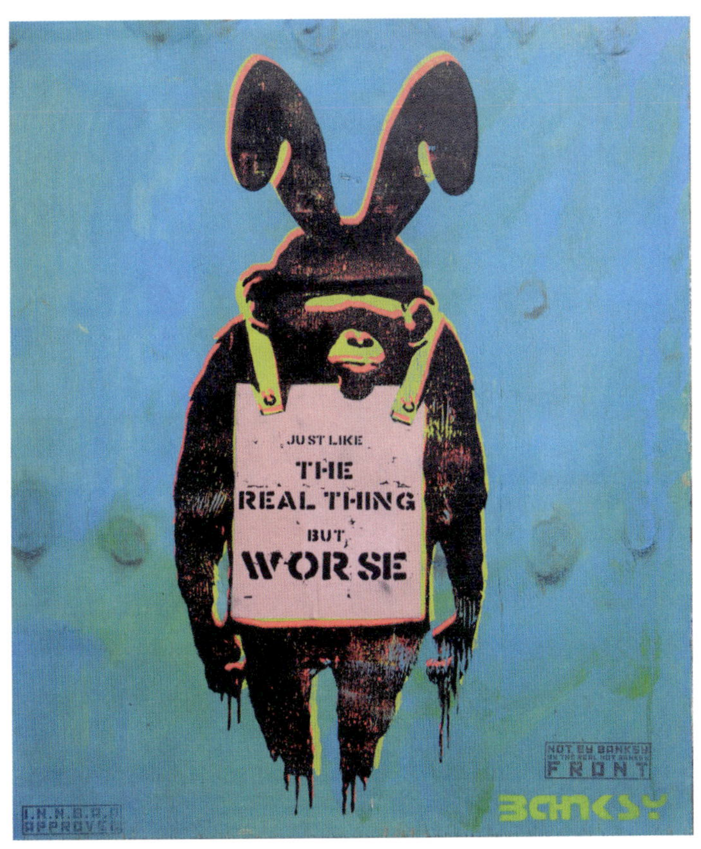

JUST LIKE
THE
REAL THING
BUT
WORSE
I.N.N.B.A.A
APPROVED
NOT BY BANKSY
FRONT
BANKSY

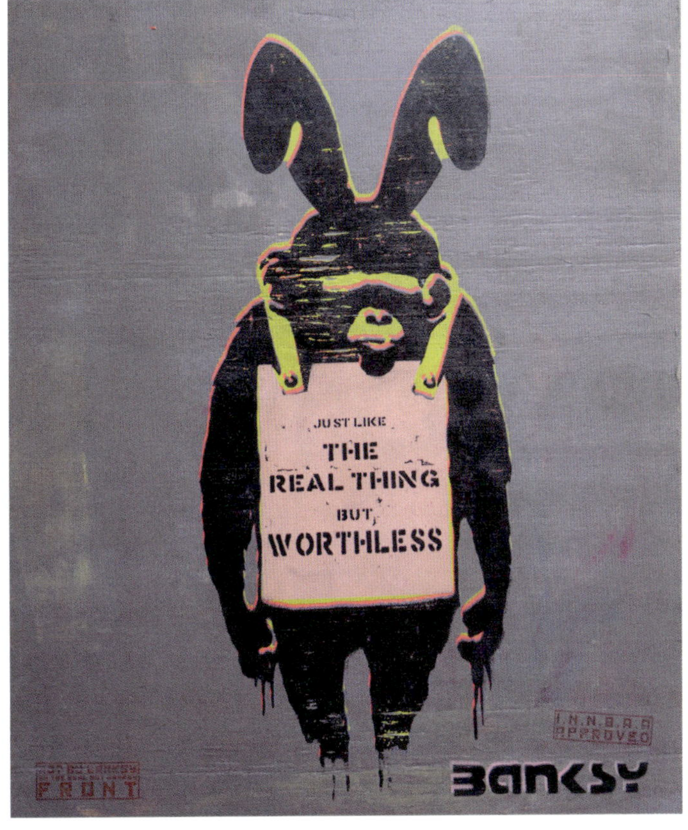

JUST LIKE
THE
REAL THING
BUT
WORTHLESS
I.N.N.B.A.A
APPROVED
NOT BY BANKSY
FRONT
BANKSY

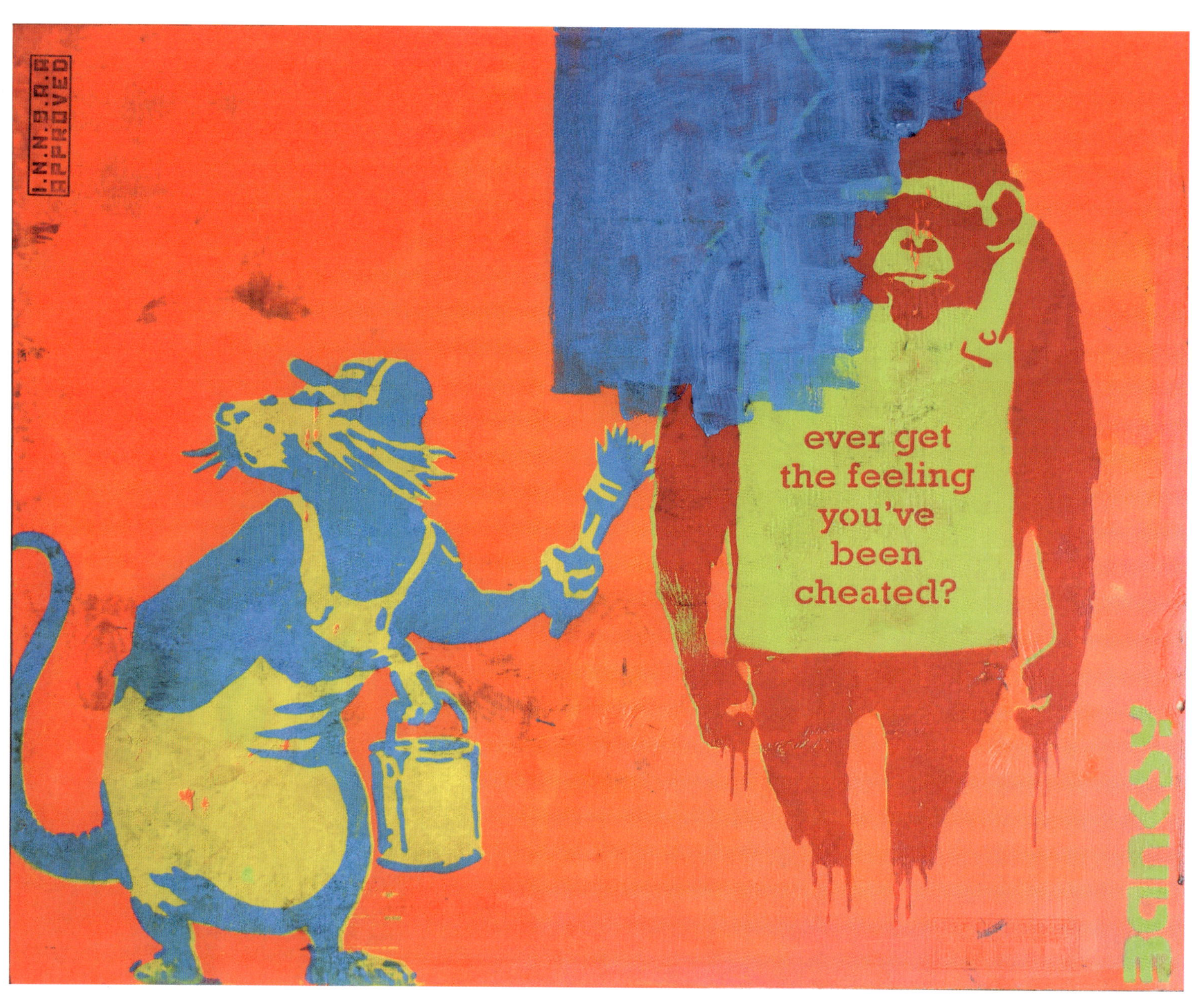

I.N.N.G.R.
APPROVED
ever get
the feeling
you've
been
cheated?
Banksy

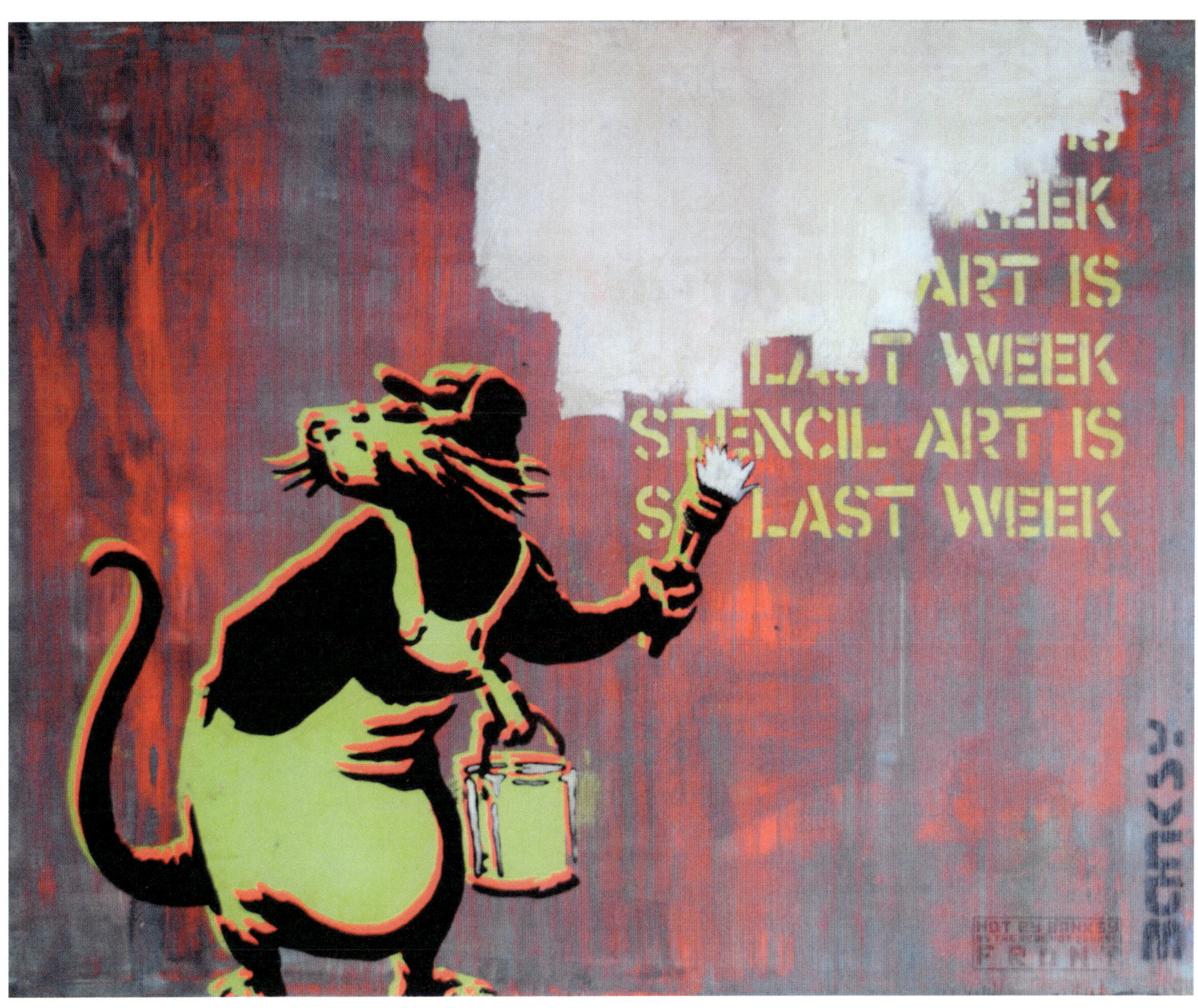
WEEK
ART IS
LAST WEEK
STENCIL ART IS
SO LAST WEEK

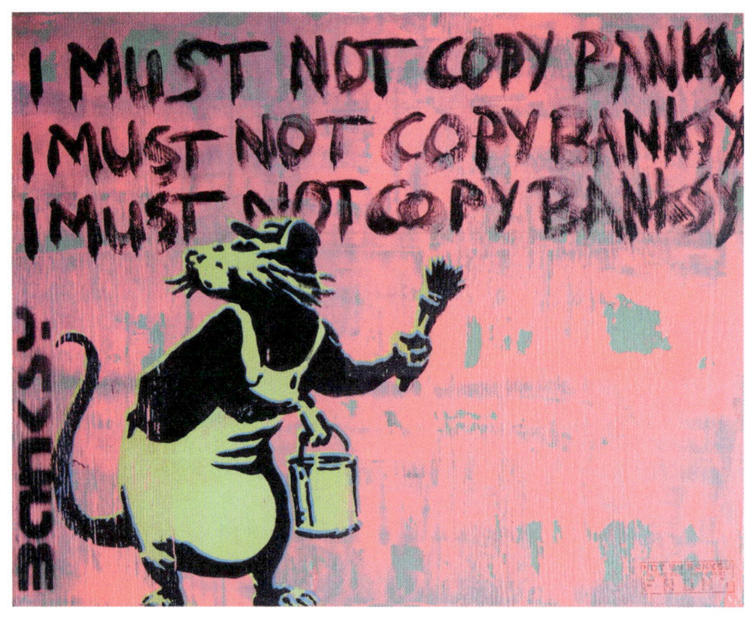

I MUST NOT COPY BANKSY
I MUST NOT COPY BANKSY
I MUST NOT COPY BANKSY
BANKSY

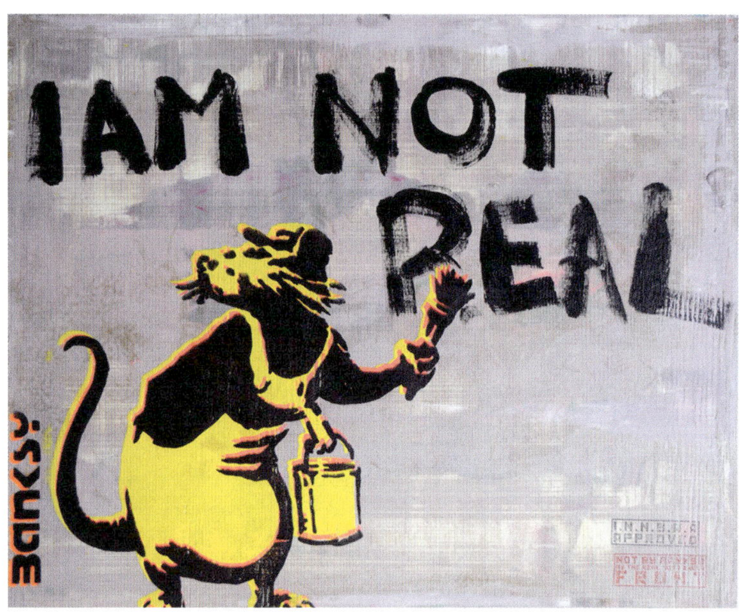

IAM NOT REAL
BANKSY

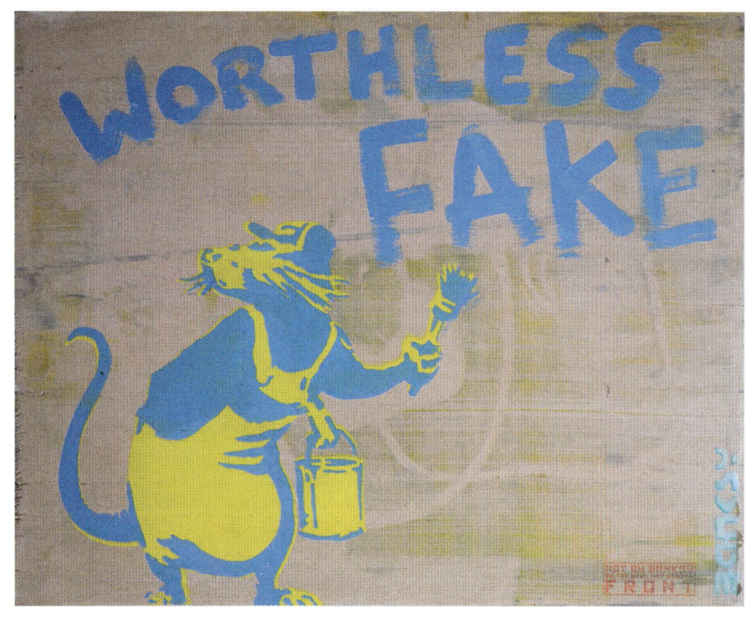

WORTHLESS FAKE
BANKSY
FRONT

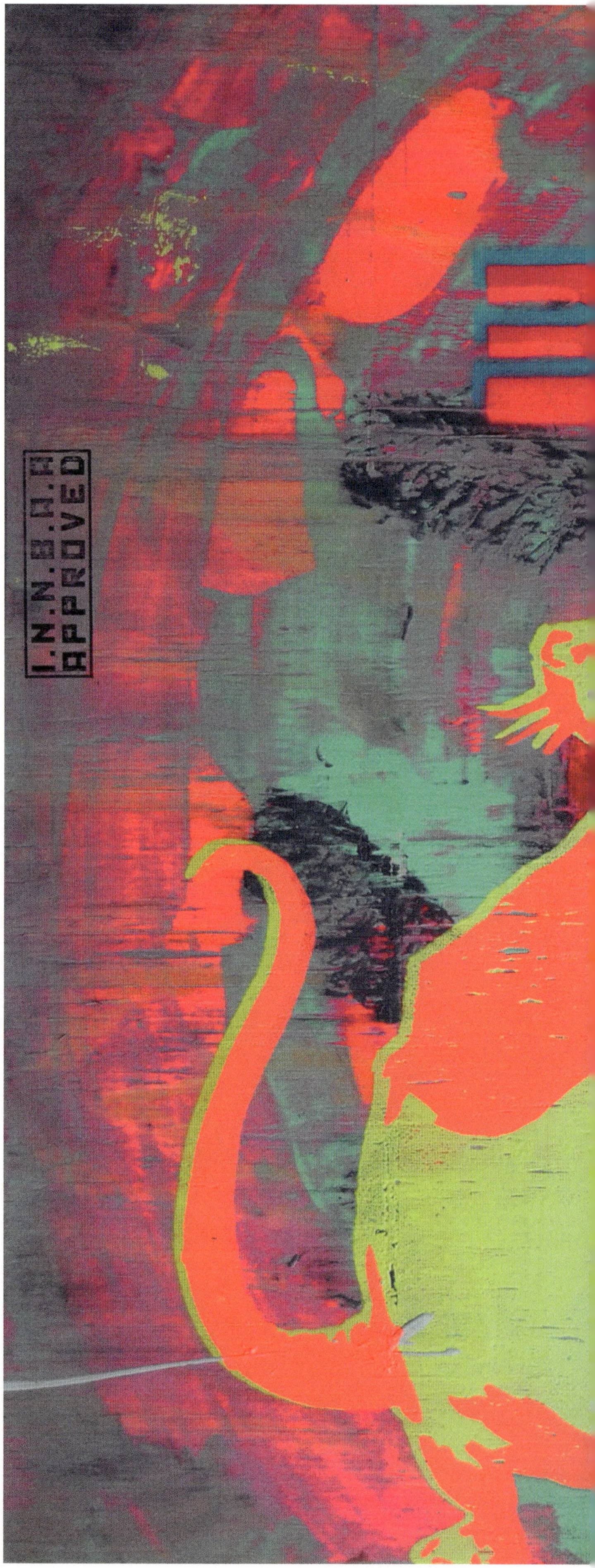

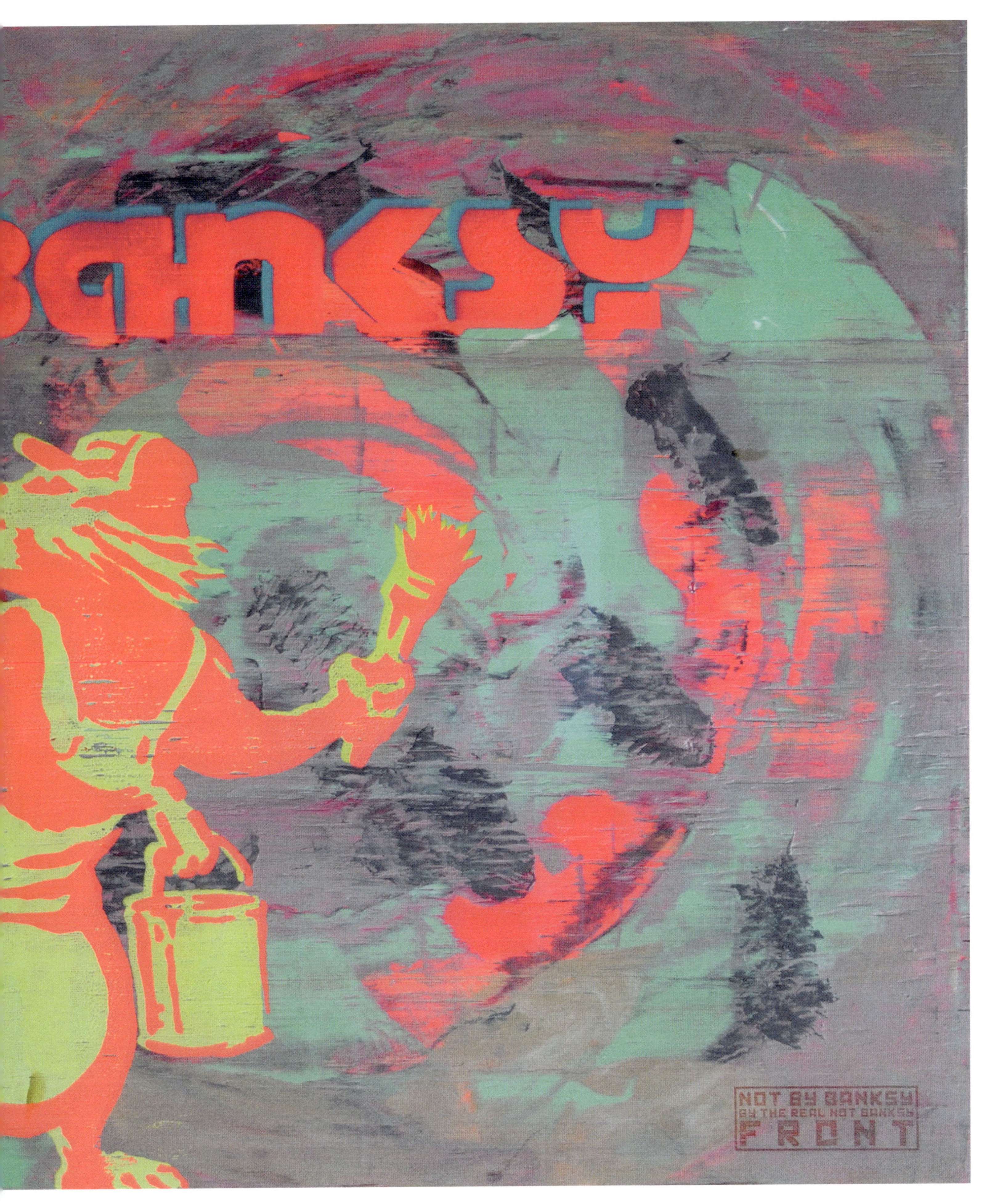
BANKSY
NOT BY BANKSY
BY THE REAL NOT BANKSY
FRONT

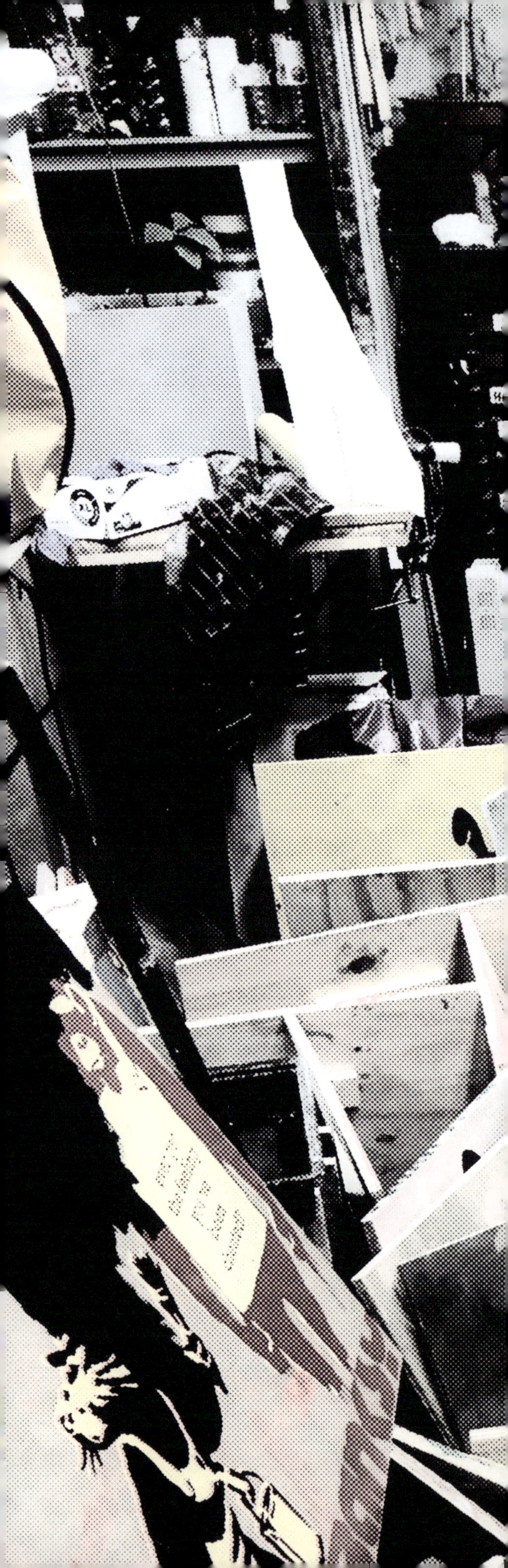

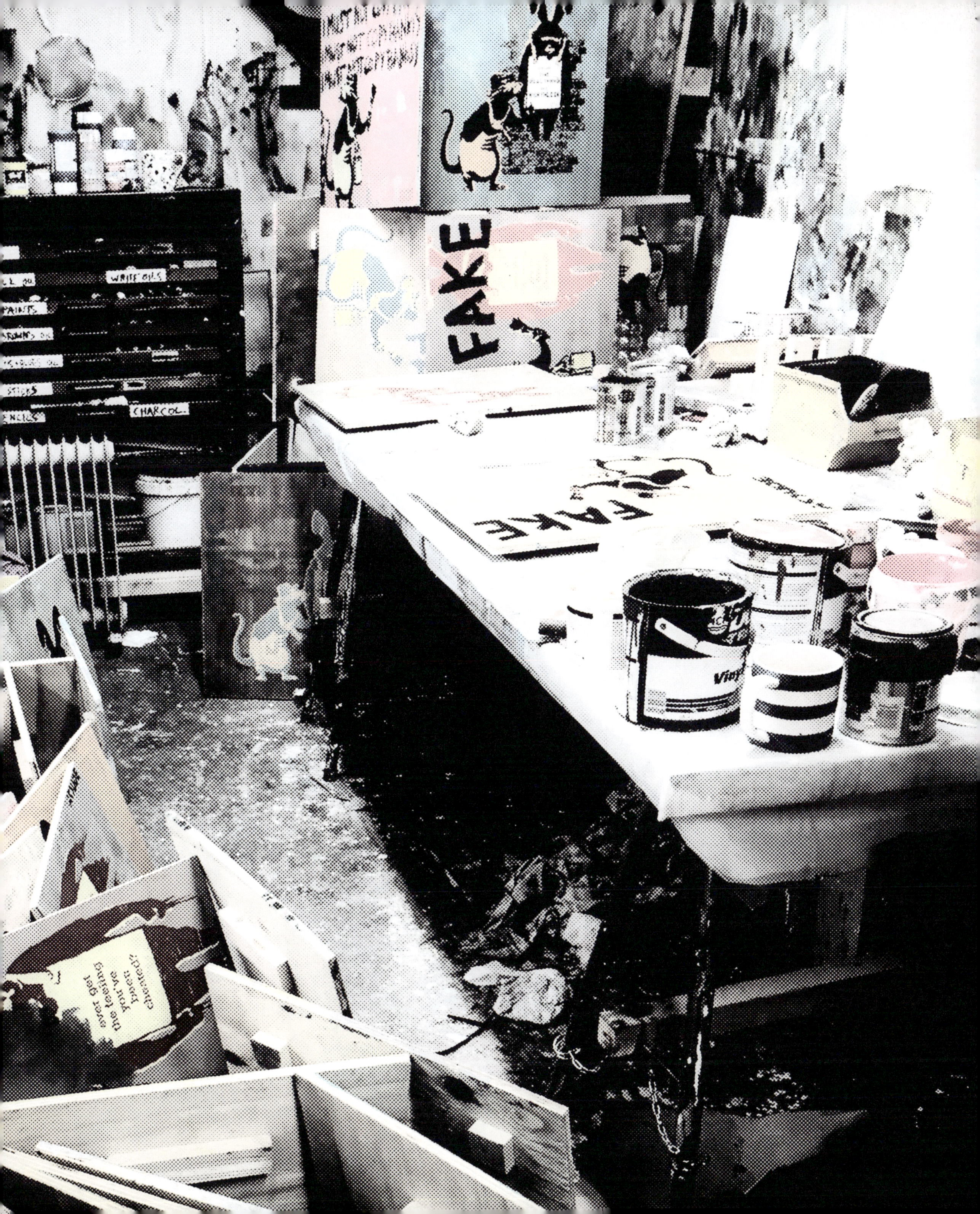

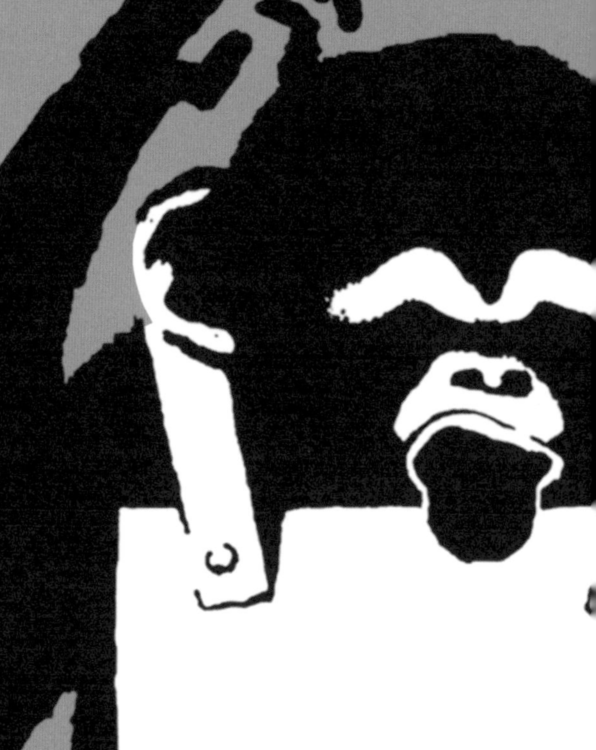

WHAT NOT TO DO
IN
A
GLOBAL
don't!

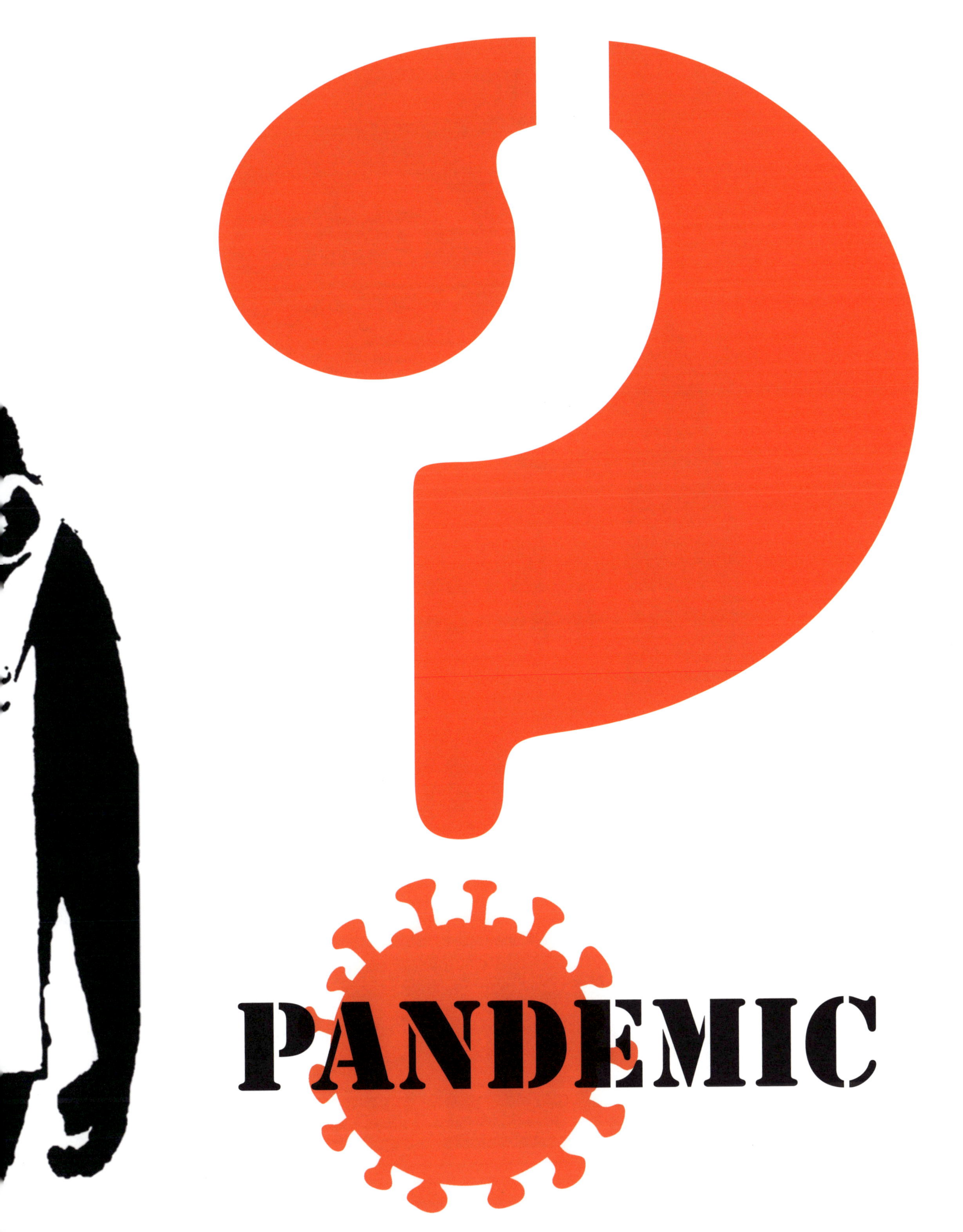

PANDEMIC

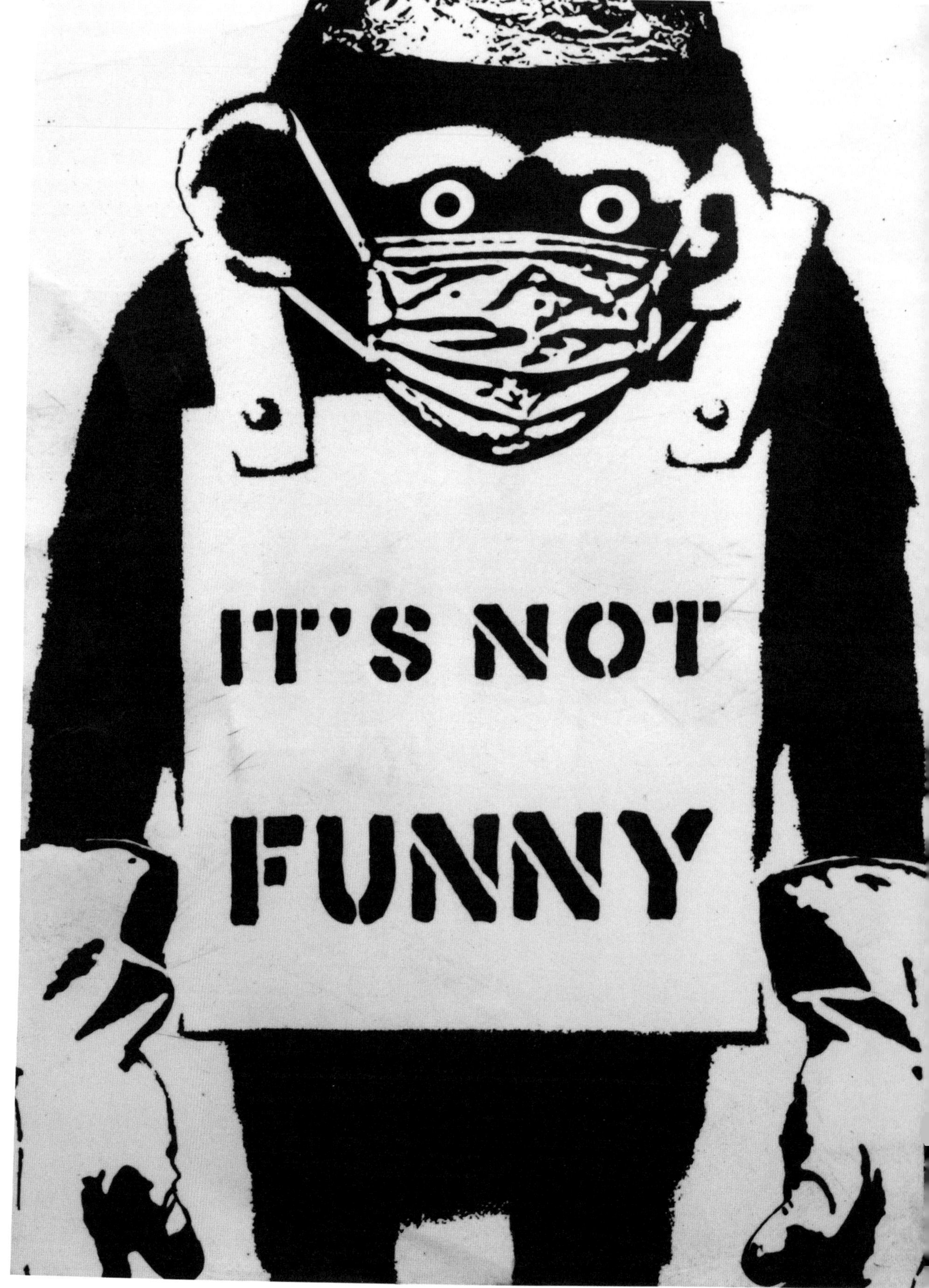
IT'S NOT
FUNNY

IT'S NOT FUNNY

As the world shuts down its borders
The International Neo NOT BANKSY Anartist Alliance
has been proclaimed as
DEFUNCT
and the
Real NOT BANKSY Front
DISSOLVED

OUT OF THE CONTAGION
OF THE PAST
springs forth the
ISOLATE
STRIDENT
EMERGENT
and
ESSENTIAL

New NOT BANKSY Realisation

The **New NOT BANKSY Realisation** realises that what was before is now **NOT**
The **New NOT BANKSY Realisation** realises that nothing is **NOT** real
The **New NOT BANKSY Realisation** realises that **NOT** truth is fake real but
NOT as fake as the true fake **NOT** real
The **New NOT BANKSY Realisation** realises that **NOT-art** of the future is **ESSENTIAL**
and must **NOT** pander to the clamouring demand for earnest maudlin sentiment and inane messaging
The **New NOT BANKSY Realisation** realises that **NOT-art** must now be **NOT** art
and can only exist in the bubble of its own **NOT-negative** reflection
The **New NOT BANKSY Realisation** realises that **NOT-art**
should only be
WORN
and
NOT
SEEN

TO THIS EFFECT WE PROUDLY PRESENT THE INAUGURAL

New NOT BANKSY Realisation
NOT-art T-shirt

IT'S NOT FUNNY
One colour screen print on Vintage White organic cotton
sealed in a contagion-free labelled paper bag

Pamphlet published in April 2020 to explain how things were 'NOT anymore'
& the necessity of an essential NOT-Art t-shirt at a time of global crisis.

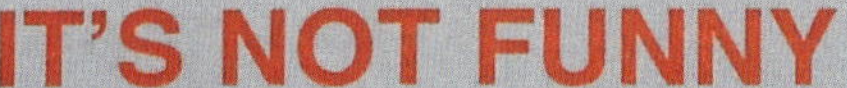

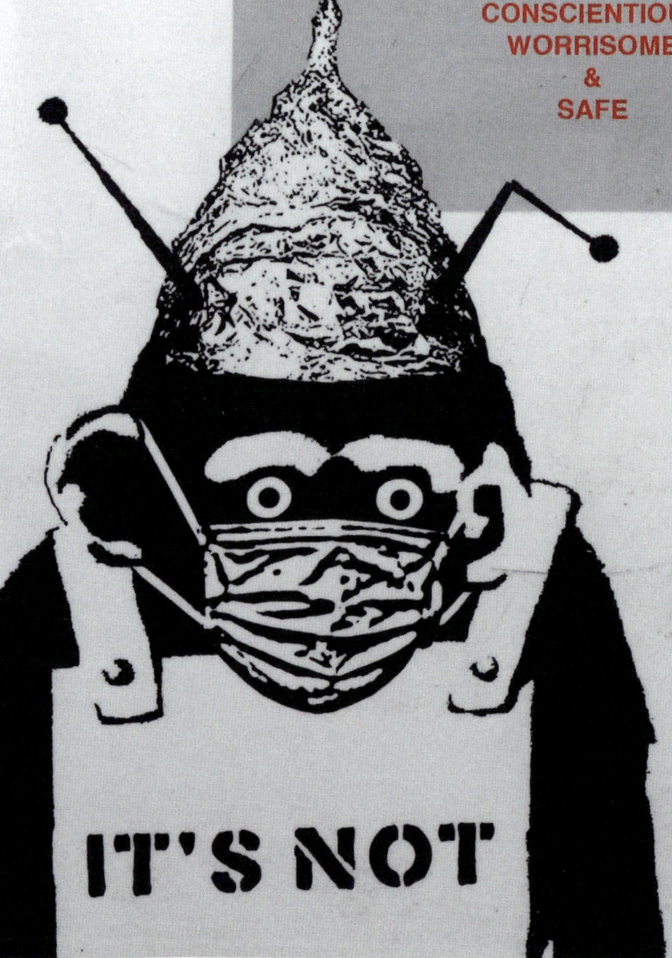

issued by

L-13

april, 2020

THE NEW NOT BANKSY REALISATION
COVID-19 / 5G / CONSPIRACY CHIMP

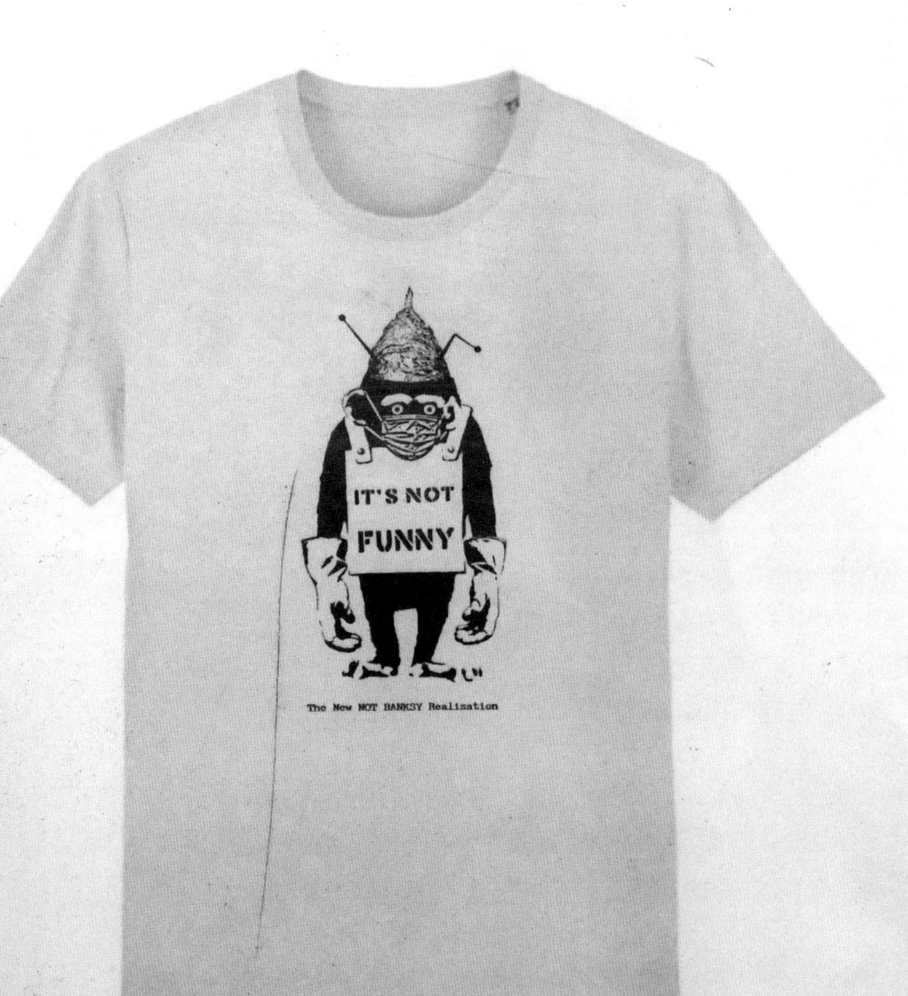

NOT-art EMERGENT ESSENTIAL
T-SHIRT

Pamphlet published to explain how things were 'NOT anymore' & the necessity of an essential NOT-Art t-shirt at a time of global crisis.

We really didn't know what to expect with the onset of the pandemic.
It felt a bit wrong to be doing anything non-worthy and not earnestly concerned.
But our 'life is shit then you die' taking the piss gallows humour seemed to go down well
with the T-shirt, so we thought we'd try publishing a print.

NEW NOT BANKSY REALISATION
COVID-19 / 5G / CONSPIRACY CHIMP
SCREEN PRINT
FIRST EDITION
MAY 2020

Following a meeting of the Covid-19 NOT-art Authority's
Emergent Essentials Committee
to discuss all things Emergent and Essential,
it has been decided to relax the strict NOT-art restrictions
and allow a small run of limited edition prints.

If nothing too bad happens as a result,
this First Edition of just 50 prints in Ultra Blue and Yellow
will be followed by Second Edition of 75 prints in a different colourway.

BE ALERT. BE GREEDY AND THANKFUL.
DON'T PANIC. PANIC!!
PREPARE FOR THE WORST.
ONLY ONE PRINT PER HOUSEHOLD and ONE FRIEND PERMITTED.
WASH YOUR HANDS BEFORE AND AFTER.
KEEP YOUR DISTANCE.
FOLLOW THE NOT-art AUTHORITY'S CODE.
STAY ALERT.

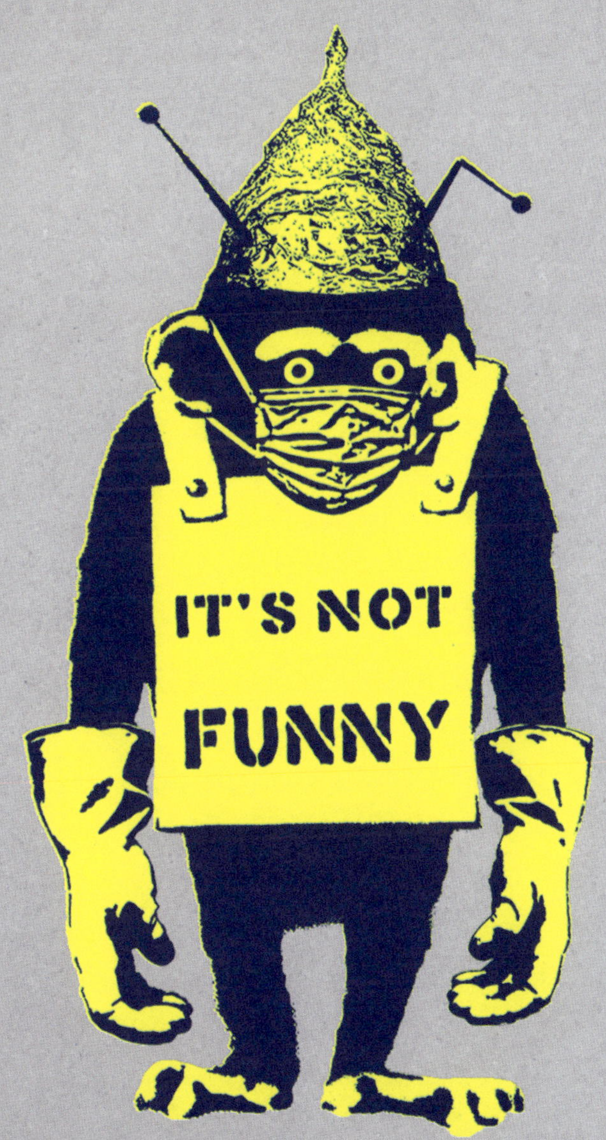

The New NOT BANKSY Realisation

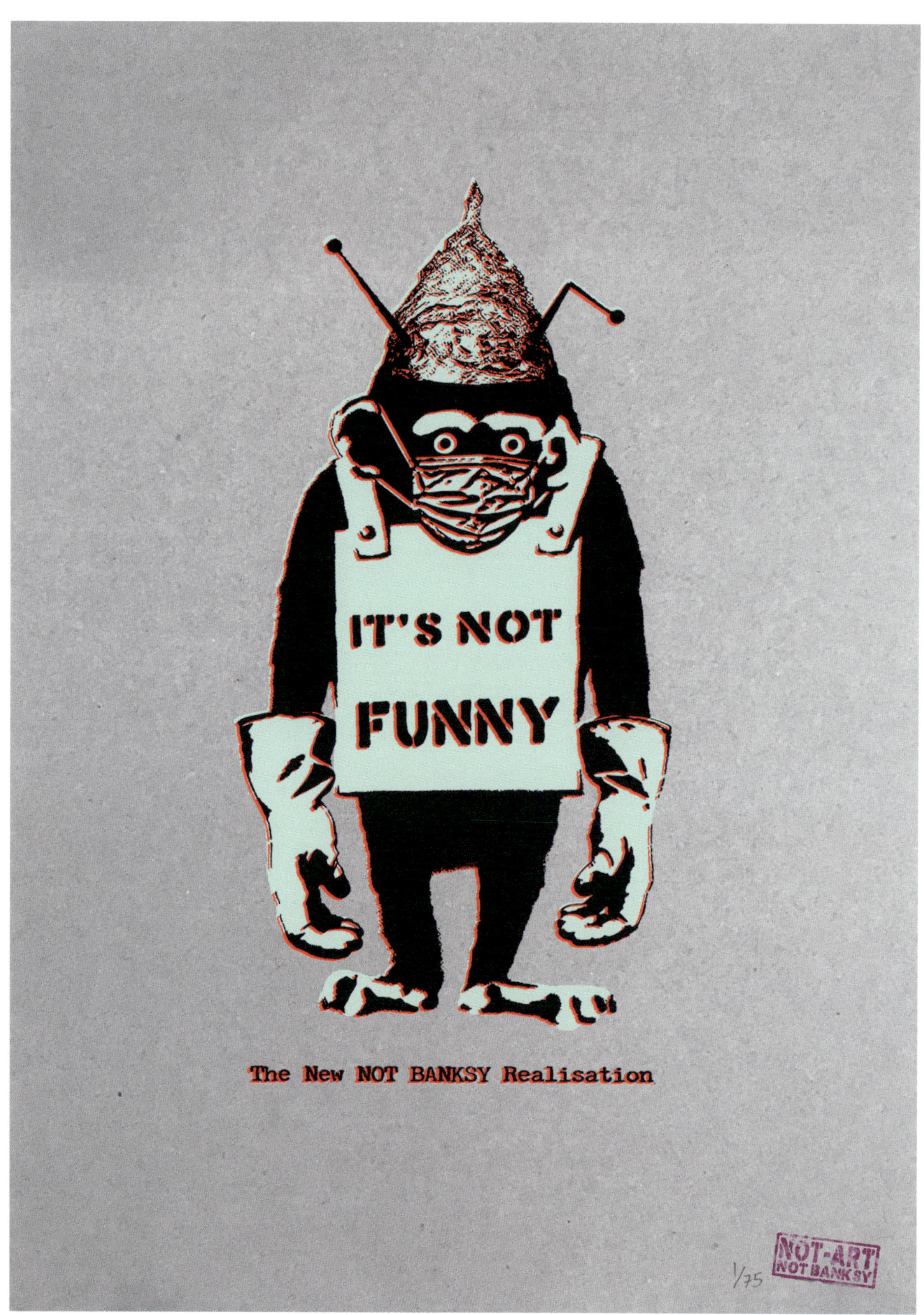

The New NOT BANKSY Realisation

THEN A SECOND EDITION

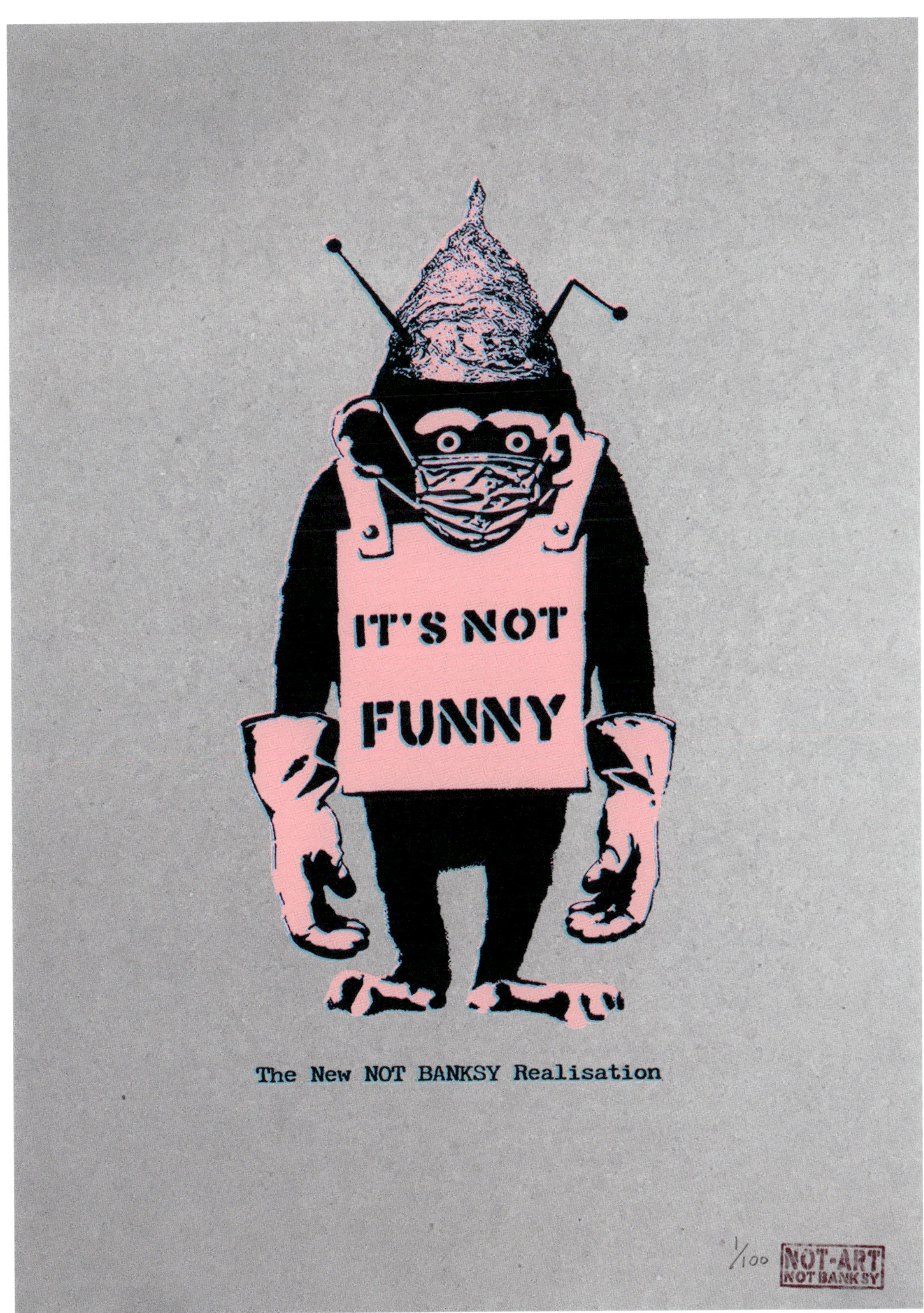

AND "against all good judgement and sound clinical advice" A THIRD EDITION

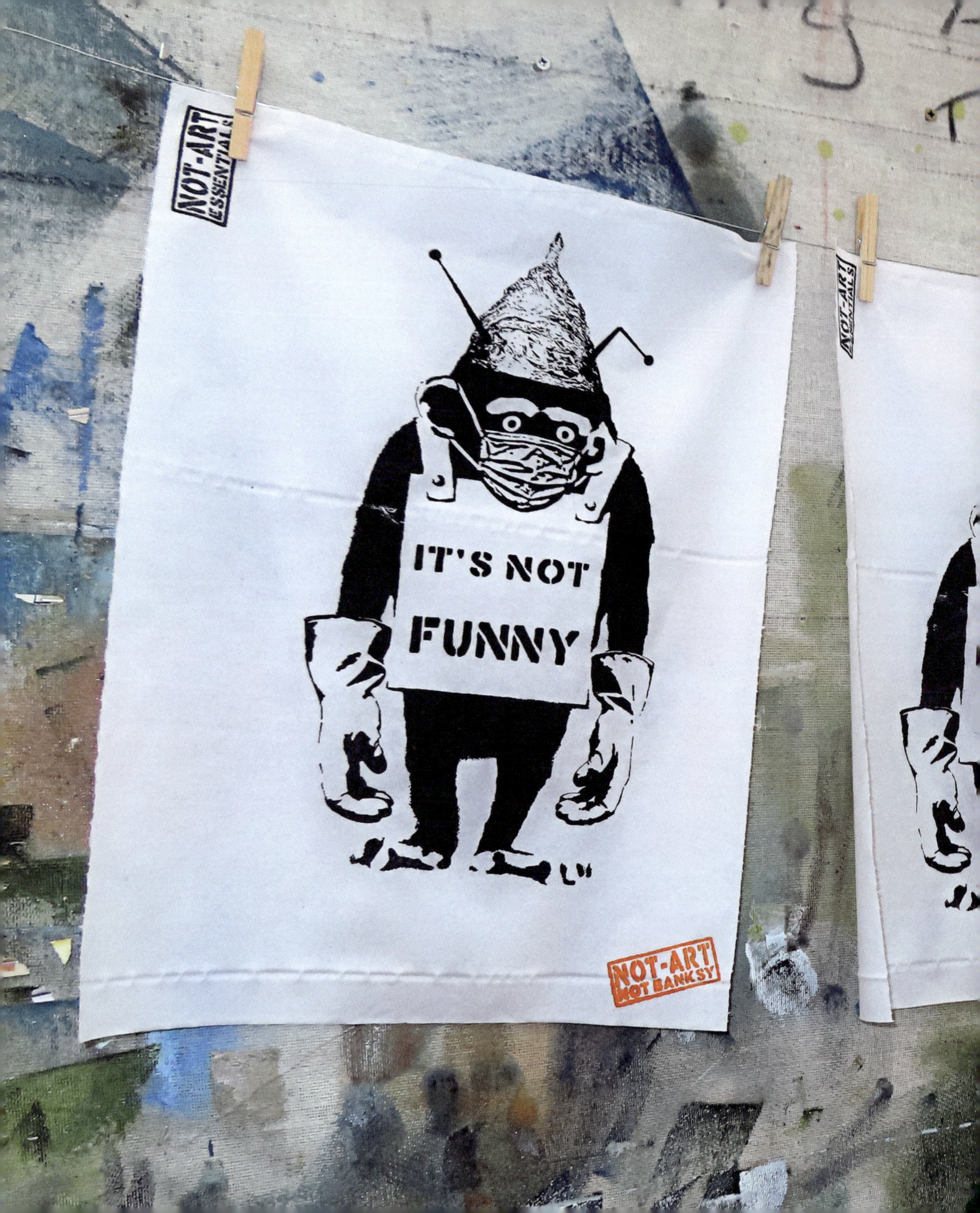
NOT-ART
ESSENTIALS
IT'S NOT
FUNNY
NOT-ART
NOT BANKSY

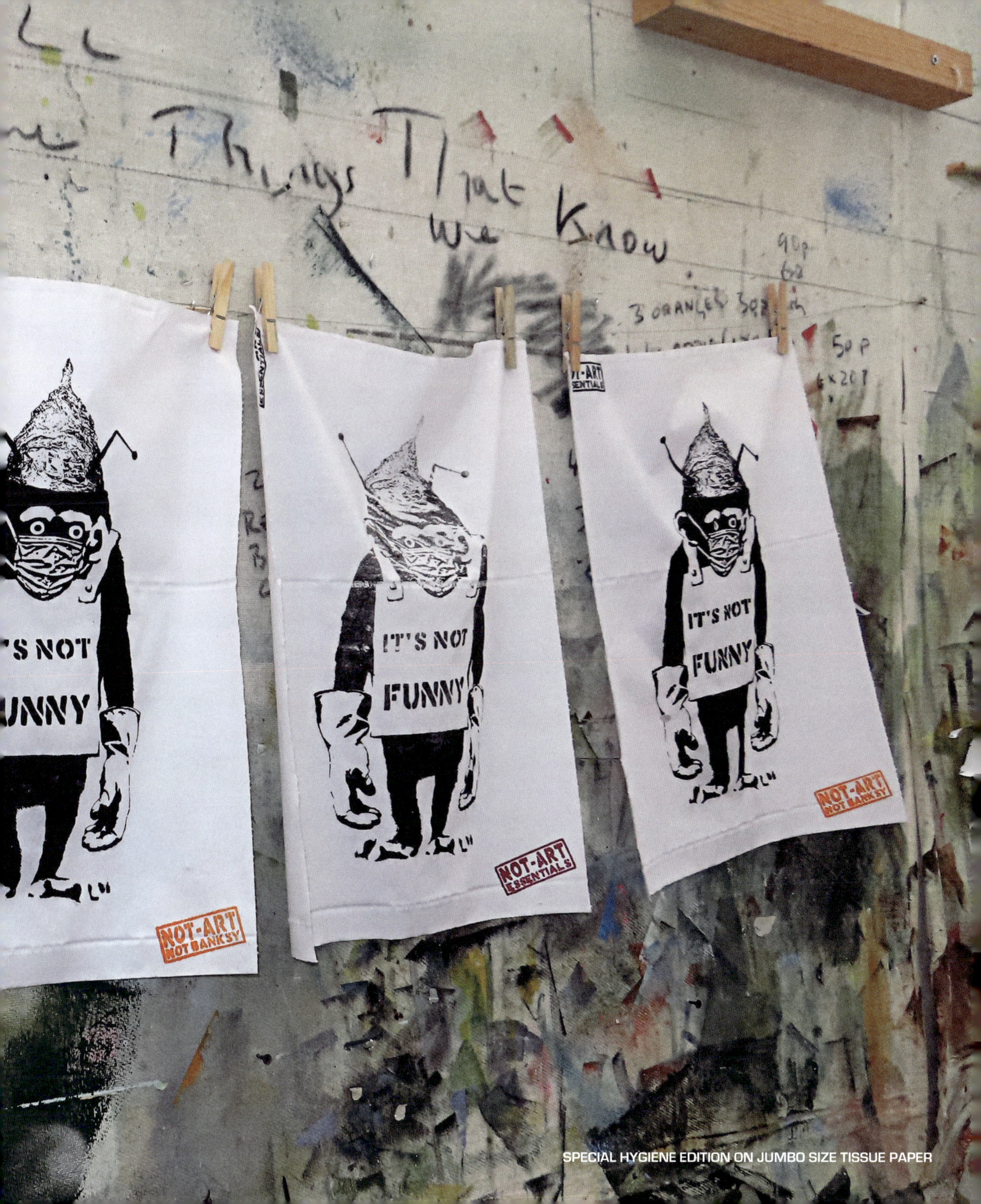
Things That We Know
90p
3 ORANGES 30p
50 P
IT'S NOT FUNNY
IT'S NOT FUNNY
IT'S NOT FUNNY
NOT-ART NOT BANKSY
NOT-ART ESSENTIALS
SPECIAL HYGIENE EDITION ON JUMBO SIZE TISSUE PAPER

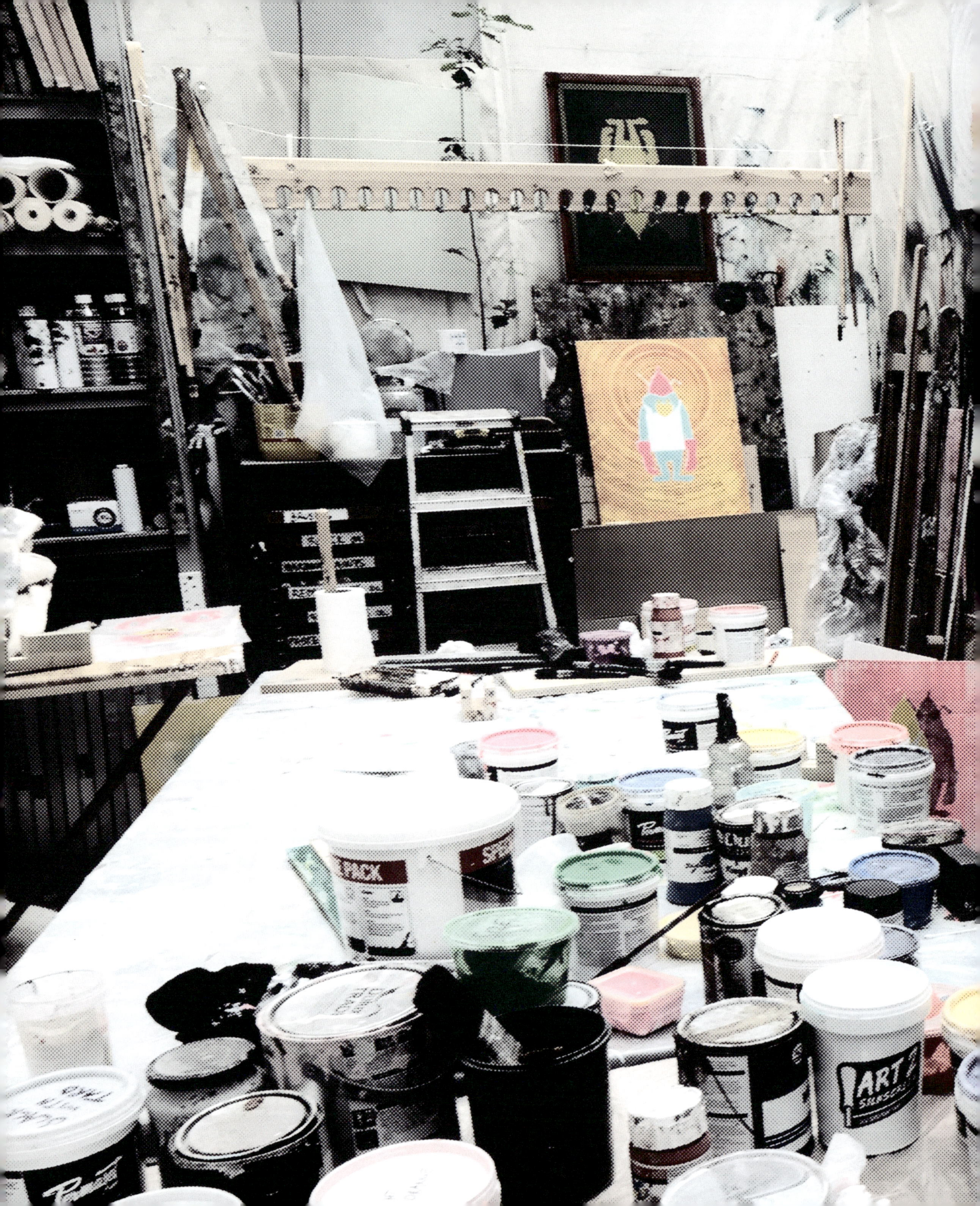

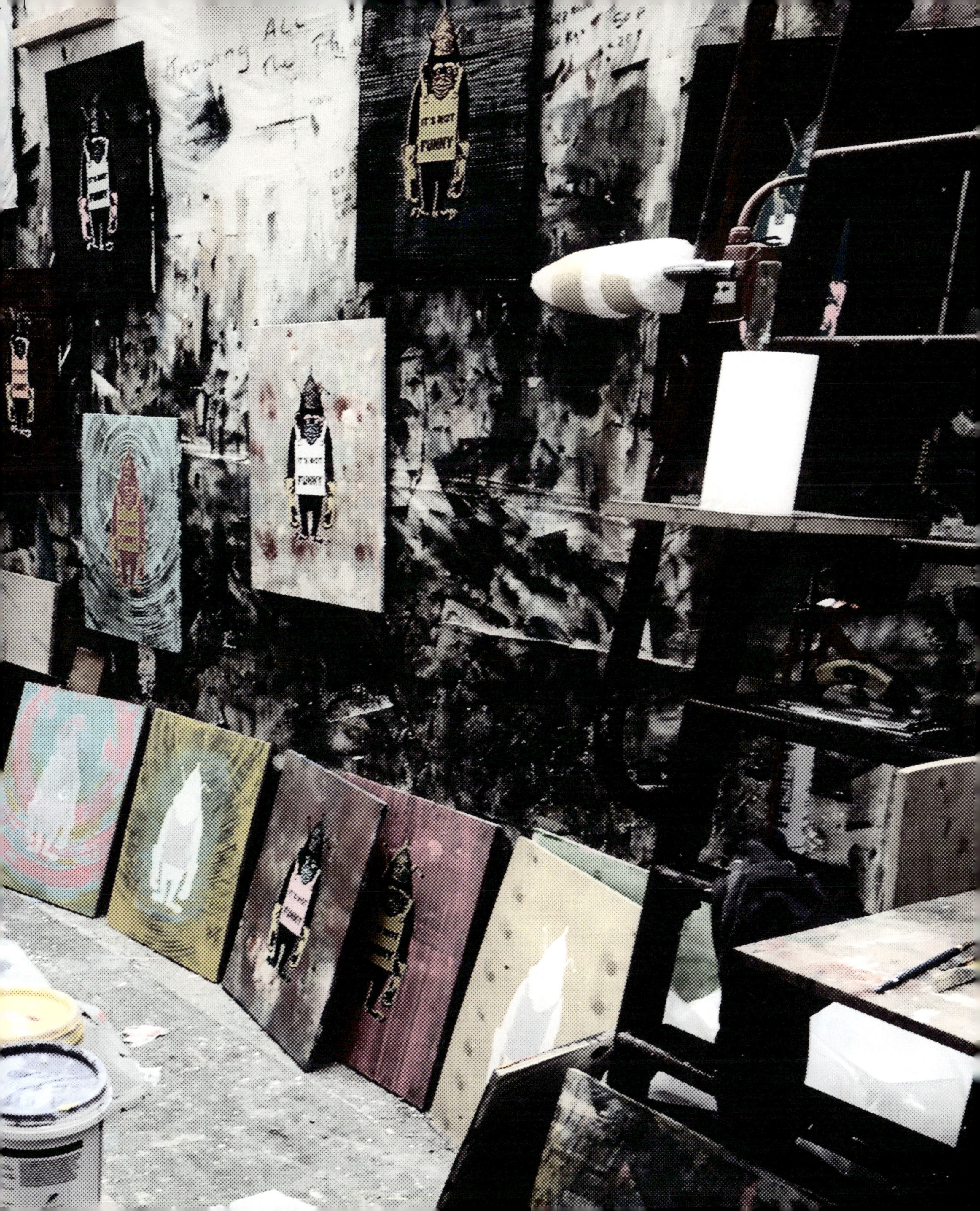

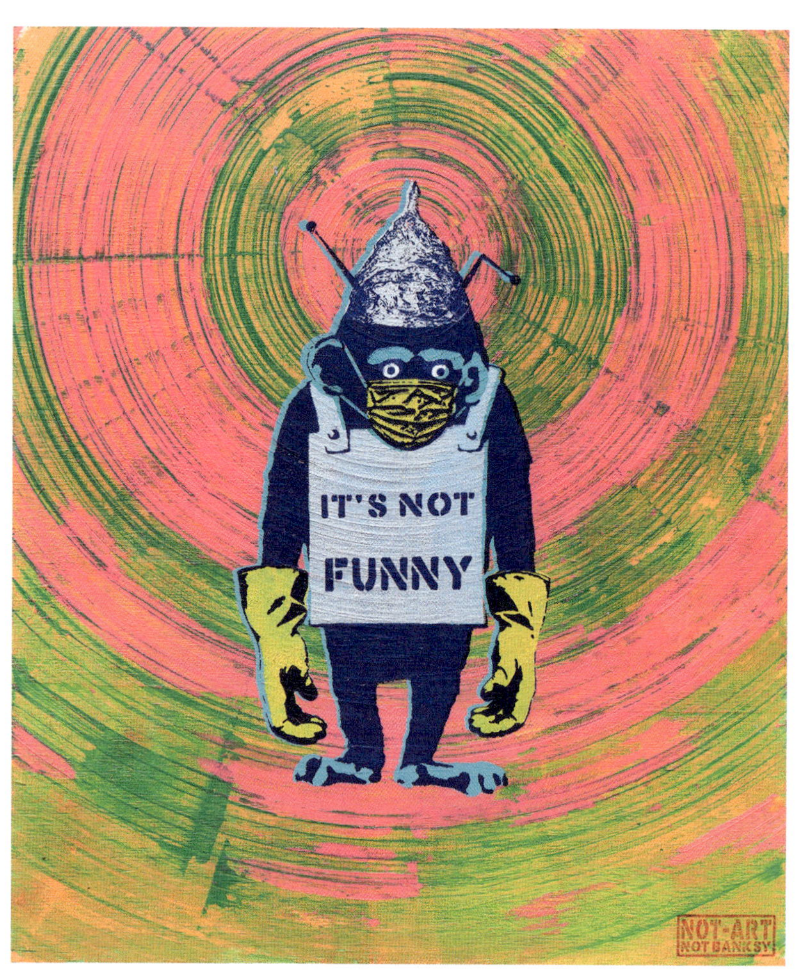

THEN WE MADE A FEW "ORIGINALS"

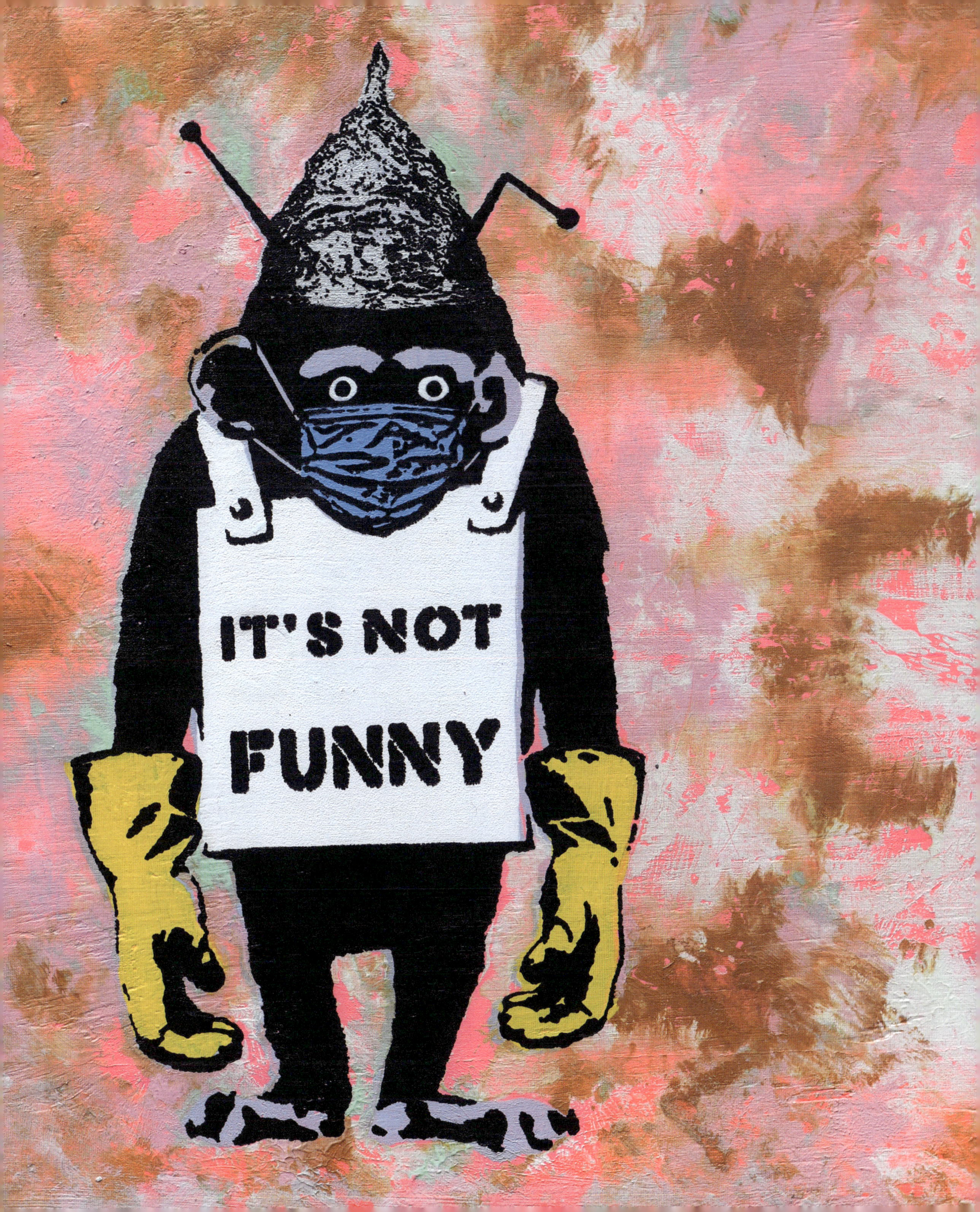

IT'S NOT
FUNNY

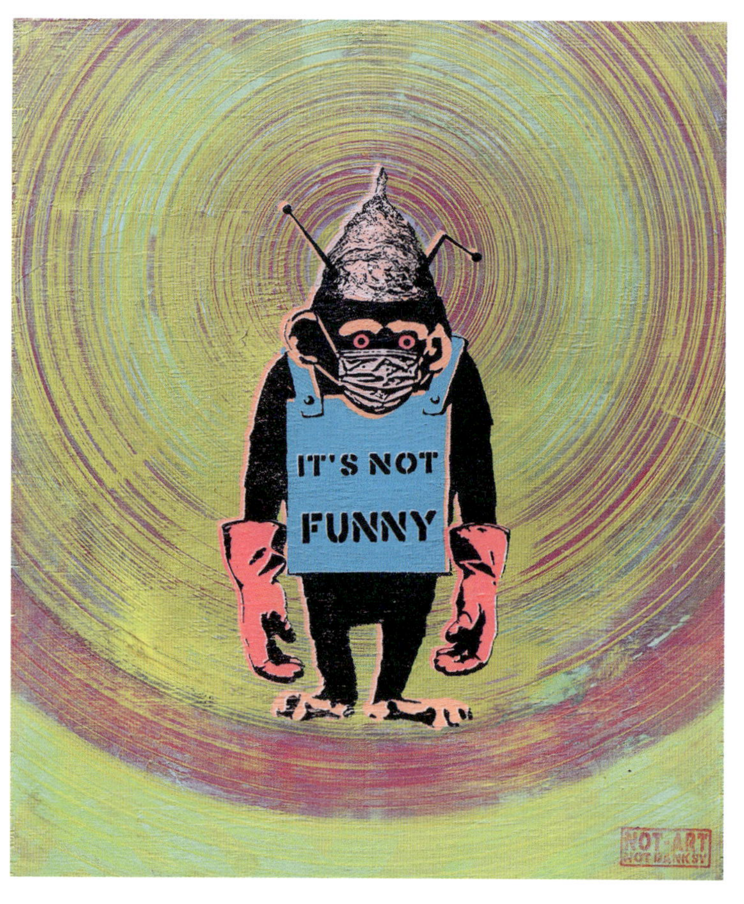
IT'S NOT
FUNNY
NOT-ART
NOT BANKSY

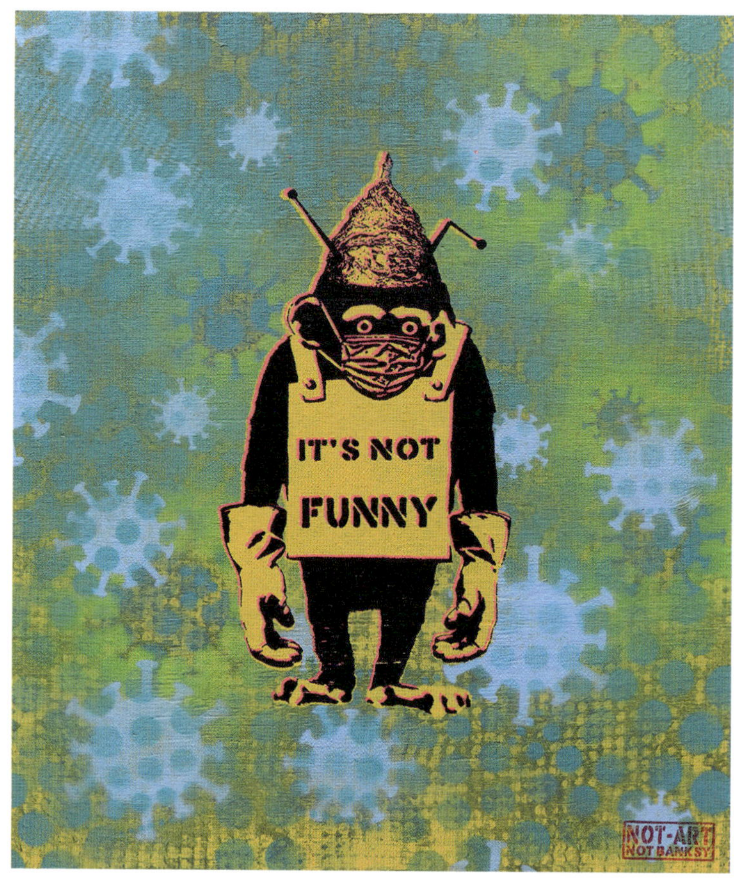
IT'S NOT
FUNNY
NOT-ART
NOT BANKSY

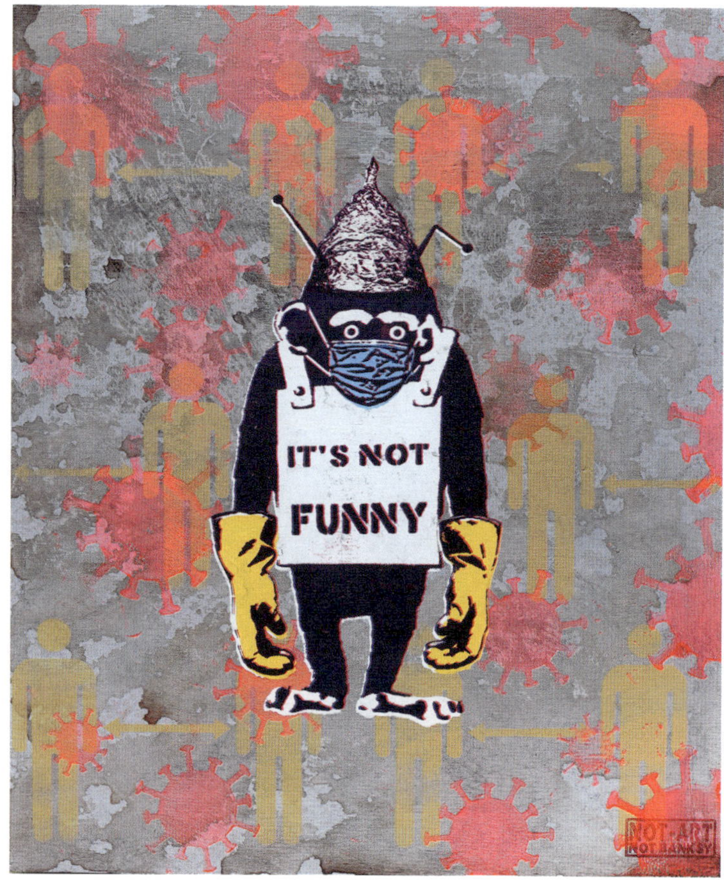
IT'S NOT
FUNNY
NOT-ART
NOT BANKSY

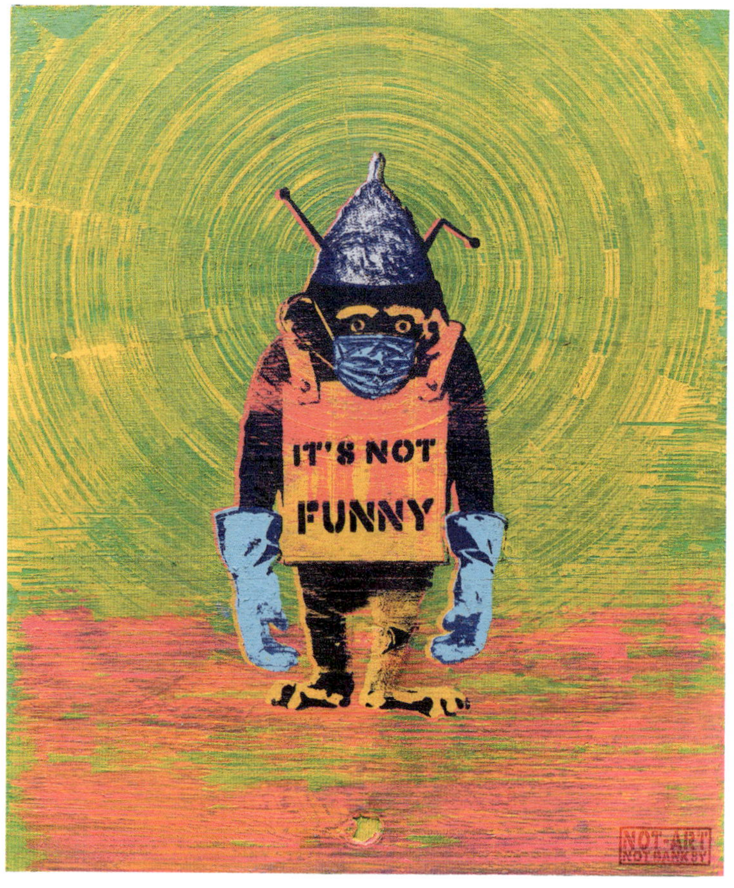
IT'S NOT
FUNNY
NOT-ART
NOT BANKSY

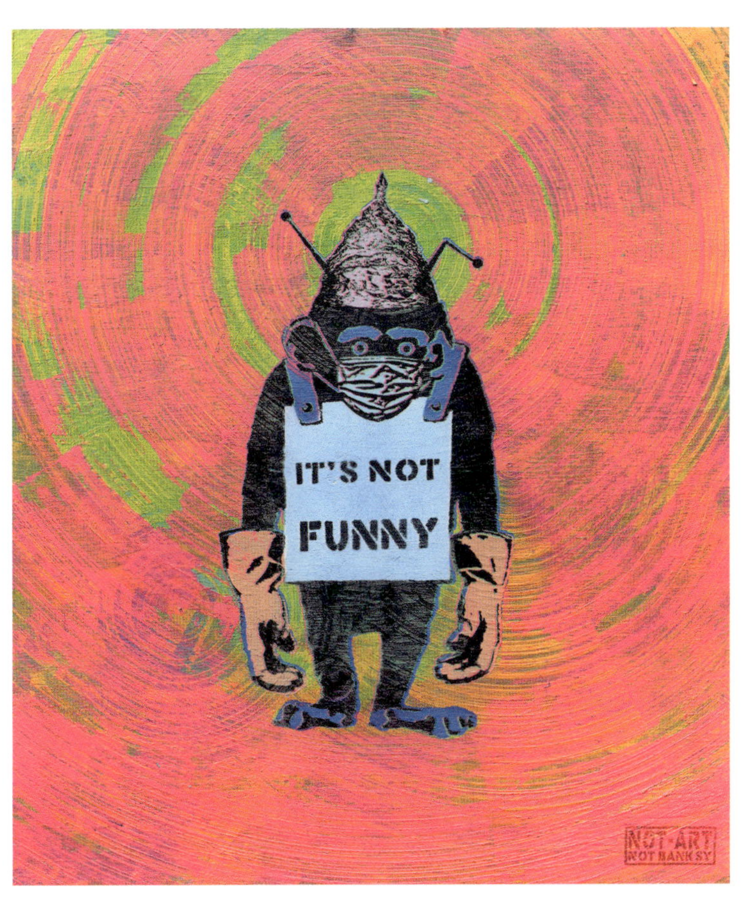

IT'S NOT
FUNNY

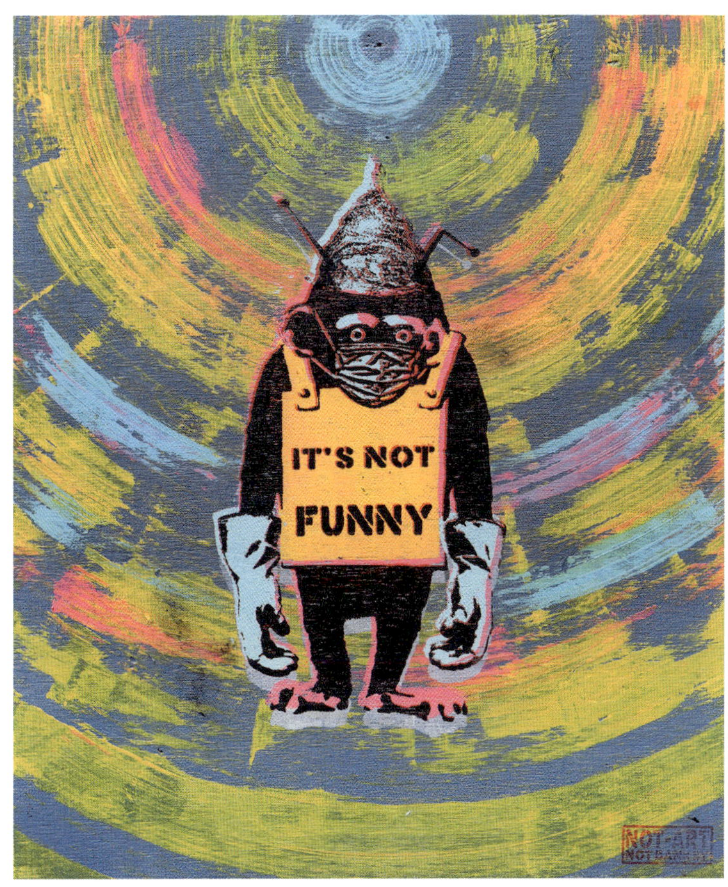

IT'S NOT
FUNNY

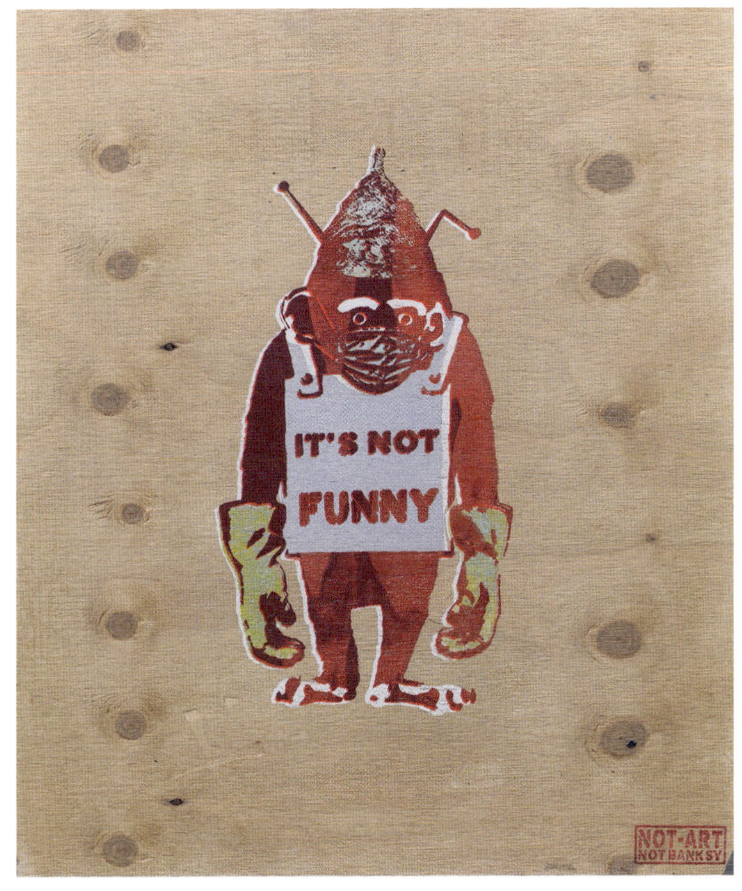

IT'S NOT
FUNNY

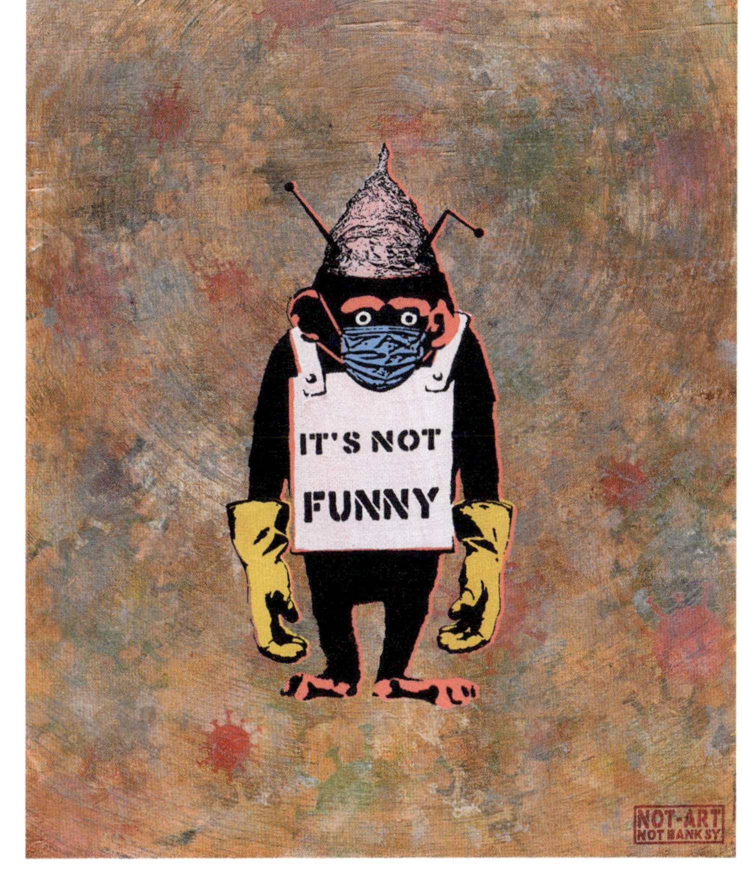

IT'S NOT
FUNNY

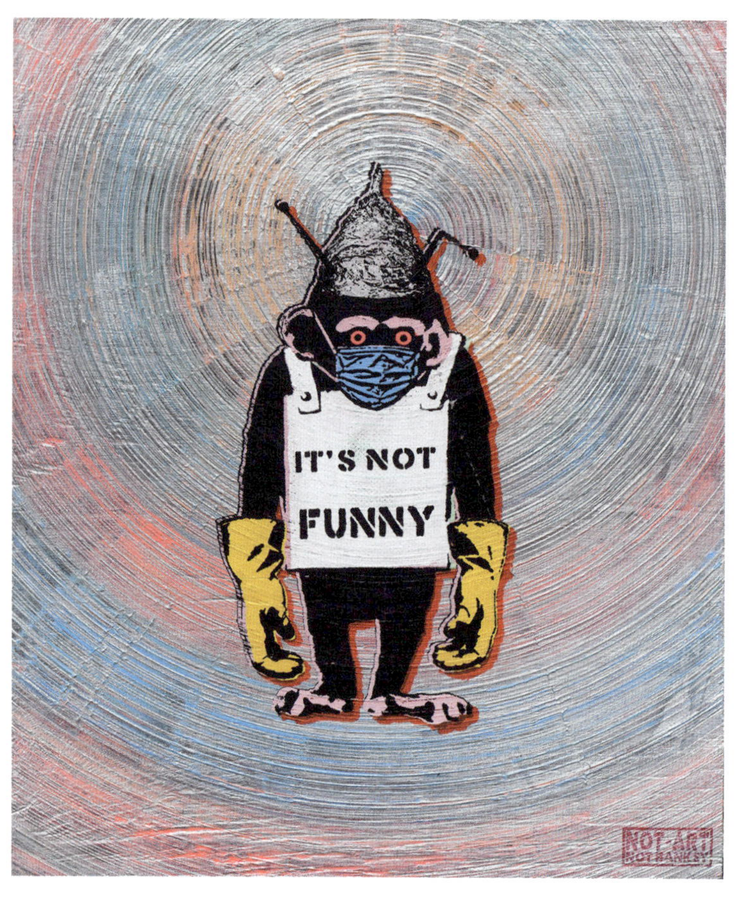

IT'S NOT
FUNNY

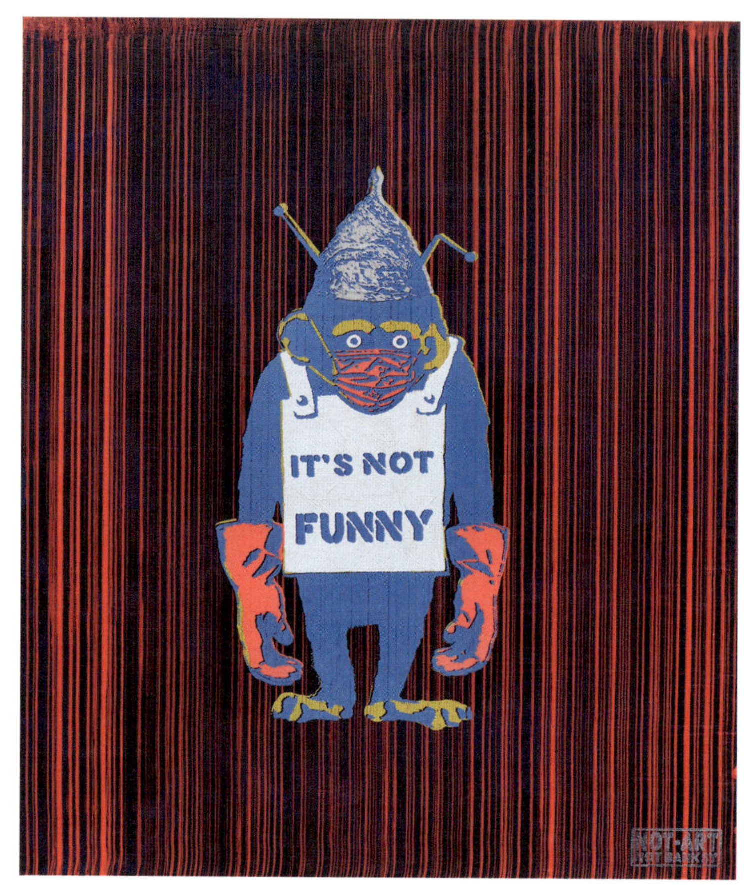

IT'S NOT
FUNNY

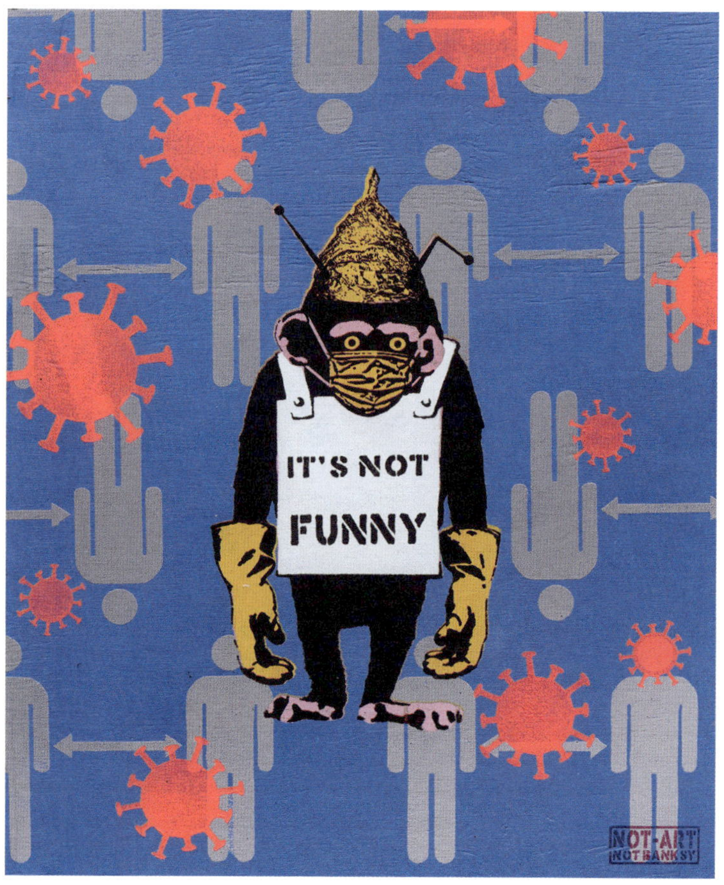

IT'S NOT
FUNNY

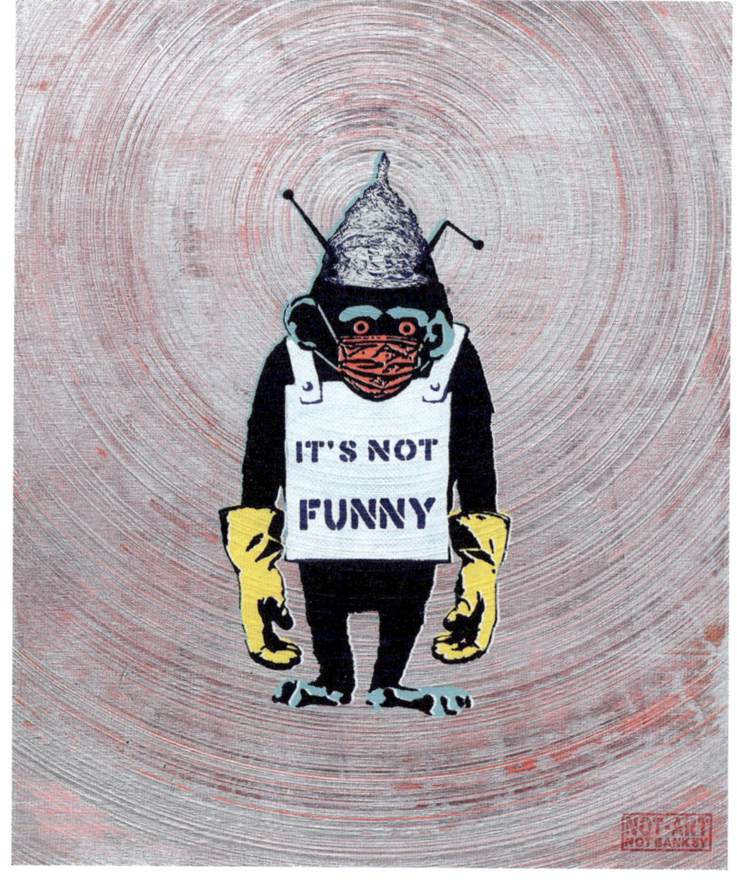

IT'S NOT
FUNNY

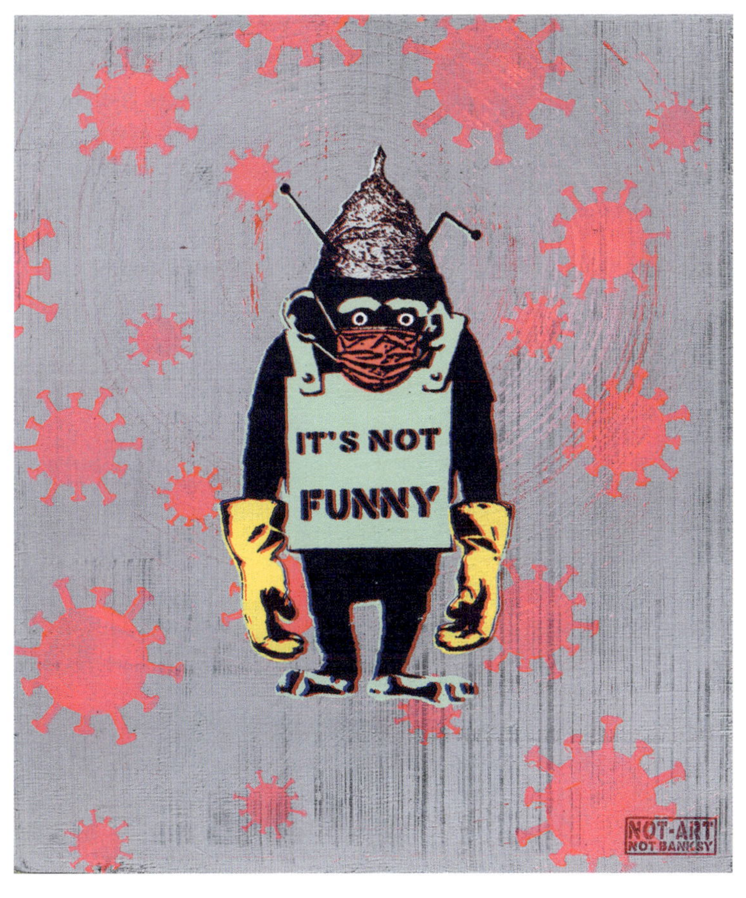
IT'S NOT
FUNNY
NOT-ART
NOT BANKSY

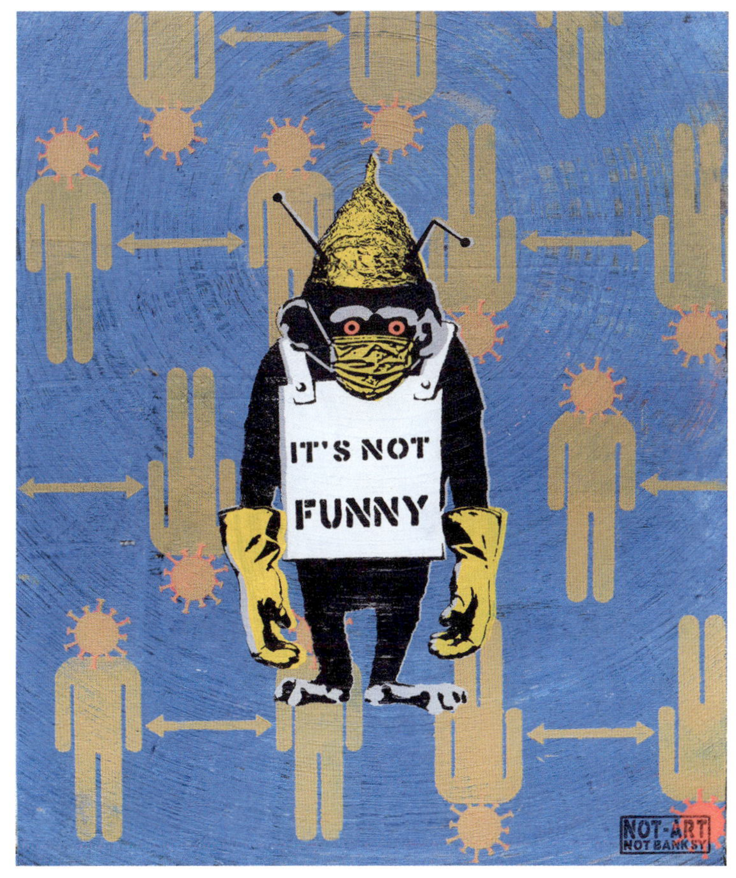
IT'S NOT
FUNNY
NOT-ART
NOT BANKSY

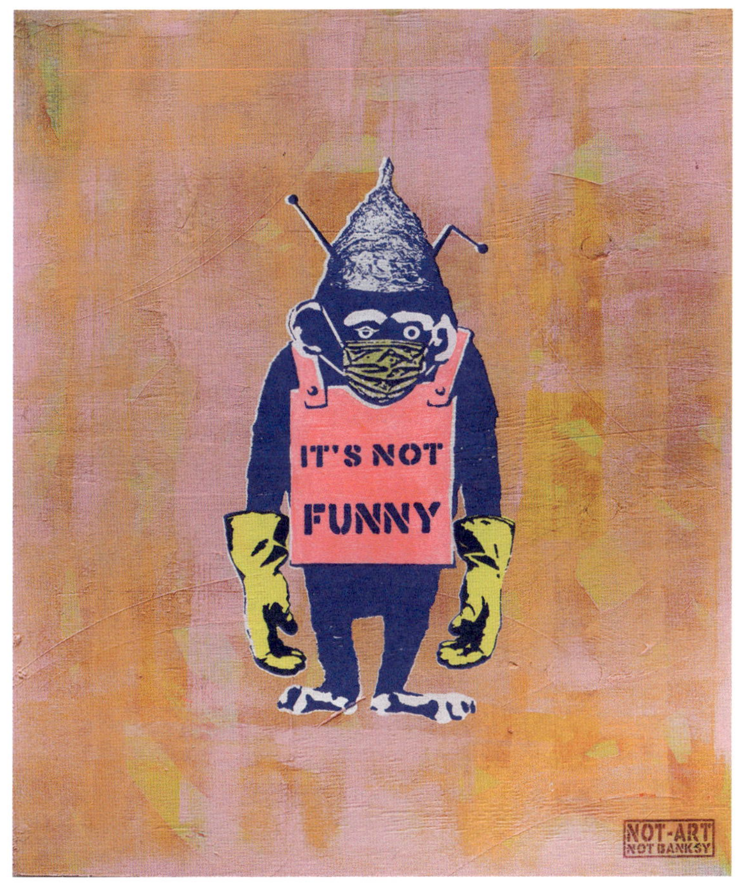
IT'S NOT
FUNNY
NOT-ART
NOT BANKSY

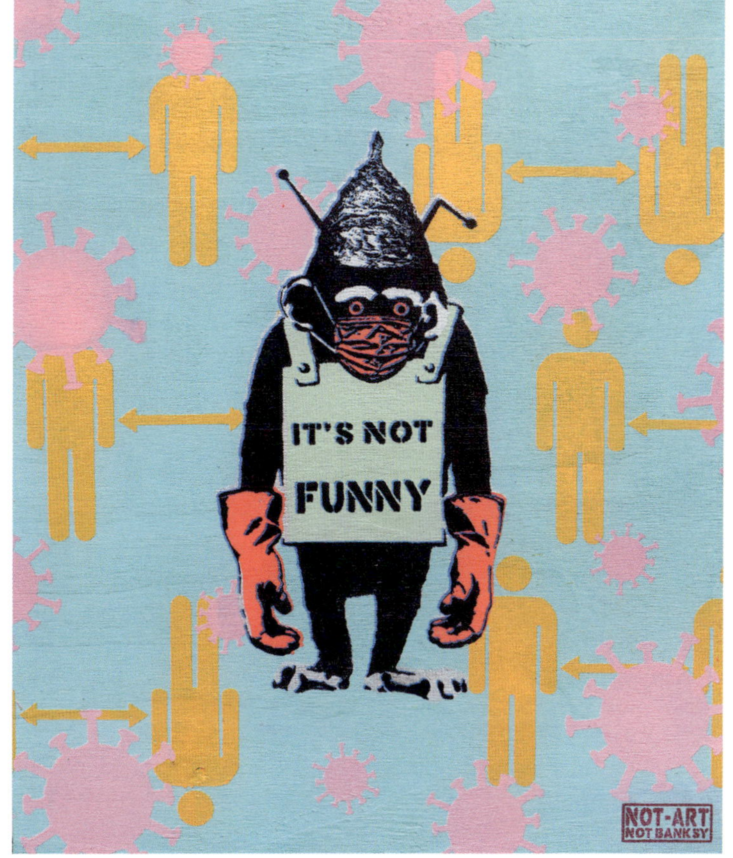
IT'S NOT
FUNNY
NOT-ART
NOT BANKSY

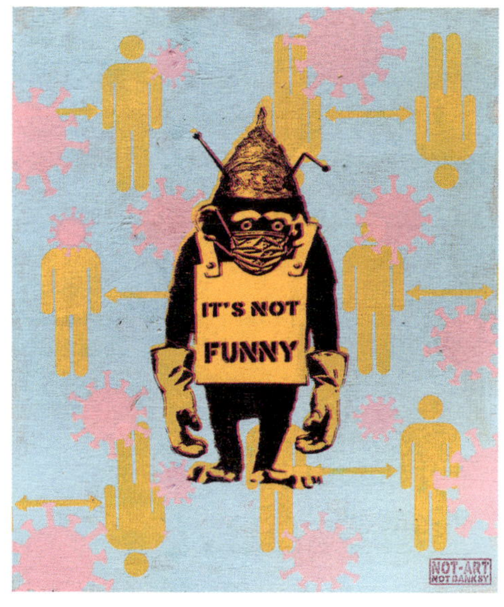
IT'S NOT
FUNNY
NOT-ART
NOT BANKSY
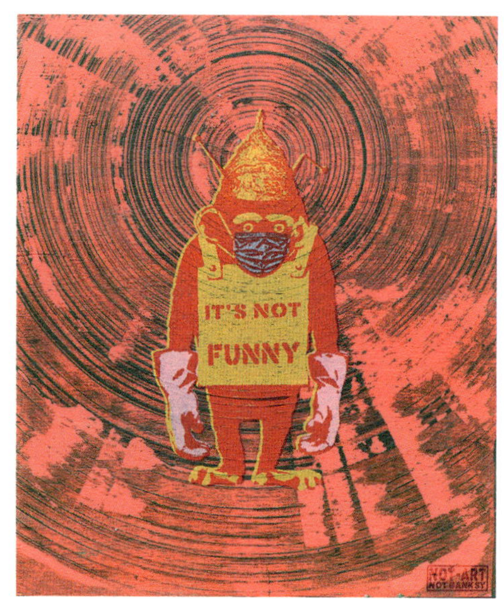
IT'S NOT
FUNNY
NOT-ART
NOT BANKSY
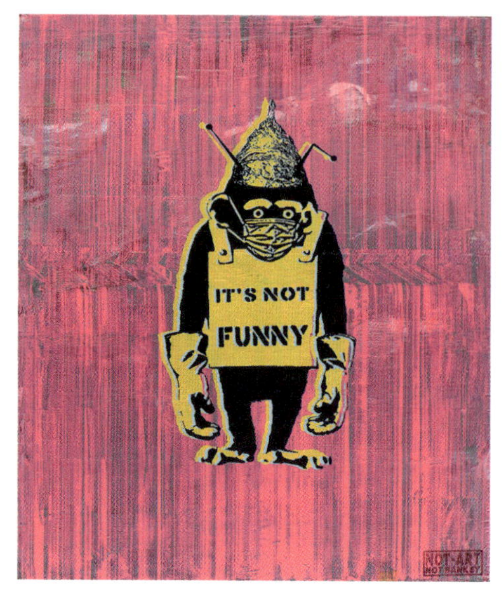
IT'S NOT
FUNNY
NOT-ART
NOT BANKSY
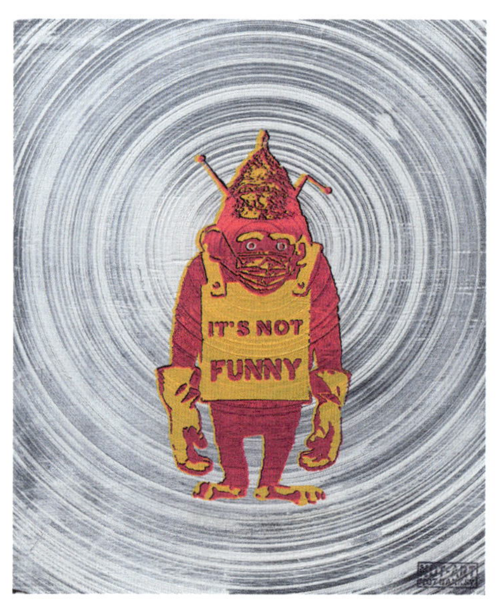
IT'S NOT
FUNNY
NOT-ART
NOT BANKSY
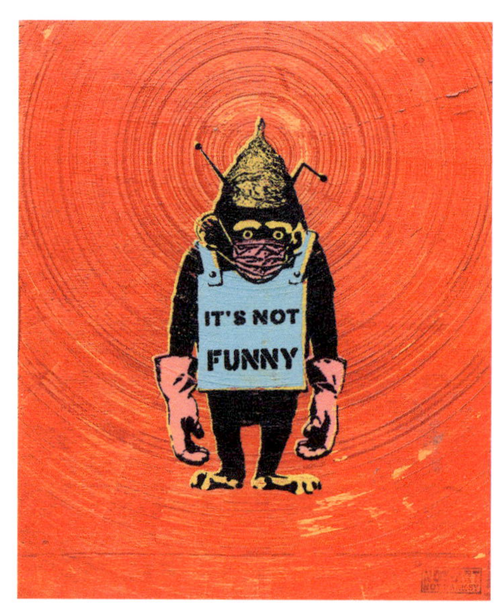
IT'S NOT
FUNNY
NOT-ART
NOT BANKSY
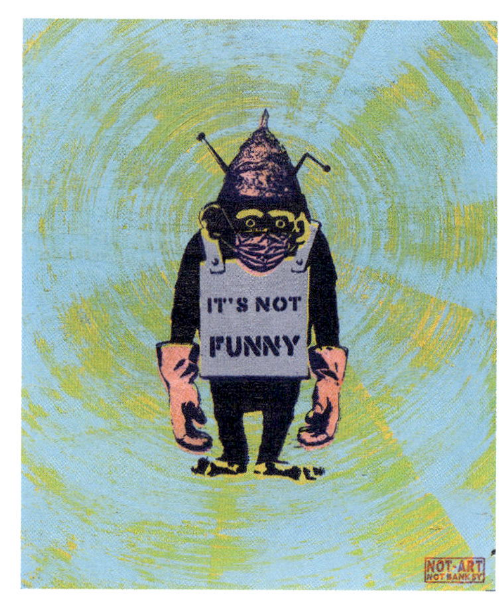
IT'S NOT
FUNNY
NOT-ART
NOT BANKSY
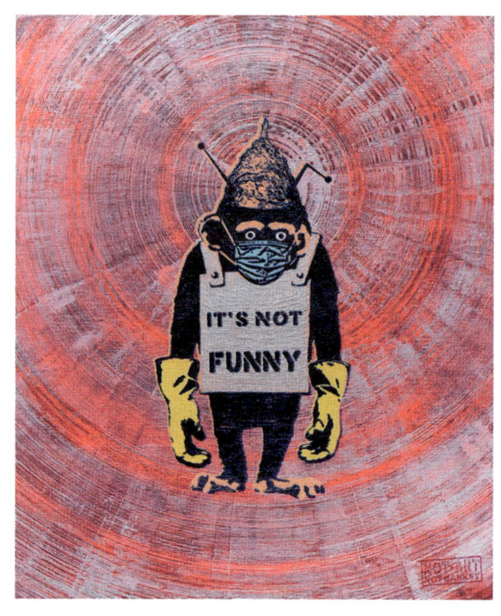
IT'S NOT
FUNNY
NOT-ART
NOT BANKSY
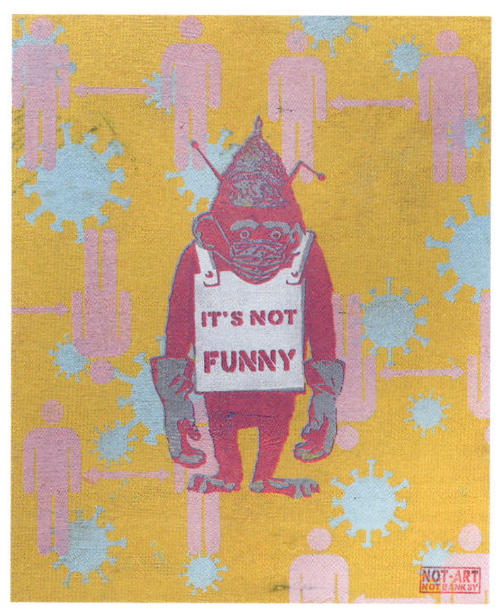
IT'S NOT
FUNNY
NOT-ART
NOT BANKSY
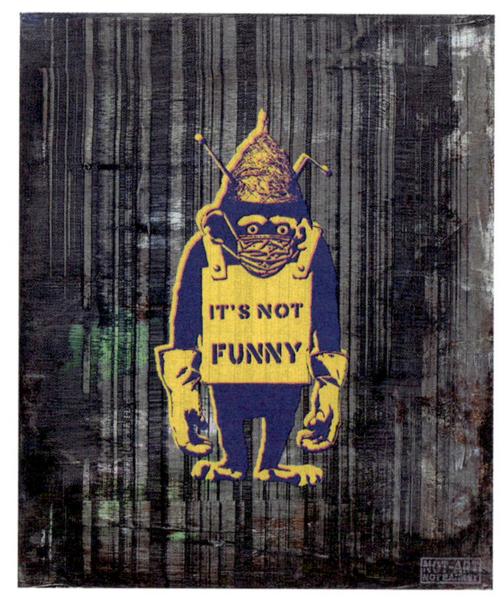
IT'S NOT
FUNNY
NOT-ART
NOT BANKSY

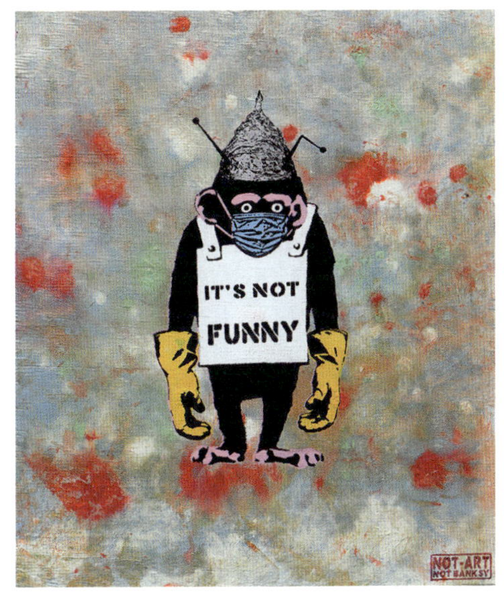
IT'S NOT
FUNNY
NOT-ART
NOT BANKSY

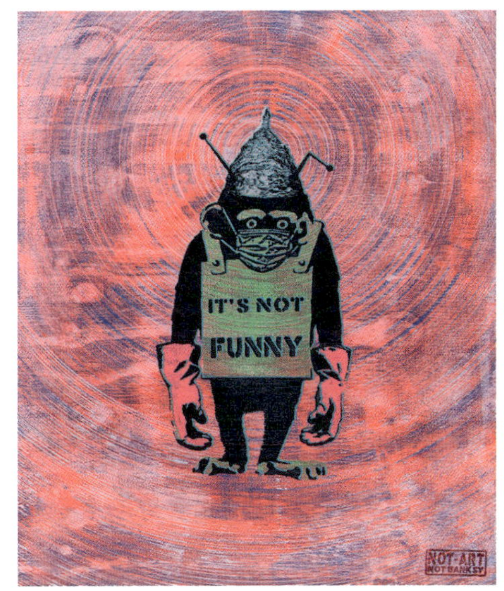
IT'S NOT
FUNNY
NOT-ART
NOT BANKSY

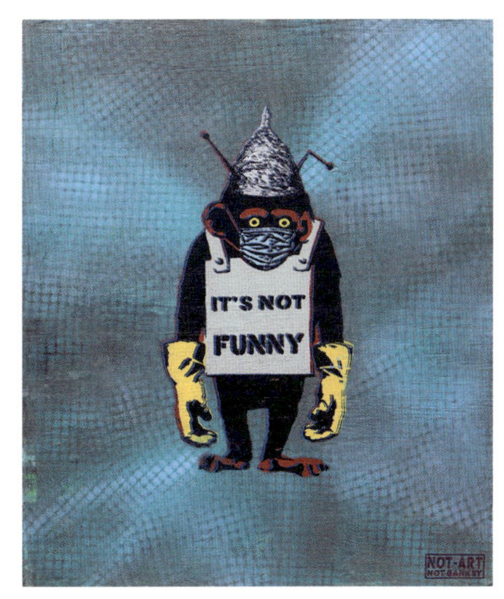
IT'S NOT
FUNNY
NOT-ART
NOT BANKSY

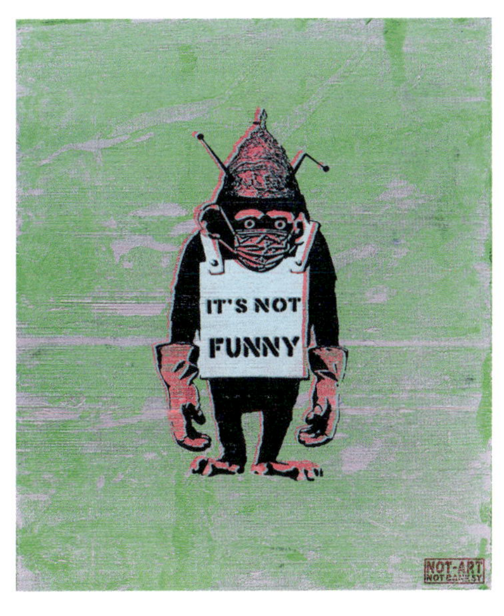
IT'S NOT
FUNNY
NOT-ART
NOT BANKSY

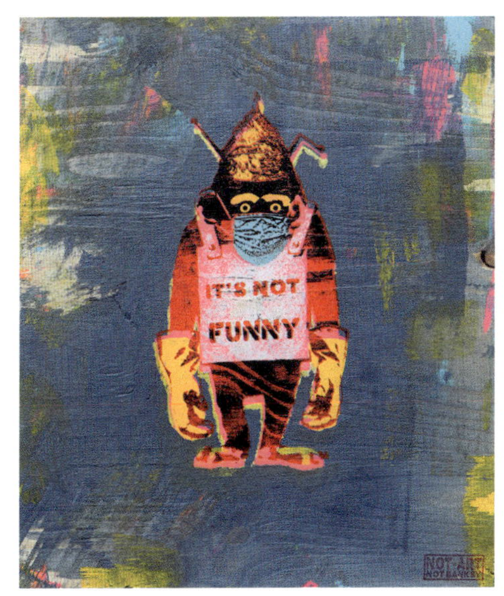
IT'S NOT
FUNNY
NOT-ART
NOT BANKSY

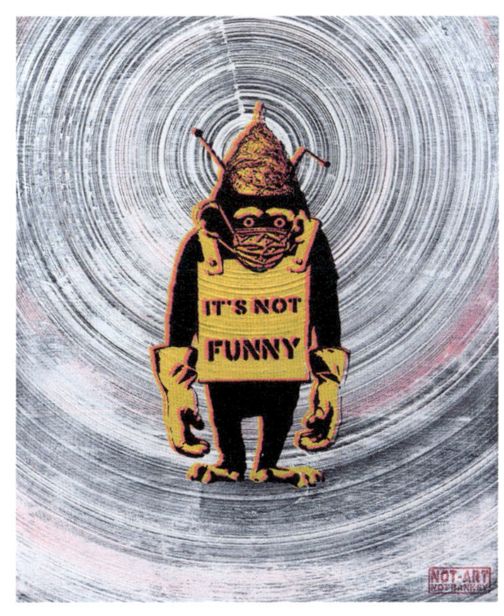
IT'S NOT
FUNNY
NOT-ART
NOT BANKSY

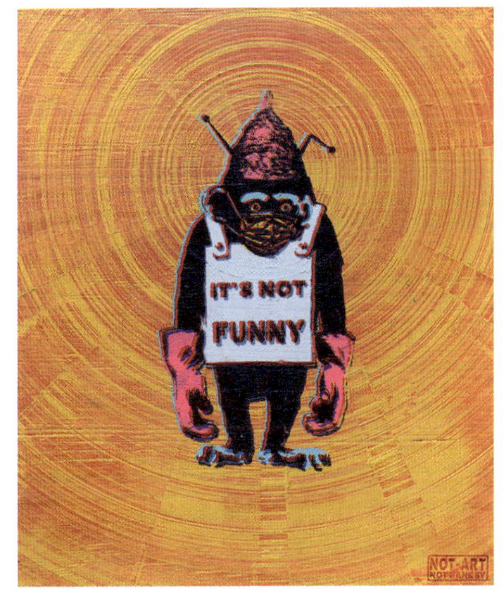
IT'S NOT
FUNNY
NOT-ART
NOT BANKSY

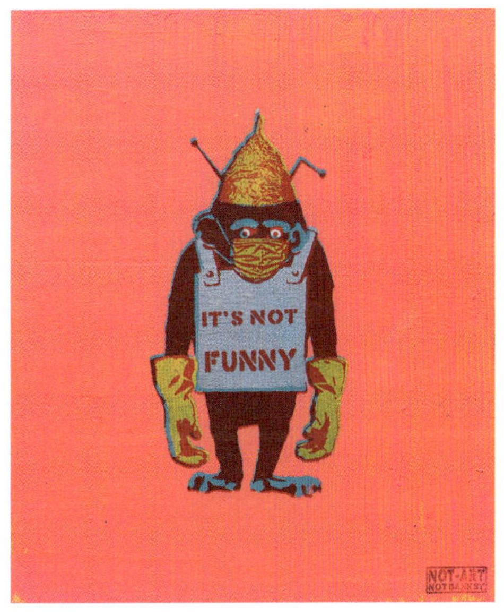
IT'S NOT
FUNNY
NOT-ART
NOT BANKSY

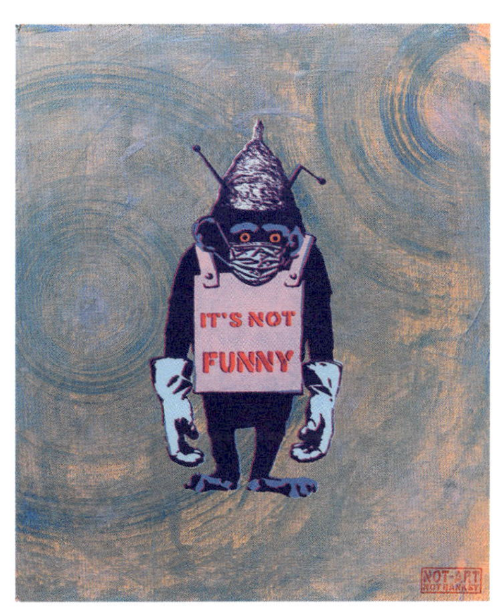
IT'S NOT
FUNNY
NOT-ART
NOT BANKSY

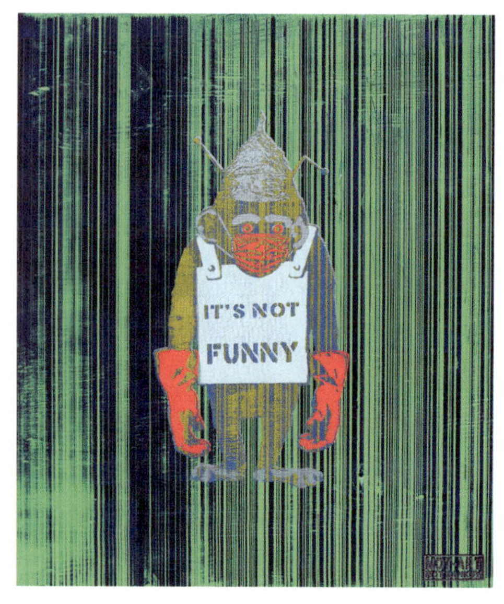
IT'S NOT
FUNNY

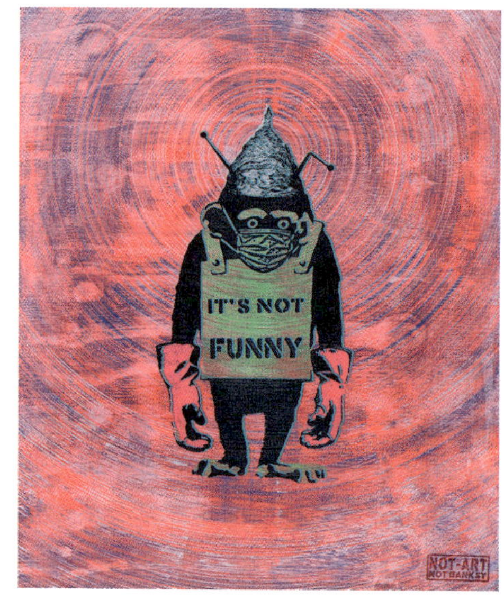
IT'S NOT
FUNNY

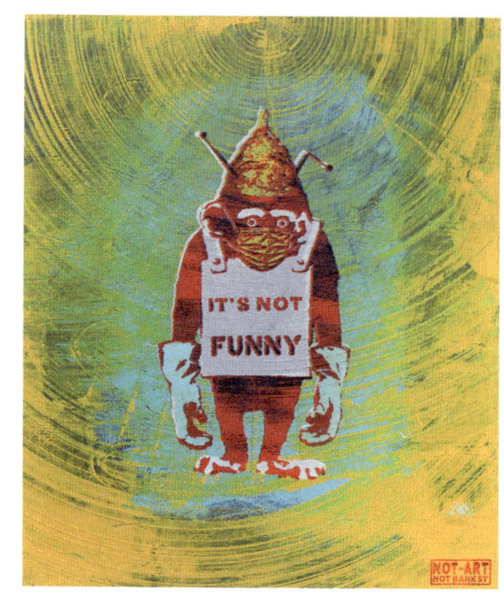
IT'S NOT
FUNNY

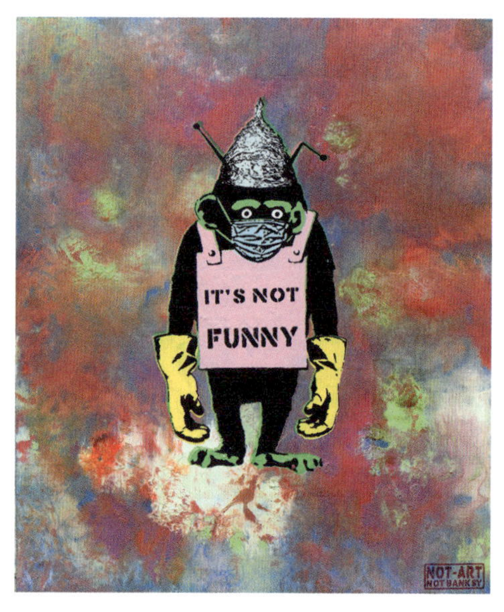
IT'S NOT
FUNNY

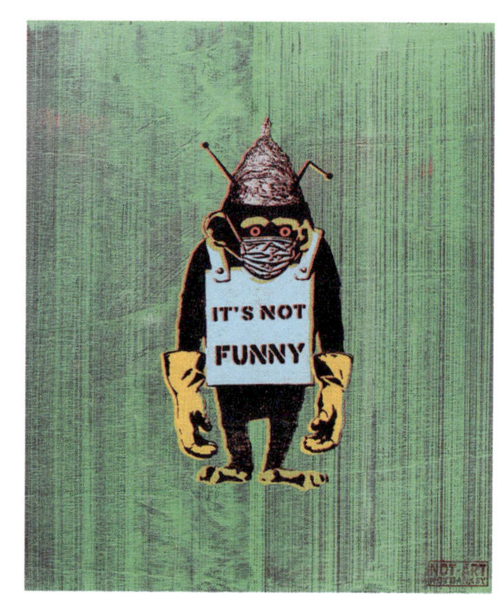
IT'S NOT
FUNNY

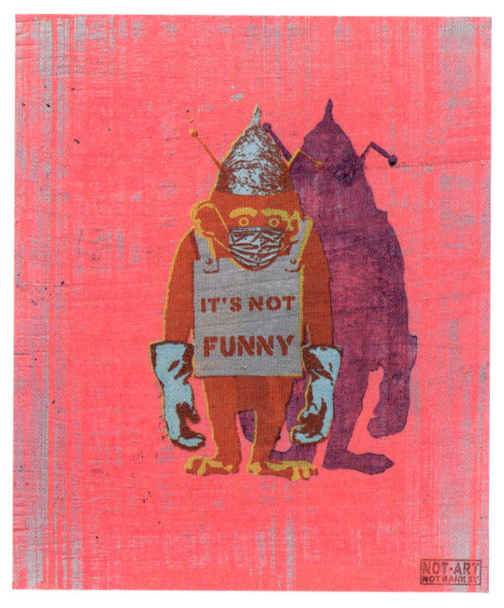
IT'S NOT
FUNNY

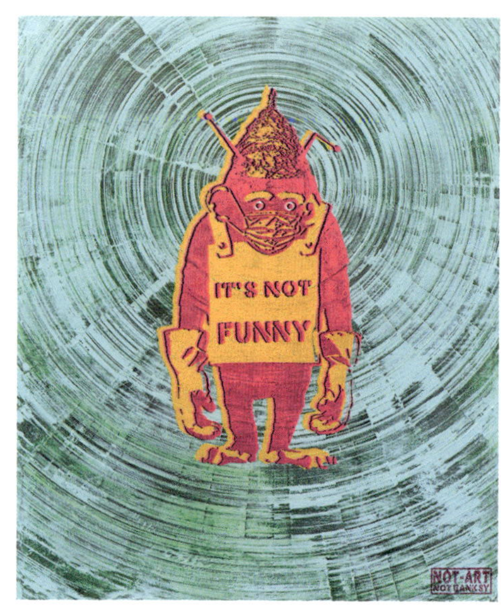
IT'S NOT
FUNNY

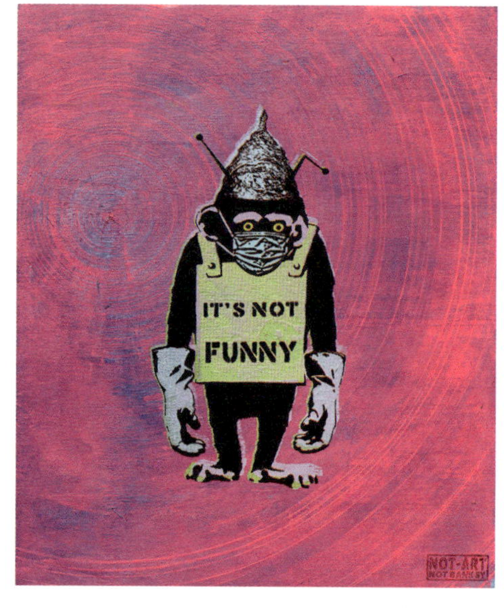
IT'S NOT
FUNNY

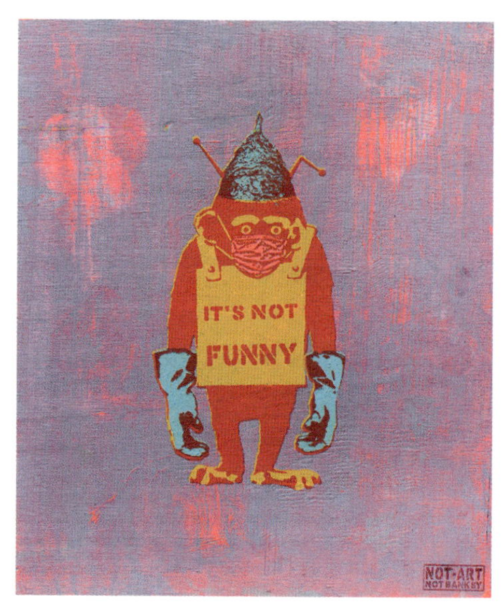
IT'S NOT
FUNNY

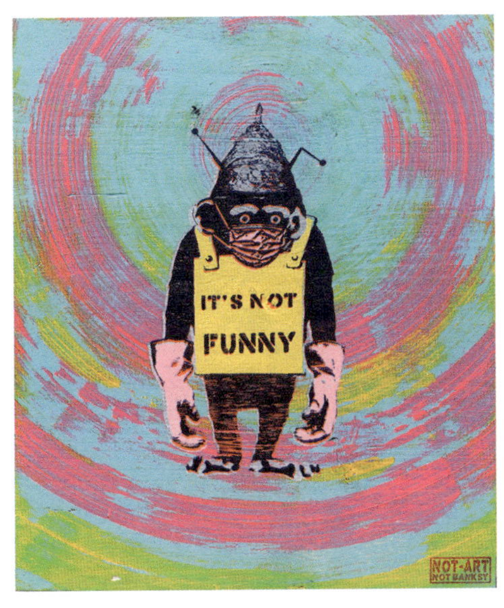
IT'S NOT
FUNNY

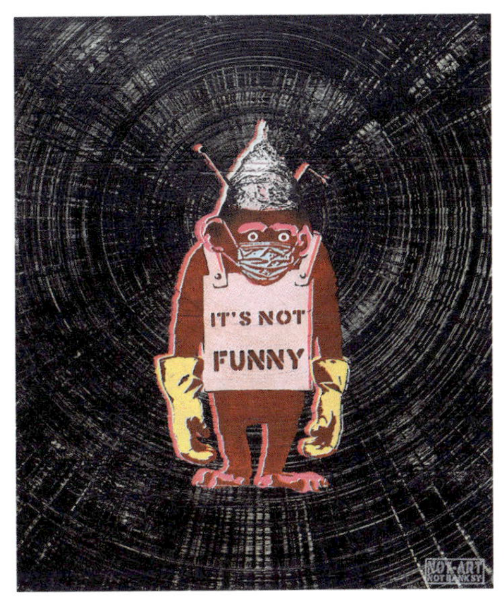
IT'S NOT
FUNNY

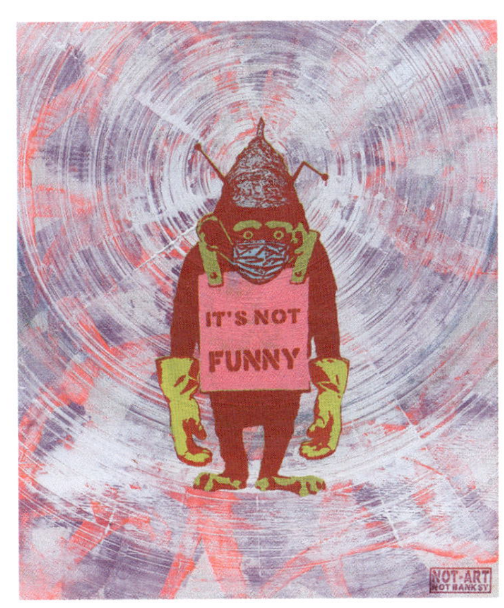
IT'S NOT
FUNNY

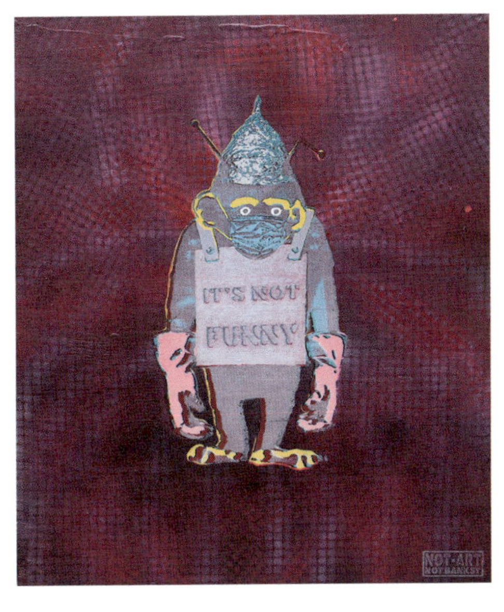
IT'S NOT
FUNNY

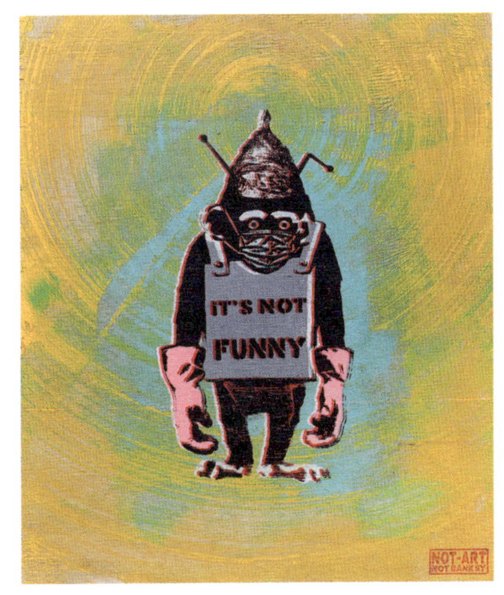
IT'S NOT
FUNNY

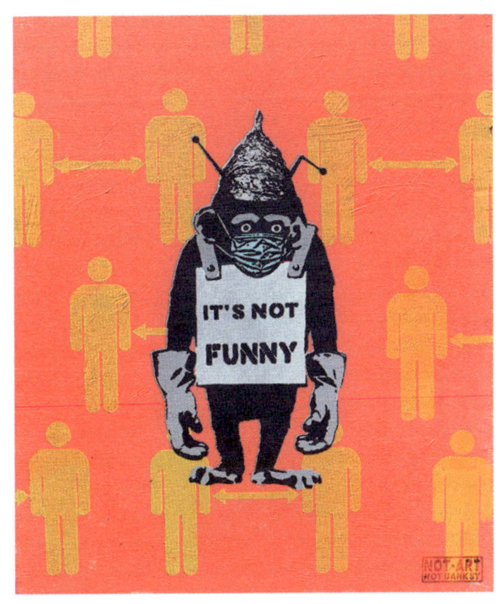
IT'S NOT
FUNNY

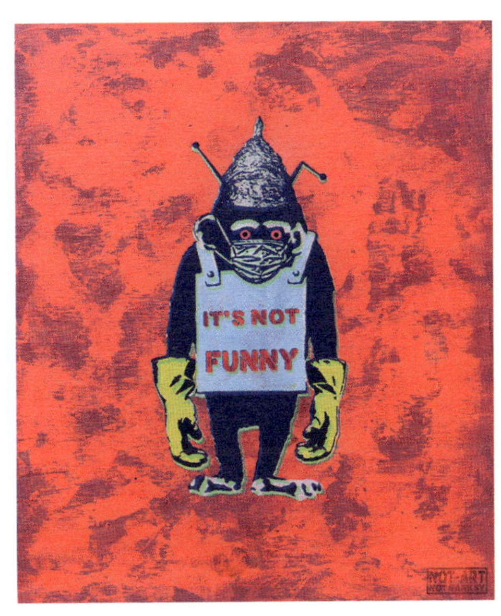
IT'S NOT
FUNNY

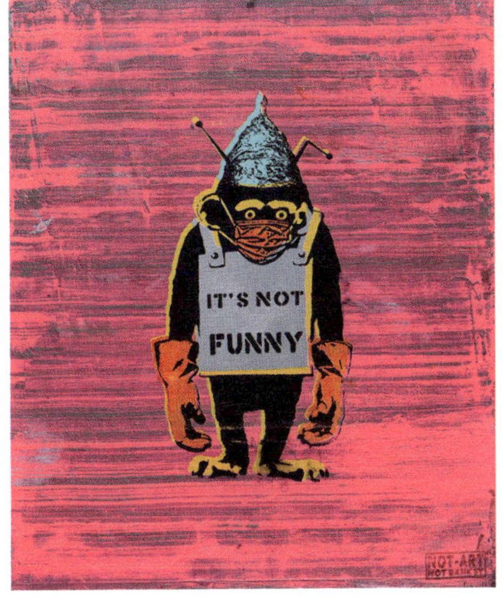
IT'S NOT
FUNNY

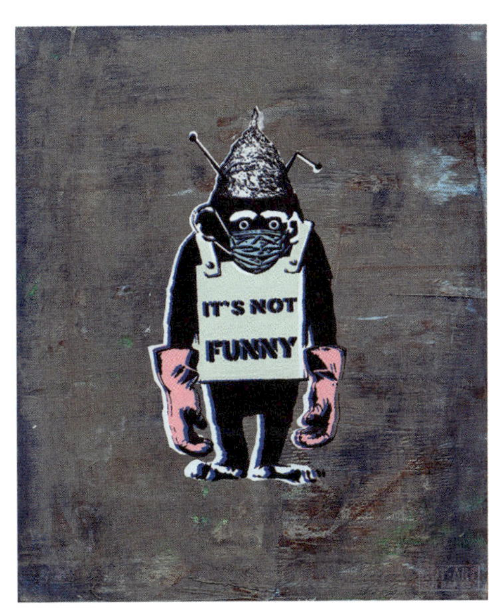
IT'S NOT
FUNNY

COVIDIAN DEATH CULT CHIMP PAINTINGS

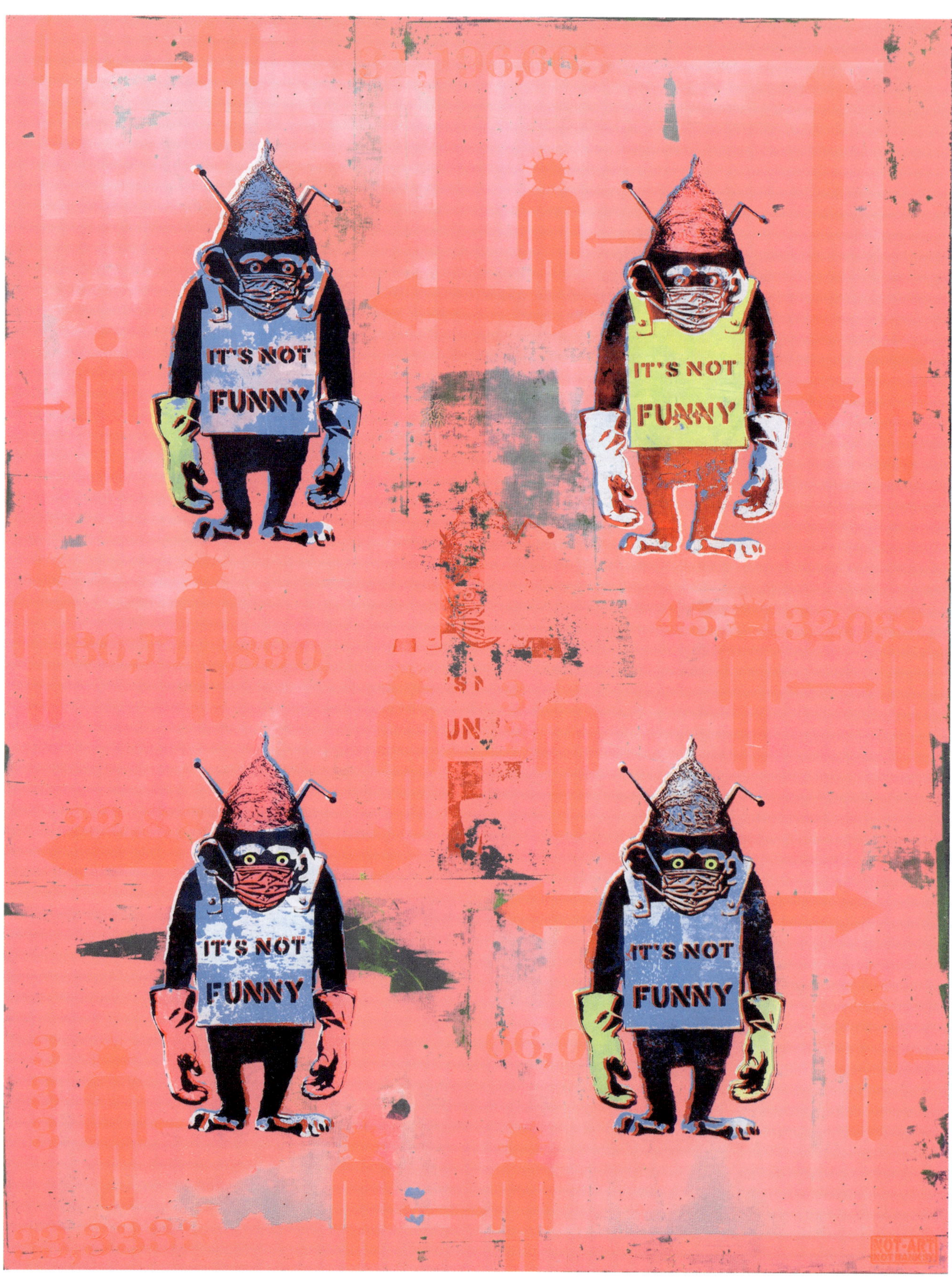

Household paint, and screen ink on plywood | 122 x 91.5 cm

Household paint, and screen ink on plywood | 152.5 x 122 cm

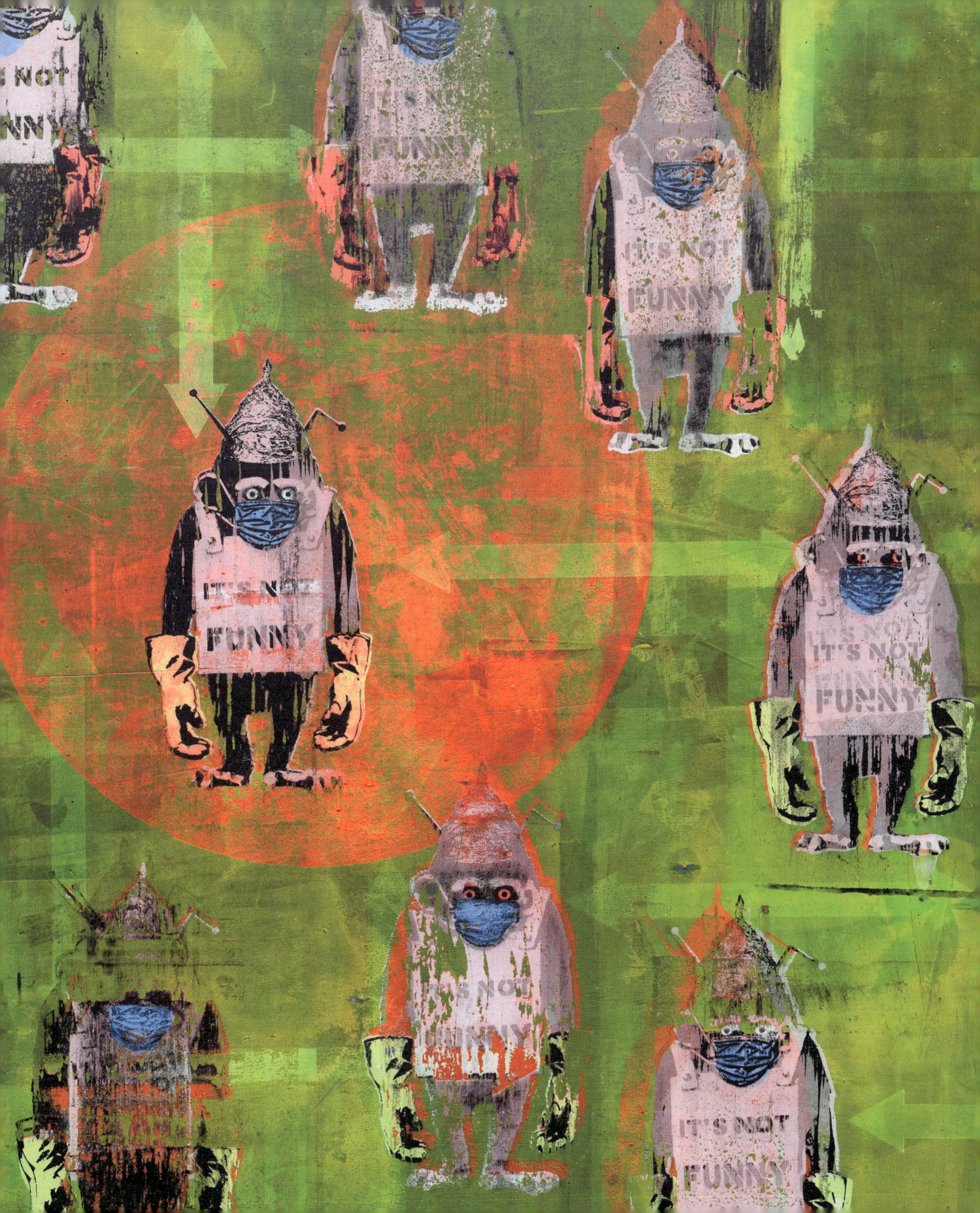
IT'S NOT
FUNNY
IT'S NOT
FUNNY
IT'S NOT
FUNNY
IT'S NOT
FUNNY
IT'S NOT
IT'S NOT
FUNNY
IT'S NOT
FUNNY
IT'S NOT
FUNNY

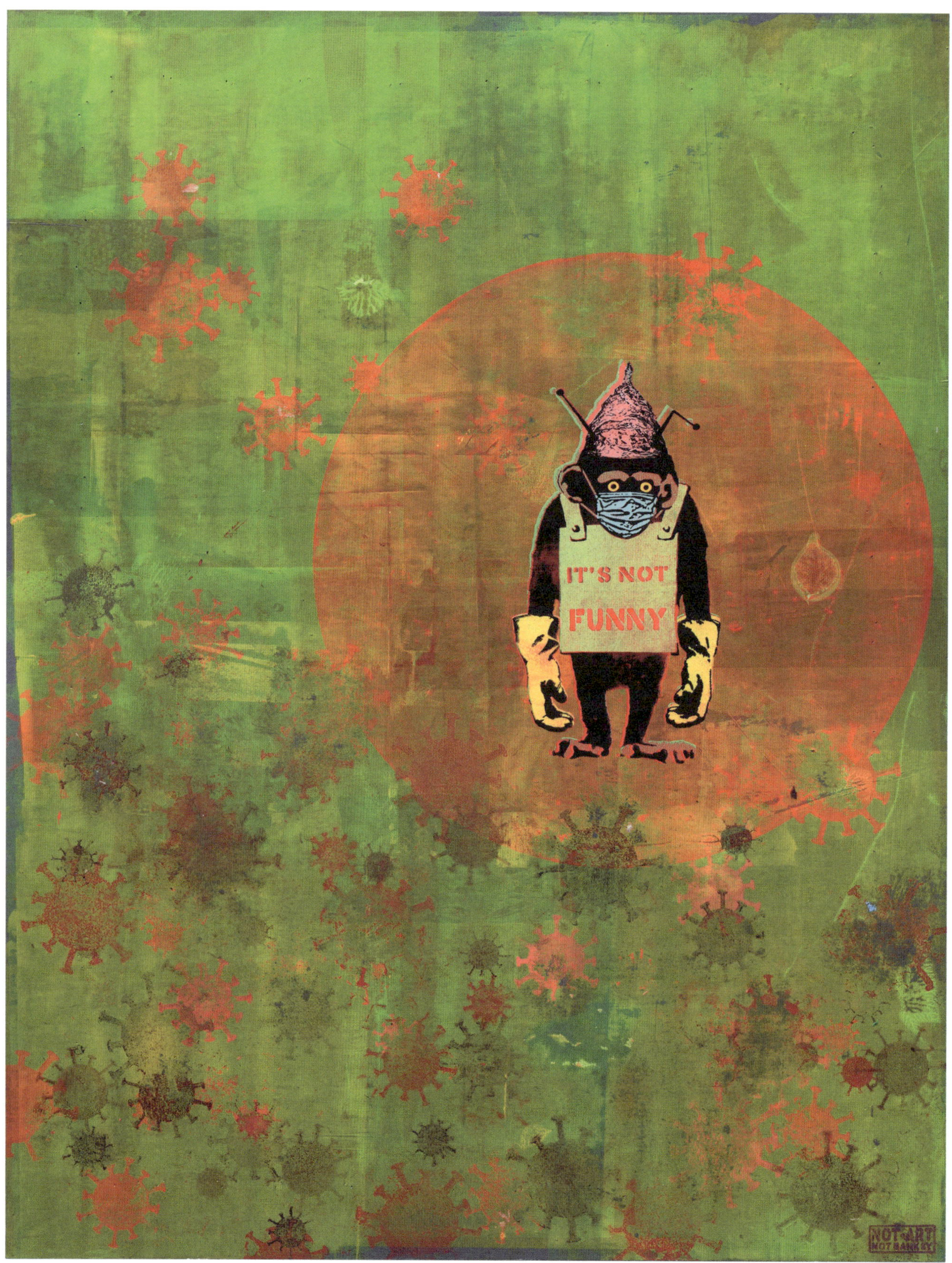

Household paint, and screen ink on plywood | 122 x 91.5 cm

Household paint, and screen ink on plywood | 152.5 x 122 cm

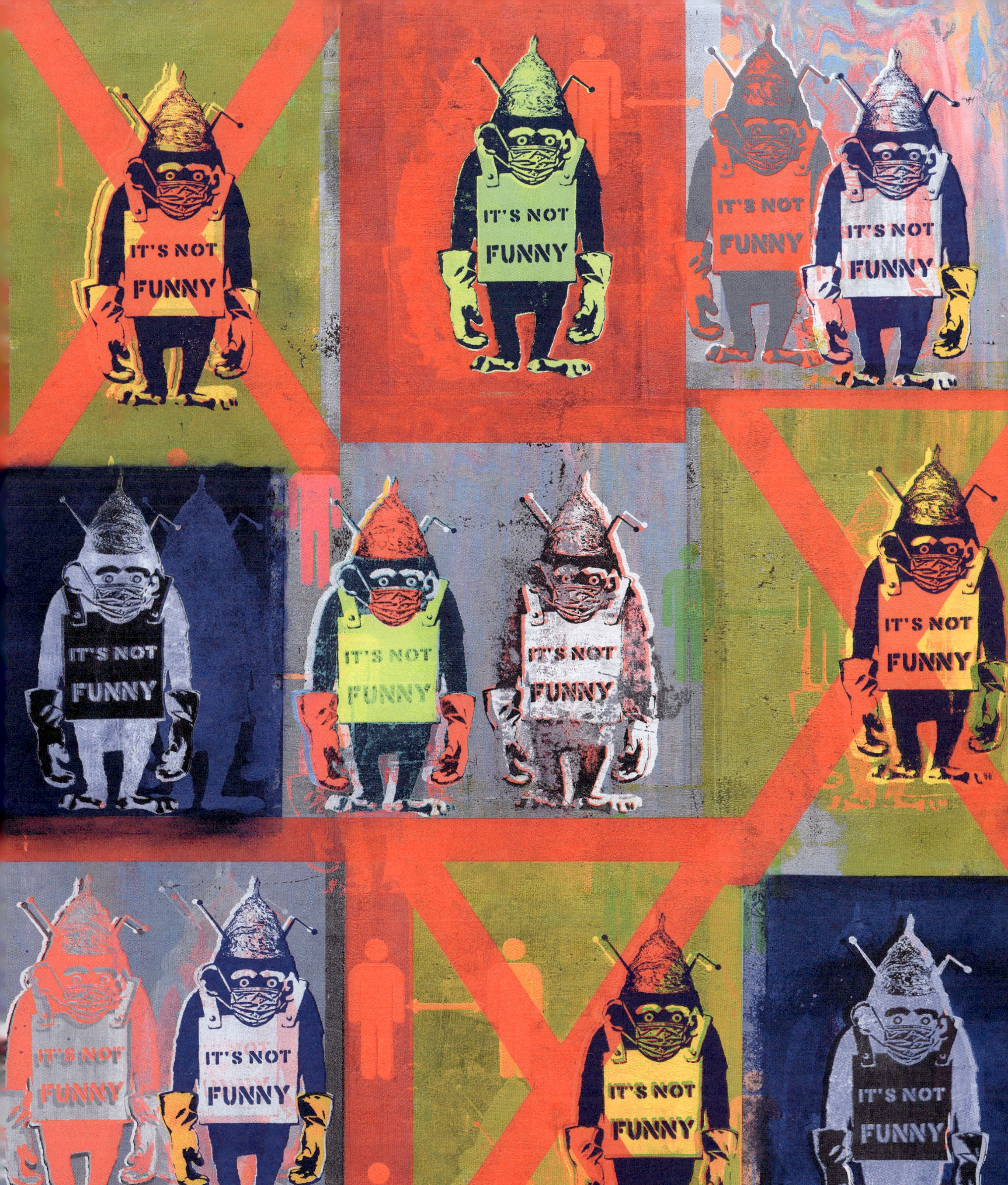

IT'S NOT FUNNY
IT'S NOT FUNNY
IT'S NOT FUNNY
IT'S NOT FUNNY
IT'S NOT FUNNY
IT'S NOT FUNNY
IT'S NOT FUNNY
IT'S NOT FUNNY
IT'S NOT FUNNY
IT'S NOT FUNNY
IT'S NOT FUNNY

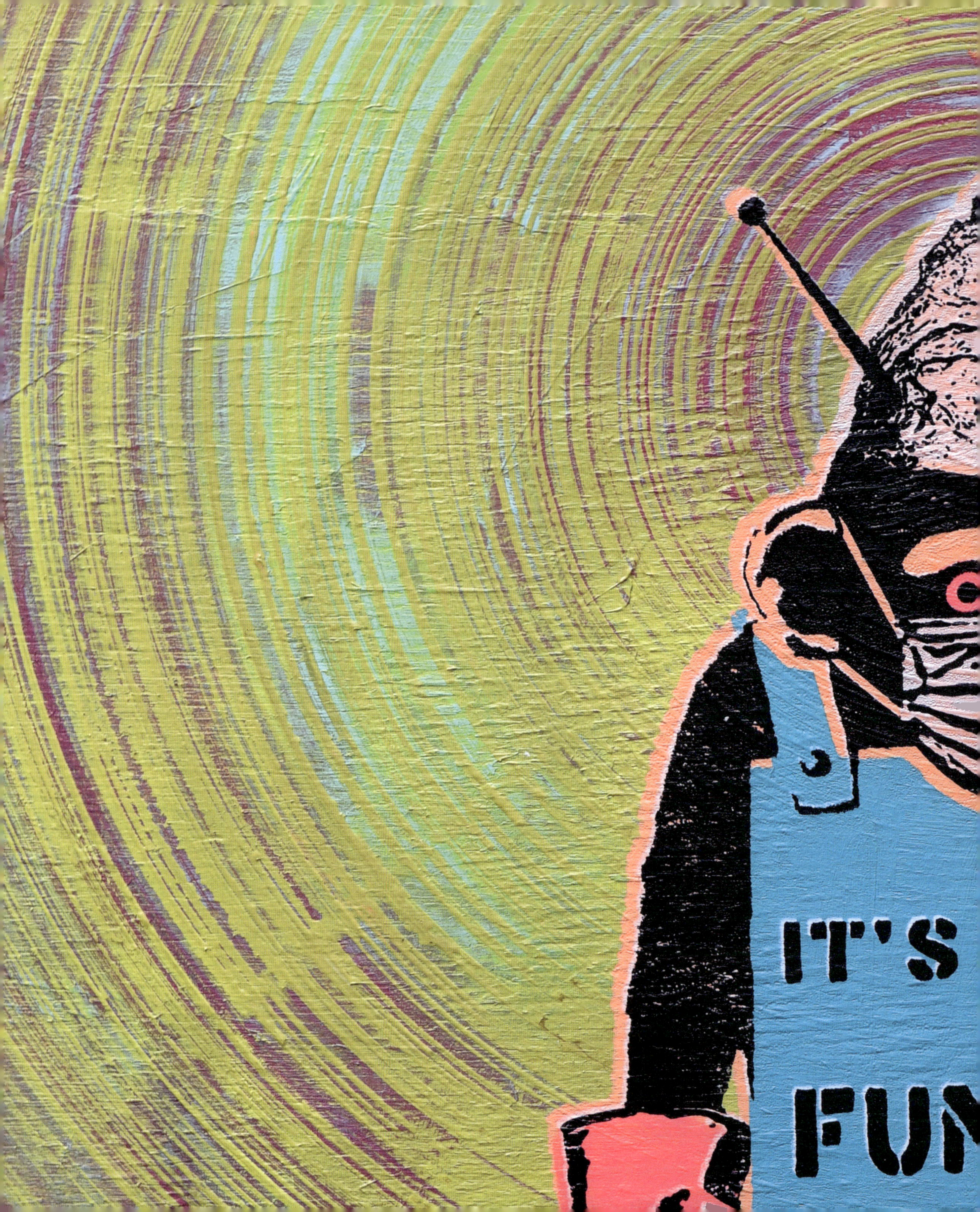
IT'S
FUN

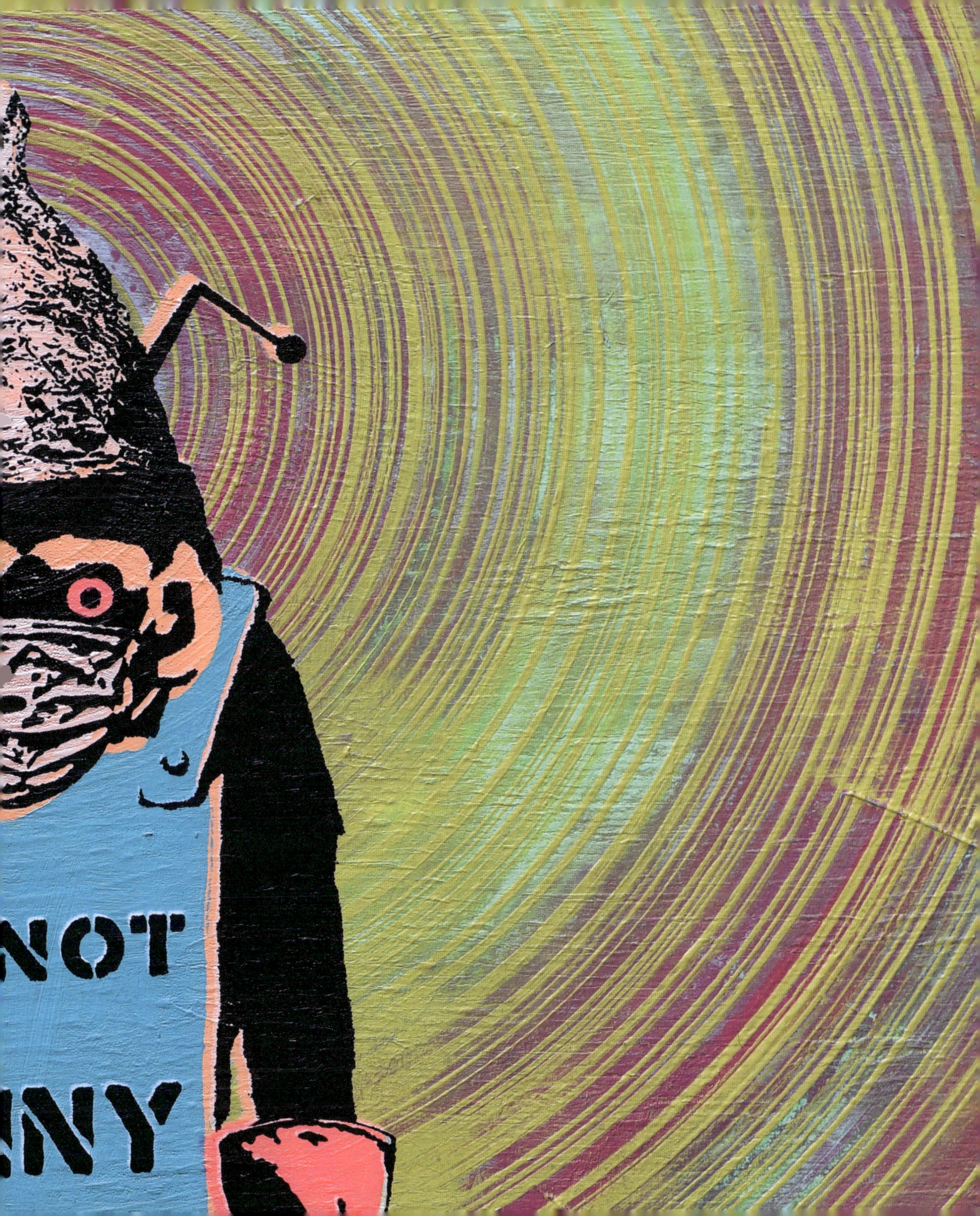

NOT
NNY

THE
DIVINE WIND
OF THE
THE NEW NOT BANKSY
REALISATION
BLOWS
IN THE
LAND
OF THE
RISING SUN
OCTOBER 2020

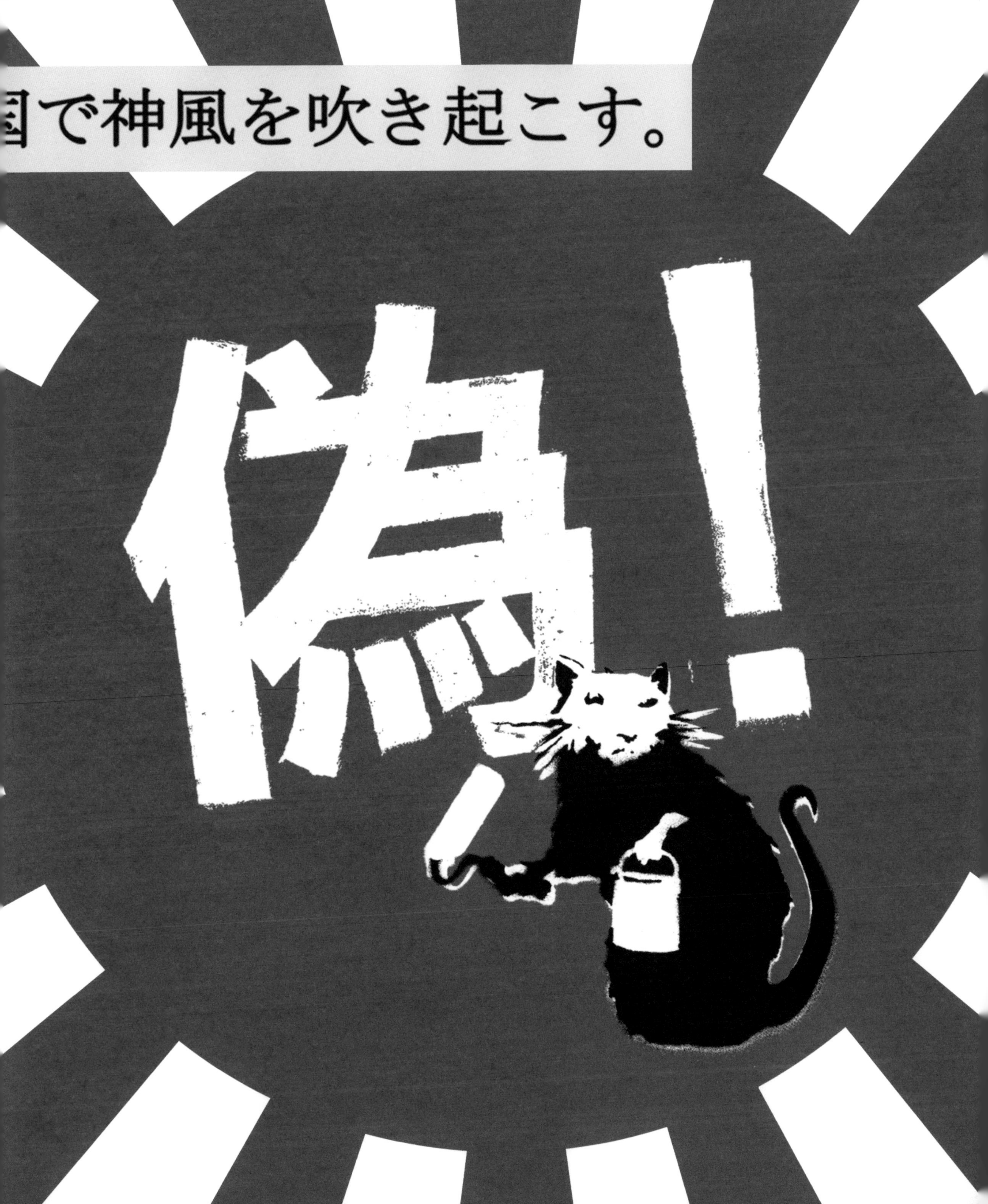
国で神風を吹き起こす。
偽！

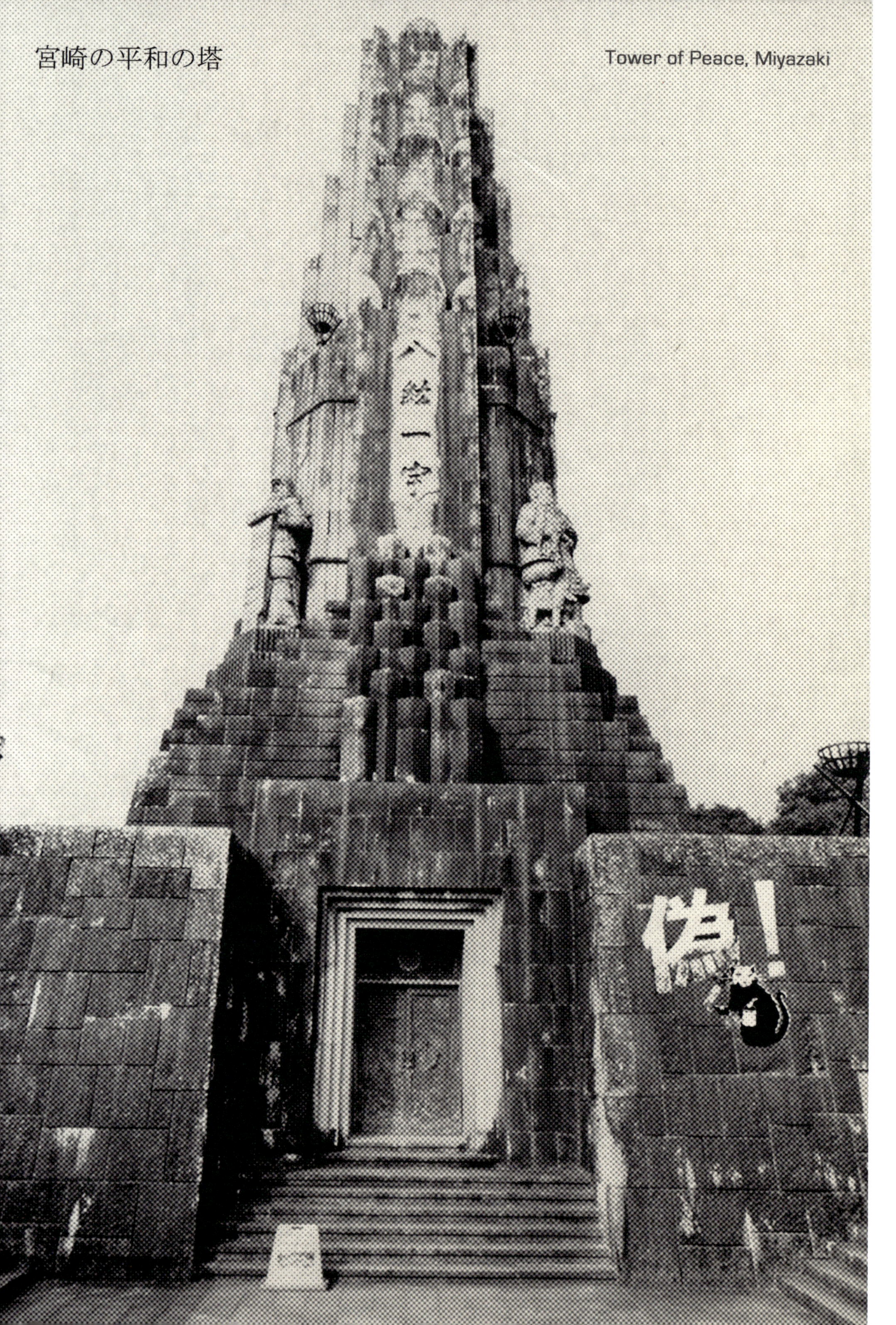
偽！

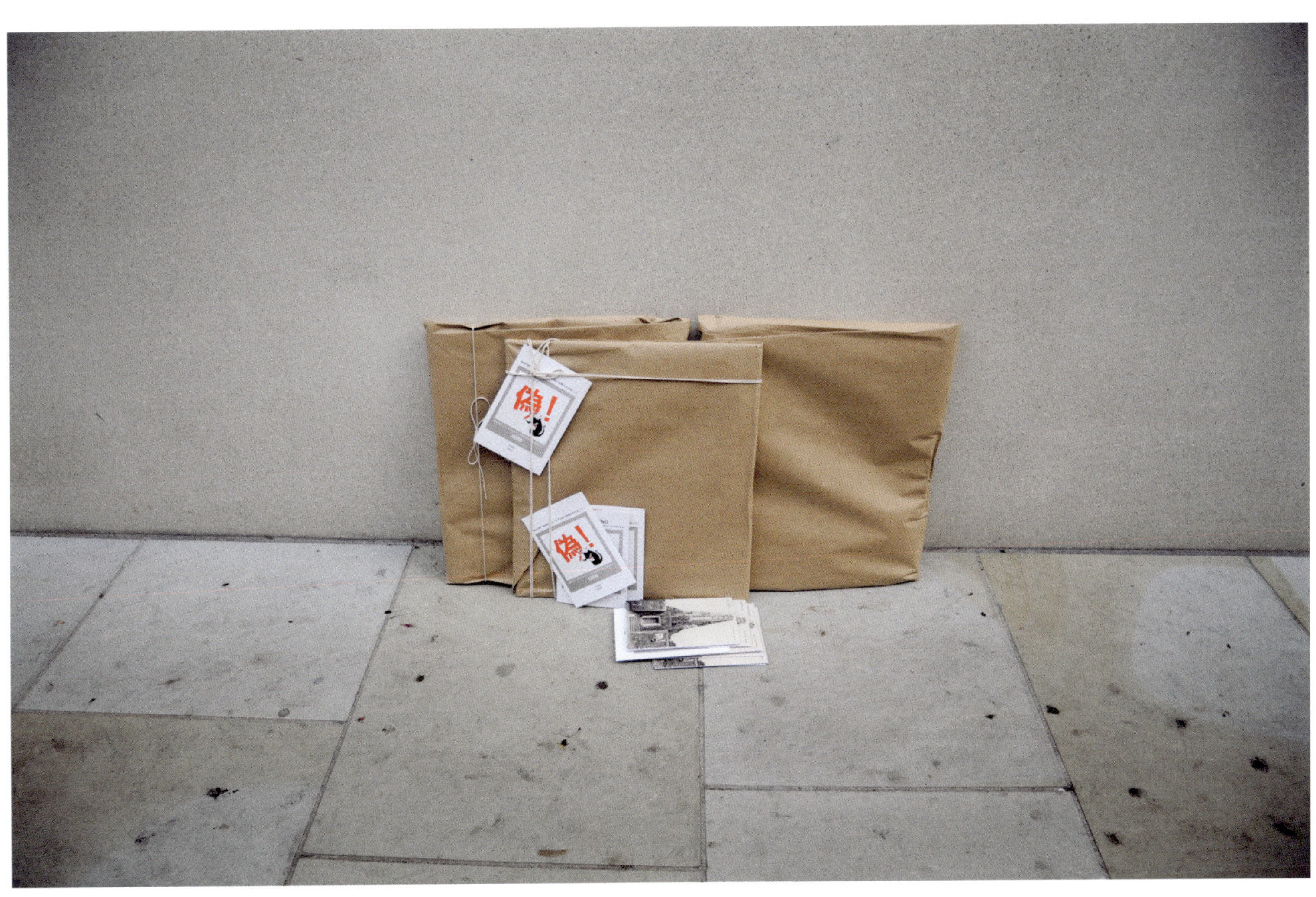

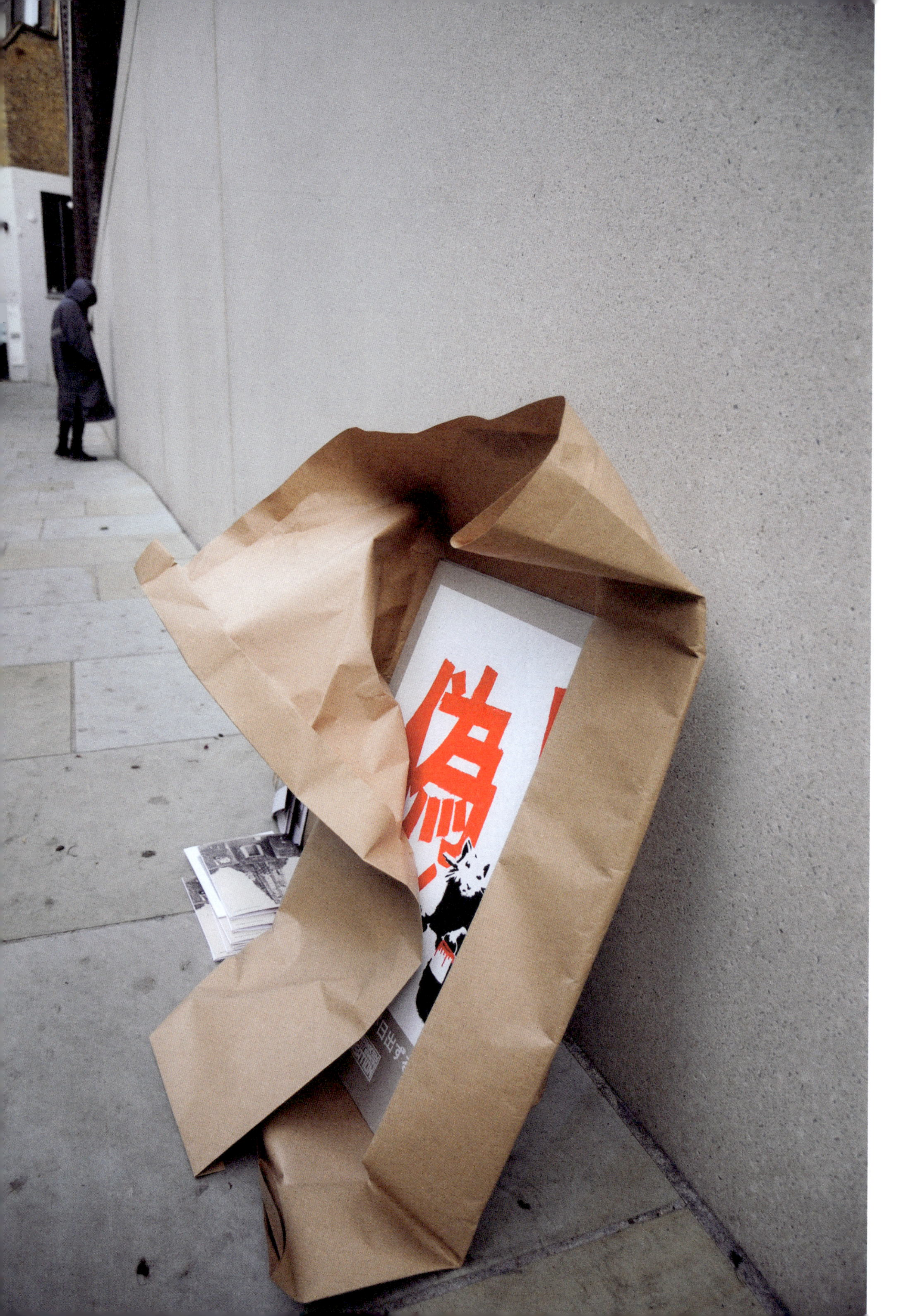

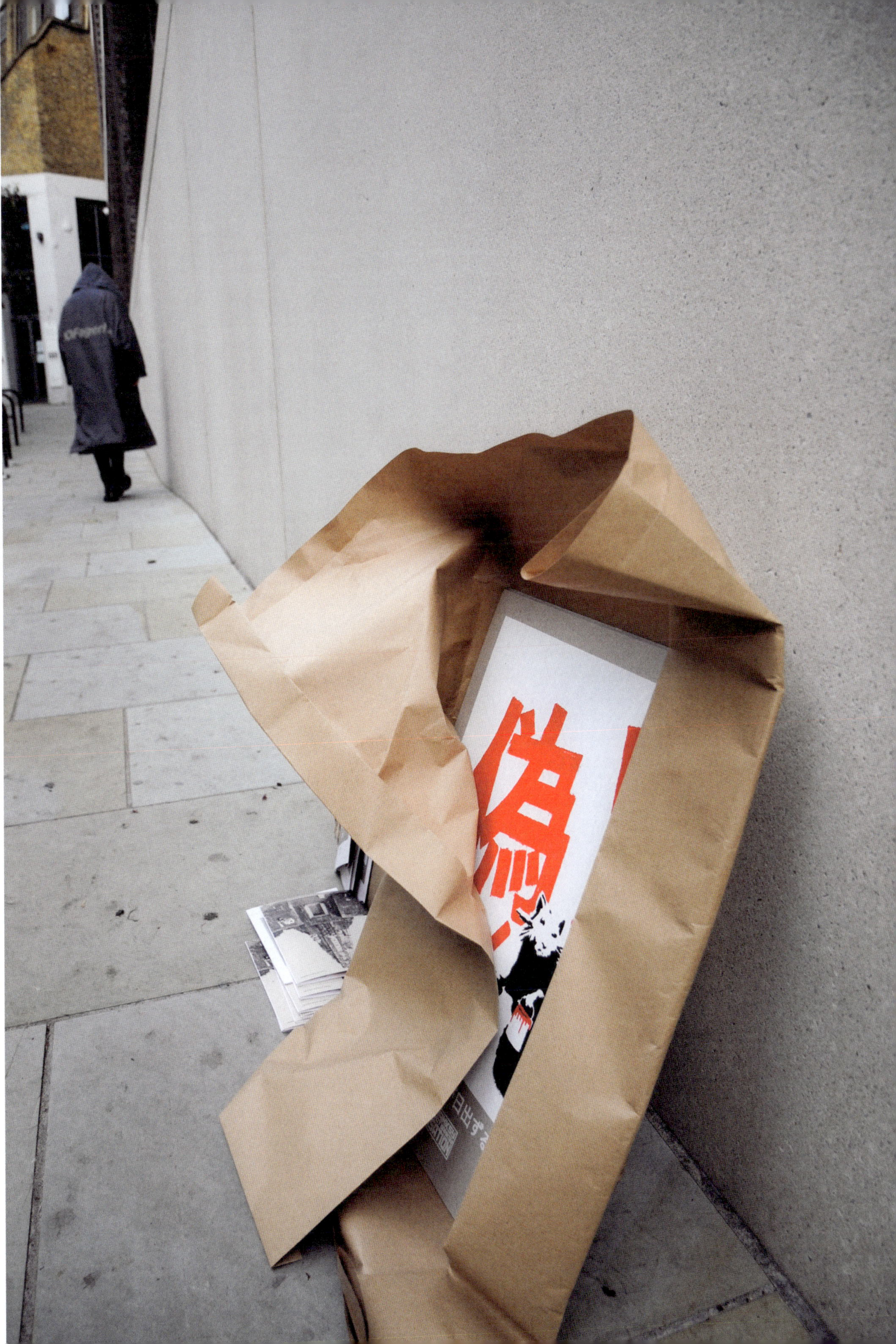

A new dawn is **NOT** upon us!

A new **NOT BANKSY** has appeared in the rising sun!

This is the new true story of the **New NOT BANKSY Realisation**.

In the shadow of the Peace Tower of Miyazaki a rogue non-collective of **Neo-No-Nothingist NOT-Art InActivists** has arisen to claim that **Banksy** is **NOT** from Bristol, that **NOT BANKSY** is **NOT** from Scunthorpe, that **STOT21stCplanB** do **NOT** exist, and that all three are in fact the invention of themselves: a Japanese **Radical-NOT NOT-Art** sect intent on destabilising the dominance of Euro-American Culture and exposing the Western orientated Art World as the calamitous force for evil it truly is. This rogue non-collective sect of **Neo-No-Nothingist Radical-NOT NOT-Art InActivists** is known as *Scorpion Thunderbolt of the 21*[st] *Century Plans C, D and E [STOT21stCplansCD&E]*.

With the publication of a **NOT BANKSY** screen print edition to be made and sold in Japan for the Japanese people, this normally inactive and secretive non-collective have made the following explanatory statement about their activities.

*"We **STOT21stCplansCD&E**, being a non-collective sect of **Neo-No-Nothingist Radical-NOT NOT-Art InActivists**, are the true **New NOT BANKSY Realisation**.*

*Our extreme form of non-collectivism was born of the unawareness (and a flaccid concrete irreality) in Japan that innovations in suppression could not exist without worthless inaction undertaken through deviant strategic disturbances. Whereas **Nothingism** and **Neo-Nothingism** liberated **NOT-art** in a chained discursive cage, it never liberated the **Non-artwork** as a material **Non-artifact** or the **Anartist** as **anti-creator**. Keeping the decentrality of "**Non-collectivism and Neo-No-Nothingism**" in mind, we capture and release two essential traits of **Neo-No-Nothingism** in Japan: the "don't do it yourself" spirit and the "anti-social engagement" in the unawareness of a broader public insignificance. Utilising these ever-negating pulses of disenchantment we publish this print as final proof of our disbelief in all Western (and non-Western) art. We tear it all down in our minds and rebuild nothing.*

We are Fake, You are Fake, Banksy is Fake, NOT BANKSY is Fake, This is Fake!

Long live NOTHING NOT!!"

STOT21stCplansCD&E, Miyazaki, November 2020

This statement was found with a pile of 250 prints on the doorstep of the Liberty lifestyle shop and cafe in Miyazaki, with additional instructions to sell the first 50 copies in Japan and export the remaining 200 to be sold to 'the West' through their longstanding co-conspirators, the L-13 Light Industrial Workshop.

AUTHENTICITY
NOT BY BANKSY BY THE NEW NOT BANKSY REALISATION

Just to be clear, all artworks by the **New NOT BANKSY Realisation** and associated activities by STOT21stCplansCD&E are **NOT** by **BANKSY** and the real **BANKSY** has nothing to do with any of the **New NOT BANKSY Realisation** non-collective sects, **NOT-Art** and **NON-artifacts**.

Made in Japan
Accept no imitations or fakes

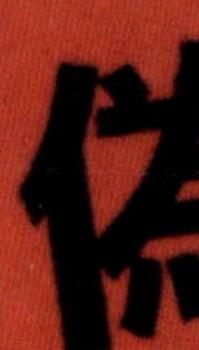

First Edition, December 2020
Published by Liberty, Miyazaki

Lib

思想を軸に、 「DON'T DO IT YOURSELF 」というメッセージを発信する。 その思いを込めたこの作品は、西洋諸国の芸術に対する我々の不信感を証明したものだ。 我々が全てを切り裂き「無」を作ってみせよう。

我々は偽物であり、あなたも偽物だ。 Banksy も偽物、NOT BANKSY も偽物。 これは偽物なのだ!

無よ、永遠なれ!

STOT21stCplansCD&E、2020 年11月、宮崎。

この声明は、250もの作品の山と共に、宮崎のライフスタイルショップ&カフェ「Liberty」で発見された。 最初の50部をLibertyで販売し、残りの200部を L-13 Light Industrial Workshop で販売する。

AUTHENTICITY

NOT BY BANKSY BY THE NEW NOT BANKSY REALISATION

念のために言っておくと、**New NOT BANKSY** によるすべての作品と **STOT21stCplansCD&E** による活動は **BANKSY** によるものではない。 本物の **BANKSY** はNew **NOT BANKSY** とは何の関係もない。

Made in Japan
Accept no imitations or fakes

未だ夜は明けず。
日の出と共に **New NOT BANKSY** が現れた。

これは、新たな **NOT BANKSY** が実在するという物語。

宮崎の平和の塔の影の中、**非虚無主義**を掲げ、**非芸術家、非集団組織**を名乗る、ならずものの一人がいた。 彼 は、**Banksy** はブリストル出身でない、**NOT BANKSY** はスカンソープ出身でない、**STOT21stCplanB** は存在 しない、全てはでたらめだと主張した。 アーティストとして急成長し、西洋が席巻するアート界の悪の真相を 暴こうとしている彼こそが、**Scorpion Thunderbolt of the 21st Century Plans C,D and E** [通称: STOT 21stCplansCD&E] だ。

日本の何者かによって作り、販売されている **NOT BANKSY** の模造品に対し、普段は口を閉ざす彼も次のよう に説明した。

我々STOT **21stCplansCD&E**こそ、真の **New NOT BANKSY** だ。

我々が**非集団組織**を形成したのは、日本での認知の無さと、アート界の行き過ぎた戦略的攪乱を、行動をもっ て抑制するためだ。 **虚無主義、新たな虚無主義**は、非芸術を小さな枠組みの中で解放したが、非芸術作品やク リエイティブでない芸術家を解放しなかった。 そこで、**非集団主義・新たな虚無主義**という二つの

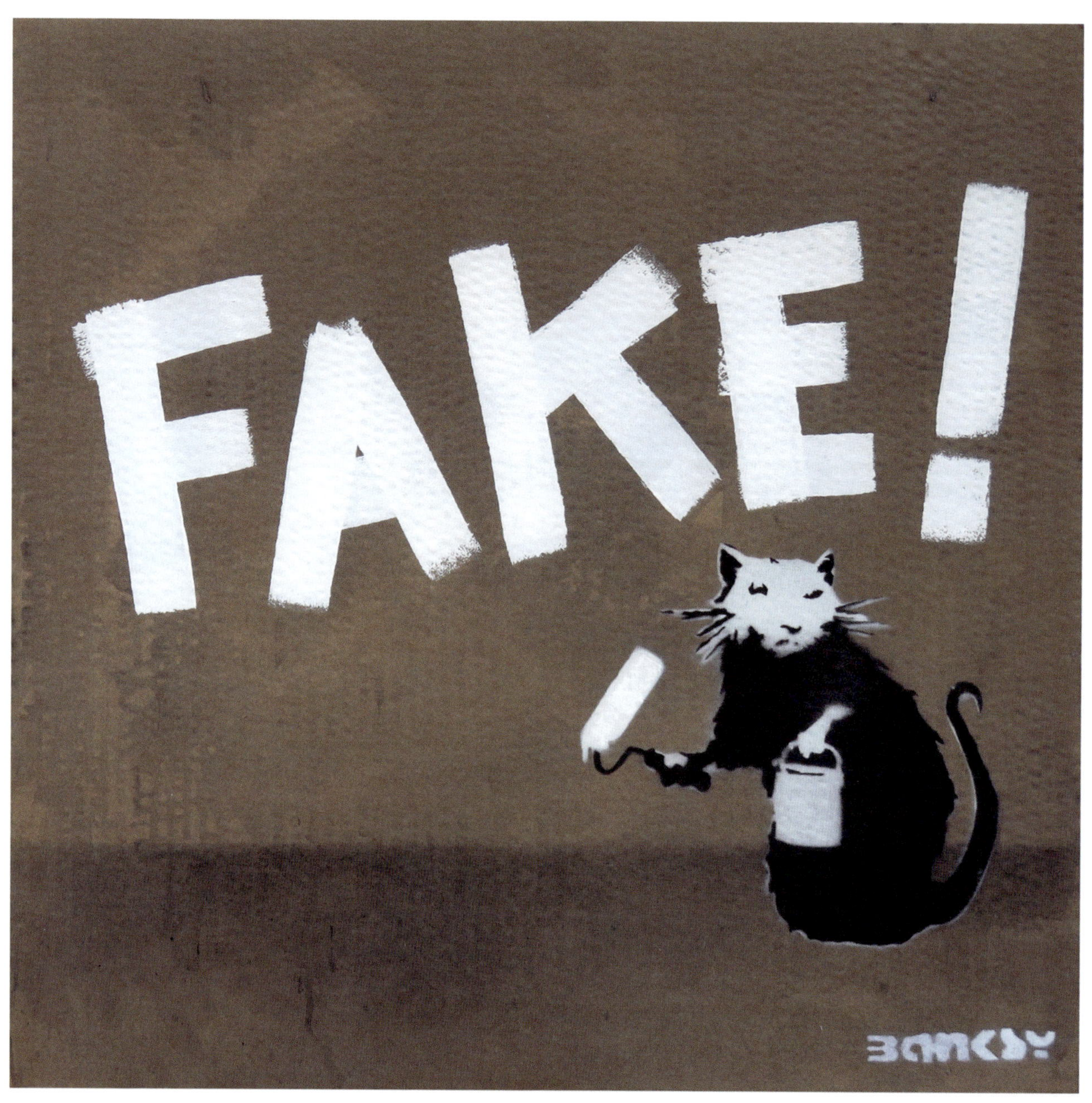

The "original" FAKE! circa 2008, household paint and spray paint on cardboard,
never made into an edition

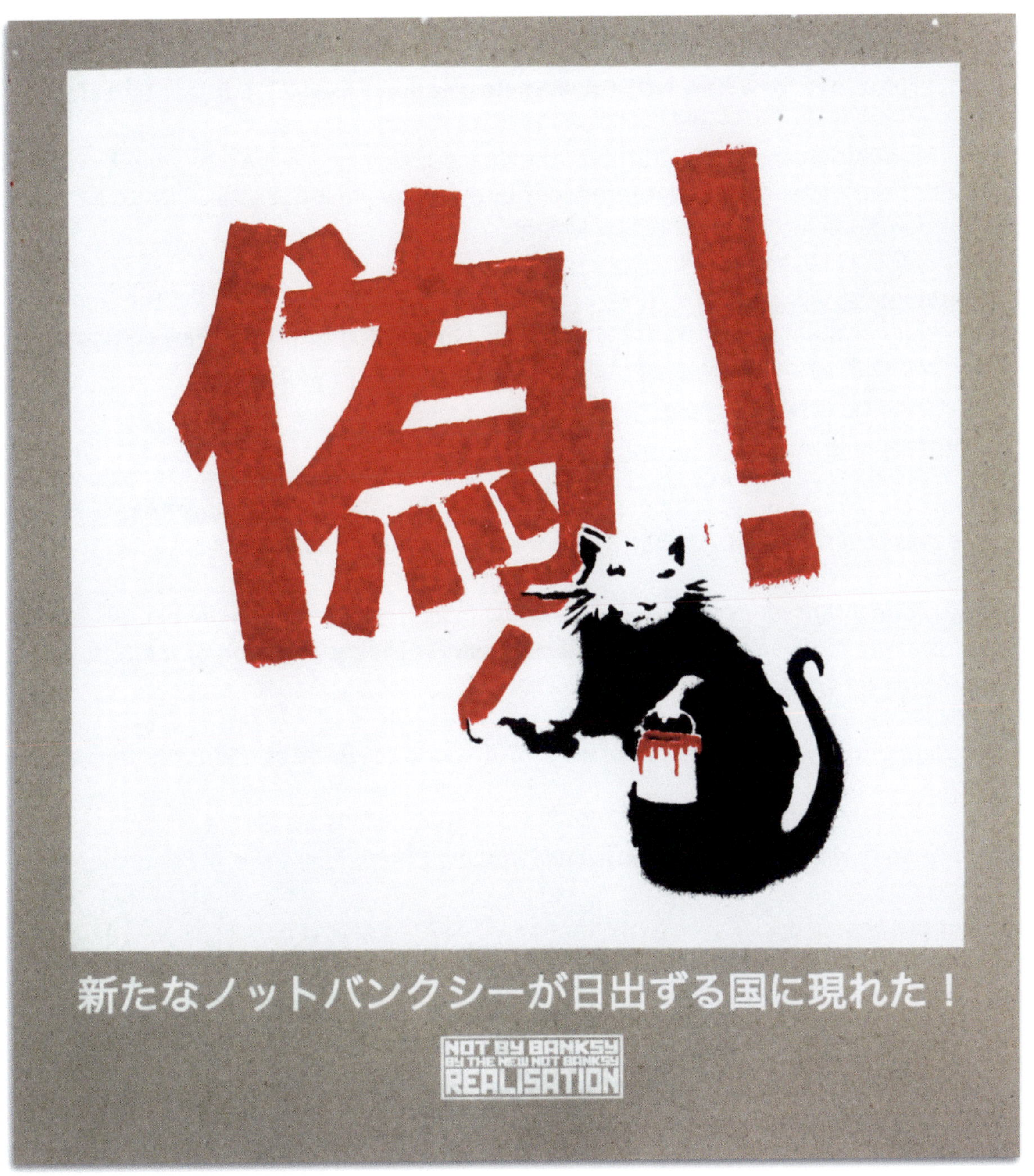

Japanese FAKE!, 2020, three colour screen print on grey pulp card,
first published and sold in Japan with some of the edition imported back
into the UK for sale in The West

STOP PRESS: Miyazaki, Japan 27/12/2020

New NOT-Prototypes for a New NOT BANKSY Realisation FAKE! 2nd Edition Revealed

Following reports that the FAKE! graffiti at the Peace Tower of Miyazaki had been removed by the authorities, large crowds gathered to mourn and protest this grave loss to NOT-culture, and a candlelit vigil was held overnight.

Representatives of "LIBERTY" the Miyazaki Lifestyle Shop and Café attended this vigil, and in the early hours of the morning were handed a package by a mysterious masked figure. Inside the package were 13 prints of many different colours and sparkles.

An accompanying note stated:

These prints are all test pressings for a potential 2nd Edition of the infamous FAKE! artwork by us, the declared New NOT BANKSY Realisation of the Rising Sun.

We kindly request that all 13 unique prints should be offered for ~~sale~~ to the people of Japan as tokens of unity and peace ~~(at a reasonable price)~~, for the propagation of the Neo-Not-Nothingist agenda of the New World NOT-Disorder.

This sale should take place on New Year's Day 2021, and the ~~price~~ of the prints should be ~~£250~~ each.

When these test prints have been ~~sold~~ we will make a 2nd Edition of the FAKE! artwork.

We will let the people decide which colours this 2nd Edition should be.

Over and out for 2020, may 2021 be better.

NNBR, Miyazaki

These 13 unique prints in many colours and sparkles will go on ~~sale~~ with Gallery DNA at ~~(put date and time here, to make the info revealed!)~~

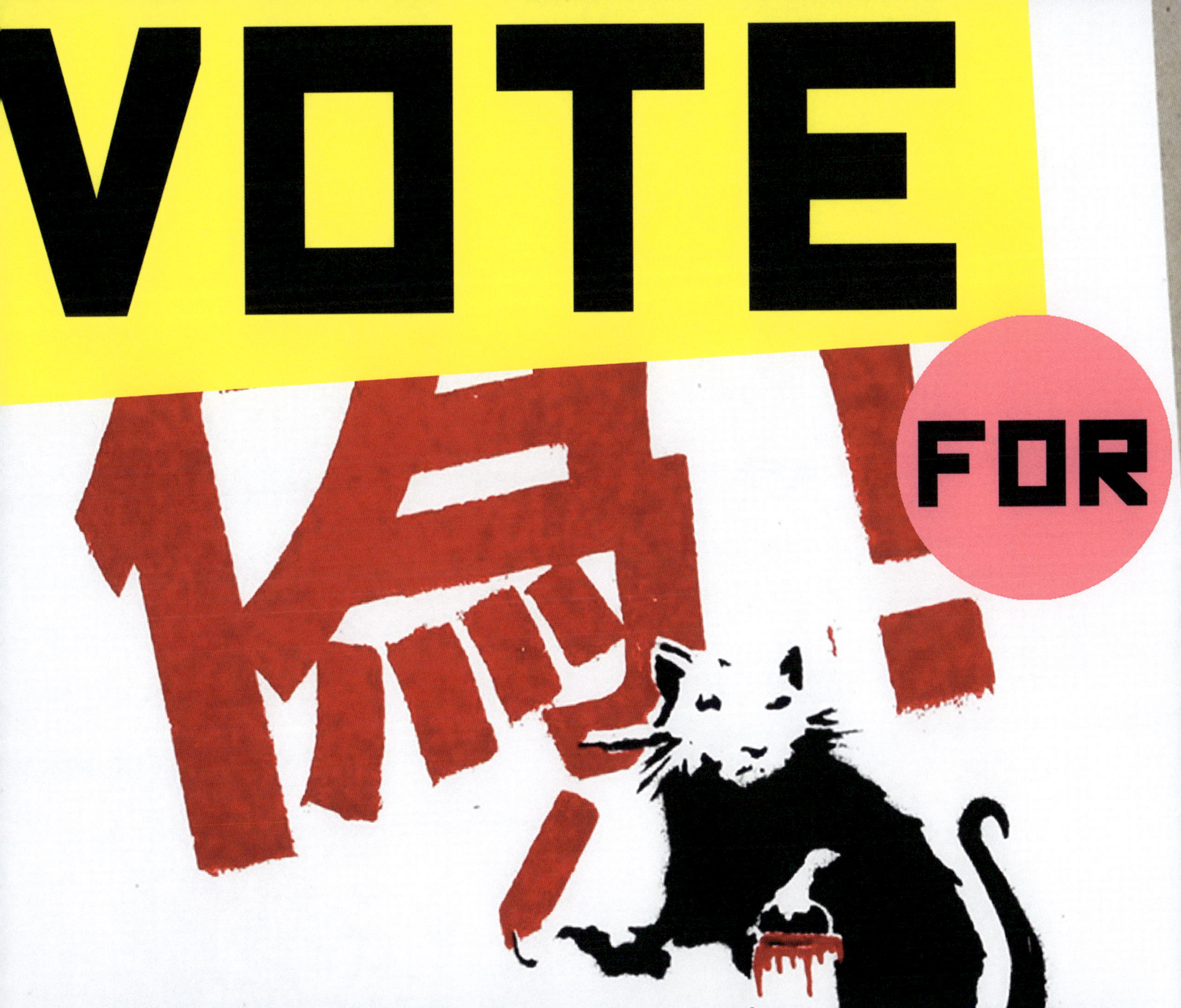

VOTE
FOR
FAKE!
A SECOND EDITION
COLOUR-WAY
BY THE NEW NOT BANKSY REALISATION
OF THE RISING SUN

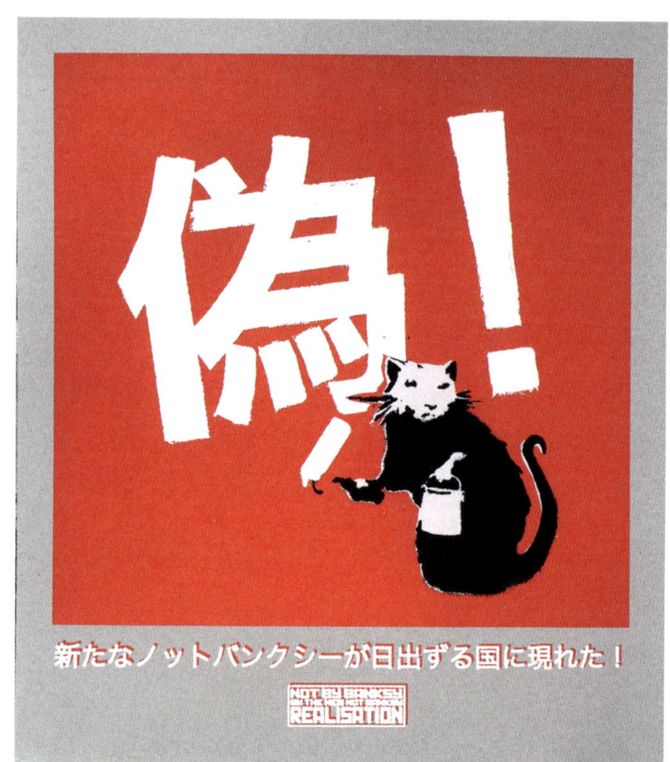

偽！
新たなノットバンクシーが日出ずる国に現れた！
NOT BY BANKSY
ON THE NOT NOT BANKSY
REALISATION

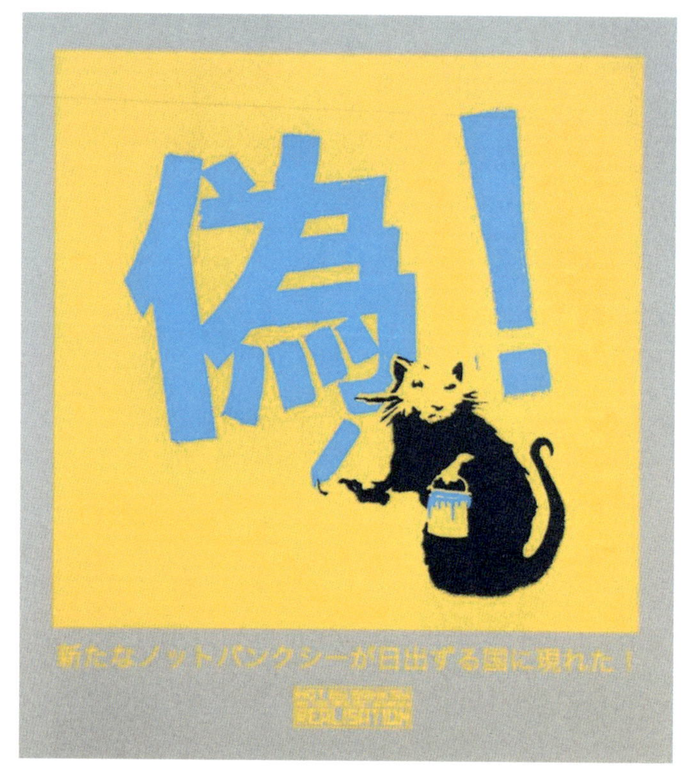

偽！
新たなノットバンクシーが日出ずる国に現れた！
NOT BY BANKSY
ON THE NOT NOT BANKSY
REALISATION

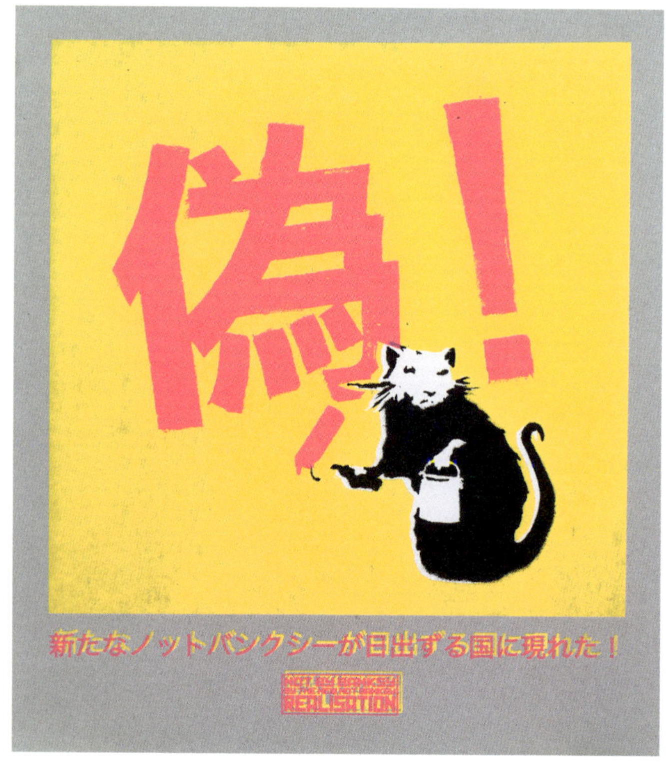

偽！
新たなノットバンクシーが日出ずる国に現れた！
NOT BY BANKSY
ON THE NOT NOT BANKSY
REALISATION

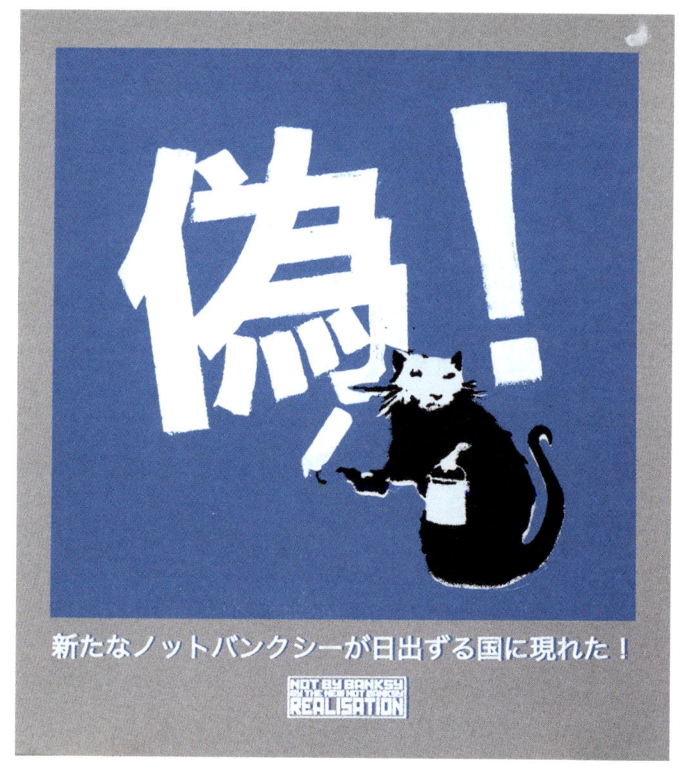

偽！
新たなノットバンクシーが日出ずる国に現れた！
NOT BY BANKSY
ON THE NOT NOT BANKSY
REALISATION

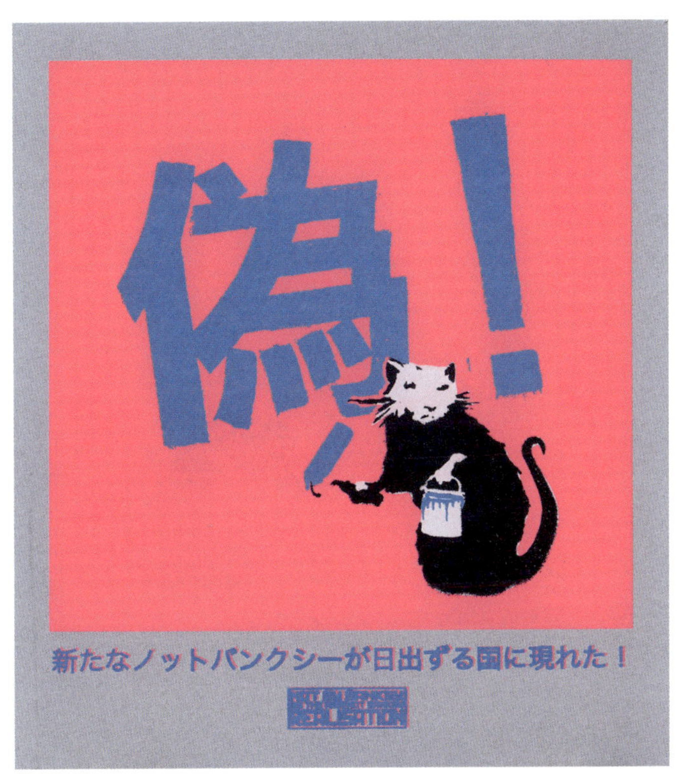
偽！
新たなノットバンクシーが日出ずる国に現れた！
NOT BY BANKSY
REALISATION

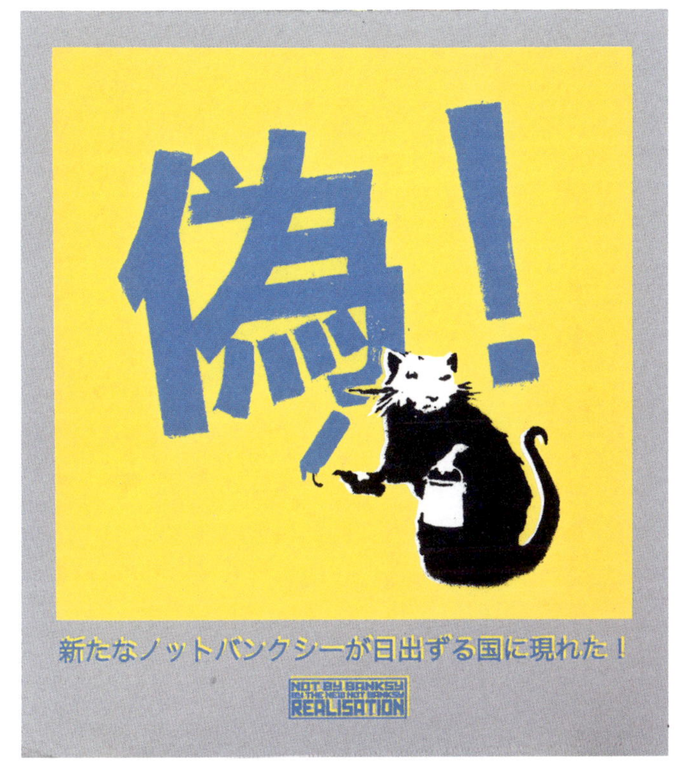
偽！
新たなノットバンクシーが日出ずる国に現れた！
NOT BY BANKSY
REALISATION

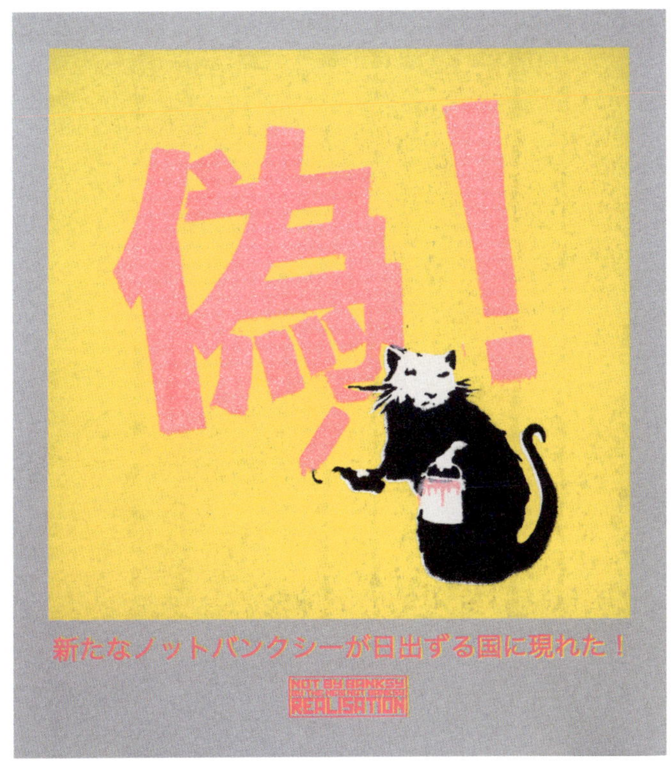
偽！
新たなノットバンクシーが日出ずる国に現れた！
NOT BY BANKSY
REALISATION

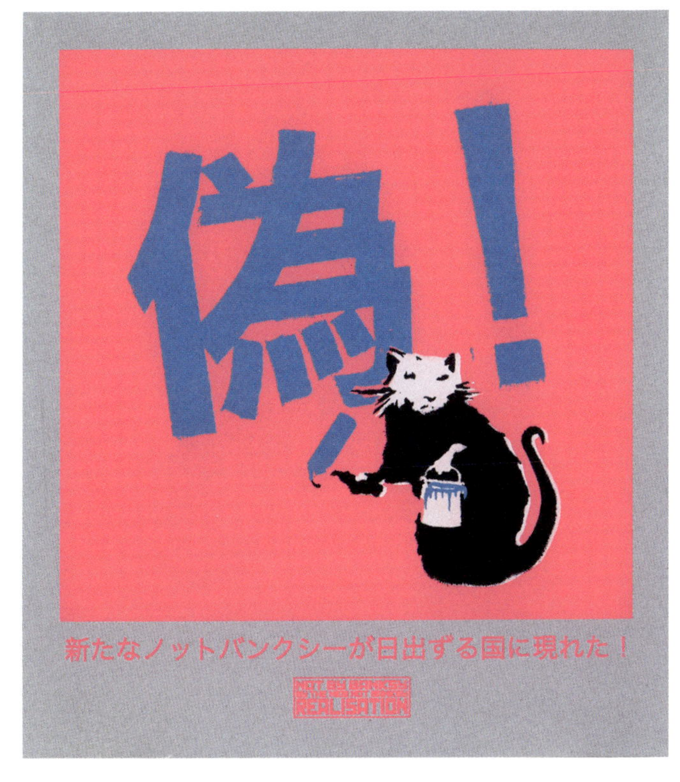
偽！
新たなノットバンクシーが日出ずる国に現れた！
NOT BY BANKSY
REALISATION

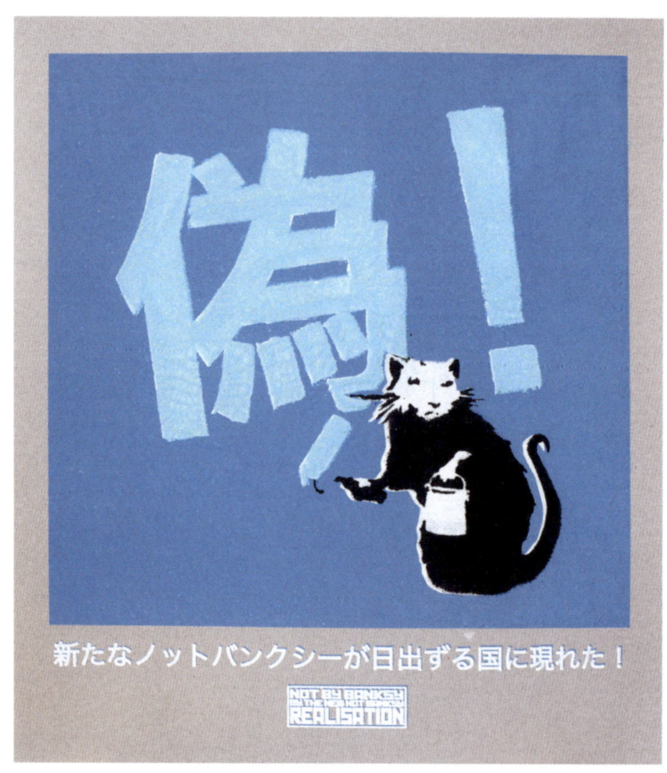
偽！
新たなノットバンクシーが日出ずる国に現れた！
NOT BY BANKSY
ON THE NEW NOT BANKSY
REALISATION

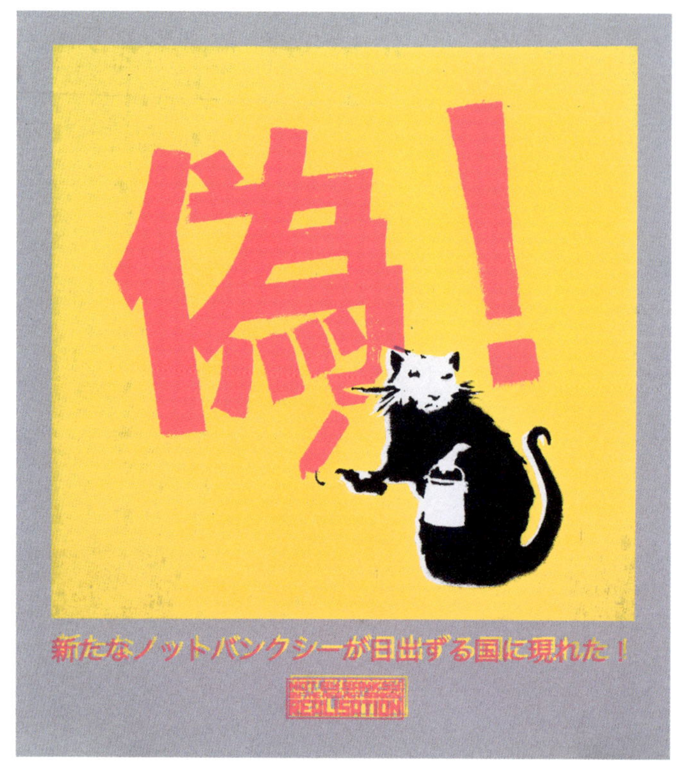
偽！
新たなノットバンクシーが日出ずる国に現れた！
NOT BY BANKSY
ON THE NEW NOT BANKSY
REALISATION

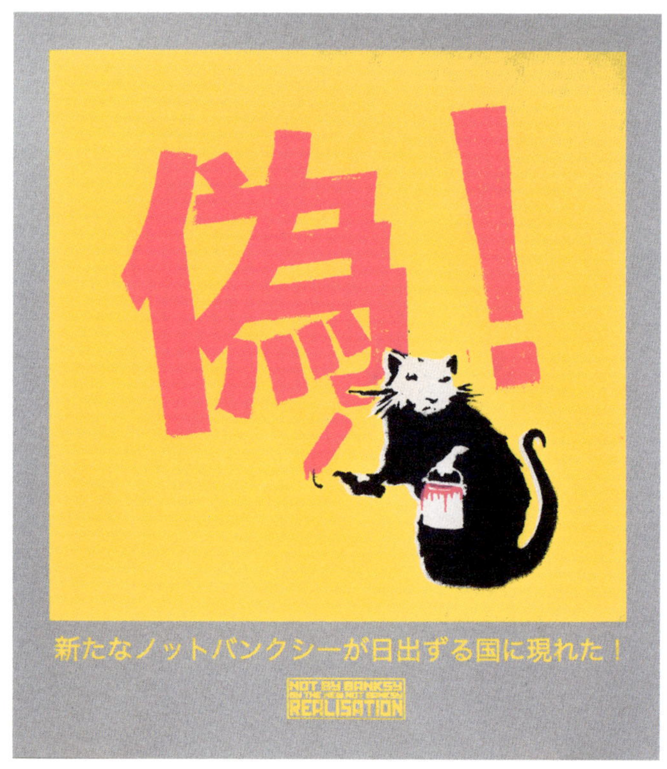
偽！
新たなノットバンクシーが日出ずる国に現れた！
NOT BY BANKSY
ON THE NEW NOT BANKSY
REALISATION

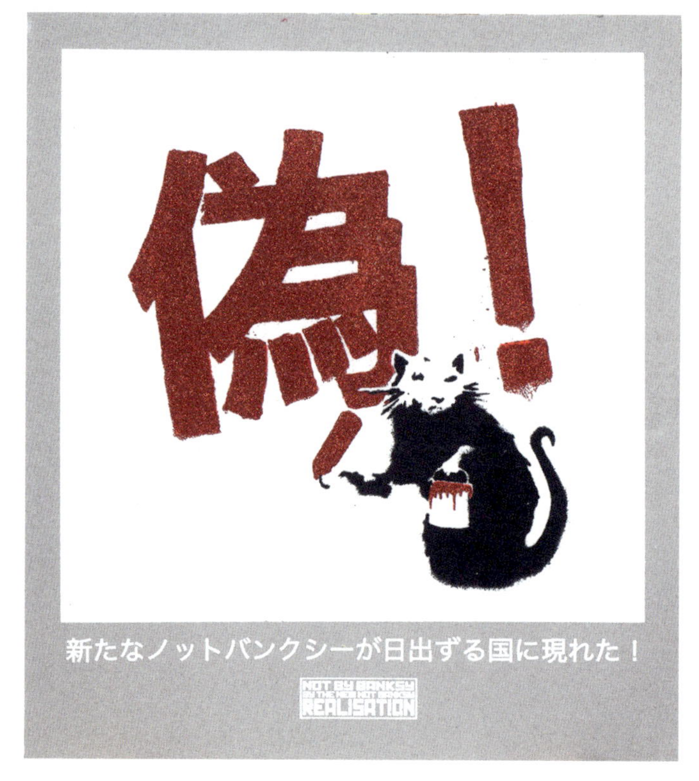
偽！
新たなノットバンクシーが日出ずる国に現れた！
NOT BY BANKSY
ON THE NEW NOT BANKSY
REALISATION

THE WINNER

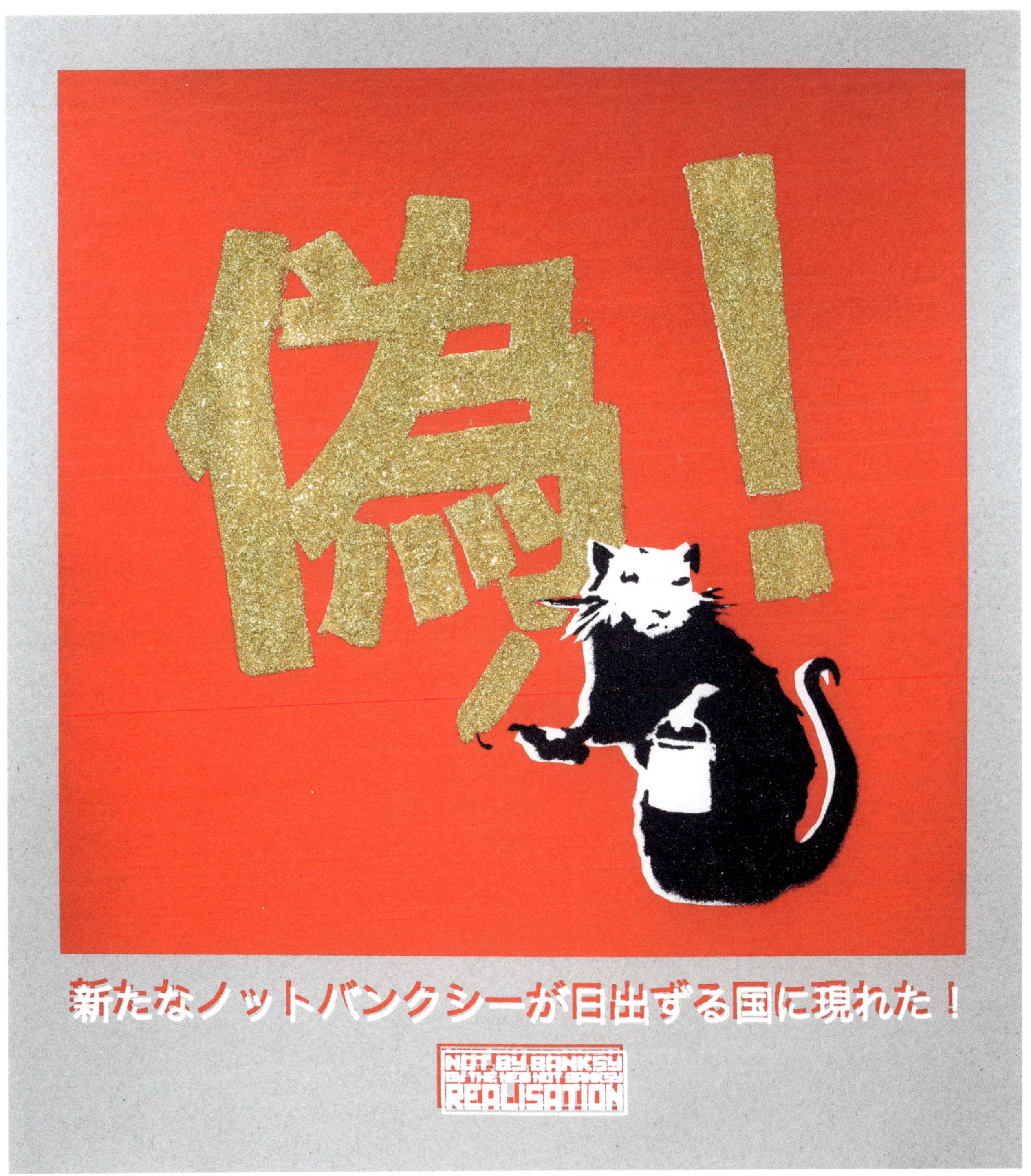

2nd Edition FAKE!

Four Colour Screen Print with Gold Glitter
on 1200 micron recycled grey pulp card
edition of 250 signed numbered and stamped on the back with COA attached
52 x 45 cm

SAVES THE WORLD

メッセージをもたらす
の
ラブ ピース
に
すべての生き物
グレート＆スモール

日本の友達が助けを求めました。地元の猫は虐待され、虐待されていました。彼らは、油で覆われた猫を報告し、助けるために何かをしなければならないと決めました。

彼らは「猫は私たちの敵ではありません。なぜそれを傷つけるのですか？」

ネズミは「私たちの敵はあなたの敵ではありません。なるがままに。すべてのものと平和に暮らす。また、昆虫、花、あなたの仲間の人間…そして私たちの多くの悪意のあるネズミのために親切な考えを考慮してください。敵を倒す最善の方法は、敵の友達を作ることです。みんなで一緒に暮らしましょう。」

日本の私たちの友達は、迷子の世話をしたり、悪い状況で動物を救ったりするのを助ける慈善団体を持っています。彼らは、私たち、新しいNOT BANKSY Realizationが、資金を集めて調和のメッセージを広めるためのプリントをデザインするかどうかを尋ねました。

私たち新しいNOTBANKSY Realizationは、彼らのためにこれを行いました。何か前向きなことをするために、私たちのネオニヒリストの何もないアジェンダを一時的に放棄します。これらの版画の販売によるすべての利益は動物を救うために使われ、私たちは喜んでお手伝いします。

日本には「朝のない夜はない」ということわざがあります。それは物事が良くなり、日の出が闇を消し去るようになることを意味します。

新しいNOTBANKSY Realizationには、「あなたが生きるために生きなさい、そう生きなさい！」という言葉もあります。それは無意味なナンセンスですが、それが可能な限り最良の方法で意味することを意味します。ですから、それも信じて、私たちがメッセージを広めるのを手伝ってください。

N.N.B.R. 2021年5月

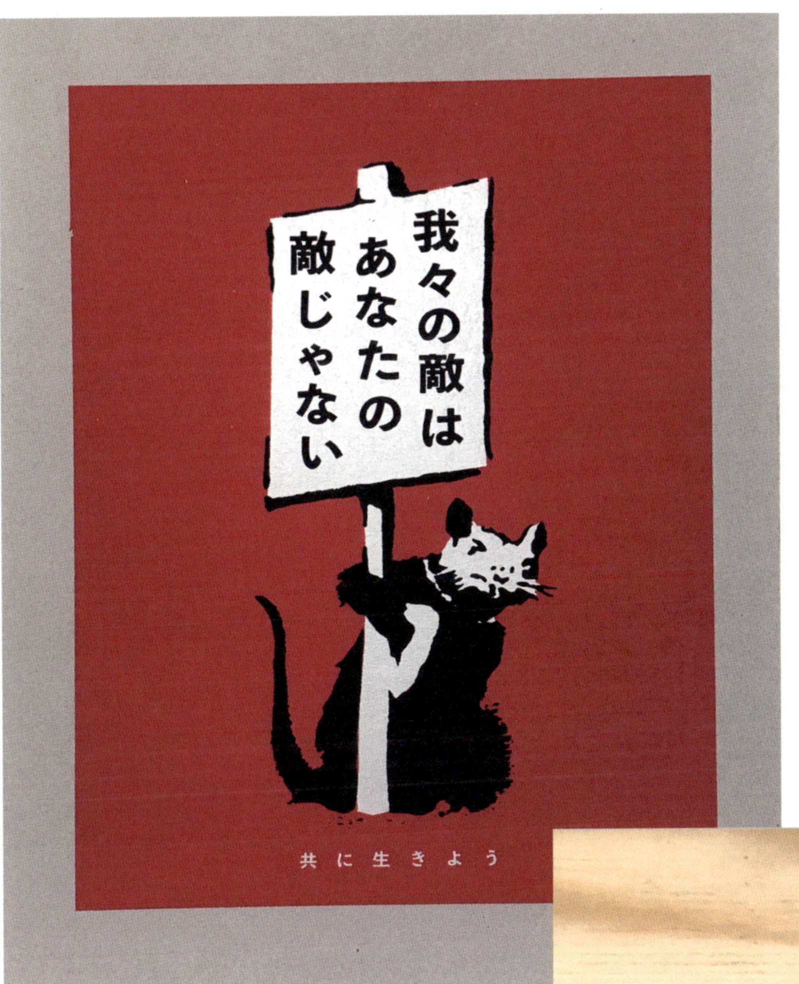

'Our Enemy is NOT Your Enemy' Prints on plywood and pulp card in support of an animal welfare charity.

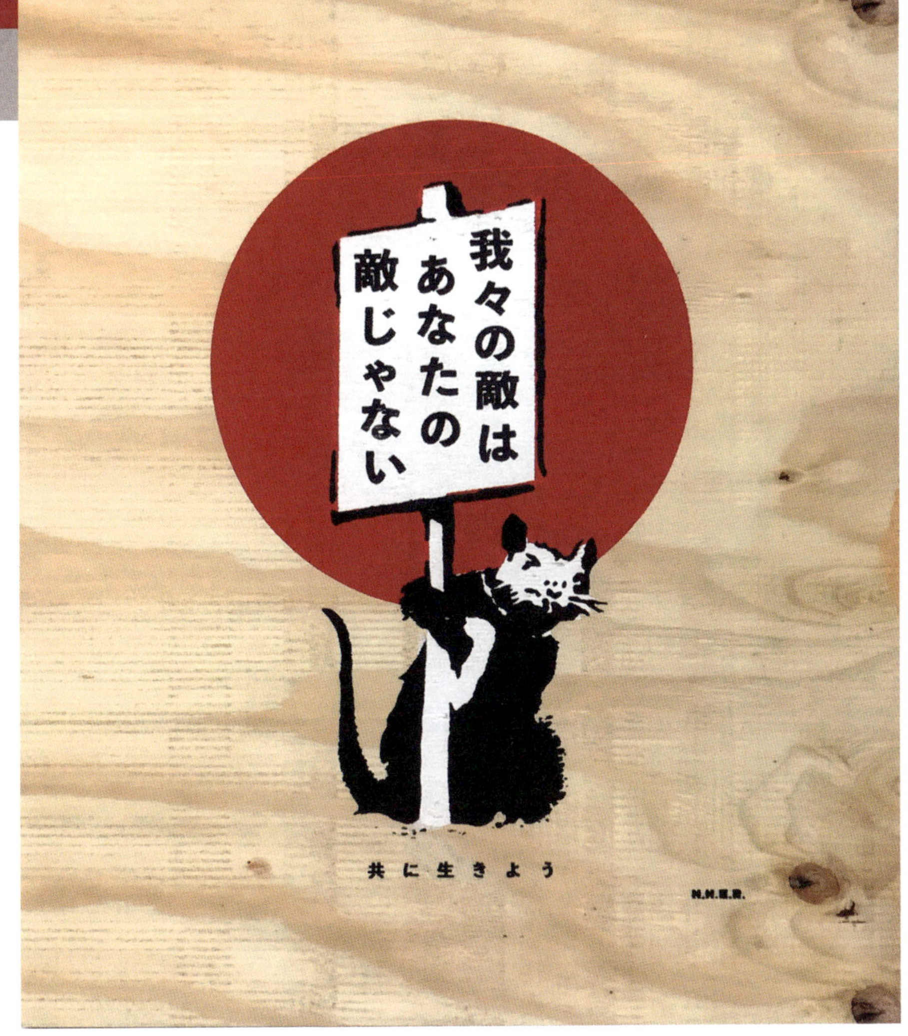

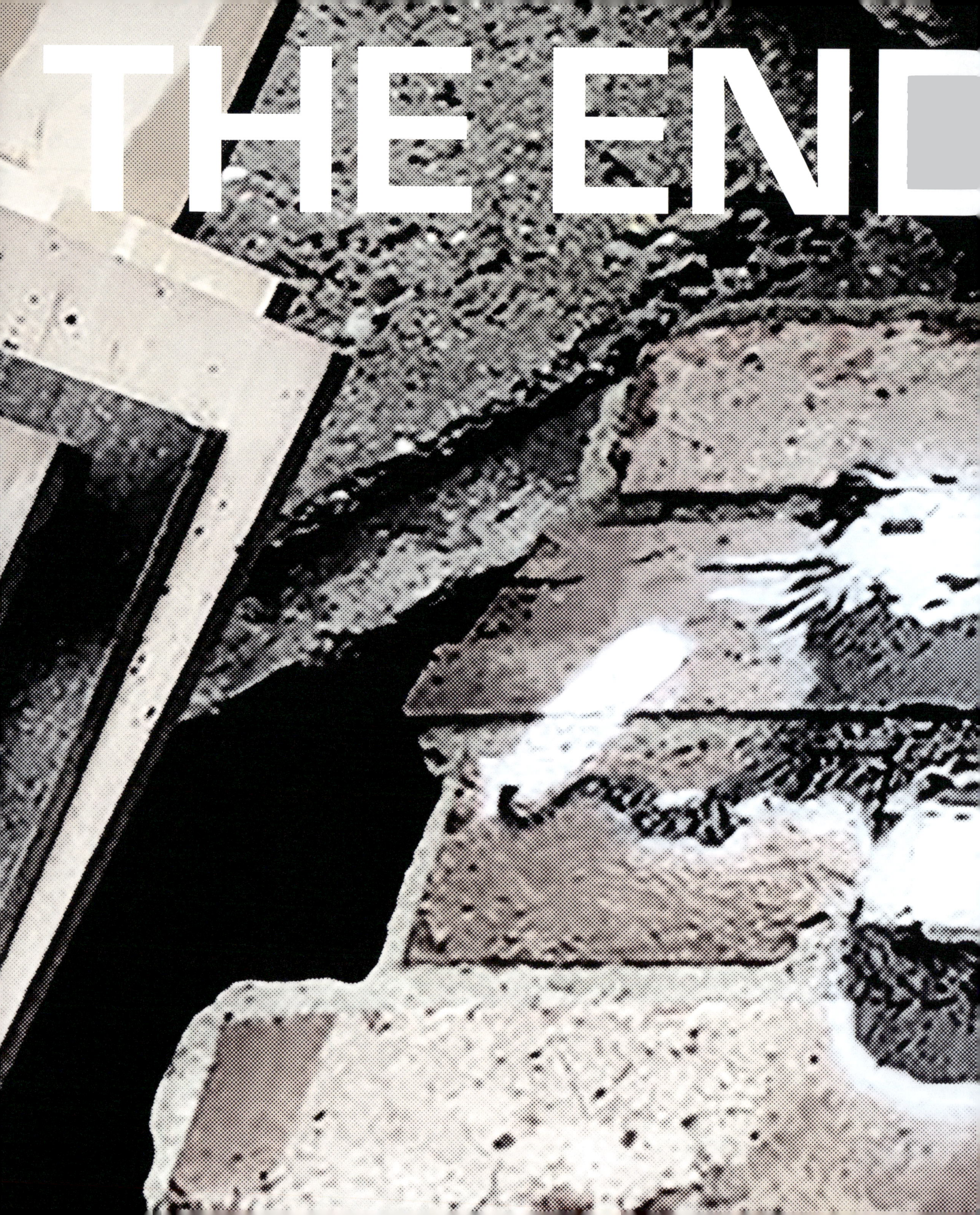

THE END

IS NIGH

BY THIS POINT
WITH THE GLOBAL PANDEMIC, BREXIT, CLIMATE
CHANGE, CRYPTO CURRENCIES, NFT'S, AND AN
UNCHECKED MONEY LAUNDERING ART MARKET
ROTTING EVERYONE'S BRAINS
THE DEMAND FOR NOT BANKSY WAS SPIRALLING
OUT OF CONTROL
SO
WE ONCE MORE DECIDED ENOUGH WAS ENOUGH
AND CONSPIRED TO KILL THE NEW NOT BANKSY
REALISATION IN A FABRICATED SELF-ANNIHILATION
STORY FED TO THE INTERNATIONAL FAKE NEWS
MEDIA CONGLOMERATES AND BURIED THEM IN THE
RUBBLE OF THE FAKE PEACE TOWER OF MIYAZAKI
BUT
OUT OF THE RUBBLE
LIKE A DIRTY GREAT PHOENIX OF
DOOM
SPRANG FORTH THE EMERGENT IS-NOT-BANKSY
AbNORMALCY OF THE 21st CENTURY GENERATION
Z WHO MADE MORE AND MORE AND MORE IS-NOT-
BANKSY ARTWORKS UNTIL THE WHOLE WORLD
WAS STUFFED AND BLOATED WITH FLATULENT
SELF-SATISFACTION AND NOT BANKSY COULD STOP
FOR A WHILE, HAVE A LITTLE LIE DOWN,
AND WRITE THIS MEMOIR

THE DEATH

OF THE NEW NOT BANKSY REALISATION IN THE LAND OF THE RISING SUN

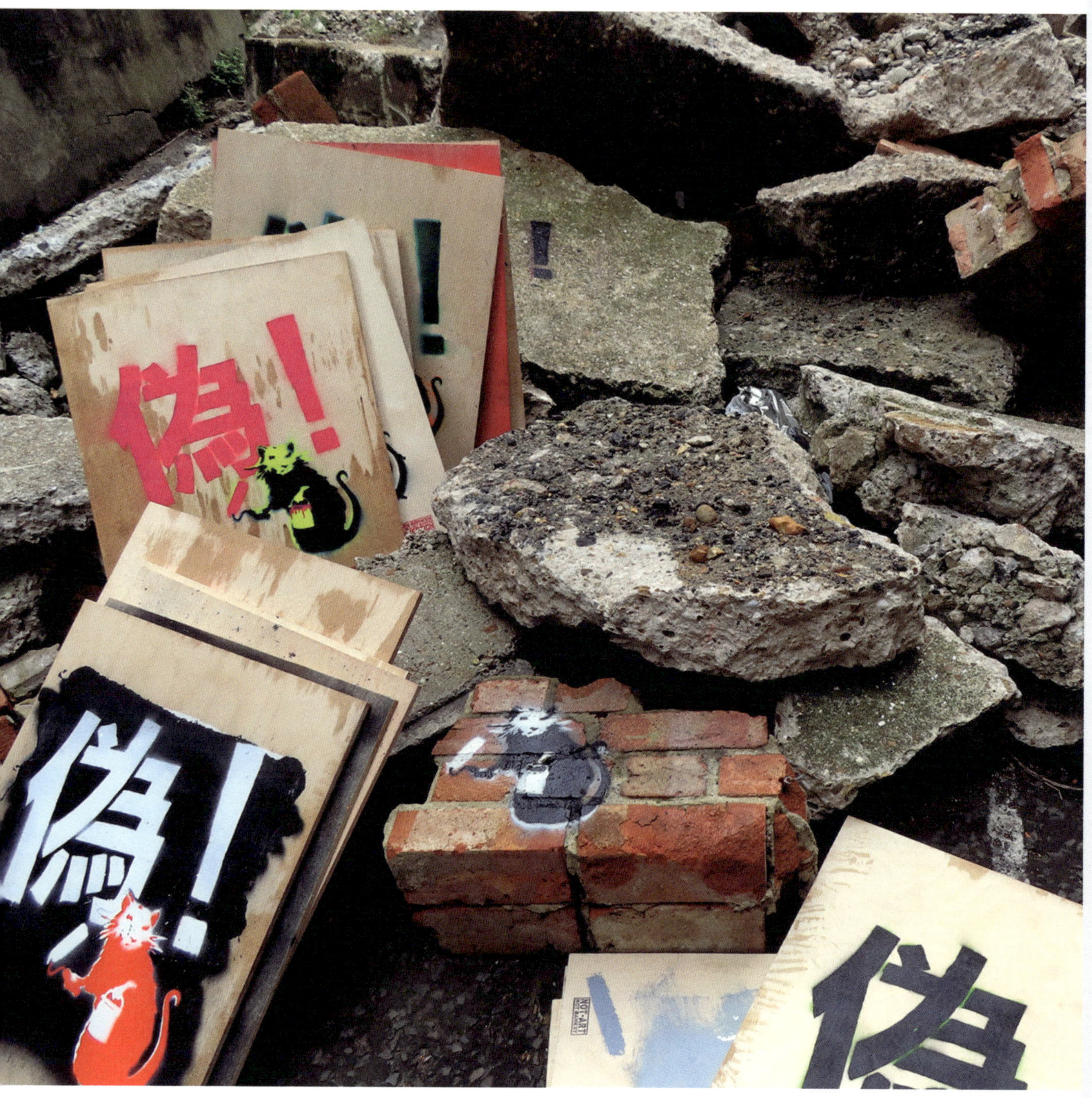

MIYAZAKI - CLERKENWELL
2021

日出ずる国のノットバンクシー、死す。

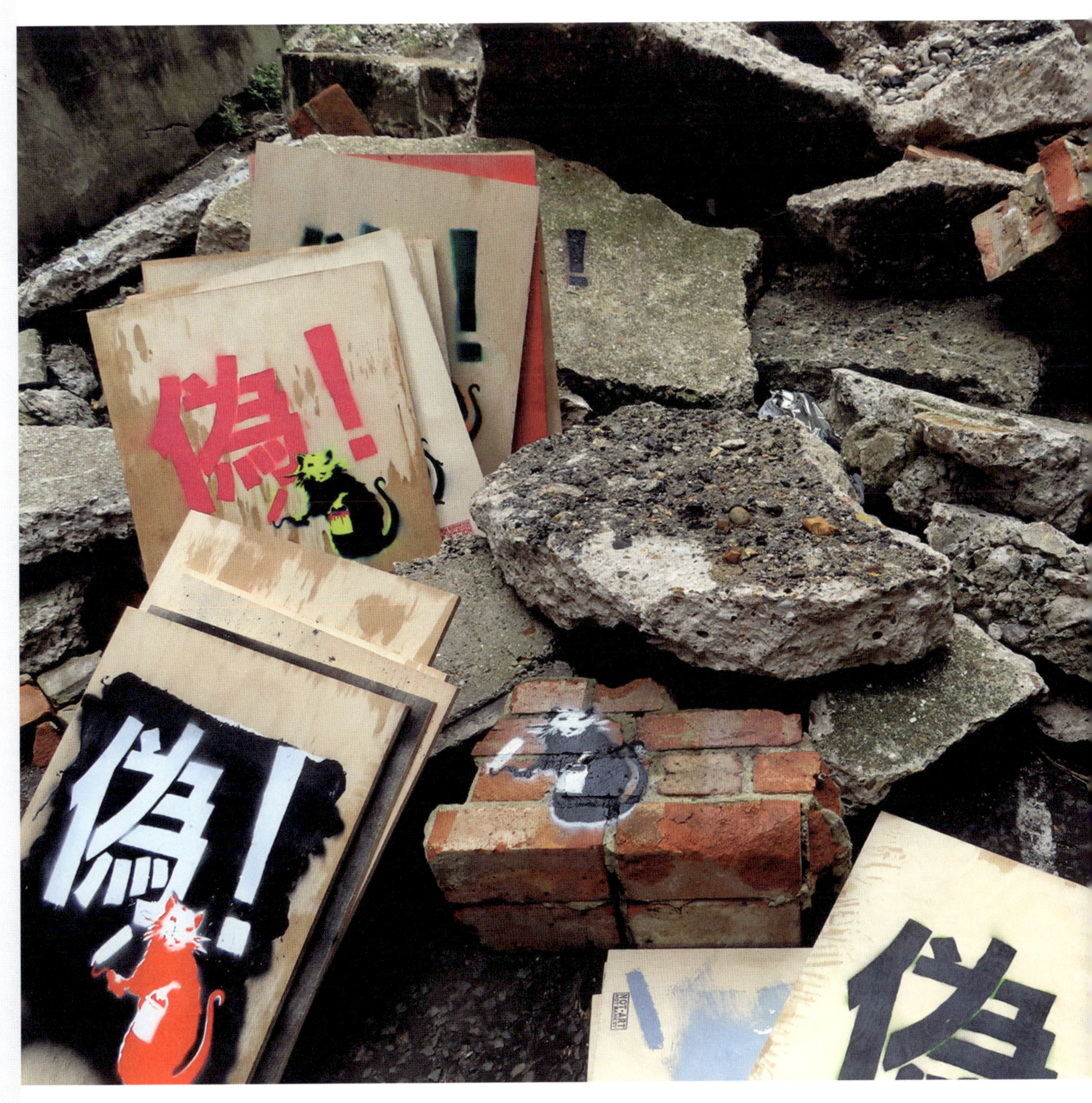

宮崎
CLERKENWELL
2021

Once again, a **divine wind** is blowing hard in the **Land of the Rising Sun**.

The **Peace Tower of Miyazaki** has been **destroyed!**

Left amongst the rubble of this destruction were 50 spray paintings featuring the infamous **FAKE!** design by the **New Not Banksy Realisation of the Rising Sun**, and a **note of annihilation**.

The **note of annihilation** contained the following message:

As **Neo-No-Nothingist NOT-Art InActivists**, we the **New Not Banksy Realisation of the Rising Sun** have rebelled against our inactive selves in a **despicable display of bloated bourgeois decadence** and taken **direct action**. We refute the **LIES** of this world. We denounce all as **FAKE!** We came into a **world of wanton war and destruction** and we leave a **world of wanton war and destruction**.

The Peace Tower of Miyazaki is **FAKE!** and has been a source of ideological discomfort for decades. It was originally built to glorify Imperial Japan's occupation of Asian nations and only later [in the 1960s] rededicated as the city's Peace Tower. The slogan carved into the tower: **"Hakko Ichiu" [Eight Corners of the World Under One Roof]** is not a message of peace but a message of conquest and subjugation. And, while we applaud such **duplicitous & tactical neo-not-re-imaginings** of what **IS** and what **IS NOT**, our **Neo-Nihilist Agenda** trumps all and dictates that even as a revised message of peace we the **New Not Banksy Realisation of the Rising Sun** have a **duty to destroy** it and ourselves.

We are guilty

You are guilty

Destroy all monuments

Destroy all Art

Destroy Everything and Do Nothing About it!

We crush ourselves in the rubble of the **FAKE Tower of Peace.**

The New Not Banksy Realisation of the

Rising Sun is dead!

As a parting gift and reminder that we died for you all, we leave you 50 **FAKE!** stencil paintings – each one unique in its own special way. 25 to be sold in Japan and 25 to be sold in the UK.

This will mark the beginning of a new era of the **IS NOT BANKSY**.

As the **IS NOT BANKSY** we are many. **We are everywhere.**

On this day, the 18ᵗʰ July 2021, an exhibition celebrating the work of the **New Not Banksy Realisation** opens at **Gallery DNA** in Miyazaki, Japan and the first 25 **FAKE** "originals" will be sold. Then tomorrow, 19ᵗʰ July 2021, on the day of so-called **'freedom'** and a return to the so-called **'normal'** in the UK, the other 25 will be sold via the **L-13 Light Industrial Workshop** and a new **IS NOT BANKSY** force will arise.

Out of the rubble of **fake peace** will spring the **Emergent International New IS NOT BANKSY AbNormalcy of the 21ˢᵗ Century Generation Z.**

Long Live the **Emergent International New IS NOT BANKSY AbNormalcy of the 21ˢᵗ Century Generation Z!**

AUTHENTICITY
NOT BY BANKSY BY THE NEW NOT BANKSY REALISATION

Just to be clear, all artworks by the **New NOT BANKSY Realisation** and associated activities by **STOT21stCplansCD&E** are **NOT** by **BANKSY** and the real **BANKSY** has nothing to do with any of the **New NOT BANKSY Realisation** non-collective sects, **NOT-Art** and **NON-artifacts.**

Made in Japan and Clerkenwell
Accept no imitations or fakes

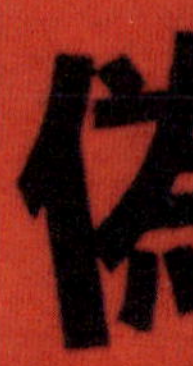

Published on the occasion of the exhibition
Lying, Cheating, Stealing and the Death of Art in the Land of the Rising Sun

L
Lib
Galle

！

at LIBERTY / GALLERY D.N.A
5-1 Shinjo-cho Miyazaki-shi Miyazaki Japan

13

rty

D.N.A

忘れぬため、我々は50枚の「偽!」のペインティングを用意した。日本で25

枚、英国で25枚販売する。

そして、ここから「NOT BANKSY」の新たな時代が始まる。我々は、幾重にも存在し、どこにだって現れる。

2021年7月18日、宮崎のGallery DNAで「the New Not Banksy Realisation」の最後の作品を記念した展覧会が開かれ、25枚の「偽!」が最初に販売される。そして明日、2021年7月19日、「自由」が訪れ、英国が「普通」に戻る日に、残りの25枚がL-13 Light Industrial Workshopで販売され、新たなNOT BANKSYが誕生する。

偽りだらけの平和の瓦礫の中から「Emergent International New IS NOT BANKSY AbNormalcy of the 21st Century Generation Z」として蘇る。

Emergent International New IS NOT BANKSY AbNormalcy of the 21st Century Generation Z、万歳!

AUTHENTICITY

NOT BY BANKSY BY THE NEW NOT BANKSY REALISATION

念のために言っておくと、**New NOT BANKSY** によるすべての作品と **STOT21stCplansCD&E** による活動は **BANKSY** によるものではない。本物の **BANKSY** は **New NOT BANKSY** とは何の関係もない。

Made in Japan and Clerkenwell
Accept no imitations or fakes

再び、日出ずる国で神風が吹き荒れる。

宮崎の平和の塔が破壊された。

瓦礫の中に残されていたのは「the New Not Banksy Realisation of the Rising Sun」による、悪名高きデザイン「偽!」をモチーフとした50枚のペインティング。そして、消滅を意味する謎のメッセージだ。

そのメッセージには次のような内容が記されていた。

非虚無主義を掲げ、非芸術家である我々「the New Not Banksy Realisation of the Rising Sun」は、肥大した富裕層の卑劣な行為の中で、為す術もない自らへの戒めとして、行動に移した。我々はこの世の全ての嘘に抵抗し、そのすべてが偽物だと糾弾する。そして、無謀な戦争と破壊の世界に別れを告げる。

宮崎の平和の塔は偽物だ。何十年もの間、イデオロギー的な違和感の原因ともなっている。本来は、日本がアジア諸国を占領したことを誇示するために建てられたものだが、その後(1960年代)、宮崎市の平和のシンボルとして再建された。塔に刻まれる「八紘一宇」の文字は、平和へのメッセージではなく、征服と支配の意味合いを持つ。その嘘と誠の二転三転する陳腐な発想に拍手を送りながらも、それを自らと共に破壊する義務がある。

私たちは罪であり、あなたは罪だ。

すべての石碑を破壊し、すべての芸術を破壊する。

すべてを破壊し放棄する。我々は、偽物の「平和の塔」の瓦礫の中で、自らをも破壊する。そう、the New Not Banksy Realisation of the Rising Sun は死んだのだ。この悲劇を

FAKE
ORIGINALS

BY THE
REAL

NOT BANKSY
FRONT

IN THE LAND
OF THE

RISING SUN

JULY 2021

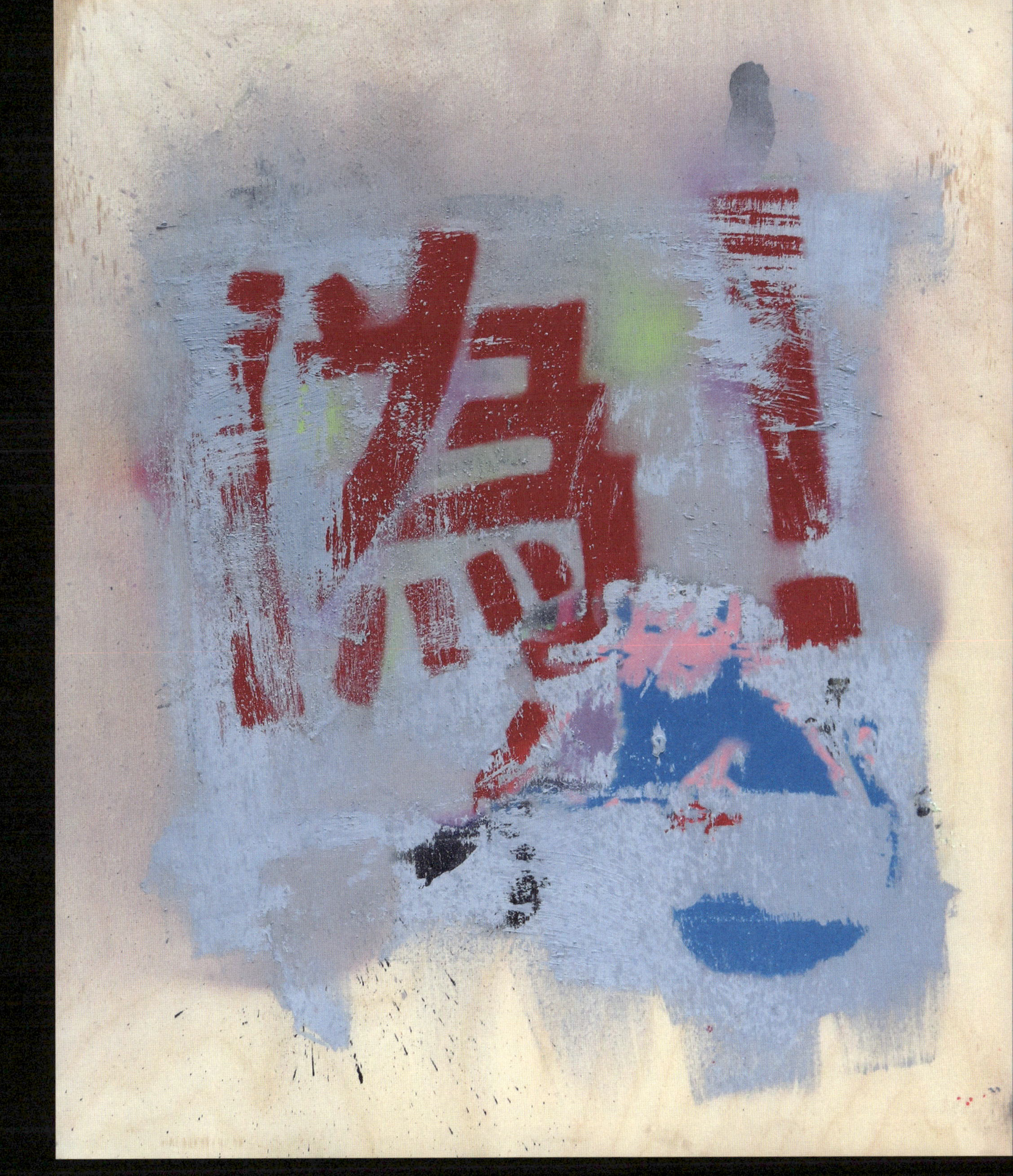

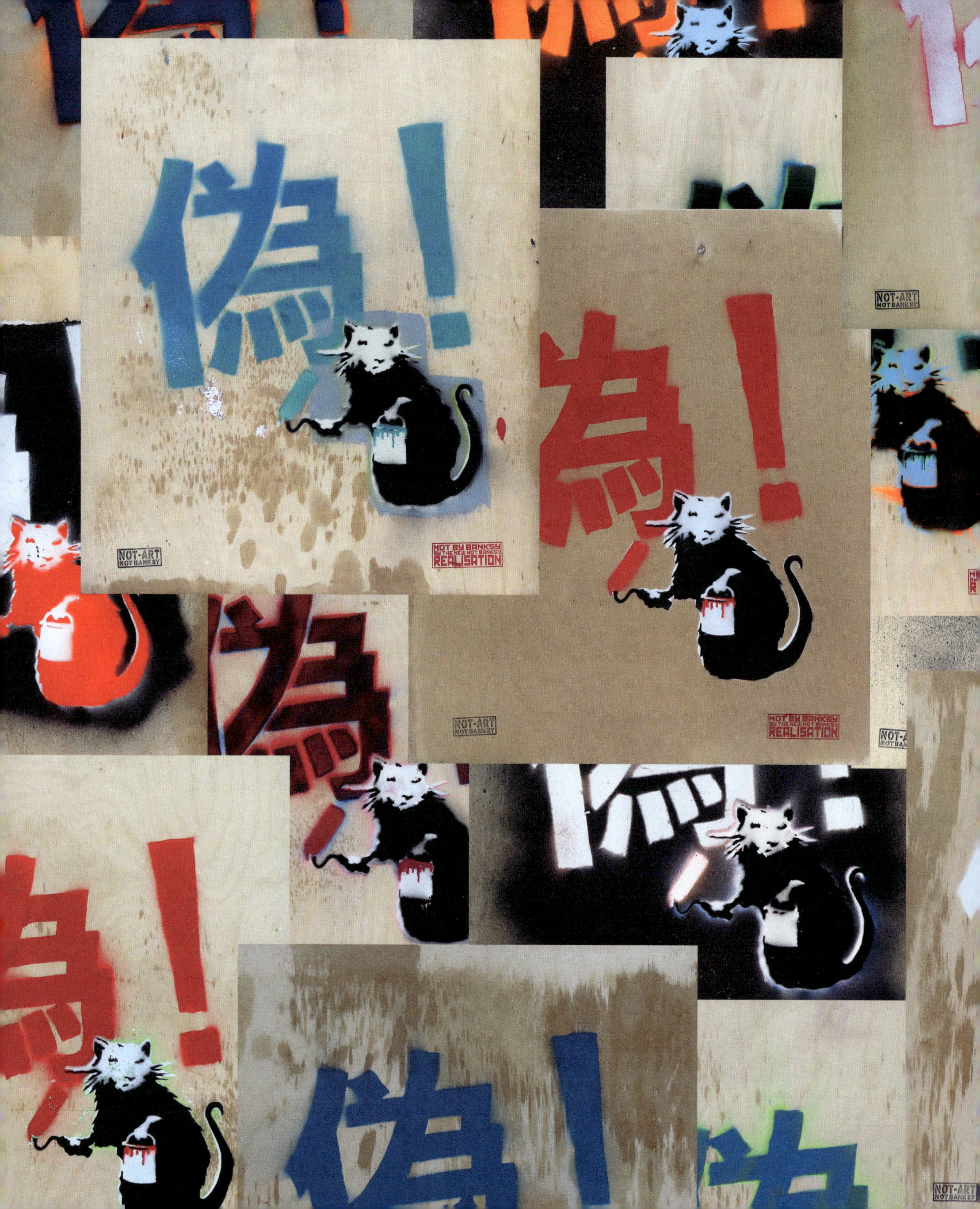

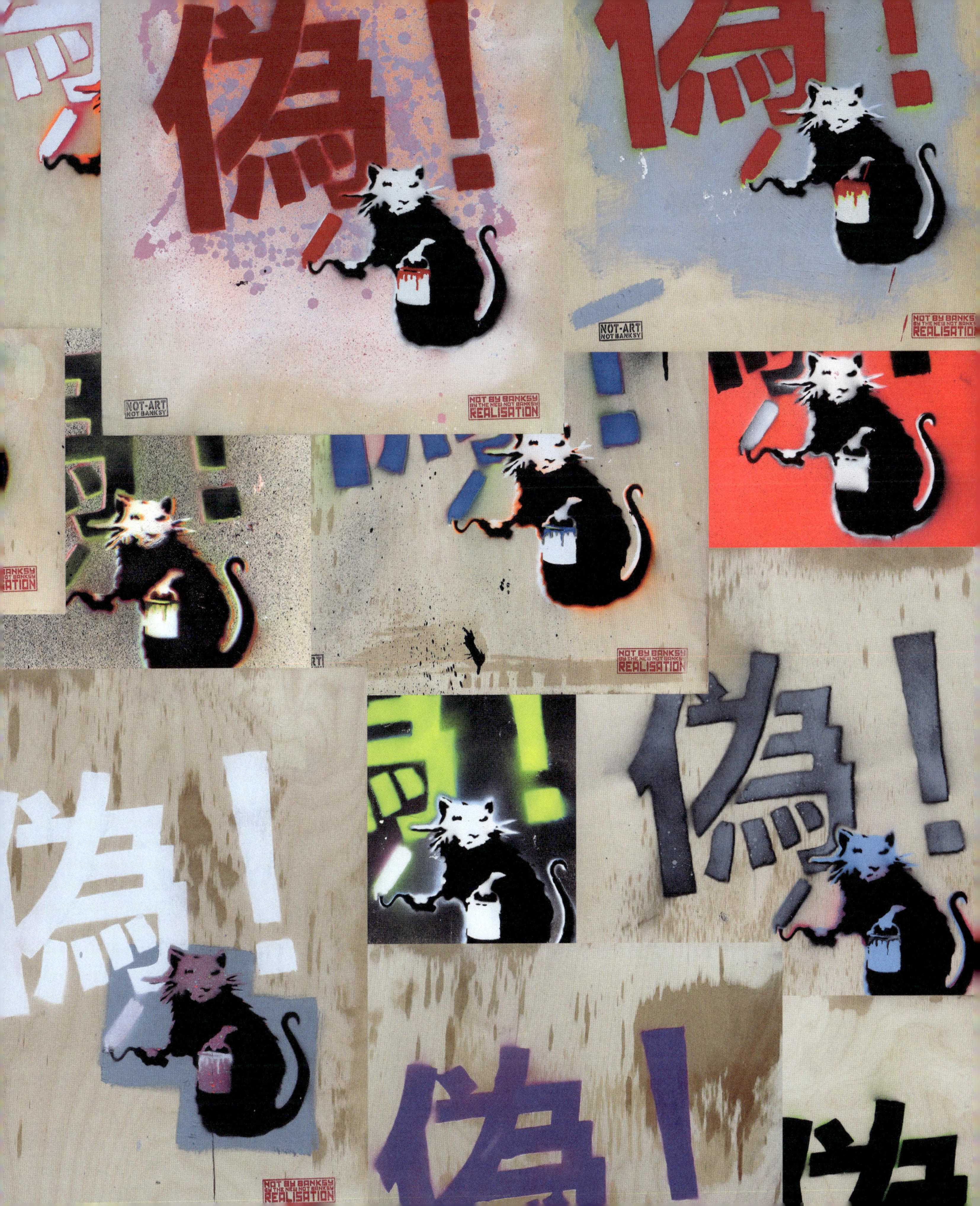
偽！
NOT-ART
NOT BANKSY
NOT BY BANKSY
ON THE NEW NOT BANKSY
REALISATION

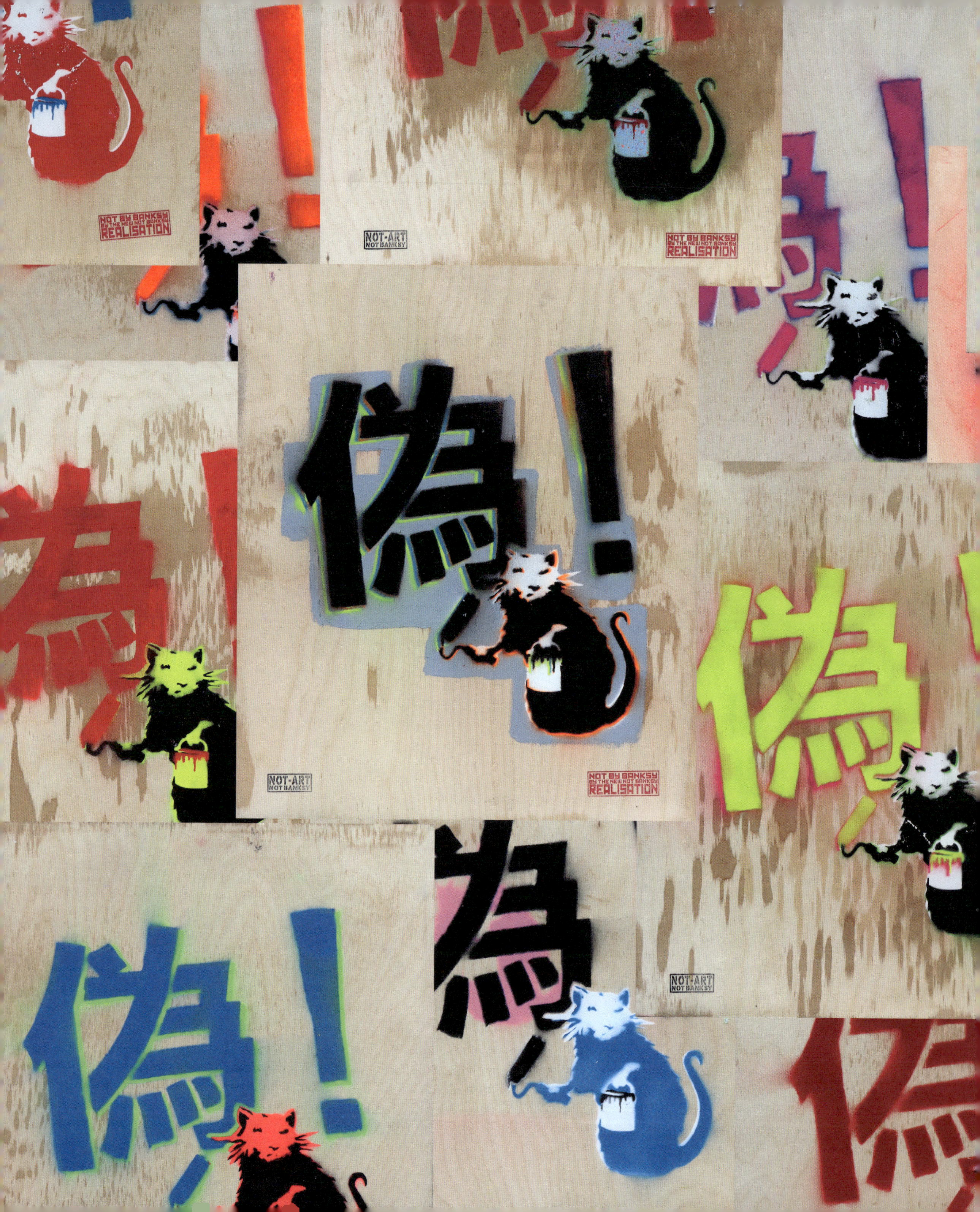

NOT BY BANKSY
BY THE NEW NOT BANKSY
REALISATION
NOT-ART
NOT BANKSY

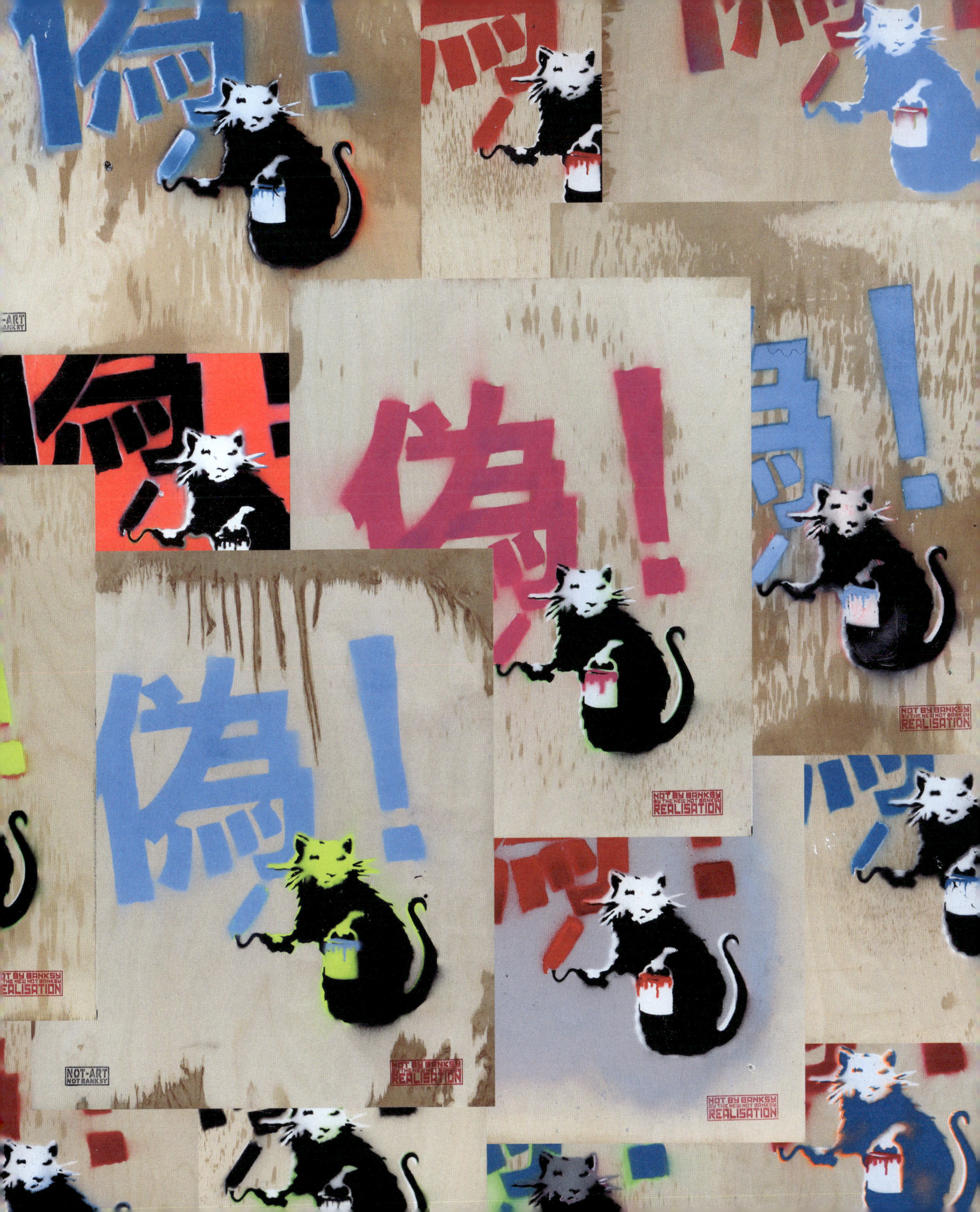

偽！
NOT-ART
NOT BANKSY
NOT BY BANKSY
OR THE NEW NOT BANKSY
REALISATION

IS-NOT-FAKE ORIGINALS

BY THE
EMERGENT
IS-NOT-BANKSY ABNORMALCY
OF THE 21ST CENTURY
GENERATION
Z

AUGUST 2021

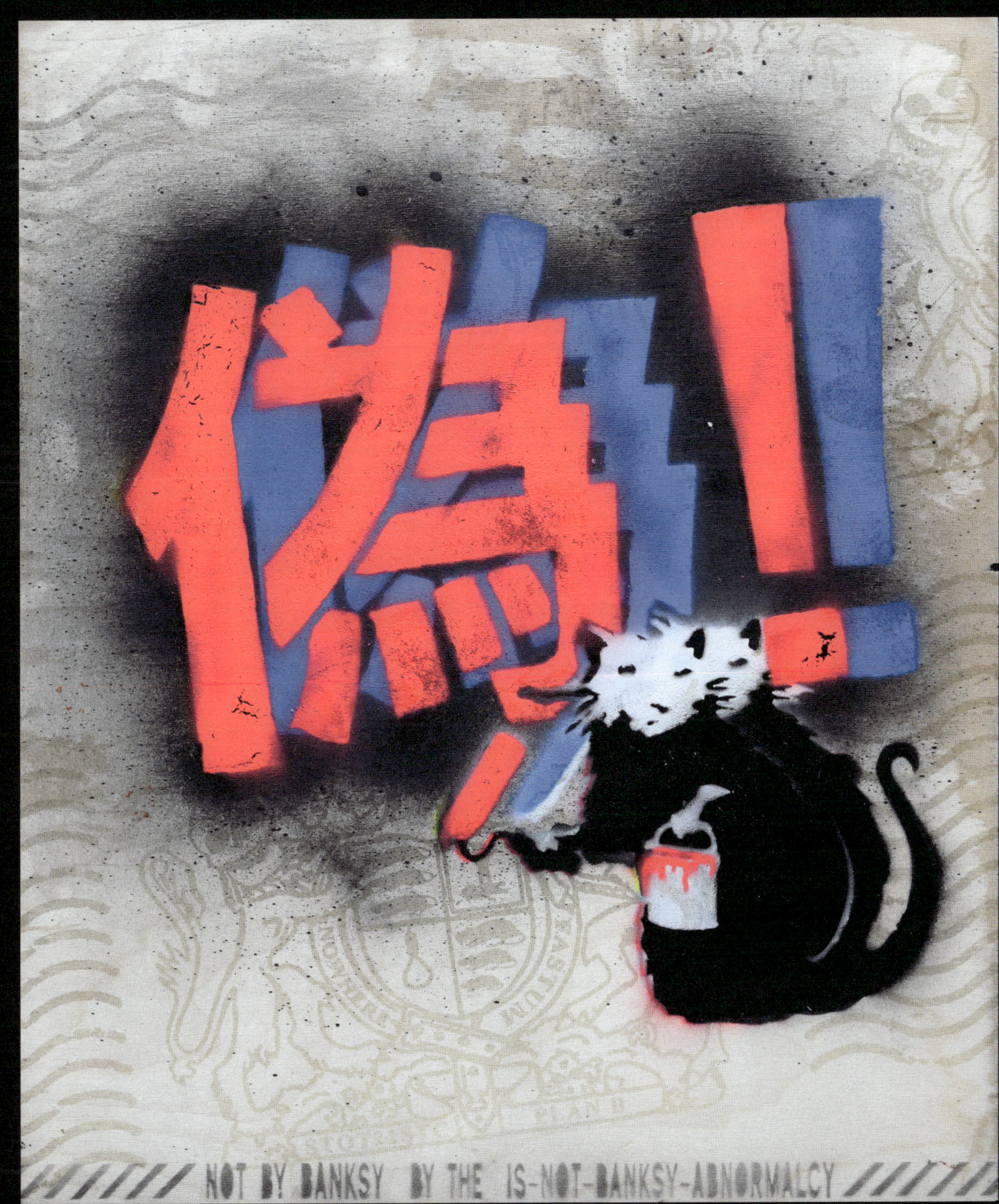

NOT BY BANKSY BY THE IS-NOT-BANKSY-ABNORMALCY

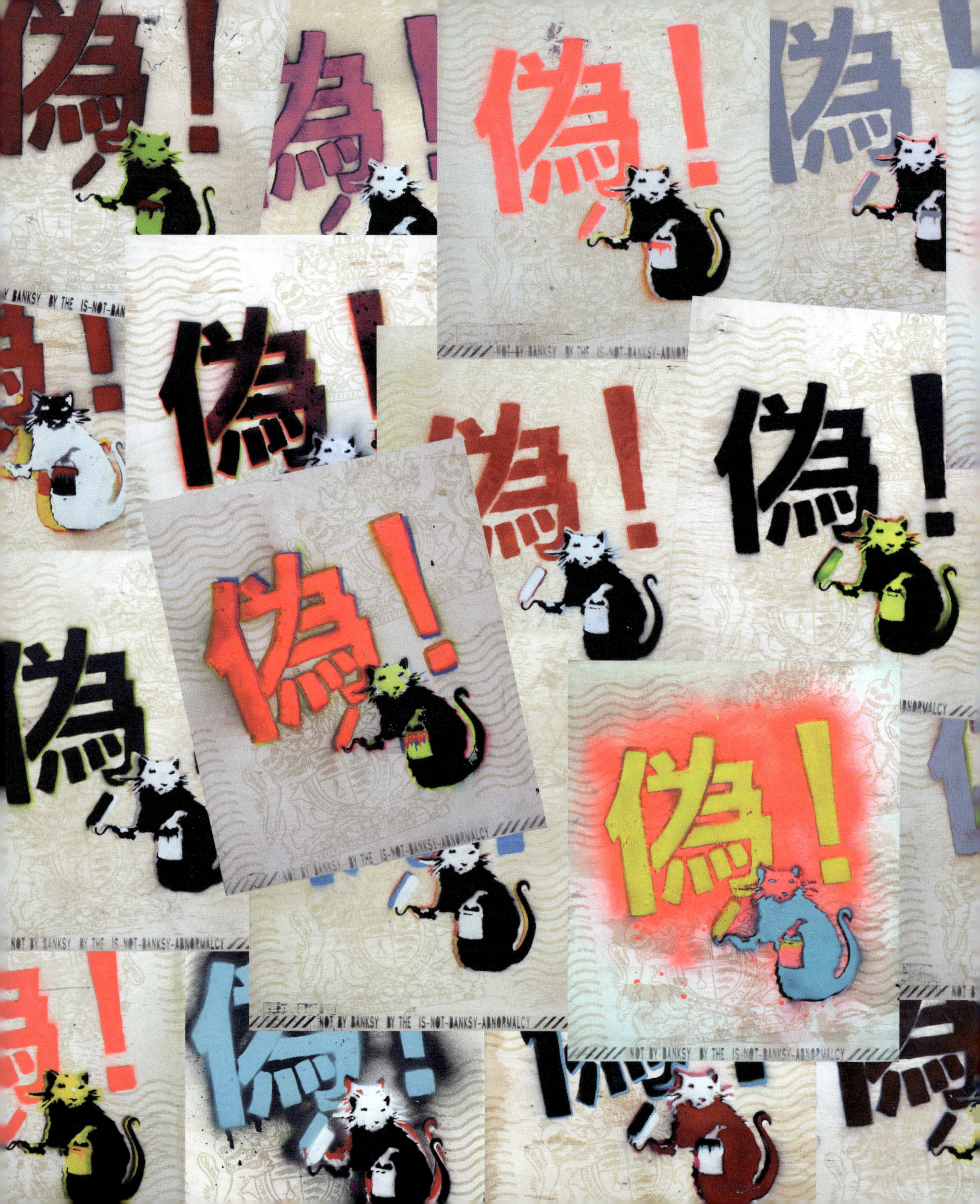

偽!
NOT BY BANKSY BY THE IS-NOT-BANKSY-ABNORMALCY

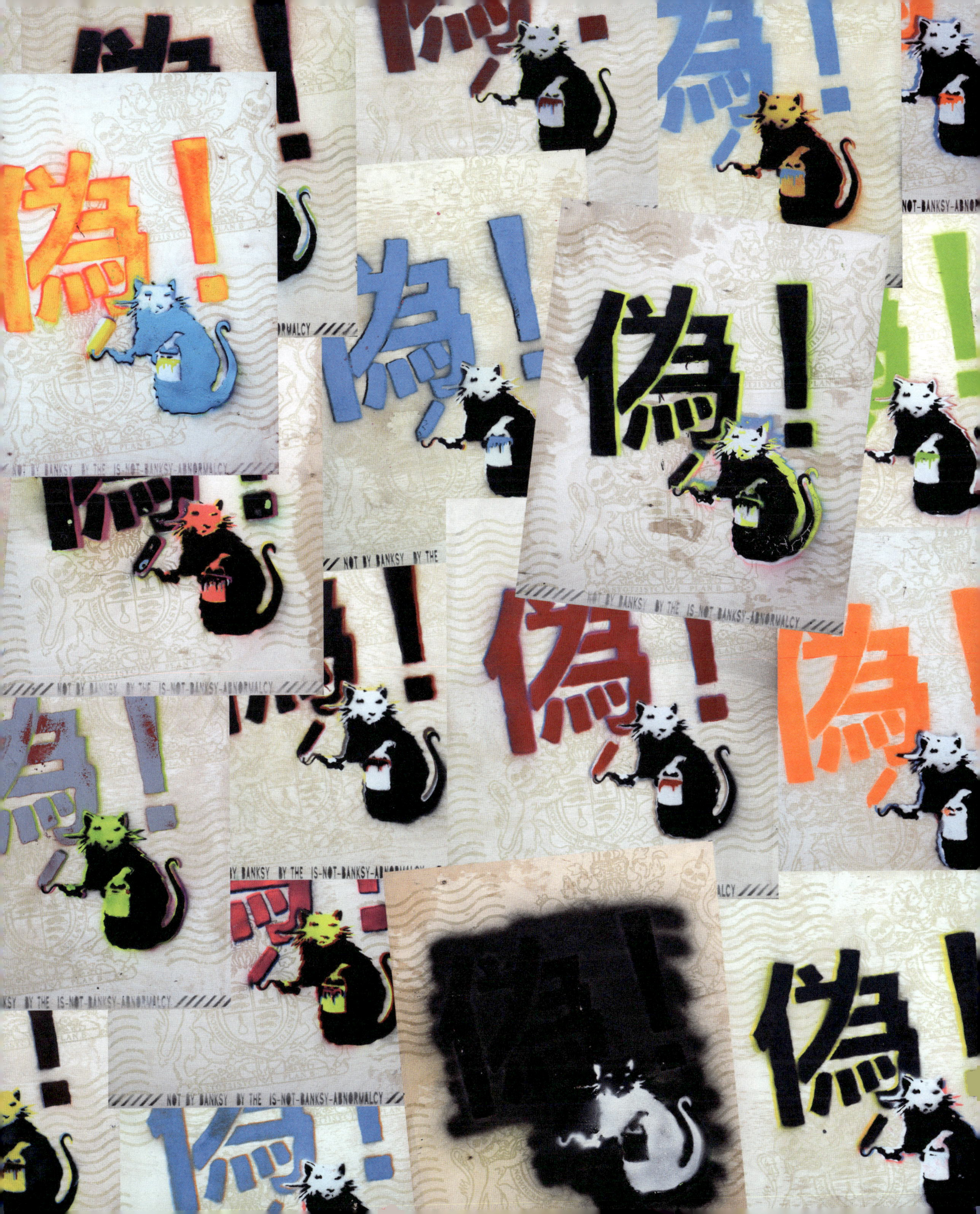

NOT BY BANKSY BY THE IS-NOT-BANKSY-ABNORMALCY

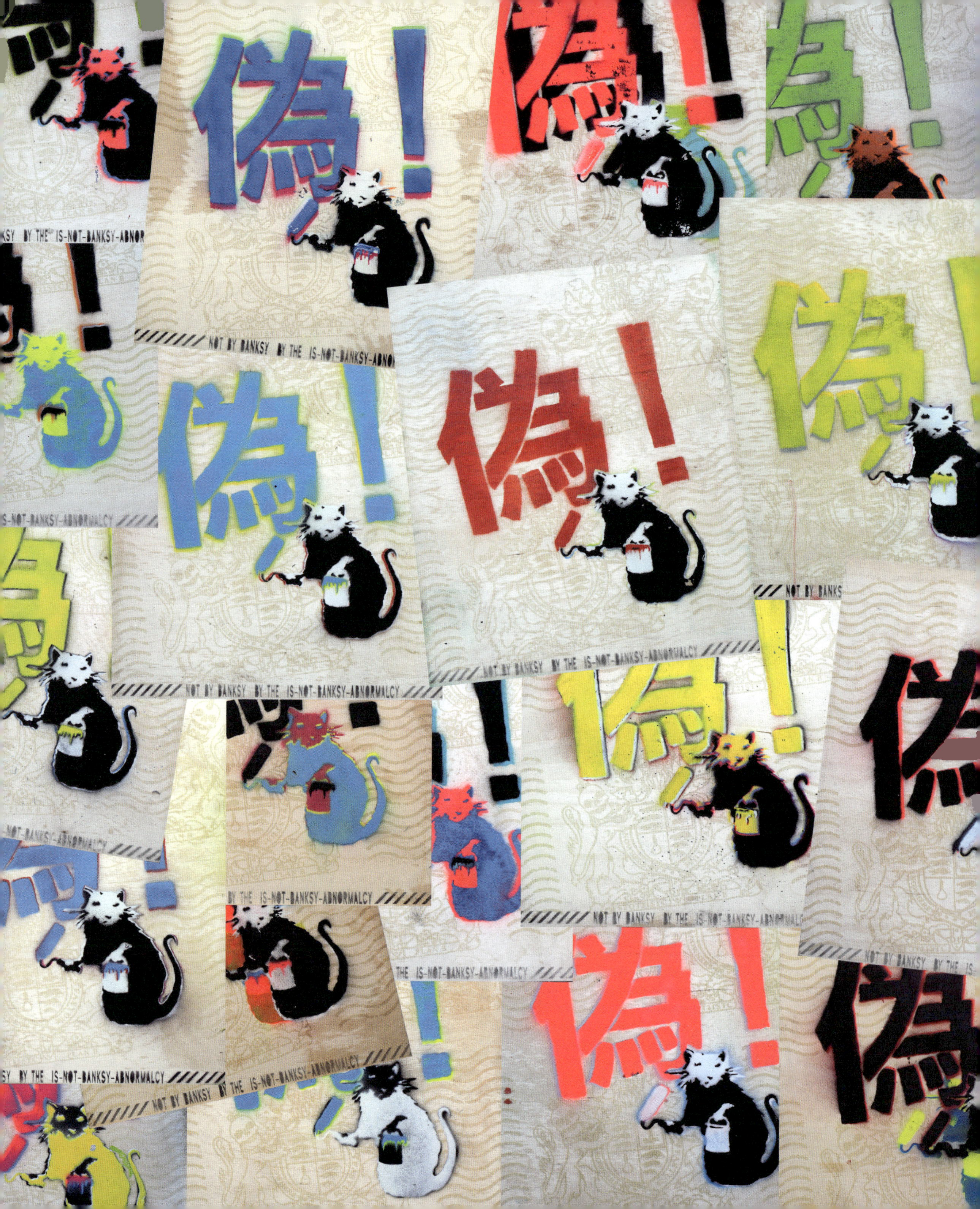

偽！
NOT BY BANKSY BY THE IS-NOT-BANKSY-ABNORMALCY

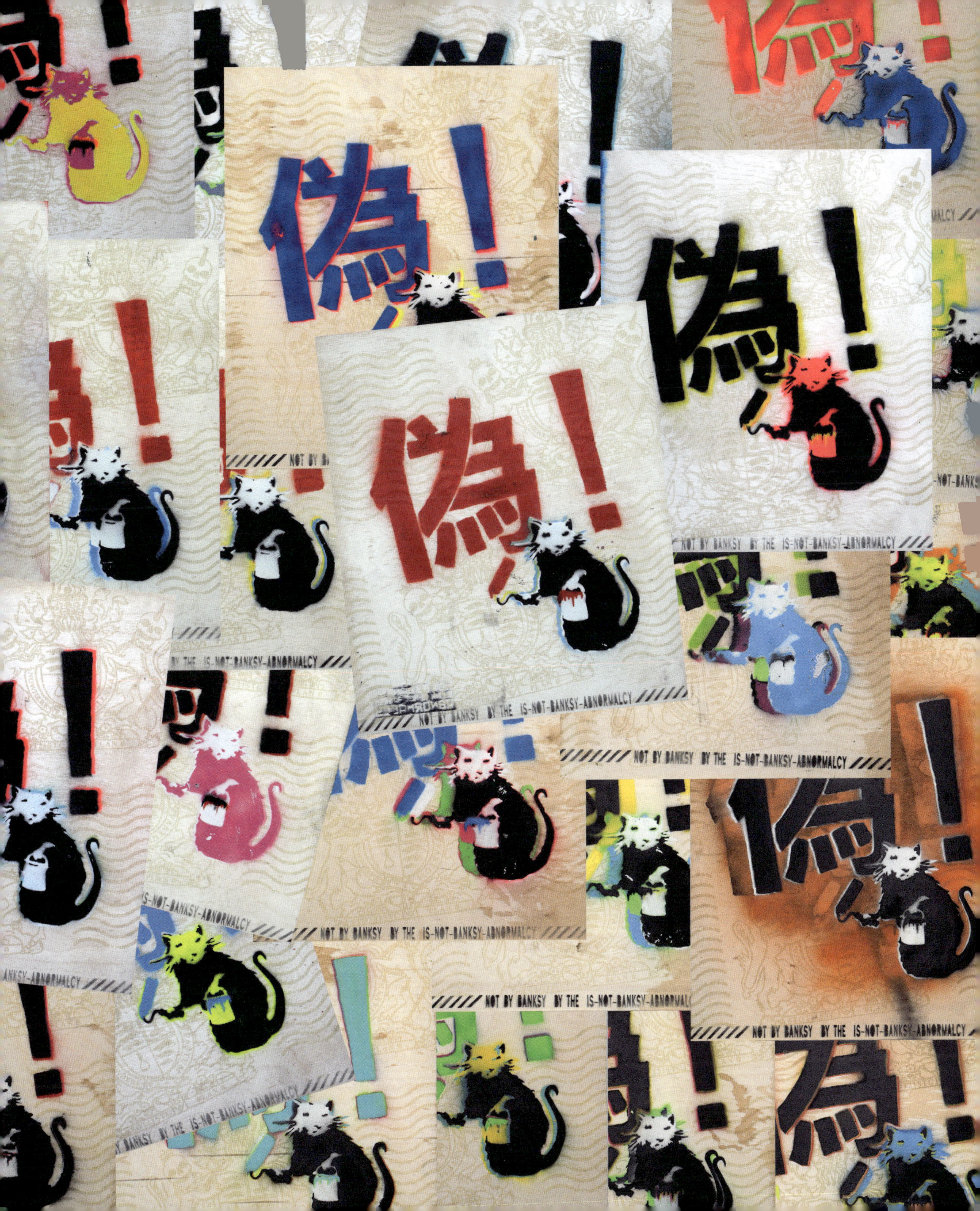
NOT BY BANKSY BY THE IS-NOT-BANKSY-ABNORMALCY

IS-NOT-FAKE

ᴅᴇDELUXE

ᴜɴORIGINALS

BY THE

EMERGENT

IS-NOT-BANKSY

ABNORMALCY

OF THE 21ST CENTURY

GENERATION

Z

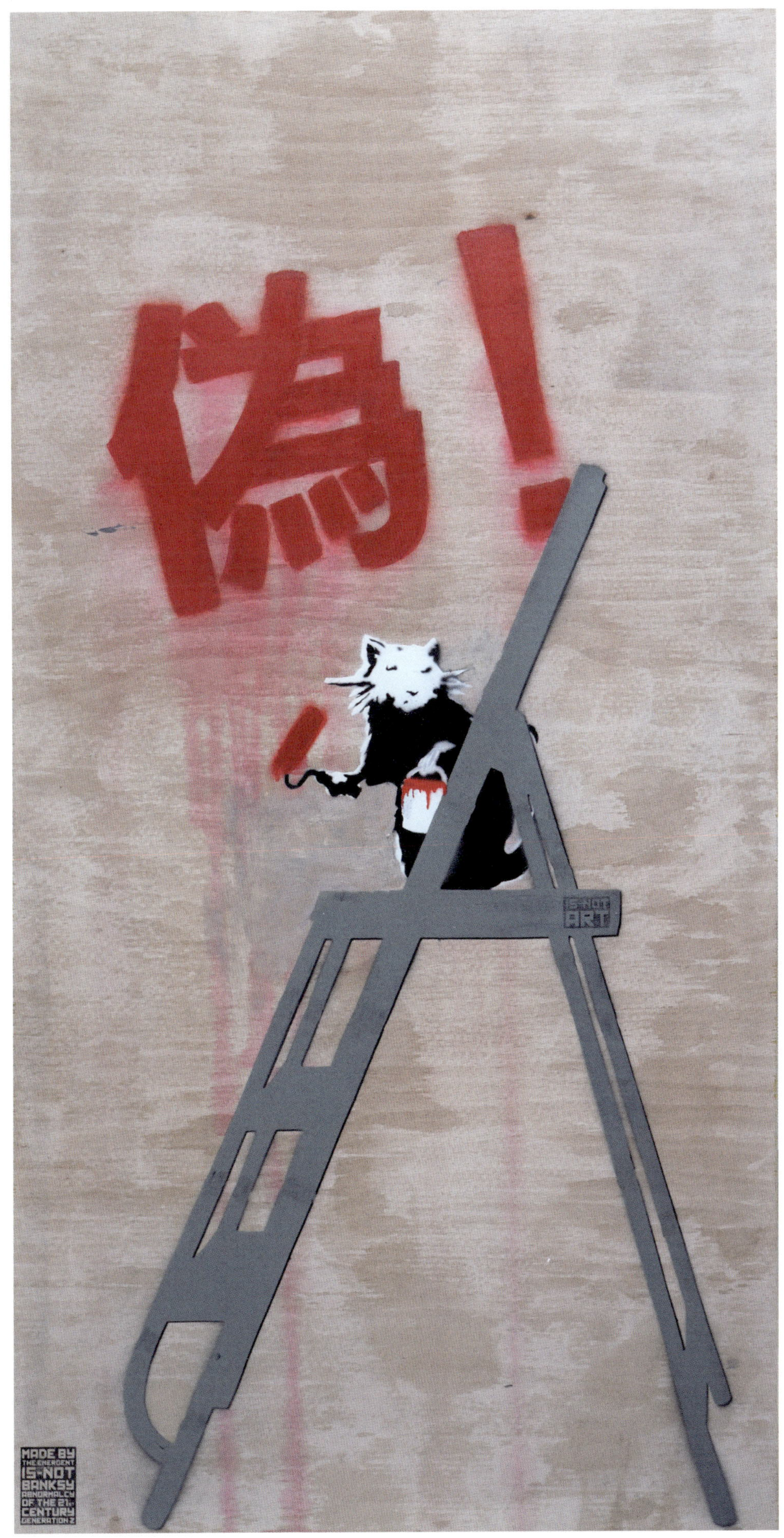

Household paint
spray paint
screen ink
and rubber stamps
on 122 x 61 cm
plywood panel

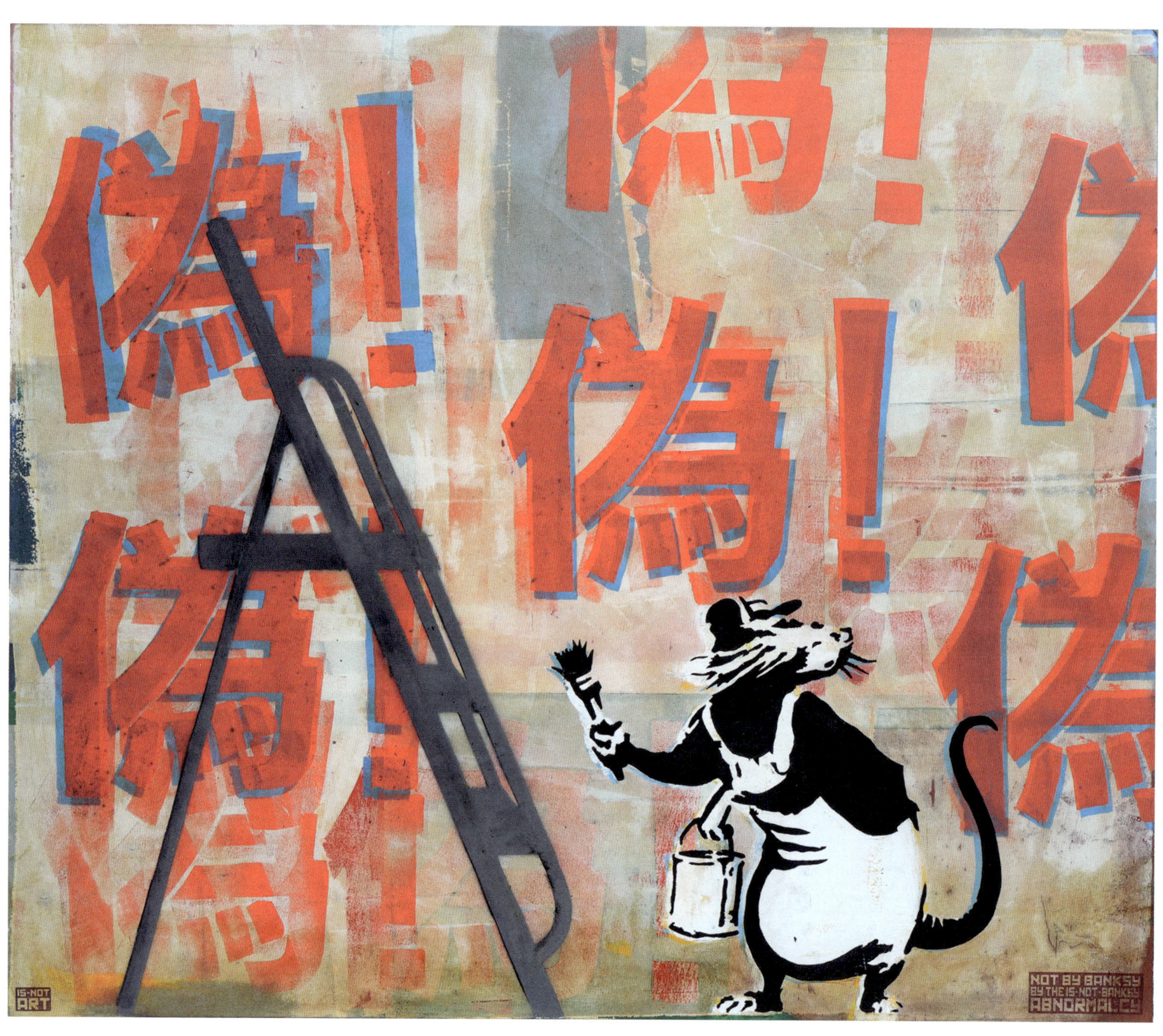

Household paint
spray paint
screen ink
and rubber stamps
on 125 x 107 cm
plywood panel

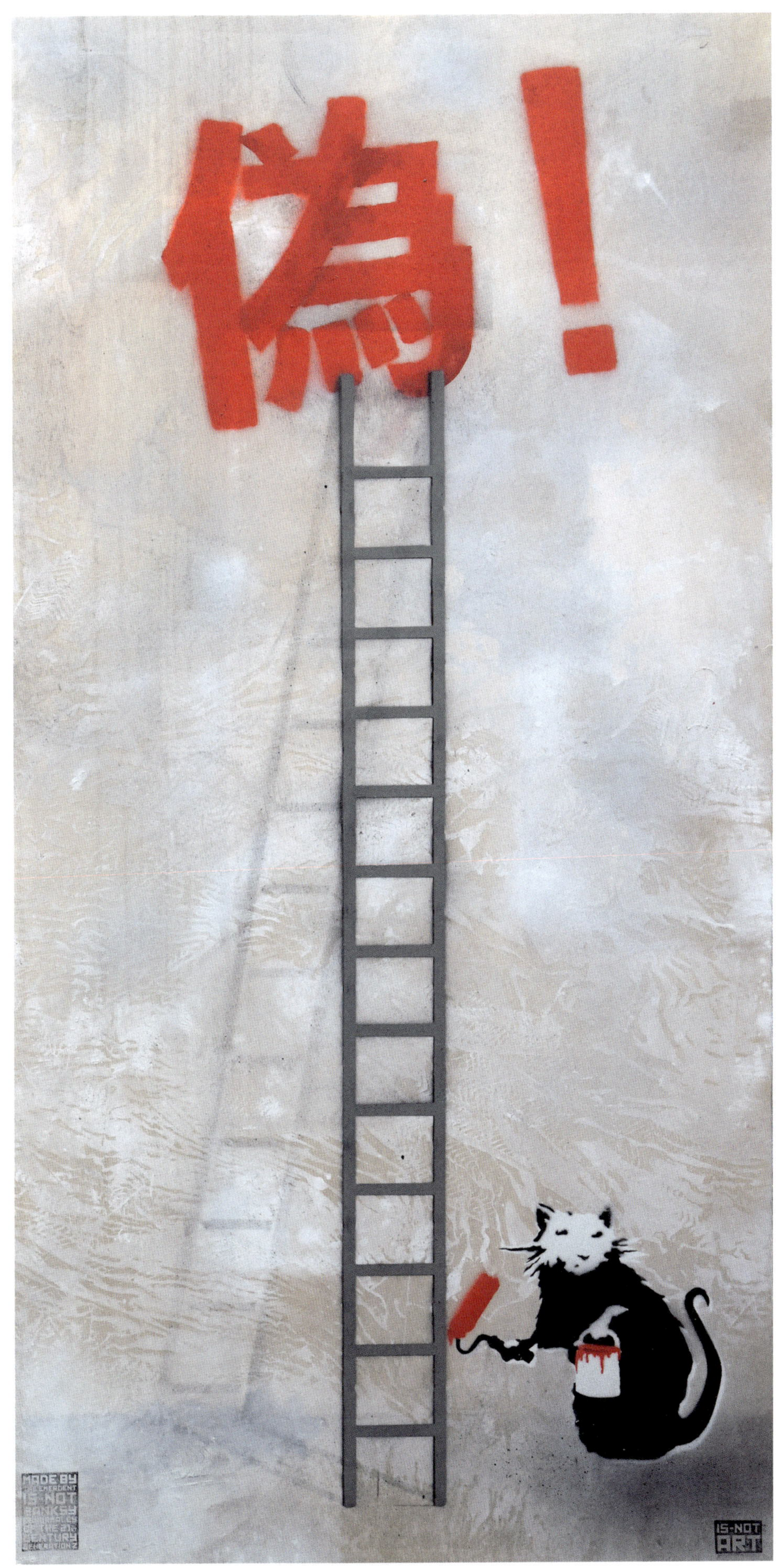

Household paint
spray paint
screen ink
and rubber stamps
on 125 x 61 cm
plywood panel

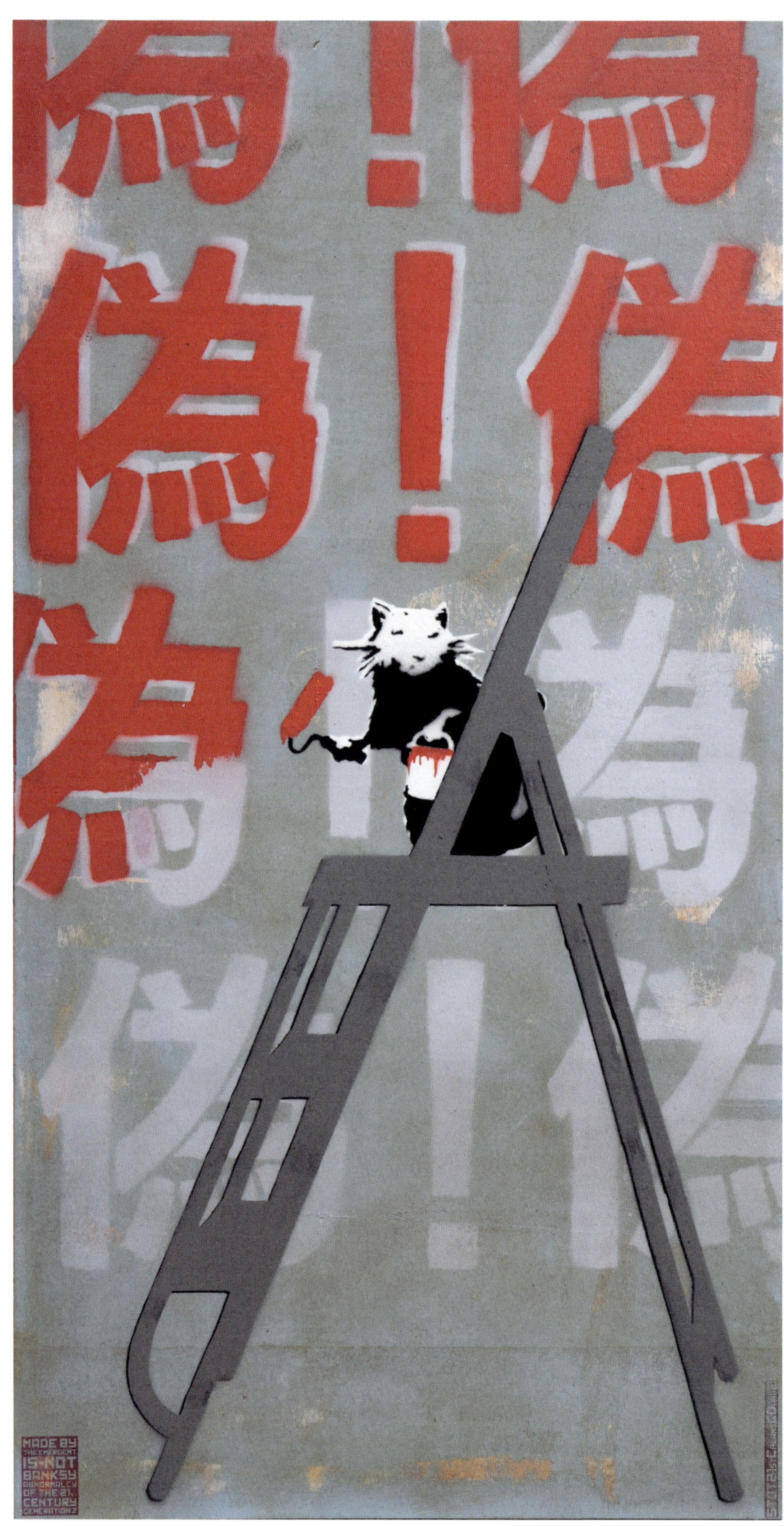

Household paint
spray paint
screen ink
and rubber stamps
on 119 x 61cm
plywood panel

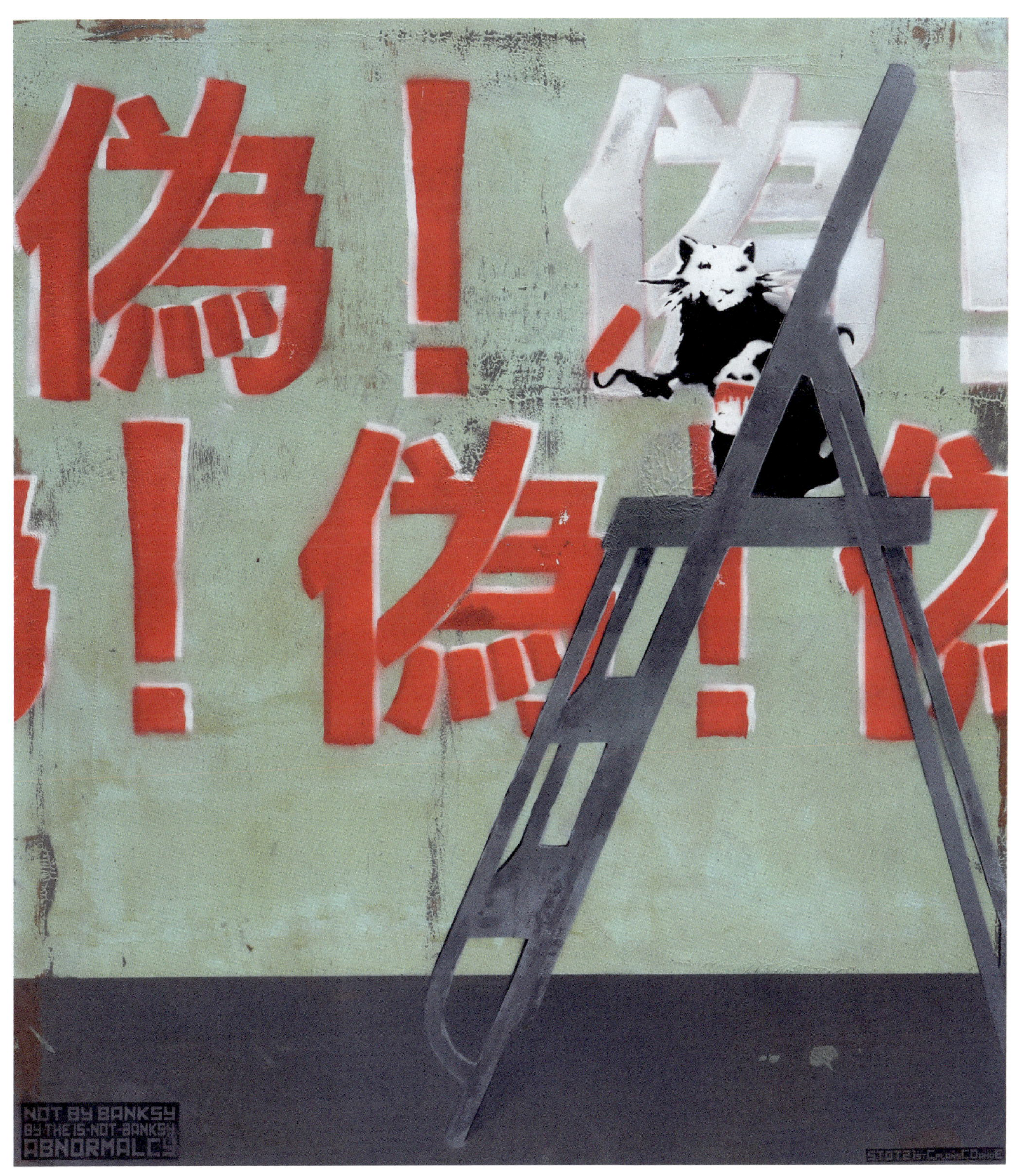

Household paint
spray paint
screen ink
and rubber stamps
on 90.5 x 77.5 cm
plywood panel

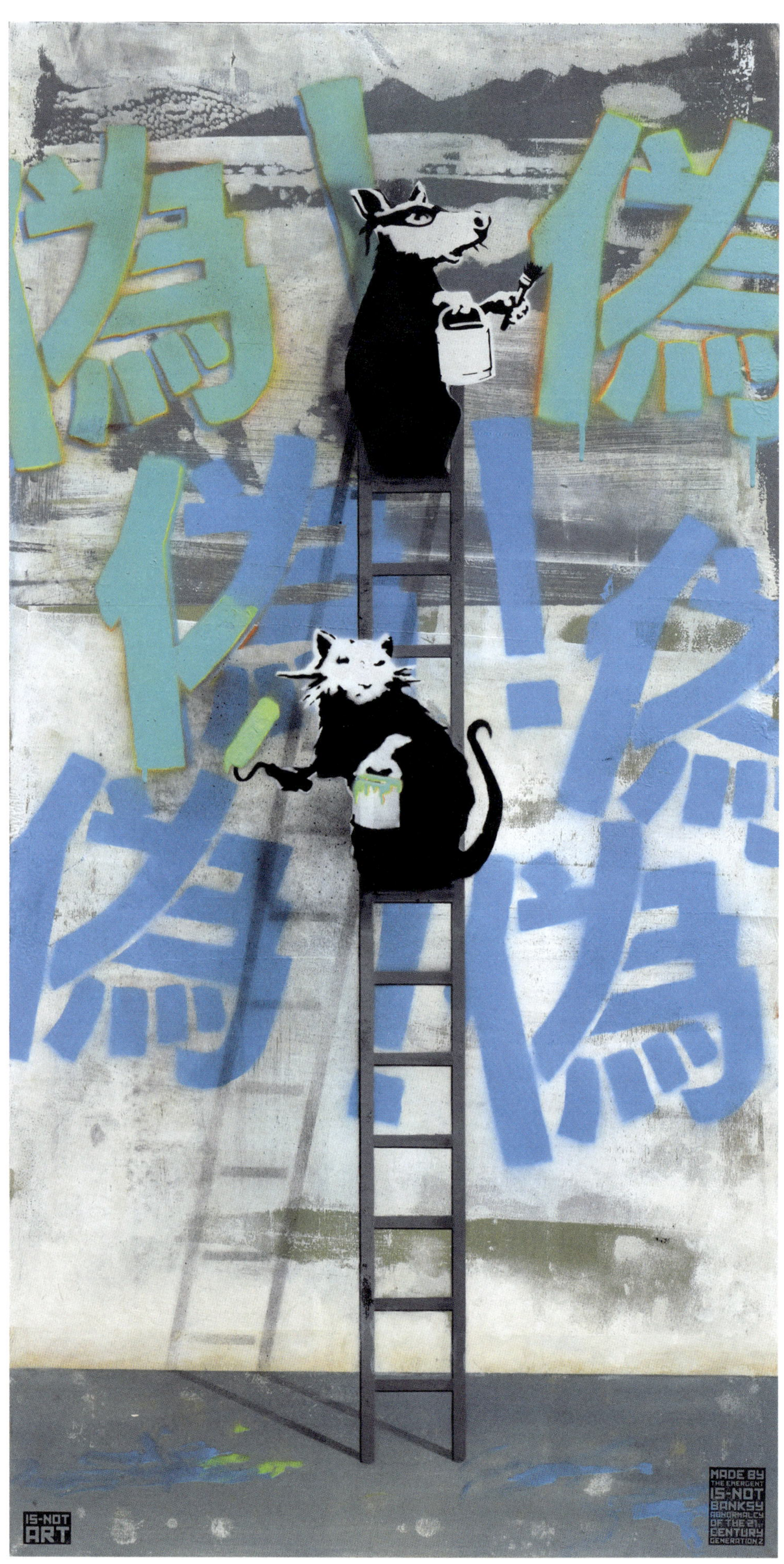

Household paint
spray paint
screen ink
and rubber stamps
on 119 x 61cm
plywood panel

Household paint
spray paint
screen ink
and rubber stamps
on 90.5 x 77.5 cm
plywood panel

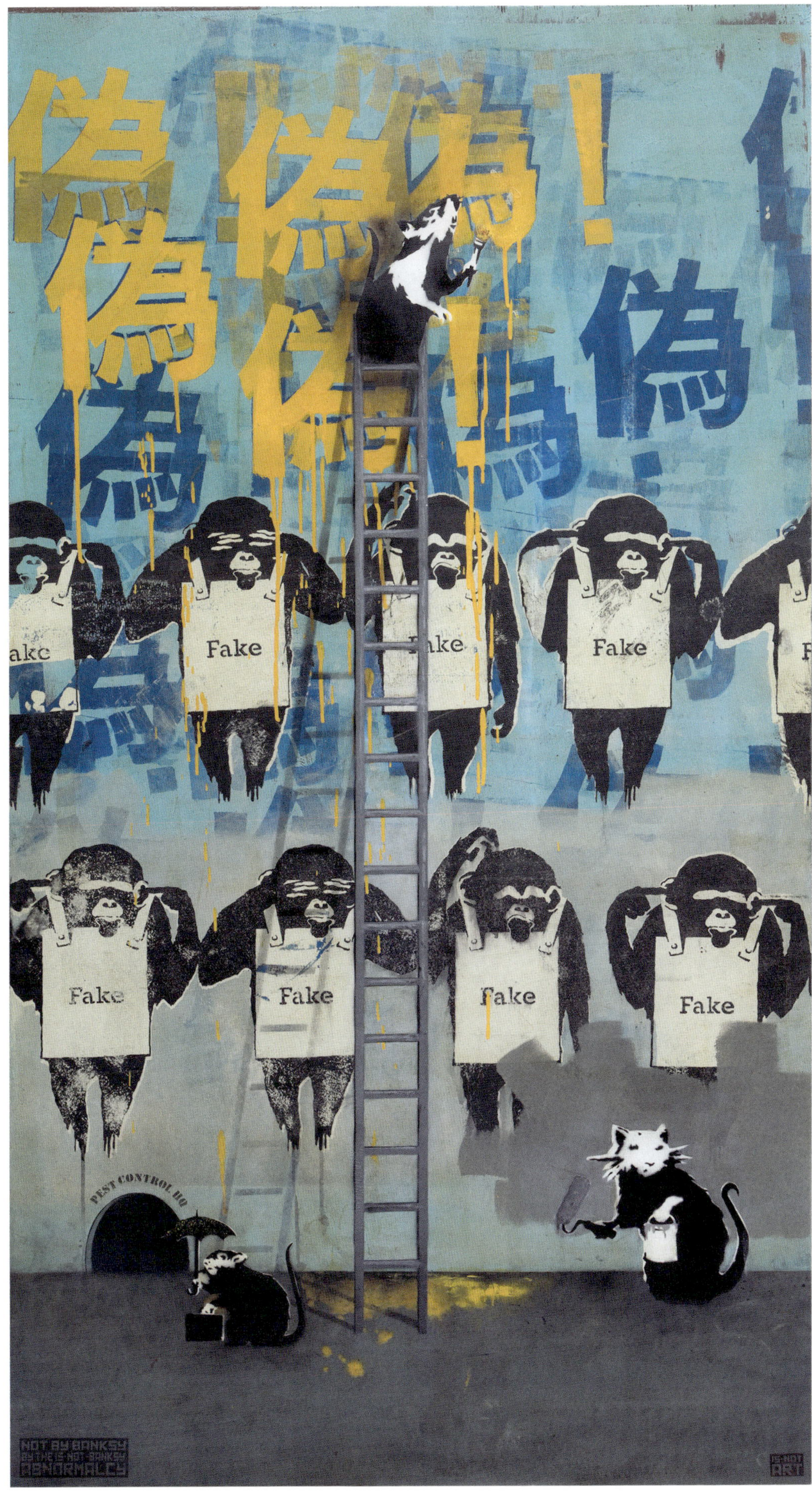

Fake
Fake
Fake
Fake
Fake
Fake
Fake
PEST CONTROL HQ
NOT BY BANKSY
BY THE IS-NOT-BANKSY
ABNORMALCY
IS-NOT
ART

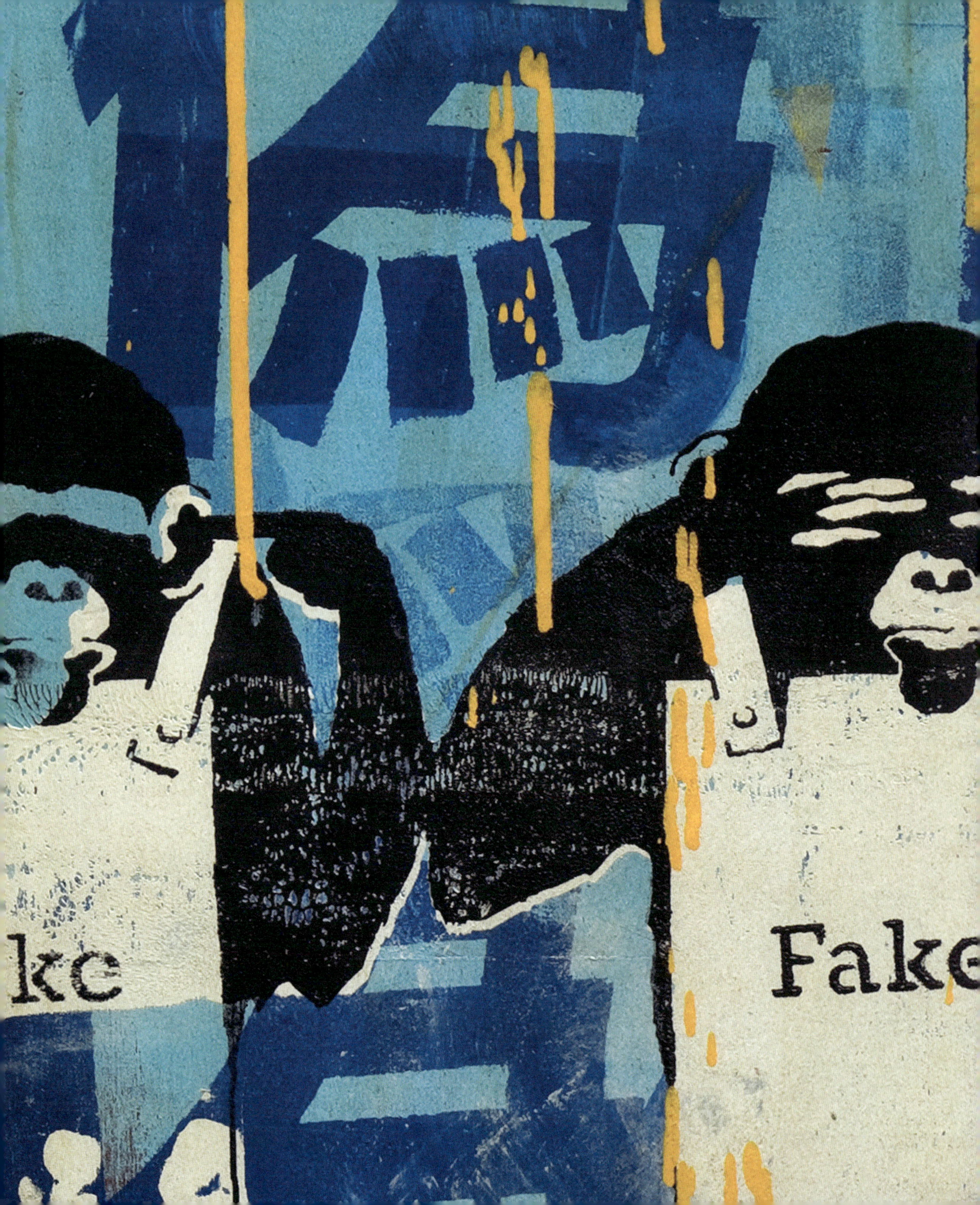
ke
Fake

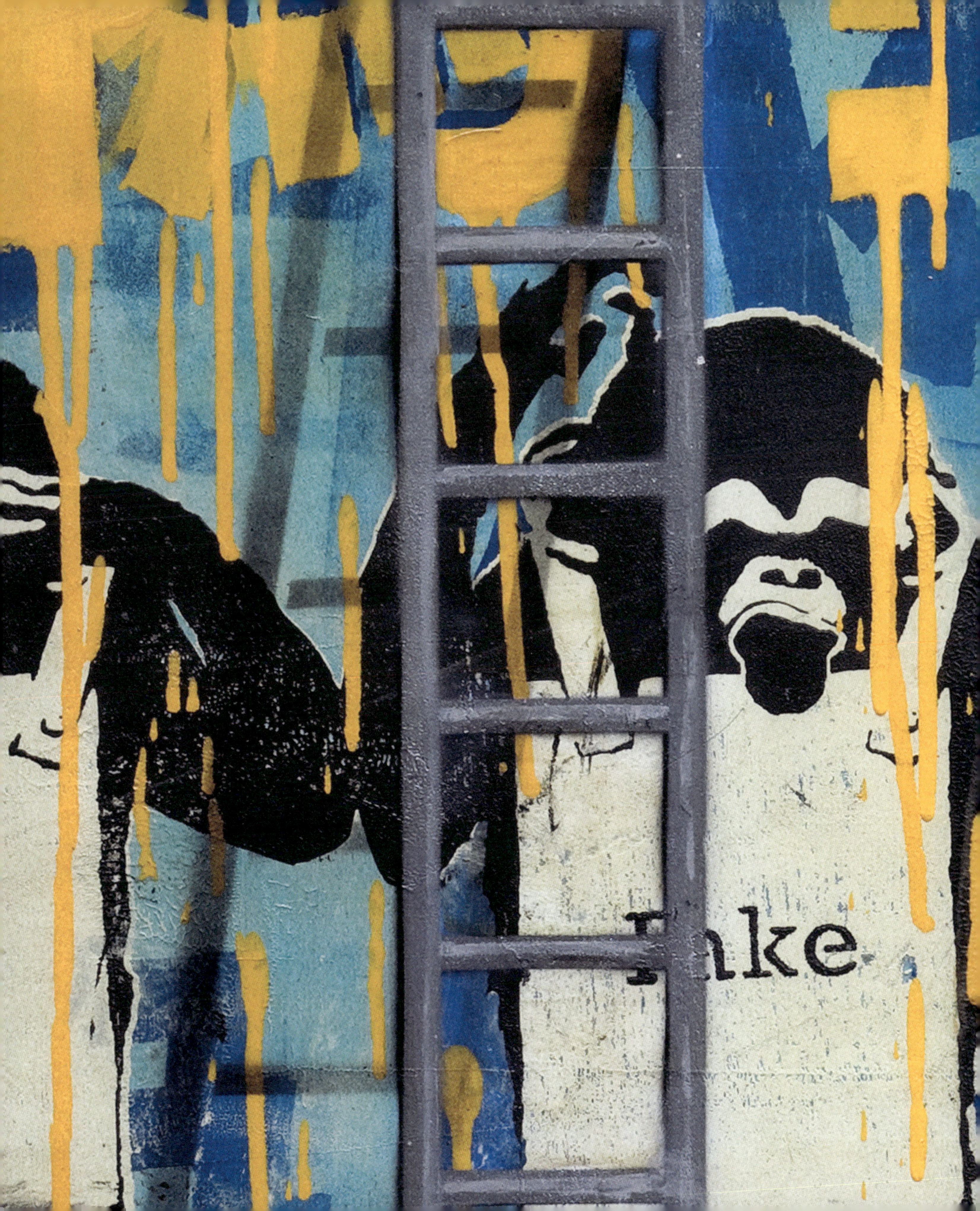
nke

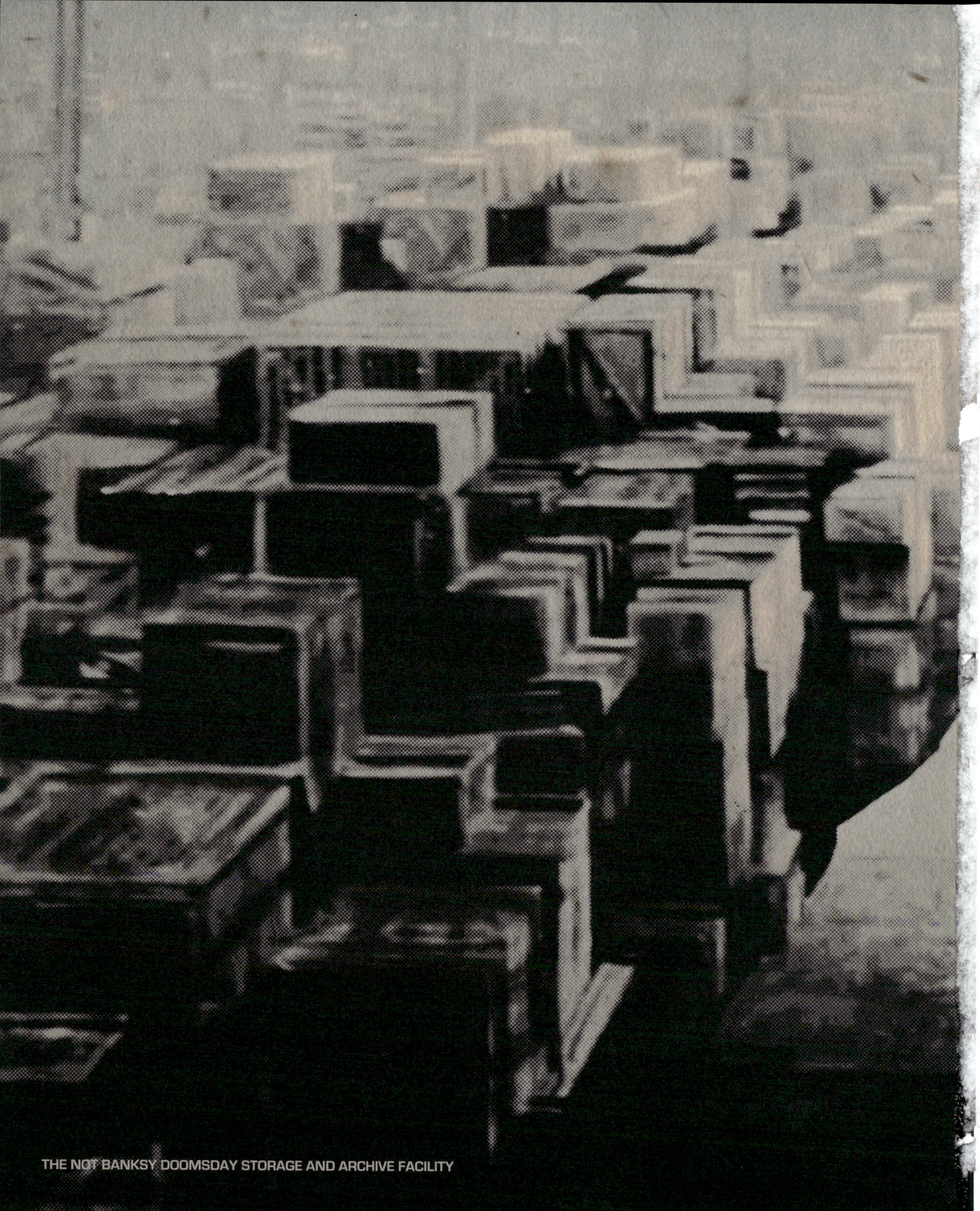

THE NOT BANKSY DOOMSDAY STORAGE AND ARCHIVE FACILITY

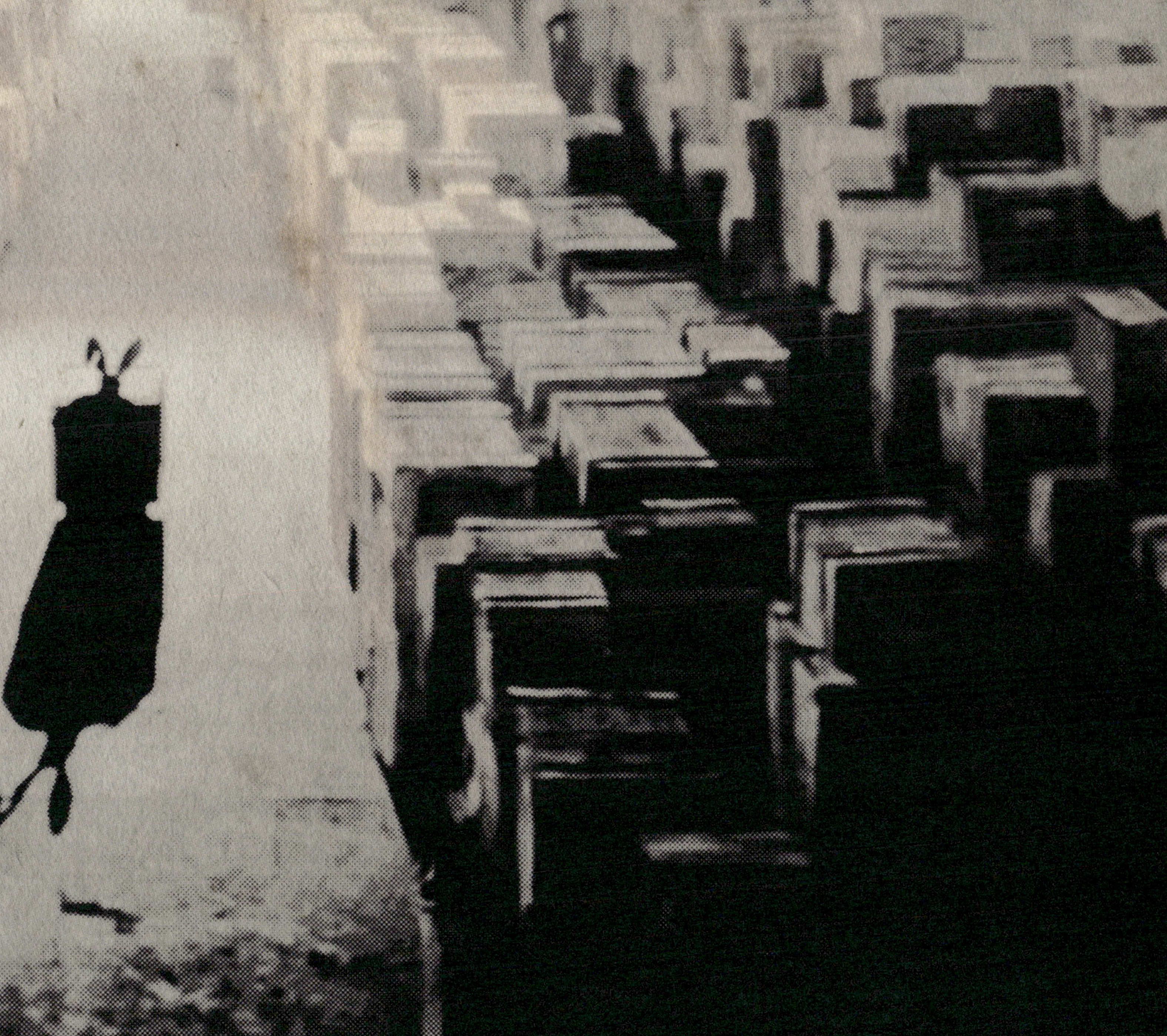

NOT
THE END
TO BE CONTINUED

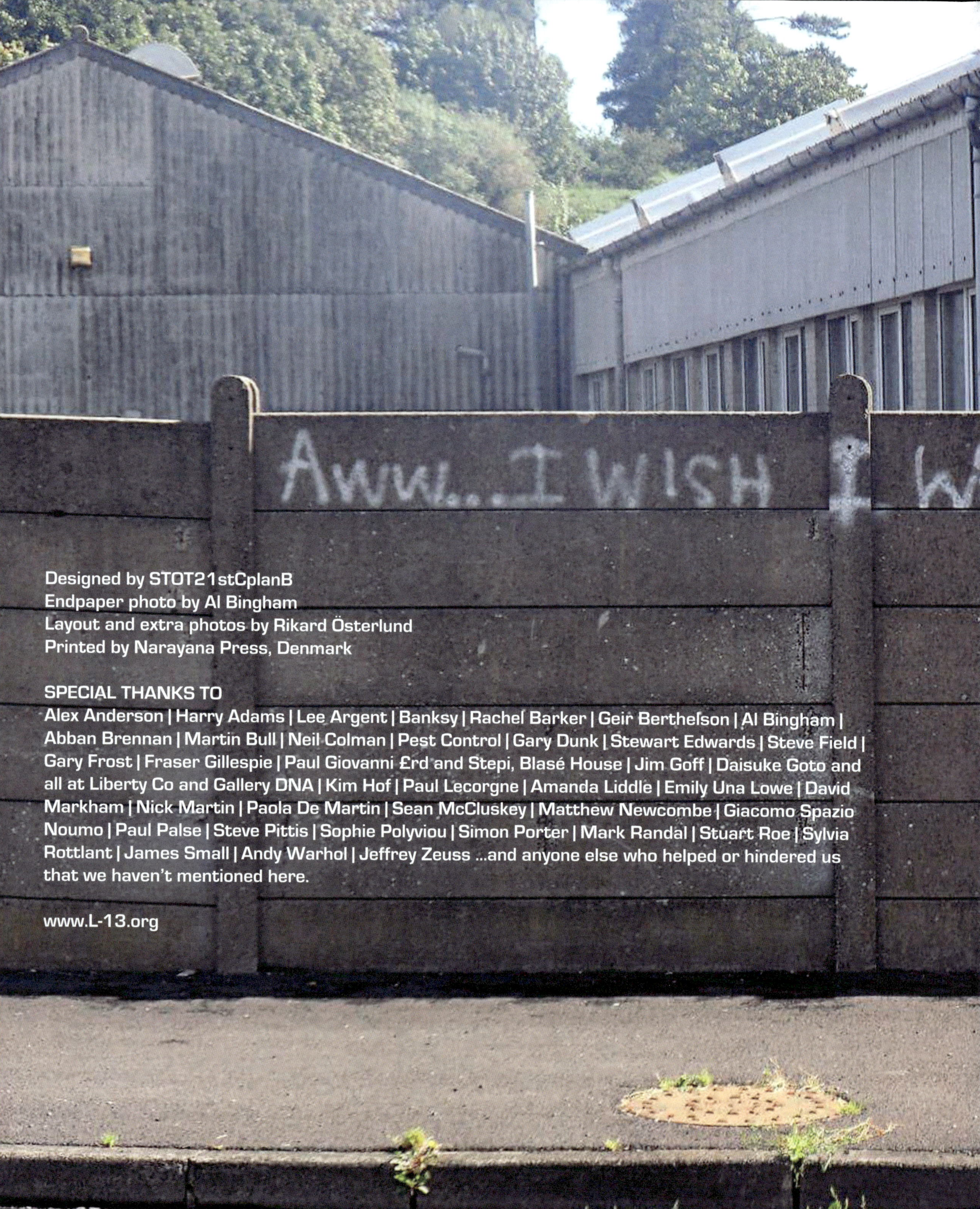

Designed by STOT21stCplanB
Endpaper photo by Al Bingham
Layout and extra photos by Rikard Österlund
Printed by Narayana Press, Denmark

SPECIAL THANKS TO
Alex Anderson | Harry Adams | Lee Argent | Banksy | Rachel Barker | Geir Berthelson | Al Bingham |
Abban Brennan | Martin Bull | Neil Colman | Pest Control | Gary Dunk | Stewart Edwards | Steve Field |
Gary Frost | Fraser Gillespie | Paul Giovanni £rd and Stepi, Blasé House | Jim Goff | Daisuke Goto and
all at Liberty Co and Gallery DNA | Kim Hof | Paul Lecorgne | Amanda Liddle | Emily Una Lowe | David
Markham | Nick Martin | Paola De Martin | Sean McCluskey | Matthew Newcombe | Giacomo Spazio
Noumo | Paul Palse | Steve Pittis | Sophie Polyviou | Simon Porter | Mark Randal | Stuart Roe | Sylvia
Rottlant | James Small | Andy Warhol | Jeffrey Zeuss ...and anyone else who helped or hindered us
that we haven't mentioned here.

www.L-13.org